Watford Natural History Society

Transactions of the Watford Natural History Society and Hertfordshire Field Club

Watford Natural History Society

Transactions of the Watford Natural History Society and Hertfordshire Field Club

ISBN/EAN: 9783337795931

Printed in Europe, USA, Canada, Australia, Japan

Cover: Foto ©Suzi / pixelio.de

More available books at **www.hansebooks.com**

TRANSACTIONS

OF THE

WATFORD
NATURAL HISTORY SOCIETY

AND

HERTFORDSHIRE FIELD CLUB.

EDITED BY THE HONORARY SECRETARY.

VOLUME I.

JANUARY, 1875, TO JUNE, 1877.

WATFORD:
SOLD AT THE PUBLIC LIBRARY, QUEEN'S ROAD.
LONDON :
HARDWICKE & BOGUE, 192, PICCADILLY, W.

1878.

CONTENTS.

PAGE

1. The Cretaceous Rocks of England. By J. LOGAN LOBLEY, F.G.S., F.R.G.S. (With 5 woodcuts.) 1

2. Notes on the Flora of the Watford District. By ARTHUR COTTAM, F.R.A.S... 14

3. Notes on a proposed re-issue of the Flora of Hertfordshire, with Supplementary Remarks on the Botany of the Watford District. By R. A. PRYOR, B.A., F.L.S. 17

4. On the Observation of Periodical Natural Phenomena. By JOHN HOPKINSON, F.L.S., F.G.S., Hon. Sec. .. 33

5. Notes on the Plants on which the Meteorological Society invites Observations as to their Time of Flowering. By the Rev. W. M. HIND, LL.D. 43

6. Notes on the Observation of Insects in Connexion with Investigations on Seasonal Phenomena. By ARTHUR COTTAM, F.R.A.S... 50

7. On the Pleasures and Advantages to be derived from a Study of Natural History, and more particularly from the Observation of Birds. By J. E. HARTING, F.L.S., F.Z.S. 52

8. Miscellaneous Notes and Observations 63

9. On the Botanical Work of the Past Season. By R. A. PRYOR, B.A., F.L.S. (With a Map of Hertfordshire.) 65

10. List of Works on the Geology of Hertfordshire. By W. WHITAKER, B.A., F.G.S. 78

11. A Few Words about our Local Ferns. By JOHN E. LITTLEBOY 83

12. The Physical Structure of the London Basin, considered in its Relation to the Geology of the Neighbourhood of Watford. By Professor JOHN MORRIS, F.G.S. (With 6 woodcuts.) 89

13. Miscellaneous Notes and Observations 108

14. On the supposed Chalybeate Spring at Watford, and on other Medicinal Waters in Herts. By R. A. PRYOR, B.A., F.L.S. 109

15. The Rainfall in 1875.. 112

16. Anniversary Address. By the President, JOHN EVANS, F.R.S., F.S.A., F.G.S., etc. 113

PAGE

17. The Geology and Water Supply of the Neighbourhood of Watford. By the Rev. J. C. CLUTTERBUCK, M.A.. 125

18. Meteorological Observations taken at Cassiobury House from May to December, 1875. By the Right Hon. the EARL OF ESSEX 132

19. Miscellaneous Notes and Observations 135

20. The Hertfordshire Bourne. By JOHN EVANS, F.R.S., V.P.S.A., F.G.S., etc., President 137

21. The Hertfordshire Ordnance Bench Marks, from the 'Abstracts of Levelling' of the Ordnance Survey. By JOHN HOPKINSON, Hon. Sec.. 141

22. The Polarisation of Light. By JAMES U. HARFORD. (With a Plate.) 152

23. The Eocenes of England and their Extension in Hertfordshire. By J. LOGAN LOBLEY, F.G.S., F.R.G.S. .. 161

24. Miscellaneous Notes and Observations 172

25. Notes and Queries on the River Colne, Watford. By ALFRED T. BRETT, M.D. 175

26. Fish-hatching and Fish-culture in Hertfordshire. By A. T. BRETT, M.D. With Notes on Pisciculture in Hertfordshire, by PETER HOOD, M.D... 179

27. Anniversary Address. By the President, JOHN EVANS, F.R.S., V.P.S.A., F.G.S., etc. 187

28. The Fertilisation of Plants. By the Rev. GEORGE HENSLOW, M.A., F.L.S., F.G.S... 201

29. Instructions for taking Meteorological Observations. By WILLIAM MARRIOTT, F.M.S... 211

30. Meteorological Observations taken at Holly Bank, Watford, during the year ending 28th February, 1877. By JOHN HOPKINSON, F.L.S., F.M.S., Hon. Sec. .. 217

31. Report on the Rainfall in Hertfordshire in 1876. By the Honorary Secretary 225

32. Notes on a Remarkable Storm in Hertfordshire, April 4th, 1877. By Lieut. R. B. CROFT, R.N., F.L.S. .. 230

33. On Microscopic Fungi. By E. M. CHATER. (With 3 woodcuts.) 231

34. Notes on the Otter and Badger in Hertfordshire. By ALFRED T. BRETT, M.D., President 236

35. Miscellaneous Notes and Observations 238

Index, etc. 241

PROCEEDINGS, January, 1875, to June, 1878, pp. ix–lxiv.

LIST OF ILLUSTRATIONS.

PLATES.

I. Map of Hertfordshire showing the Districts into which
it is proposed to divide the County for the illustration of its Botanical Geography .. .. .. *To face* p. 65
II. The Polarisation of Light .. .. *To face* p. 160

WOODCUTS.

	PAGE
Section showing the approximate relative thickness of the British Sedimentary Rocks	3
Map showing the extension of the Cretaceous Rocks in England	5
Foraminifera from the Chalk..	9
Foraminifera from the Atlantic Ooze	9
Section across the London Tertiary Basin	11
General Section of the Tertiary Beds at Bushey Kiln, Watford	94
Ditto at Watford Heath Kiln	95
Ditto at Hatfield Park Kiln	98
Ditto at Mr. Lines' Brickyard, near Hertford	99
General Section on Railway, Bushey Cutting	100
Wheat Mildew—*Puccinia graminis*	232
Bramble Leaf Brand—*Aregma bulbosum*	233
Maple Blight—*Uncinula bicornis*	234

Dates of publication of the several parts contained in this volume :

Part 1.	Pages 1-32	July, 1875.
„ 2.	„ 33-64	Nov. 1875.
„ 3.	„ 65-88, and ix-xvi	March, 1876.
„ 4.	„ 89-112, and xvii-xxiv.	June, 1876.
„ 5.	„ 113-136, and xxv-xxxii.	Oct. 1876.
„ 6.	„ 137-160, and xxxiii-xl.	March, 1877.
„ 7.	„ 161-200, and xli-xlviii.	July, 1877.
„ 8.	„ 201-216, and xlix-lvi	Dec. 1877.
„ 9.	„ 217-240, and lvii-lxiv	April, 1878.
„ 10.	„ 241-248, and i-viii	August, 1878.

PROCEEDINGS

OF THE

WATFORD NATURAL HISTORY SOCIETY.

MEETING TO FOUND THE SOCIETY, 23RD JANUARY, 1875.

ALFRED T. BRETT, Esq., M.D., in the Chair.

Present: Dr. Brett, Mr. E. M. Chater, Mr. George Chippindale, Mr. Arthur Cottam, Mr. Thomas Heather, Mr. John Hopkinson, Dr. Iles, Mr. J. Logan Lobley, Mr. F. W. Silvester, Mr. W. Lepard Smith, Mr. C. R. Smith, and Mr. J. Watson Walker, jun.

The Chairman, having read a notice of the intention to found a Natural History Society for Watford and its neighbourhood (from the 'Watford Observer' of the 2nd of January), stated the object of the present meeting, and the reasons which had induced him, in conjunction with Mr. Cottam and Mr. Hopkinson, to take the initiative in proposing the formation of the Society at the commencement of the present year.

It was then moved by Mr. Cottam, seconded by Dr. Iles, and carried—"That it is desirable to establish a Society at Watford for the promotion of the study of Natural History, to be called the Watford Natural History Society and Hertfordshire Field Club."

Moved by Mr. Chater, seconded by Mr. W. L. Smith, and carried—"That the Society be now founded, and shall consist of those ladies and gentlemen who have signified their desire to become members, with power to add to their number."

By this resolution the following were elected Members :—

Dr. Alfred T. Brett and Miss Brett, Watford House; Mr. H. W. Bridges, Upper Nascot, Watford; Mr. R. H. Carter, Ashlands, Watford; Mr. E. M. Chater, High Street, Watford; Mr. George Chippindale, Rough Down Villas, Boxmoor; Mr. Alfred J. Copeland and Mrs. Copeland, Dell Field, Watford; Mr. Arthur Cottam, F.R.A.S., St. John's Road, Watford ; Mr. John E. Dawson, F.R.G.S., F.R.M.S., Oak Lodge, Watford; Dr. J. R. Bathurst Dove, Chesnut Cottage, Pinner; the Rev. C. E. Drew, M.A., Queen's Road, Watford; the Right Honourable the Earl of Essex and the Countess of Essex, Cassiobury Park, Watford ; Mr. John Evans, V.P.R.S., V.P.S.A., Pres.G.S., etc., Nash Mills, Hemel Hempstead; Mr. H. Sugden Evans, F.R.M.S., F.C.S., Barham Lodge, Elstree ; the Rev. W. Falconer, M.A., F.R.A.S., The Rectory, Bushey; Admiral E. G. Fanshawe, F.R.G.S., Delrow, Aldenham ; Mr. W. M. Fawcett, Winsmore Lodge, Watford; Mr. C. E. Fry, The Little Elms, Watford; Mr. T. Gardner, Queen's Road, Watford; Mr. George Green, Hyde Lodge, Watford; Mr. James U. Harford, Upper Nascot, Watford; Mr. Thomas Heather,

Queen's Road, Watford; Mr. Clement Heaton, Verulam House, Watford; the Rev. W. Marsden Hind, LL.D., The Parsonage, Pinner; Mr. James Hopkinson and Mr. John Hopkinson, F.G.S., Holly Bank, Watford; Mr. Charles F. Humbert, F.G.S., Little Nascot, Watford; Dr. F. H. Wilson Iles and Mrs. Iles, High Street, Watford; the Rev. R. Lee James, LL.B., The Vicarage, Watford; Dr. J. Gwyn Jeffreys, F.R.S., F.L.S., Treas.G.S., etc., Ware Priory; Mr. J. Logan Lobley, F.G.S., F.R.G.S., 59, Clarendon Road, Notting Hill, London; Mr. W. H. Petty and Miss Petty, Lady's Close, Watford; Mr. George Ryan and Mr. Robert Ryan, Belmont House, Watford; Mr. John Sedgwick, Elmcote, Watford; Mr. Alfred O. Sedgwick and Mrs. Sedgwick, North End House, Watford; Mr. F. J. Sedgwick, High Street, Watford; Mr. F. W. Silvester, Hedges, St. Albans; Mr. J. J. Smith, Miss Smith, Mr. W. L. Smith, and Mr. C. R. Smith, Lady's Close, Watford; Mr. George Tidcombe, jun., C.E., Chalk Hill, Bushey; Mr. William A. Tooke, Pinner Hill; Mr. George Wailes, Park Road, Watford; Mrs. Walker and Mr. J. Watson Walker, jun., Fairfield House, Watford; Miss E. S. Wilkie, Bushey Grange; and the Rev. T. Wiltshire, M.A., F.L.S., Sec.G.S., etc., 25, Granville Park, Lewisham.

Moved by Mr. Chippindale, seconded by Mr. Silvester, and carried—"That Mr. John Hopkinson be the Honorary Secretary of the Society."

Moved by Mr. Lobley, seconded by Dr. Iles, and carried—"That the following gentlemen constitute the Provisional Committee, to consider the organization, constitution, and laws of the Society, and to report thereon to the next general meeting: Dr. Brett, Mr. Alfred Copeland, Mr. Arthur Cottam, Mr. C. E. Fry, Mr. Thomas Heather, Mr. C. F. Humbert, Mr. F. W. Silvester, Mr. W. L. Smith, Mr. G. Tidcombe, jun., and Mr. John Hopkinson."

A vote of thanks to the Chairman having been moved by Mr. Lobley, seconded by Dr. Iles, and carried, Dr. Brett briefly replied, wishing success to the Society.

INAUGURAL MEETING, 11TH FEBRUARY, 1875.

Charles F. Humbert, Esq., F.G.S., having first been voted to the Chair, stated that this meeting had been convened by the Provisional Committee to elect a President and other officers, and to pass the laws.

He then proposed the election of Mr. John Evans, F.R.S., etc., as the first President of the Society. Dr. Brett seconded, and the resolution was carried unanimously.

Mr. Evans, on taking the Chair, said that, owing to his time being so fully occupied, he had with great reluctance consented to accept the office of President: he had, however, been pressed to do so in so kind a manner, that he could not refuse, and would do all in his power to further the objects of the Society.

The following ladies and gentlemen were elected Members of the Society by resolution:—

Miss Benskin and Mr. John P. Benskin, High Street, Watford; Mr. C. A. Booth, Westfield, Watford; Miss F. Cazalet, St. Albans Road, Watford; Mr. Jonathan Chater, High Street, Watford; Miss Clarke, The Lindens, Watford; Mr. A. Basil Cottam, St. John's Road, Watford; Miss Ada Cotterell, The Stanboroughs, Watford; the Right Honourable the Lord Ebury, Moor Park, Rickmansworth; Miss Diggle and Mr. William A. Diggle, Queen's Road, Watford; Mr. Robert Etheridge, F.R.S., F.R.S.E., V.P.G.S., Palæontologist to the Geological Survey of England, Museum, Jermyn Street, London; Miss Evans and Miss Beatrice Evans, Barham Lodge, Elstree; Mr. Walter J. Green, High Street, Watford; the Honourable Norman Grosvenor, Moor Park, Rickmansworth; Mr. Edward Harrison, Upper Nascot, Watford; Mr. John Hart, Miss Hart, and Miss Fanny Hart, Wansford House, Watford; Mr. J. E. Harting, F.L.S., F.Z.S., 27, Carlton Hill, St. John's Wood, London; Mr. Charles Henson, Rutland Lodge, Watford; Mr. Henry Hicks, M.R.C.S., F.G.S., Heriot House, Hendon; Mr. John E. Littleboy, Hunton Bridge; Mr. Richard Morgan, Clarendon Hotel, Watford; Mr. Simpson Noakes, Bushey Heath; Mr. Bernard Piffard and Mrs. Piffard, Hill House, Hemel Hempstead; Mr. R. A. Pryor, B.A., F.L.S., Hatfield; Mr. George Rooper, F.Z.S., Nascot House, Watford; Dr. Alfred T. Rudyard, St. Albans Road, Watford; Mr. J. G. Smith, Hamper Mills, Watford; Mr. W. T. Stone, Watford Heath; Mr. William Verini, The Ferns, Bushey Heath; and the Rev. W. Walsh, M.A., The Parsonage, St. Andrew's, Watford.

The following gentlemen were elected as the Officers and Council for the ensuing year, in addition to Mr. John Evans, already elected President:—

Vice-Presidents.—Alfred T. Brett, M.D.; the Right Honourable the Earl of Essex; Charles F. Humbert, F.G.S.; J. Gwyn Jeffreys, LL.D., F.R.S., F.L.S., F.G.S.

Treasurer.—Arthur Cottam, F.R.A.S.

Hon. Secretary and Librarian.—John Hopkinson, F.L.S., F.G.S.

Hon. Curator.—W. Lepard Smith.

Other Members of the Council.—E. M. Chater; George Chippindale; John E. Dawson, F.R.G.S., F.R.M.S.; H. Sugden Evans. F.R.M.S., F.C.S.; the Rev. W. Falconer, M.A., F.R.A.S.; Admiral E. G. Fanshawe, F.R.G.S.; W. M. Fawcett; Thomas Heather; the Rev. R. Lee James, LL.B.; J. Logan Lobley. F.G.S., F.R.G.S.; John Sedgwick; Frank W. Silvester.

The following Laws, proposed for adoption by the Provisional Committee, were then read and passed *seriatim*:—

I.—The Society shall be called the WATFORD NATURAL HISTORY SOCIETY AND HERTFORDSHIRE FIELD CLUB, and shall have for its object the investigation of the Meteorology, Geology, Botany, and Zoology of the neighbourhood of Watford and the County of Hertford, and the dissemination amongst its members of information on Natural History and Microscopical Science.

II.—The Society shall consist of Ordinary and Honorary Members, including Ladies; the number of Ordinary Members being unlimited, and the number of Honorary Members being limited to twenty.

III.—The management of the Society shall be vested in a Council consisting of a President, four Vice-Presidents, a Treasurer, an Honorary Secretary and Librarian, an Honorary Curator, and twelve other members, to be elected annually, by ballot, at the Ordinary Meeting in February, which shall be the Annual Meeting. The President shall not hold office for a longer term than two years, and in each year the senior Vice-President, and the three senior ordinary members of the Council, shall not be eligible for re-election; but the Council shall have power to fill up, from these or other Members of the Society, any vacancy that may occur during the year.

IV.—The Ordinary Meetings of the Society shall be held in the rooms of the Watford Public Library on the second Thursday in each month (except during the months of July, August, and September), at half-past seven o'clock in the evening, the Council having power to alter the day and hour of meeting; and during the summer months Field Meetings shall also be held at such time and place as the Council may direct.

V.—Minutes shall be kept of the Ordinary Meetings of the Society and of the meetings of the Council, and the minutes of each meeting shall be read as the first business of the next ensuing meeting of the same kind.

VI.—Members shall have the privilege of attending all the Ordinary and Field Meetings of the Society, and of introducing one Visitor at any such meeting, and shall be entitled to a copy of all Publications issued by the Society during their membership.

VII.—The Annual Subscription for Ordinary Members shall be Ten Shillings, payable immediately after their election, and afterwards due in advance on the 1st of January in each year; and all Members elected after the year of the foundation of the Society shall pay an Entrance Fee of Ten Shillings. No Member shall be entitled to any of the privileges of the Society whose subscription is twelve months in arrear; and any Member whose subscription is two years in arrear may be excluded from the Society by the Council.

VIII.—Any Ordinary Member may compound for his or her Annual Subscriptions by a payment of Five Pounds.

IX.—The Honorary Members shall be ladies or gentlemen of eminence in Natural Science, or who shall have done some special service to the Society, and whose usual place of residence is not in the County of Hertford or within twelve miles of the town of Watford; and they shall be elected only by the Members upon the recommendation of the Council, not more than five to be elected in any one year.

X.—Every Candidate for admission shall be proposed by two or more Members, who shall sign a certificate in recommendation of such candidate, one of the proposers from personal knowledge. The certificate shall be read from the Chair at the Ordinary Meeting following its receipt by the Secretary, and the candidate shall then be balloted for, one black ball in six excluding.

XI.—Members wishing to resign at the termination of any year are required to inform the Honorary Secretary, in writing, of their intention to do so, on or before the 30th of November in that year.

XII.—The Accounts of the Society shall be made up to the 31st of December in each year, and audited by two Auditors appointed at the Ordinary Meeting following; and the Balance Sheet, together with a Report on the general progress of the Society during the preceding year, shall be submitted to the Annual Meeting in February.

XIII.—The Society shall discourage the practice of removing rare plants from the localities of which they are characteristic, and of exterminating rare birds, fish, and other animals, and shall use its influence with landowners and others for the protection of the characteristic birds of the County, and of the neighbourhood of Watford in particular; the rarer botanical specimens collected at the Field Meetings shall be chiefly such as can be gathered without disturbing the roots of the plants; and notes on the habits of birds shall be accumulated instead of specimens, either of the birds or of their eggs.

XIV.—No Law shall be altered except by a majority of votes of the Members present at a Special Meeting called for that purpose. The Council may at any time, and shall, upon a requisition signed by not less than twelve Members, convene a Special Meeting; and a printed notice stating the objects for which the meeting is convened shall be sent to each Member not less than ten days before such meeting, at which no business shall be considered except that for which it was convened.

XV.—A copy of these Laws shall be sent by the Secretary to each Member upon election to membership of the Society.

The President then delivered an address on the work that might be done by the Society in the investigation of the Natural History of the County, treating briefly of some of the most important points for inquiry in the sciences of Meteorology, Geology and Palæontology, Botany, and Zoology, and of the value of the microscope in scientific investigation.

A vote of thanks to the President having been moved by Mr. John Hopkinson, seconded by Dr. Brett, and carried, Mr. Evans briefly responded.

The meeting then resolved itself into a Conversazione, at which the following gentlemen exhibited objects under their microscopes :— Dr. Brett, Mr. E. M. Chater, Mr. Arthur Cottam, Mr. A. Basil Cottam, Mr. H. Sugden Evans, Mr. John Hopkinson, and Mr. J. Watson Walker.

ORDINARY MEETING, 11TH MARCH, 1875.

JOHN EVANS, Esq., V.P.R.S., etc., President, in the Chair.

Mrs. John Evans, Nash Mills, Hemel Hempstead; Mr. George H. Gisby, Widbury Hill, Ware; Mrs. James Hopkinson, Holly Bank, Watford; Miss Juliette Scholz, Aldenham Lane, Bushey; Miss Ethel Sedgwick, Elmcote, Watford; Mr. C. K. Smith, The Hawthorns, Watford; Mr. John Wilson, 159, New Bond Street, London; and Miss Mary Wilson and Miss Rose Wilson, Grove House, Bushey, were elected Members of the Society.

The following lecture was delivered :—
"The Cretaceous Rocks of England." By J. Logan Lobley, F.G.S., F.R.G.S. (*Vide* page 1).

A discussion ensued, in which Mr. W. Whitaker, of the Geological Survey of England, Mr. James U. Harford, Mr. Arthur Cottam, and the President, took part.

The following specimens were exhibited :—

Fossils from the Cretaceous Rocks, in illustration of his lecture, by Mr. Lobley.

Fossils from the Cretaceous Rocks; and, under the microscope, Foraminifera from the Chalk of Norfolk, and from the Mediterranean, by Mr. John Hopkinson.

Foraminifera from the Chalk of Watford, and from the Red Sea, under the microscope, by Mr. Arthur Cottam.

The lecture was also illustrated by numerous maps and diagrams; the Geological Society's Geological Map of England having been lent for the occasion by the Geologists' Association; a Section across the Wealden, by the Geological Survey; and Diagrams of Cretaceous Fossils, by Professor Morris.

ORDINARY MEETING, 8TH APRIL, 1875.

ALFRED T. BRETT, Esq., M.D., Vice-President, in the Chair.

Mr. Stephen Austin, Bayley Lodge, Hertford; Mr. William Barber, M.A., and Mrs. Barber, Wood Hall, Pinner; Major Francis Duncan, Royal Artillery, M.A., D.C.L., LL.D., F.G.S., F.R.G.S., 29, The Common, Woolwich; Mr. Thomas F. Halsey, M.P., Gaddesden Place, Hemel Hempstead; Mr. J. Cardinal Harford, Upper Nascot, Watford; Dr. Peter Hood, Upton House, Watford; Mrs. Humbert, Little Nascot, Watford; Mr. J. Henry James, Kingswood, Watford; Dr. M. Drury Lavin, Bushey; Mr. W. Jones Loyd, Langleybury, Watford; the Rev. C. M. Perkins, M.A., Abbey Gateway, St. Albans; the Rev. Newton Price, Belmont House, Watford; Mr. Robert Pryor, High Elms, Watford; Mrs. Ransom, Essex Road, Watford; Mr. Henry Rogers and Mrs. Rogers, Portman House, Watford; Mr. F. J. Thairlwall, 169, Gloucester Road, Regent's Park, London; Miss Ward, Chalk Hill, Bushey; and Mr. George Waterman, Derby Road, Watford, were elected Members of the Society.

George James Allman, M.D., F.R.S., F.R.S.E., Pres.L.S., Emerson Professor of Natural History in the University of Edinburgh; James Glaisher, F.R.S., F.R.A.S., F.R.M.S., F.M.S., Superintendent of the Magnetic and Meteorological Department, Royal Observatory, Greenwich; Joseph Dalton Hooker, M.D., R.N., C.B., D.C.L., LL.D., Pres.R.S., F.L.S., F.G.S., Director of the Royal Gardens, Kew; Sir John Lubbock, Bart., M.P., F.R.S., F.L.S., F.G.S.; and John Morris, F.G.S., Goldsmid Professor of Geology and Mineralogy in University College, London, were elected Honorary Members.

The following communications were read :—

1. A Letter from Mr. H. A. Warne, Oneida, Madison Co., New York, to the Honorary Secretary, dated 17th Feb., 1875, offering to exchange North American for British Plants.

Mr. Warne wishes to obtain the more striking and characteristic plants of the British Isles, and " would prefer species of Ranunculaceæ, Rosaceæ (only a few *Rubus* species), the showier Scrophulariaceæ, Polemoniaceæ, Solanaceæ, Gentianaceæ, Ericaceæ, and the most interesting Compositæ and Liliaceæ," not represented in North America. Any peculiarly interesting or striking plants from other orders would be acceptable, and he would be glad to get specially peculiar mosses and all the ferns not found also in America. Parasitic fungi *on leaves*, and lichens, are also desired. For these he states that he can return "a large proportion of the species of phænogamous plants found east of the Mississippi, and a number from Colorado and California." He has also many ferns, mosses, liverworts, lichens, and fungi. He recommends that packages should be sent " by mail." No package should exceed two pounds in weight. " No writing should be put in the packages—the specimens must simply be numbered, with a slip of paper attached, and the names, with corresponding numbers, sent by letter. This," he says, "will insure second or third rates of postage, and safe delivery."

2. "Notes on a Proposed Re-issue of the Flora of Hertfordshire, with Supplementary Remarks on the Botany of the Watford District." By R. A. Pryor, B.A., F.L.S. (*Vide* p. 17).

3. "On the Botanical Geography of Hertfordshire." By Arthur Cottam, F.R.A.S.

Mr. Cottam stated that the 'Flora Hertfordiensis' was now very much out of date. It was published in 1849, and had two appendices—one dated 1851, and the other 1859. The boundary lines on the map, dividing the county into districts for botanical purposes, were to a great extent artificial, rendering it impossible to make them out on the ground. On a large map he showed where the natural lines of division should be, forming the districts from the drainage areas of the different rivers and their tributaries.

4. "Notes on the Flora of the Watford District." By Arthur Cottam, F.R.A.S. (*Vide* p. 14).

The Secretary then read extracts from letters he had received, as follows:—(1) from Mr. William A. Tooke, Pinner Hill, offering to render assistance to Members of the Society desirous of examining the flora of the district, as far as his property extends; (2) from Mr. H. George Fordham, Odsey, near Royston, saying that if at any time an excursion should be made to that neighbourhood—to the coprolite pits or other places of interest—he would do what he could to further the objects of the Society; (3) from Mr. John E. Ingpen, Honorary Secretary of the Quekett Microscopical Club, London, inviting the Members of the Society to join in any of the Excursions of the Club; and (4) from Mr. Henry Walker, Honorary Secretary of the West London Scientific Association and Field Club, to the same effect as the preceding.

A Collection of Mosses was exhibited by Dr. Brett; collections of Hertfordshire Plants, by Mr. Cottam and Mr. W. L. Smith; and spore-cases of Ferns, under the microscope, by Mr. J. Hopkinson.

FIELD MEETING, 1ST MAY, 1875.

Rain was falling heavily, when a train arrived at Watford, conveying about five-and-twenty members of the Geologists' Association, who, in spite of the prospect of a thoroughly wet afternoon, had left London to join in the first Field Meeting of the Watford Natural History Society. The President, the Secretary, and several other members received them; and as there seemed no prospect of anything but a thoroughly wet afternoon—for it had been raining continuously most of the day—the programme which had been announced was abandoned, and the members of the two Societies assembled at the residence of the Secretary—Holly Bank—where Professor Morris had kindly consented to give a lecture on what would have been seen had the day been fine.

Soon, however, the rain almost ceased, and it was decided to visit a chalk-pit in Berry Wood, near Aldenham, as being the nearest spot known where an instructive geological section could be seen.

Crossing the Colne at Bushey Mill, a gravel-pit near Berry Wood was first examined, and Professor Morris showed that the gravel here was Drift re-arranged and brought down from higher levels; some of its flint pebbles being slightly rolled; others more or less angular; and others again, elliptical, kidney-shaped, or round, and perfectly black—these being derived from the waste of beds of Lower Tertiary age. Fragments also of hardened slate, grit, quartzite, and white quartz here were seen—the latter being derived from slaty rocks which do not occur *in situ* in this part of England, and were most probably brought by the action of ice from Palæozoic rocks some hundreds of miles north of this spot.

The Chalk-pit in Berry Wood was then visited. Here the Upper Chalk has a very irregular surface underlying a thick bed of gravel, which was shown not to repose now on the surface on which it was originally deposited; the Chalk having been at one time nearly level, and afterwards irregularly dissolved away by the percolation through the gravel and into cracks, or its more pervious portions, of water holding carbonic acid in solution.

In the Chalk here are the remains of sponges and ventriculites inclosed in mere shells of flint, containing "spicules," Foraminifera, and even Polyzoa, beautifully preserved; and amongst others, specimens of *Globigerina haloides* were detected by Professor Morris, who stated that a similar form was now living in the Atlantic, where the chalk now being accumulated frequently contains 90 per cent. of Foraminifera, specimens of which he exhibited, and also of the chalk from which they were washed, dredged from a depth of a mile and a half.

The President here, choosing a solid flint with one surface somewhat even, showed how by striking the plane surface sharply in a vertical direction with a round-headed hammer, a perfectly regular cone may be produced, the single blow depressing the flint at the point hit, and thus causing an increased density of the slightly elastic particles of which it is composed, immediately under this point, which forms the apex of the cone; the surrounding flint being afterwards removed by giving it a few sharp taps with the hammer.

The beautiful grounds of "Otterspool," the residence of Mr. S. T. Holland, were by his kind permission next visited. Here there is a remarkable pool, at the bottom of which are several springs which now yield about 300,000 gallons of water a day, and are said at times some years ago to have yielded a million. These springs are part of a series which rise along the valley by lowering the reservoir of water in the chalk, and here seem mostly due to the rain which falls on the adjoining Eocene area, and percolates through the Lower Eocene sands and Drift gravels into the Chalk. The pool was by sounding found to be 16 feet deep at the deepest part; and the water is so clear that the springs themselves, and the sides of the fissure in the chalk which forms the pool, can be distinctly seen, and so cold that wine is iced in it.

Although this Field Meeting was chiefly devoted to geology, a few plants were collected by the botanists; and the following list of mollusca collected by one of the party—Mr. H. J. J. Lavis—will show that the conchology of Berry Wood is also worthy of attention:

Clausilia, sp. Berry Wood Chalk-pit, "amongst moss."

Cochlicopa (Jeffreys), sp. Near Otterspool, Berry Wood, "in some moss around an old tree stump."

Helix aspersa,
    „ cantiana (?),   } Near Otterspool, Berry Wood, "under some bricks and
    „ nemoralis,   } stones," abundant.

Lymnea peregra,
    „ stagnalis,   } "In a pond by the side of the road, just after crossing
Physa fontinalis,   } the river bridge" (Bushey Mill).
Planorbis carinatus,
    „ corneus,

Zonites glabra,   } Near Otterspool, Berry Wood, "under some bricks and
    „ radiatula,   } stones."

On their return to Watford the members of the Geologists' Association had tea at Holly Bank before leaving for London by an evening train, to which the saloon carriage in which they had arrived—kindly provided by the Railway Company—was attached.

ORDINARY MEETING, 13TH MAY, 1875.

ALFRED T. BRETT, ESQ., M.D., Vice-President, in the Chair.

The Honourable Arthur Capel, Cassiobury Park, Watford; Mr. William T. Eley, Oxhey Grange, Watford; Mr. John B. Fairman, Aldenham; the Rev. Canon Gee, D.D., The Vicarage, Abbot's Langley; Mr. Frank Hollingsworth, The Netherwyld, St. Albans; Mrs. Jones Loyd, Langleybury, Watford; Miss Willshin, Kingsbury, St. Albans; and Major J. Andover Wood, 11, Princes Square, Bayswater, London, were elected Members of the Society.

Letters were read from Professor Allman, Dr. Hooker, and Sir John Lubbock, thanking the Society for their election as Honorary Members.

The following papers were read:—

1. "On the Observation of Periodical Natural Phenomena." By John Hopkinson, F.L.S., F.G.S., Hon. Sec. (*Vide* p. 33).

2. "Notes on the Plants on which the Meteorological Society invites Observations as to their Time of Flowering." By the Rev. W. Marsden Hind, LL.D. (*Vide* p. 43).

3. "Notes on the Observation of Insects in Connexion with Investigations on Seasonal Phenomena." By Arthur Cottam, F.R.A.S. (*Vide* p. 50).

4. "On the Pleasure and Advantages to be derived from a Study of Natural History, and more particularly from the Observation of Birds." By J. E. Harting, F.L.S., F.Z.S. (*Vide* p. 52).

The Rev. Dr. Hind exhibited a number of plants, freshly gathered, in illustration of his paper.

Mr. Cottam exhibited a collection of insects.

Mr. J. Hopkinson exhibited living plants of *Dentaria bulbifera* (coral root) from Red Heath, in flower; and also, under the microscope, one of the axillary bulbs which produce new plants by falling to the ground and there growing—the coral root being usually propagated in this way, as the pod seldom ripens.

Living plants of *Dentaria bulbifera*, from the same locality, were also exhibited by Mr. W. L. Smith.

FIELD MEETING, 29TH MAY, 1875.

COLNE VALLEY WATER WORKS, BUSHEY KILN, AND WATFORD HEATH KILN.

As the weather had prevented the route arranged for the 1st of May being then taken, it was decided upon for this occasion, and a party of about fifty ladies and gentlemen, many of whom were members of the Geologists' Association, who had been invited to take part in this meeting, assembled at Bushey Station at three o'clock.

The Chalk-pit near the station was first visited. A good section of the Upper Chalk is here seen, and overlying it a bed of flint-pebbles from the Woolwich and Reading series proved the former presence of this formation. This bed completely thins out in the pit, and is succeeded by clay-drift and sandy gravel (terrace-gravel), which repose, in other parts of the pit, immediately on the Chalk.

At the Colne Valley Water Works, adjoining this pit, the party were received by Mr. William Verini, who gave an account of the sinking of the well, which he stated had been excavated to a depth of 70 feet, or to 108 feet above ordnance datum, abundance of water having been obtained. Professor Morris here stated that the Chalk is one of our best reservoirs, when exposed over a considerable area absorbing a large amount of rainfall, which, in more impervious rocks, instead of sinking, would at once form rivers on the surface. The water is retained in the Chalk by impermeable beds of clay—the Gault clay—below it, and in boring an underground channel is sometimes tapped.

Leaving the Water Works,—which when complete will supply Bushey, Stanmore, Edgware, and other places, with water from the Chalk, softened by what is called the "lime process,"—the party proceeded to Bushey Kiln, where a section of the higher beds of the Woolwich and Reading series, and of the basement-bed of the London Clay, is exposed.

Crossing then the fields to Watford Heath Kiln, several plants were collected, and the ragged Robin *(Lychnis Flos-cuculi)*, one of the species in the Meteorological Society's list, was seen to be just coming into flower, fully a week later than usual.

At Watford Heath there is a more extensive section of the beds seen at Bushey—the Woolwich series being visible almost to its junction with the Chalk, and several feet of the London Clay, above its basement-bed, being exposed. Here Professor Morris stated that we were just on or near the edge of the London Basin, but that we do not get the lowest beds of the Tertiary series immediately overlying the Chalk, thirty or forty feet of marine sands known as the Thanet sands, not represented here, being found on the opposite side of the Thames, between the Chalk and the Woolwich and Reading beds, and thinning out under London. Here also, he said, the Woolwich series consists of marine beds, containing marine shells, while south of London the shells are all of fresh-water or estuarine species, showing that in the old Tertiary times in the south there was land over which rivers flowed, while there was more or less open sea to the north. Overlying the Woolwich and Reading beds the pebble beds at the base of the London Clay, rounded on an old sea-shore, mark the commencement of a change—a change here from temperate to tropical conditions, as shown by the fauna and flora.

Leaving Watford Heath, and descending the steep slope of the Tertiary escarpment, along the edge of which flows the river Colne, the gravel-pits at Colney Butts were soon reached, and afforded evidence of a climate—within comparatively recent times —very different from that of the London Clay period; for the gravel here is of glacial origin, and pebbles of quartzite and other rocks which could not have come from a nearer point than Charnwood Forest, and may have been brought by the agency of ice from Cumberland or Wales, were found associated with flints from the Hertfordshire Chalk, and with fragments of the Hertfordshire conglomerate.

Here the party dispersed, and most of those who had come from London were very kindly entertained at tea, at Watford House, by Dr. Brett.

FIELD MEETING, 9TH JUNE, 1875.

BRICKET WOOD AND MUNDEN PARK.

As on the 1st of May, rain, though in heavy partial showers instead of as then in a continuous general downpour, threatened to put a stop to the intended arrangements; but fortunately it was late in the afternoon when the start was to be made, and the rain had ceased when the members left Watford for Bricket Wood, where it was proposed to spend most of the evening in collecting plants, insects, and microscopic objects.

Amongst the rarer plants found in flower, *Limosella aquatica*, and *Neottia Nidus-avis* (the bird's-nest orchis), may be mentioned; and several insects of considerable rarity were collected.

Here the party separated,—some remaining in the wood to return to Watford by train, and others returning on foot by Bricket Wood Common, Munden Park, and Berry Wood. In crossing the Colne in Munden Park, the yellow water-lily *(Nuphar lutea)* and the yellow flag *(Iris Pseudacorus)* were seen in profusion in full bloom, and in the hedges the dog-wood *(Cornus sanguinea)* was observed to be just coming into flower. "Otterspool" was again visited, by the kind permission of the proprietor, and the pool, after several trials, was found to be remarkably free from microscopic organisms. A little starwort (*Callitriche verna*), growing in profusion and flowering freely, attracted much attention, being seldom found in flower in the ponds in the neighbourhood of Watford.

In addition to the plants already mentioned, the following were observed in flower in the course of the walk :—*

Thalictrum flavum (meadow rue).—Bushey Mill.
Ranunculus Flammula (lesser spearwort). – Bricket Wood.
Lychnis Flos-cuculi (ragged Robin).—Otterspool.
Orobus tuberosus (bitter vetch).—Bricket Wood.
Potentilla Tormentilla (tormentil).—do.
Sanicula europæa (wood sanicle).—do.
Viburnum Opulus (guelder-rose).—do.
Solanum Dulcamara (bittersweet).—do.
Veronica officinalis (common speedwell).—do.
Pedicularis sylvatica (lousewort).—do.
Rhinanthus Crista-galli (yellow rattle).—do.
Melampyrum pratense (cow-wheat).—do.
Stachys sylvatica (hedge woundwort).—do.
Myosotis palustris (forget-me-not).—Otterspool.
Symphytum officinale (comfrey).—Munden Park.
Lysimachia nemorum (wood loosestrife). – Bricket Wood.
Orchis maculata (spotted orchis).—do.
Habenaria bifolia (butterfly orchis).—do.
Listera ovata (tway-blade orchis).—do.

ORDINARY MEETING, 10TH JUNE, 1875.

ALFRED T. BRETT, Esq., M.D., Vice-President, in the Chair.

Miss Laura Healey, Lady's Close, Watford ; Mr. Arthur Henry Holland, Munden House, Aldenham ; Mr. W. R. Masaroon, Belmont House, Watford ; Mr. Matthew Moggridge, F.G.S., M.A.I., Scientific Club, Savile Row, London ; Mr. E. H. Norris, Belmont House, Watford ; and Miss Clara E. Serle, Woodhall, Pinner, were elected Members of the Society.

The following communications were read :—

1. Reports of the Rainfall for the first quarter of the year :— (1) at Watford House, by Dr. Brett ; (2) at Harwood's Farm, Cassiobury, by Mr. Swanston ; and (3) at Nash Mills, Hemel Hempstead, by Mr. John Evans, F.R.S., President (*Vide* p. 63).

2. A Letter from Dr. Brett, to the Secretary, dated June 5th, asking for information about a Mineral Spring said to have been discovered at Watford in 1689 (*Vide* p. 63).

Mr. Henry Rogers mentioned that this spring was alluded to in the 'Post Office Directory of Hertfordshire' for 1874.

Dr. Brett stated that Mr. J. G. Smith had told him that the water from a well which was dug at Hamper Mills some years ago was so impregnated with iron as to be of no use in paper making.

3. Extract of a Letter from Mr. R. A. Pryor, B.A., F.L.S., to the Secretary, dated Hatfield, 9th June, 1875, giving some account of his recent work in the investigation of the Botany of Hertfordshire (*Vide* p. 63).

* From a list kindly furnished by Mr. E. M. Chater.

4. A Letter from Mr. J. H. James to Dr. Brett, dated Kingswood, Watford, 23rd April, 1875, on the destruction of an Oak Tree by the Larvæ of the Goat Moth, and on the occurrence of the Death's Head Moth at Watford (*Vide* p. 64).

Mr. Arthur Cottam said that the larvæ of the goat moth usually attacked the elm and willow—seldom the oak. They always kept to one tree, and so long as it was in existence would not attack others in the neighbourhood. He had not found them easy to rear beyond the chrysalis state.

Mr. C. E. Fry stated that he had reared the death's head moth from the chrysalis state, but they were usually malformed, having a distorted wing.

The Rev. C. M. Perkins said that he had had a pear tree completely eaten off by the larvæ of the goat moth, and that it was blown down by the wind. The tree was eaten all round; there were three generations in it; none of the younger larvæ lived, but of the three-year-olds he reared several through the chrysalis state to the perfect moth.

Mr. J. Logan Lobley mentioned that he had had poplar and sycamore trees attacked by this moth, and had lost several trees in consequence.

Mr. Fry, having been asked to explain the process of "sugaring," said that he used a composition of beer, sugar, and rum, which he smeared in patches on the trees, rough-barked trees being the best for the purpose. The moths became quite tipsy and fell into the collecting boxes. By sugaring at dusk the capture of moths continues all night, different species arriving at different times.

Mr. Cottam stated that Mr. Fry begins to sugar when the sallows are in bloom, which he thought accounted much for his success. The composition should be put on the leeward side of trees at dusk, when the dumble-dor beetle was on the wing.

The meeting then resolved itself into a conversazione, and numerous objects, principally collected at the Field Meeting the previous day, were exhibited.

A collection of plants from Cannes, France, presented to the Society this evening by the Earl of Essex, was also exhibited.

FIELD MEETING, 19TH JUNE, 1875.

ALDBURY, ASHRIDGE PARK, AND BERKHAMPSTEAD.

Leaving Tring Station at about three o'clock, the members, thirty-two in number, went direct to the village of Aldbury. Here the Church, dedicated to St. John the Baptist, was first visited, and its old tombs and monumental brasses were examined with much interest.

In the centre of the village, by the side of the pond, formed it was found by surface drainage, the stocks were next noticed, still remaining in their original position.

Thence climbing the hill "in the way from *Aldbury* to *Little-Gaddesden*, called *Muniborough*,"* the party entered Ashridge Park, and soon arrived at the Monument—a granite column 200 feet high—erected " In honour of Francis, third Duke of Bridgewater, 'Father of Inland Navigation,' 1832." On Moneybury Hill the President pointed out an old Roman " barrow," in which he said some few years ago Earl Brownlow (the present owner of Ashridge) and he had found about a dozen Roman coins, some forgeries of the time, and a few ancient brooches.

*Salmon, Hist. Antiq. Herts, p. 136.

An opening in the trees revealing an extensive and beautiful prospect of Buckinghamshire, Mr. Evans turned from Archæology to Geology. We are now, he said, at the edge of a false escarpment, the valley just below us being cut out in the Lower Chalk by a stream which now sometimes flows nearly to Aldbury, and sometimes disappears higher up the valley, sinking into swallow-holes in the Chalk; beyond is the true escarpment of the Lower Chalk, with the Totternhoe stone forming a projecting ridge, and passing insensibly into the Upper Greensand; in the middle distance we see, he continued, the Gault valley of Aylesbury, rising into hills here and there; and the higher hills in the extreme distance mark the outcrop of the Lower Greensand.

A peculiar gnarled and twisted beech tree, which should not be allowed to perish before it has formed a subject for pen and pencil, next attracted attention. It is, however, on the Buckinghamshire side of the avenue which extends from the Monument to Ashridge House, and we cannot therefore claim it as one of " the remarkable trees of Hertfordshire." Nor can we claim Ashridge House, for "there is but a small part of the House of *Ashridge* in this County; the rest, and most of the Park, is in Bucks. . . . ."*

Leaving the house, and the County of Buckingham, to the left, Berkhampstead Common was soon reached, and just outside the confines of the park a brick-field was entered.

The clay here is apparently an " outlier "—a portion of the old London Basin cut off from the main body—the intermediate Tertiary beds, which once extended over a very large area, having been removed by denudation, leaving patches here and there as witnesses of its former extent. In places " pipes," formed by the percolation of water through the clay, show that it is not impervious, there being a considerable amount of sand in it. Here and there, also, on its upper surface, drift is seen, apparently due to more recent submergence in glacial times.

A delightful walk across the common—a refreshing change from the more sylvan beauty of the park—brought the party to Berk-hampstead Castle, which was thus described by Salmon in 1728, in his account of " Berkamsted St. Peters:"—

" The Castle contains within its first Moat four or five Acres. There is again a Division by another Moat. The South Part, consisting of about two Acres, is upon a Level, with most of the Walls and Chimneys remaining: the Windows opened all to the Inside. Toward the North, across a Moat, is a high Hill or Keep, capable of defending itself against the former, if possessed by the Enemy. Here are the Traces of the Bridge of Communication, and the Moat dividing these two Places of Strength is continued to the grand one, that takes in the whole Seite of the Fortification. The Bridge for Entrance from the Town was on the South Side, the Remains of it visible; answering exactly to the other on the North of the first Area, which led to the Hill." †

After strolling about the Castle grounds, and resting for a while, the members returned by an evening train to their respective destinations.

Although the eight miles' walk proved rather fatiguing to a few

* Salmon, *l.c.* p. 134.   † *ib.* p. 123.

of the lady members, all seemed to thoroughly enjoy their afternoon, spent in as varied and beautiful scenery as any in the county.

ORDINARY MEETING, 14TH OCTOBER, 1875.

JOHN EVANS, Esq., V.P.R.S., etc., President, in the Chair.

Mr. Edward H. Ambler, Hemel Hempstead; Mr. R. Russell Carew, F.C.S., F.R.G.S., and Mrs. Carew, Carpenders Hall, Watford ; Mr. George Cawston, F.R.Hist.S., Heathbourne, Bushey Heath; Mrs. George Chippindale, Rough Down Villas, Boxmoor; Surgeon-Major J. G. Gibbs, Braziers, Chipperfield; Mr. Charles F. Hancock, jun., Hendon Hall, Hendon ; and Dr. Charles Wotton, King's Langley, were elected Members of the Society.

The President announced the discovery of *Impatiens fulva* on the banks of the canal between Hunton Bridge and Nash Mills.

An extract was read from a Letter from the Rev. Dr. Hind to the Secretary, asking for any information on the Botany of the neighbourhood of Harrow the members of the Society could give, a new edition of the ' Flora of Harrow ' being ready for the press.

Mr. Arthur Cottam read a note on the Appearance of *Sphinx Convolvuli* (*Vide* p. 108).

The following lecture was delivered, as introductory to the Second Session of the Society :—

"The Physical Structure of the London Basin, considered in its relation to the Geology of the Neighbourhood of Watford." By Professor John Morris, F.G.S. (*Vide* p. 89).

The President, in proposing a vote of thanks to Prof. Morris, made a few remarks on the subject of the lecture.

Fossils from the London Clay were exhibited by Prof. Morris ; and Cretaceous and Eocene Fossils by Mr. J. Hopkinson.

Maps and Diagrams, in illustration of his lecture, were also exhibited by the Professor; and the Greenough Geological Map of England was kindly lent for the occasion by the Geological Society of London.

ORDINARY MEETING, 11TH NOVEMBER, 1875.

JOHN EVANS, Esq., V.P.R.S., etc., President, in the Chair.

Mr. Robert Philips Greg, F.G.S., F.R.A.S., Coles Park, Buntingford, and Mr. Stephen Taprell Holland, Otterspool, Aldenham, were elected Members of the Society.

The following communications were read :—

1. Reports of the Rainfall for the second and third quarters of the year :—(1) at Cassiobury House, by the Right Hon. the Earl of Essex ; (2) at Watford House, by Dr. Brett ; (3) at Harwood's Farm, Cassiobury, by Mr. Swanston ; (4) at Ouklands, Hempstead Road, Watford, by Mr. E. Harrison ; and (5) at Nash Mills, Hemel Hempstead, by the President (*Vide* p. 112).

2. Extract of a Letter from the Hon. Norman Grosvenor to the Rev. Newton Price, mentioning an exposure of the Bagshot Sands and overlying gravels in excavations which are being made for the foundations of some new buildings on Harrow Hill.

3. "On the Botanical Work of the Past Season." By R. A. Pryor, B.A., F.L.S. (*Vide* p. 65).

4. Extract of a Letter from the Rev. Dr. Hind to the Secretary, giving a few notes on the Botany of West Suffolk (*Vide* p. 108).

5. "A Few Words about our Local Ferns." By John E. Littleboy (*Vide* p. 83).

6. "Note on the Discovery of *Impatiens fulva* near Watford." By John E. Littleboy.

Mr. Littleboy stated that he was rowing in his boat on the Grand Junction Canal one evening when he noticed in a mass of the yellow flag, between Hunton Bridge and Russell Farm, a flower that was quite new to him, and which he found on examination to be *Impatiens fulva*. It was so abundant here that there was no danger of its being eradicated. He found it to be in full bloom about the middle or end of August.

The President said that although he had mentioned its occurrence at the last meeting of the Society, Mr. Littleboy had the right of prior discovery. He had found it in one or two places by the side of the Canal, but not in such abundance as where Mr. Littleboy had first discovered it.

Mr. John Hopkinson read Mr. H. C. Watson's account of its distribution, in which he states that the plant is of American origin, and is now perfectly naturalized in England. "Beginning considerably above Guildford, it may be traced," he says, "at intervals along the river Wey, down to its junction with the Thames at Weybridge. Below this point, localities occur on both sides of the Thames; as at Walton, Kingston, Barnes, Twickenham, and Isleworth. From Weybridge, again, in another direction, it ascends the course of the Basingstoke Canal, to Woking Heath, if not further; probably carried by boats or their towing ropes against the course of the slow stream of the canal." * Mr. Hopkinson also stated that Mr. Pryor had found it at Harefield, extending, he (Mr. Pryor) supposed, into Herts.

Mr. Littleboy said that if the plant were of American origin its seeds might have been brought in the American wheat now so largely used, some of which not unfrequently got into the Canal.

Mr. Hopkinson mentioned that he had found a single plant of *Œnothera biennis* (evening primrose) in a field near Langley Road, Watford. It had been noticed in the county before at Ware, Hertford, and Hitchin.

Mr. E. M. Chater said that he had found *Potentilla argentea*—mentioned in the 'Flora Hertfordiensis' as occurring in a neighbouring district—in two localities, Rousebarn Lane and the gravel-pit at Brightwell's Farm. He had also found there *Dianthus armeria*, mentioned as occurring at Chorley Wood and the Watford tunnel.

ORDINARY MEETING, 9TH DECEMBER, 1875.

ALFRED T. BRETT, Esq., M.D., Vice-President, in the Chair.

Mr. H. George Fordham, F.G.S., Odsey, Royston; Mrs. Griffits, Queen's Road, Watford; Mr. Frank E. Marshall, M.A., Harrow; Mr. Freeman C. S. Roper, F.L.S., F.G.S., F.R.M.S., Palgrave House, Eastbourne; and Mr. Charles Snewing, Holywell Farm, Watford, were elected Members of the Society.

* Cybele Britannica, vol. i. p. 298.—1847.

The following papers were read :—

1. "List of Works on the Geology of Hertfordshire." By William Whitaker, B.A., F.G.S., of the Geological Survey of England. Communicated by the Honorary Secretary (*Vide* p. 78).

2. "Note on the Occurrence of *Impatiens fulva* in Herts." By R. A. Pryor, B.A., F.L.S. (Incorporated in the paper "On the Botanical Work of the Past Season," at p. 71.)

A complete Ordnance Survey Map of the solid geology of Hertfordshire, which had been purchased by the Society, was exhibited, and the Secretary stated that as part of the map was not yet published, he had written to Mr. Bristow, Director of the Survey, asking permission to have the portion required coloured geologically. He read Mr. Bristow's reply, granting the permission of the Director-General, Professor Ramsay, on condition that no copy of this portion be made before the map of the Survey was published, and stated that the required half-sheet had been coloured at the office of the Survey by Mr. Best, without expense to the Society.

DONATIONS TO THE LIBRARY IN 1875.

TITLE.	DONOR.
BENTHAM, GEORGE. Handbook of the British Flora. [Illustrated Edition.] 2 vols. 8vo. London, 1865.	*Mr. W. L. Smith.*
BIRMINGHAM NATURAL HISTORY AND MICROSCOPICAL SOCIETY. Annual Report for 1874. 8vo. Birmingham, 1875	*The Society.*
BRISTOL NATURALISTS' SOCIETY. Proceedings, new series. vol. i. parts 1 and 2. 8vo. Bristol, 1874-75.	,,
———— Laws. *ib.* 1875.	,,
———— Annual Report for 1874-75. *ib.* 1875. .	,,
COLEMAN, W. S. British Butterflies. 8vo. London, 1860.	*Mr. J. Hopkinson.*
———— Our Woodlands, Heaths, and Hedges. 8vo. London, 1869.	,,
COOKE, M. C. Our Reptiles. 8vo. London, 1865. .	*Lord Ebury.*
———— Handbook of British Fungi. 2 vols. 8vo. London, 1871.	*Mr. A. Cottam.*
CROLL, JAMES. On the Physical Cause of Ocean Currents. (*Phil. Mag.* 1874.)	*The Author.*
CROMBIE, Rev. JAMES. The Geological Relations of the Alpine Flora of Great Britain. (*Proc. Geol. Assoc.*)	*Mr. J. Hopkinson.*
DAVIES, THOMAS. The Preparation and Mounting of Microscopic Objects. 2nd edition. Edited by John Matthews. 8vo. London, 1873 . . .	*Mr. A. Cottam.*
EASTBOURNE NATURAL HISTORY SOCIETY. Proceedings, Session 1874-75. 4to. Eastbourne, 1875 . .	*The Society.*
———— The Natural History of Eastbourne and its Vicinity. 12mo. *ib.* 1873	,,
EVANS, JOHN. The Ancient Stone Implements, Weapons, and Ornaments of Great Britain. 8vo. London, 1872	*The Author.*
GEOLOGICAL SOCIETY. Abstracts of the Proceedings, Nos. 289-305. 8vo. London, 1874-75 . .	*The Society.*

TITLE.	DONOR.
GEOLOGISTS' ASSOCIATION. Proceedings, vol. iv. Nos. 1-4. 8vo. London, 1875	*The Association.*
—— Annual Report for 1874. *ib.* 1875 . .	,,
HARTING, J. E. The Ornithology of Shakespeare. 8vo. London, 1871	*The Author.*
—— A Handbook of British Birds. *ib.* 1872 .	,,
—— "The Field" Calendar of Ornithology. General Report for 1872. *ib.* 1873 . . .	,,
—— Our Summer Migrants. *ib.* 1875 . .	,,
—— Rambles in Search of Shells, Land and Freshwater. *ib.* 1875	,,
HEATHER, J. F. Mathematical Instruments. 12mo. London, 1872	*Mr. T. Heather.*
HERSCHELL, Sir JOHN F. W. Meteorology. 8vo. Edinburgh, 1861	*Mr. J. Hopkinson.*
HOPKINSON, JOHN. On British Graptolites. (*Journ. Quek. Micr. Club*, 1869.)	*The Author.*
—— On *Dexolites gracilis*, a new Silurian Annelide. (*Geol. Mag.* 1870.)	,,
—— On the Structure and Affinities of the Genus *Dicranograptus* (*ib.* 1870.)	,,
—— On *Dicellograpsus*, a new Genus of Graptolites. (*ib.* 1871.)	,,
—— On a Specimen of *Diplograpsus pristis* with Reproductive Capsules. (*Ann. Nat. Hist.* 1871.) .	,,
—— On *Callograptus radicans*, a new Dendroid Graptolite. (*ib.* 1872.)	,,
—— On some New Species of Graptolites from the South of Scotland. (*Geol. Mag.* 1872.) .	,,
—— The Graptolites of the Arenig Rocks of St. David's, South Wales. (*Proc. Liverpool Geol. Soc.* 1873.)	,,
—— On some Graptolites from the Upper Arenig Rocks of Ramsey Island, St. David's. (*ib.* 1874.) .	,,
—— Report of the Proceedings of the Geological Section of the British Association at Edinburgh, 1871. (*Proc. Geol. Assoc.* 1872.) . . .	,,
—— Excursion of the Geologists' Association to Watford, April 13th, 1872. (*ib.* 1873.) . . .	,,
—— Excursion of the Geologists' Association to Eastbourne and St. Leonards, May 23rd and 24th, 1873. (*ib.* 1874.)	,,
INTELLECTUAL OBSERVER. Vols. i-ii. 8vo. London, 1868	*Dr. A. T. Brett.*
—— Vols. iii-iv. *ib.* 1869	*Mr. W. H. Petty.*
JARDINE, Sir WILLIAM. "The Field" Calendar of Ornithology for 18 . 8vo. London, 1873 .	*Mr. J. E. Harting.*
JOHNS, Rev. C. A. The Forest Trees of Britain. Vol. 2. 8vo. London, 1849	*Mr. J. Hopkinson.*
JOHNSON, M. H. Flint. 8vo. London, 1871. .	*The Author.*
—— The Nature and Formation of Flint and Allied Bodies. *ib.* 1874	,,
—— On the Microscopic Structure of Flint and Allied Bodies. (*Journ. Quek. Micr. Club*, 1874.) .	,,
KIRBY, Rev. W., and W. SPENCE. An Introduction to Entomology. 8vo. London, 1870 . . .	*Mr. J. Hopkinson.*
LANDSBOROUGH, Rev. D. A Popular History of British Zoophytes. 8vo. London, 1852	*Miss Donagan.*
LARDNER, Dr. The Microscope Explained. 12mo. .	*Mr. J. Hopkinson.*

TITLE.	DONOR.
LIEBIG, JUSTUS von. Familiar Letters on Chemistry. 3rd edition. 8vo. London, 1851	*Mr. W. H. Petty.*
LINDLEY, Prof. JOHN. School Botany. 8vo. London, 1847	*Mr. J. Hopkinson.*
———— Descriptive Botany. 2nd edition. *ib.* 1860 .	,,
LINDSAY, W. LAUDER. A Popular History of British Lichens. 8vo. London, 1855	*Mr. E. M. Chater.*
LOBLEY, J. LOGAN. Mount Vesuvius. 8vo. London, 1868	*The Author.*
LUBBOCK, Sir JOHN. On British Wild Flowers considered in Relation to Insects. 8vo. London, 1875 . .	.,
LYELL, Sir CHARLES. The Student's Elements of Geology. 12mo. London, 1871	*Mr. J. Hopkinson.*
MANN, Dr. JAMES. Address delivered at the Annual General Meeting of the Meteorological Society, 21st Jan. 1874. (*Journ. Meteorol. Soc.* 1874.) . .	*The Author.*
———— .—— 20th Jan. 1875. (*ib.* 1875.) . .	,,
MARLBOROUGH COLLEGE NATURAL HISTORY SOCIETY. Report for the half-year ending Midsummer, 1875. 8vo. Marlborough, 1875	*The Society.*
MELVILLE, J. C. The Flora of Harrow. 12mo. London, 1874	*Rev. Dr. Hind.*
MILLER, HUGH. My Schools and Schoolmasters, or the Story of my Education. 4th edition. 8vo. Edinburgh, 1855	*Mr. J. Hopkinson.*
NEWTON, ALFRED. On a Method of Registering Natural History Observations. (*Trans. Norfolk Nat. Soc.* 1871.)	*The Author.*
PAGE, DAVID. The Earth's Crust. 4th Edition. 8vo. Edinburgh, 1868	*Mr. J. Hopkinson.*
PHILLIPS, Prof. J. Address to the Geological Section of the British Association, Bradford, Sep. 18th, 1873 .	*Mr. W. Whitaker.*
PORTLOCK, Major-General. Rudimentary Treatise on Geology. 4th edition. 12mo. London, 1859 .	*Mr. J. Hopkinson.*
QUEKETT MICROSCOPICAL CLUB. Journal, Nos. 28–29. 8vo. London, 1875	*The Club.*
———— Report for 1874-75. *ib.* 1875 . . .	,,
RAMSAY, Prof. A. C. The Old Glaciers of Switzerland and North Wales. 8vo. London, 1860 . .	*Mr. J. Hopkinson.*
SCHLEIDEN, Dr. J. M. Principles of Scientific Botany. 8vo. London, 1849	*Mr. E. M. Chater.*
SMITH, Sir J. E. An Introduction to Physiological and Systematic Botany. 6th edition. 8vo. London, 1827	*Mr. J. Hopkinson.*
SWAINSON, WILLIAM. A Preliminary Discourse on the Study of Natural History. 8vo. London, 1834 .	,,
———— A Treatise on the Geography and Classification of Animals. *ib.* 1835	,,
———— On the Natural History and Classification of Quadrupeds. *ib.* 1835	,,
———— On the Natural History and Classification of Birds. 2 vols. *ib.* 1836	,,
———— On the Habits and Instincts of Animals. *ib.* 1840	,,
TATE, RALPH. The Land and Fresh-water Mollusks of Great Britain. 8vo. London, 1866 . . .	*Lord Ebury.*
TAYLOR, J. E. Geological Stories. 8vo. London, 1873	*Mr. J. Hopkinson.*
TYLOR, A. On Quaternary Gravels. (*Quart. Journ. Geol. Soc.* 1869.)	,,

TITLE.	DONOR.
VARLEY, D. Rudimentary Treatise on Mineralogy. 4th edition. 12mo. London, 1859	*Mr. J. Hopkinson.*
WALKER, HENRY. The Glacial Drifts of Muswell Hill and Finchley. 12mo. London, 1874 . . .	*Miss Donagan.*
WARD, J. CLIFTON. On the Advantages of a Combined Literary and Scientific Education. 8vo. Cockermouth, 1874	*Mr. W. Whitaker.*
WARINGTON, GEORGE. The Phenomena of Radiation. 8vo. London, 1865	*Mr. J. Hopkinson.*
WATSON, H. C. The London Catalogue of British Plants. 7th edition. 8vo. London, 1874 . . .	,,
WEBB, Rev. R. H., and Rev. W. H. COLEMAN. Flora Hertfordiensis. 12mo. London and Hertford, 1849-59	*Mr. Stephen Austin.*
WHITAKER, WILLIAM. The Geology of Parts of Middlesex, Hertfordshire, Buckinghamshire, Berkshire, and Surrey. 8vo. London, 1864	*The Author.*
———— On Subaërial Denudation, and on Cliffs and Escarpments of the Chalk and the Lower Tertiary Beds. (*Geol. Mag.* 1867.)	,,
———— On the Connection of the Geological Structure and the Physical Features of the South-East of England with the Consumption Death-rate. (*ib.* 1869.)	,,
———— On the Chalk of the Cliffs from Seaford to Eastbourne, Sussex. (*ib.* 1871.)	,,
———— On the Chalk of the Southern Part of Dorset and Devon. (*Quart. Journ. Geol. Soc.* 1871.) .	,,
———— On the Cliff-sections of the Tertiary Beds West of Dieppe in Normandy, and at Newhaven in Sussex. (*ib.* 1871.)	,,
———— On the Occurrence of the " Chalk Rock" near Salisbury. (*Mag. Wiltshire Nat. Hist. Soc.* 1871.)	,,
———— On the Occurrence of Thanet Beds and of Crag at Sudbury, Suffolk. (*Quart. Journ. Geol. Soc.* 1874.)	,,
———— Guide to the Geology of London and the Neighbourhood. 8vo. London, 1874 . . .	,,
WHITE, Rev. GILBERT. The Natural History of Selborne. Edited by the Rev. J. G. Wood. 8vo. London, 1853	*Mr. J. Hopkinson.*
WILTSHIRE, Rev. T. On the Chief Groups of the Cephalopoda. (*Proc. Geol. Assoc.* 1869.) . . .	,,
WINCHESTER AND HAMPSHIRE SCIENTIFIC AND LITERARY SOCIETY. Journal of Proceedings, vol. ii. part i. 8vo. Winchester, 1875	*The Society.*
WITHERING, Dr. W. A Systematic Arrangement of British Plants. Edited by W. Macgillivray. 4th edition. 12mo. London, 1837	*Mr. J. Hopkinson.*
WOODWARD, HENRY. Man and the Mammoth. (*Proc. Geol. Assoc.* 1869.)	,,

SPECIAL MEETING, 13TH JANUARY, 1876.

CHARLES F. HUMBERT, Esq., F.G.S., Vice-President, in the Chair.

The Chairman, having read the circular convening the meeting, formally proposed the adoption of the following Law :—
" Students of the Watford Public Library School of Science and Art who have obtained Queen's Prizes, when elected Members of the Society, shall be exempt from the payment of Entrance Fee."

A vote was then taken, and the meeting being unanimously in favour of the adoption of the Law, the Chairman declared it to be one of the Laws of the Society.

ORDINARY MEETING, 13TH JANUARY, 1876.

CHARLES F. HUMBERT, Esq., F.G.S., Vice-President, in the Chair.

The following communications were read :—

1. Reports of the Rainfall for the fourth quarter of the year 1875 :—(1) at Cassiobury House, by the Right Hon. the Earl of Essex ; (2) at Watford House, by Dr. Brett ; (3) at Harwood's Farm, Cassiobury, by Mr. Swanston ; (4) at Oaklands, Hempstead Road, Watford, by Mr. E. Harrison ; and (5) at Nash Mills, Hemel Hempstead, by the President (*Vide* p. 112).

The Secretary mentioned that the President's quarterly returns showed that the rainfall at Nash Mills in the year was nearly three inches in excess of the mean of the decade 1860-69, and that this excess was entirely due to the last half of the year,—the fall in the first half being about two inches below the mean, and in the second half nearly five inches above it, the month of July alone giving an excess of three inches and three-quarters.

2. " Meteorological Observations taken at Cassiobury House from May to December, 1875." By the Right Hon. the Earl of Essex (*Vide* p. 132).

3. " On the Construction, Adjustment, and Use of Meteorological Instruments." By Thomas Heather.

4. "On the supposed Chalybeate Spring at Watford, and on other Medicinal Waters in Herts." By R. A. Pryor, B.A., F.L.S. (*Vide* p. 109).

Mr. John P. Benskin and Mr. C. F. Hollingsworth were elected Auditors of the Accounts for 1875.

ANNUAL MEETING, 10TH FEBRUARY, 1876.

JOHN EVANS, Esq., F.R.S., etc., President, in the Chair.

Mrs. C. Heaton, Verulam House, Watford, and Mr. Milton Laurie, 145, Gloucester Road, Regent's Park, London, were elected Members of the Society.

George James Symons, Secretary of the Meteorological Society, Editor of ' British Rainfall,' and William Whitaker, B.A., F.G.S., of the Geological Survey of England, Editor of the ' Geological Record,' were elected Honorary Members.

The Report of the Council for 1875, and the Treasurer's Account of Income and Expenditure, were read and adopted.

The President delivered an Address (*Vide* p. 113).

A vote of thanks to Mr. Evans was moved by Mr. Arthur Cottam, seconded by Mr. John E. Littleboy, and carried.

The Balloting-glass having been removed, and the lists examined by the Scrutineers, the following gentlemen were declared to have been duly elected as the Officers and Council for the ensuing year :—

President.—John Evans, F.R.S., F.S.A., F.G.S., etc.

Vice-Presidents.—Alfred T. Brett, M.D.; the Right Honourable the Earl of Essex; Charles F. Humbert, F.G.S.; J. Logan Lobley, F.G.S., F.R.G.S.

Treasurer.—Arthur Cottam, F.R.A.S.

Hon. Secretary and Librarian.—John Hopkinson, F.L.S., F.G.S.

Hon. Curator.—W. Lepard Smith.

Other Members of the Council.—E. M. Chater; George Chippindale; W. M. Fawcett; J. E. Harting, F.L.S., F.Z.S.; Thomas Heather; J. Gwyn Jeffreys, LL.D., F.R.S., F.L.S., F.G.S.; John E. Littleboy; the Rev. C. M. Perkins, M.A.; R. A. Pryor, B.A., F.L.S.; George Rooper, F.Z.S.; John Sedgwick; F. W. Silvester.

It was then resolved—

That the thanks of the Society be given to Dr. J. Gwyn Jeffreys, F.R.S., retiring from the office of Vice-President.

Also that the thanks of the Society be given to Mr. John E. Dawson, Mr. H. Sugden Evans, the Rev. W. Falconer, Admiral Fanshawe, and the Rev. R. Lee James, retiring from the Council.

REPORT OF THE COUNCIL FOR 1875.

IN presenting their first Annual Report, the Council of the Watford Natural History Society and Hertfordshire Field Club have the pleasure of congratulating the Members on the prosperity of the Society, and on the progress that has been made in carrying out the chief object for which it was founded—the investigation of the Natural History of the County, and especially of the more immediate neighbourhood of the town of Watford.

The first year of the existence of a Society which has, in this brief period, entitled itself to rank as one of the chief County Natural History Societies of the Kingdom, must necessarily be an eventful one; and the number of subjects that have to be mentioned must be pleaded as an excuse for the brevity with which they will be alluded to.

During the year 150 Ordinary Members have been elected. Of these, four, who have recently removed from Watford, have resigned; and the Council much regret that at such an early period in the existence of the Society they have to announce the loss of one member by death—Mr. William A. Diggle.

Five members have compounded for their annual subscriptions; and five Honorary Members have been elected. The census of the Society at the end of the year was therefore :—

Honorary Members	...	...	...	...	5
Life Members	...	...	...	...	5
Annual Subscribers	...	...	...	...	140

Total	...	...	...	150

The rapid growth of the Society during the first few months of its existence was considered sufficient to justify the commencement of the publication, in a permanent form, of the lectures and papers communicated; and the first two parts of a volume of 'Transactions' have been printed and distributed to the Members. A third, with a few pages of 'Proceedings,' is now in the press.

The following are the principal papers and lectures which have been read, or delivered, at the evening meetings during the year 1875 :—

Feb. 11.—Inaugural Address; by the President.

March 11.—The Cretaceous Rocks of England; by J. Logan Lobley, F.G.S., F.R.G.S.

April 8.—Notes on a proposed re-issue of the Flora of Hertfordshire, with Supplementary Remarks on the Botany of the Watford District; by R. A. Pryor, B.A., F.L.S.

——— . On the Botanical Geography of Hertfordshire; by Arthur Cottam, F.R.A.S.

——— . Notes on the Flora of the Watford District; by Arthur Cottam, F.R.A.S.

May 13.—On the Observation of Periodical Natural Phenomena; by John Hopkinson, F.L.S.

——— . Notes on the Plants on which the Meteorological Society invites Observations as to their Time of Flowering; by the Rev. W. Marsden Hind, LL.D.

——— . Notes on the Observation of Insects in connexion with Investigations on Seasonal Phenomena; by Arthur Cottam, F.R.A.S.

——— . On the Pleasures and Advantages to be derived from a Study of Natural History, and more particularly from the Observation of Birds; by J. E. Harting, F.L.S., F.Z.S.

Oct. 14.—The Physical Structure of the London Basin, considered in its Relation to the Geology of the Neighbourhood of Watford; by Professor John Morris, F.G.S.

Nov. 11.—On the Botanical Work of the Past Season; by R. A. Pryor, B.A., F.L.S.

——— . A Few Words about our Local Ferns; by John E. Littleboy.

Dec. 9.—List of Works on the Geology of Hertfordshire; by William Whitaker, B.A., F.G.S.

Quarterly Reports of the Rainfall at a number of stations in the vicinity of Watford, and brief notes and observations in various departments of Natural History, have also been communicated; and although these are not enumerated above, they are not deemed deficient in value or interest, and have appeared, or will appear, in the 'Transactions.'

A considerable number of members have thus, it will be seen, taken an active part in the proceedings of the Society—a number that the Council hope will be largely increased during the present year.

Without a considerable accession of members, it will, however, be impossible to record the proceedings of the Society so fully as hitherto; and the Council hope that the members generally will take a lively interest in its prosperity, by attending the meetings as frequently as possible, and by using their best endeavours to extend the knowledge of the existence and objects of the Society amongst their friends and acquaintances.

Owing to the unfavourable weather, the Field Meetings that have taken place have not been so successful as could have been wished. Out of six meetings planned and arranged at a considerable expenditure of time by your Secretary, in frequent visits to the proposed places of meeting, of only three were the programmes announced carried out, the others being altered, or abandoned altogether, on account of the rain : one of these—July 17, to Pinner—was given up entirely ; and at another—Oct. 2, to Rickmansworth—the only persons who assembled at the appointed place of meeting were your Secretary and the Secretary of the Quekett Microscopical Club—Mr. John E. Ingpen. At the Field Meetings which *did* take place the following localities were visited :—

May 1.—Berry Wood.
——— 29.—Colne Valley Water Works, Bushey Kiln, Watford Heath Kiln,
         and Colney Butts Gravel Pits.
June 3.—Bricket Wood and Common, Munden Park, and Berry Wood.
——— 29.—Aldbury, Ashridge Park, and Berkhampstead Common and Castle.

The number present at each of these meetings was, as nearly as can be ascertained, as follows :—1st May—30 ; 29th—50 ; 3rd June—18 ; 29th—32.

At the first meeting, which was arranged in conjunction with the Geologists' Association, there were about twenty-five members of this Association present ; and at the second, about twenty members of the Geologists' Association availed themselves of an invitation to meet the members of our Society. If now it is taken into consideration that the 1st of May and the 3rd of June were wet days, and the 29th of May and 29th of June were fine, the disparity in these numbers will be seen to be fully accounted for.

The most successful and most enjoyable meeting of the year must now be recorded. Our President invited the members to a conversazione at his house on the 2nd of August, and provided an intellectual treat such as he alone could give, for the finest private collection of pre-historic implements, weapons, and ornaments, in existence, was displayed and commented upon by him. The kindness and hospitality of Mr. and Mrs. Evans on this occasion will ever be remembered with pleasure : nothing was wanting on their part to insure the enjoyment of their guests; and even the weather, so frequently unpropitious before, seemed to vie with them in making this a red-letter day in the annals of the Society.

To our President also the Council desire to express their thanks for the time and attention he has devoted to the affairs of the Society. With unusually heavy demands upon his time, as President of more than one of the leading scientific societies of London, and Vice-President of others, he has yet frequently presided at our evening meetings and accompanied us in our meetings in the field.

When other engagements have rendered it impossible for the President to attend the evening meetings, Dr. Brett has most frequently presided, and to him the thanks of the Society are especially due for the great exertions he has made in its behalf.

It would be impossible to mention all to whom the Society is indebted; but one of our Honorary Members must not be forgotten. In two of our field meetings we have had the advantage of the extensive and varied geological knowledge of Professor Morris; and his expositions of the structure, the physical relations, and the history of the various formations examined, were listened to with the greatest attention by those who were present on these occasions.

The Society is also indebted in various ways to several who are not its members: to Professor Ramsay, Mr. Bristow, and Mr. Best, for the portion of the geological map of Hertfordshire not yet published by the Survey; to Mr. G. J. Symons, Secretary of the Meteorological Society, for permission to print the extracts from this Society's 'Phenological Instructions' in the second part of the 'Transactions'; and to Mr. W. Whitaker, Editor of the 'Geological Record,' for information as to the local Natural History Societies for whose publications the 'Transactions' should be exchanged.

The financial position of the Society is satisfactory. Notwithstanding the expenses incurred in starting it, the income for the year is slightly in excess of the expenditure; and the amount received for life compositions has been transferred from the current account at the Bank to a deposit account, with the intention of investing it should a sufficient number of members compound for their annual subscriptions.

A library of works on Natural History and the allied sciences is in course of formation, and now numbers more than 50 volumes, all of which have been acquired by donation. To the respective donors the thanks of the Society are due; and it is hoped that, by the liberality of authors and others, a valuable Natural History Library may in time be formed.

Several donations towards a Natural History Museum have also been received, and, when cases are provided for their display, will form a not unimportant addition to the proposed Museum of the Watford Public Library.

To the Committee of the Public Library the Council desire, in conclusion, to express their thanks for the facilities afforded for holding their meetings and the evening meetings of the Society in the building in which we are now assembled.

The Council being of opinion that half-past seven in the evening may be somewhat too early for the convenience of some of the members, propose that in future the evening meetings shall be held at eight o'clock.

(*The Treasurer's Account is on the next page.*)

INCOME AND EXPENDITURE DURING THE YEAR ENDING 31st DECEMBER, 1875.

DR.	£	s.	d.	CR.	£	s.	d.
Subscriptions for 1875	64	0	0	Books and Stationery	7	9	0
Life Compositions	25	0	0	Advertising	1	11	4
Sale of 'Transactions'	0	10	0	Printing ' Transactions'	22	8	0
				Miscellaneous Printing	10	12	0
				Reporting	1	11	6
				Rent — Watford Public Library	5	0	0
				Attendance at ditto	1	2	6
				Subscription to Ray Society	1	1	0
				Ditto to ' Geological Record'	0	10	6
				Ballot Box	1	5	6
				Geological Maps	3	6	6
				Postages	6	15	10
				Sundry small expenses	0	19	10
				Amount placed to Deposit Account at the London and County Bank	25	0	0
				Balance	0	16	6
	£89	**10**	**0**		**£89**	**10**	**0**

Subscriptions received for 1876	8	10	0

We, the undersigned, having examined the above statement of Income and Expenditure, and the vouchers referring thereto, hereby certify that the said account is correct.

2nd February, 1876.   JOHN P. BENSKIN,   } Auditors.
                             C. F. HOLLINGSWORTH, }

ORDINARY MEETING, 9TH MARCH, 1876.

ALFRED T. BRETT, Esq., M.D., Vice-President, in the Chair.

Mr. Robert Clutterbuck, F.G.S , F.R.G.S., 8, Great Cumberland Place, Hyde Park, London; Mr. Jonathan King, Wiggenhall, Watford; Mr. W. McMurray McFarlane, Loudwater, Rickmansworth; and the Rev. R. Holden Webb, M.A., Essendon Rectory, Hatfield, were elected Members of the Society.

Letters were read from Mr. G. J. Symons, and Mr. W. Whitaker, thanking the Society for their election as Honorary Members.

The following lecture was delivered:—

"On some of the Simpler Methods of Microscopical Mounting." By Arthur Cottam, F.R.A.S.

Mr. Cottam illustrated his lecture practically by mounting objects dry and in Canada balsam. He recommended Mr. Davies' work,* in the Society's library, as the best guide to microscopical mounting.

* The Preparation and Mounting of Microscopic Objects. 2nd edition.

ORDINARY MEETING, 13TH APRIL, 1876.

ALFRED T. BRETT, Esq., M.D., Vice-President, in the Chair.

Mr. David Carnegie, Eastbury, Watford; Lieut. Richard B. Croft, R.N., F.L.S., F.R.M.S., Great Cozens, Ware; Mr. Charles Durham, Aldenham Abbey, Watford; Miss Littleboy, Hunton Bridge; Mr. Francis Lucas, Hitchin; Mr. William Lucas, The Firs, Hitchin; Mr. Robert McFarlane, Kildare, Rickmansworth; Miss Marfitt, Aldenham Abbey; Mr. Joseph Pollard, High Down, Hitchin; and Mr. Isaac Ridgway, Kytes, Watford, were elected Members of the Society.

The following lecture was delivered:—
" On the Polarisation of Light." By James U. Harford.

FIELD MEETING, 29TH APRIL, 1876.

ST. ALBANS.

Rain, which had been falling rather heavily in the morning, still threatened to descend, and the air was damp and chilly, when the President and a small number only of the members met together at St. Peter's Church. Leaving the church at three o'clock they proceeded direct to the brick-fields at Bernard's Heath.

Here there are extensive excavations in the brick-earth and glacial gravels capping the summit of the hill on the side of which St. Albans is situated, and which rises to some 400 feet above the level of the sea. In places the Chalk is reached in the deeper excavations or by shafts, and the Woolwich and Reading beds, an outlier of which rests upon the Chalk on the slightly higher ground towards St. Peter's Church, doubtless extend to the western edge of the brick-fields, and are probably present over some portion of them, for at one spot evidence was obtained that the surface of the Chalk seen was the actual surface upon which, in this neighbourhood, rests a layer of unworn green-coated flints forming the bottom bed of the Woolwich series.

After the examination of these excavations the party returned to St. Albans, again passing St. Peter's Church, and skirting the ancient eastern boundary of the borough. Then leaving the old boundary-wall on the right, the fields above the ruins of Sopwell Nunnery were crossed,—the ruins of the Nunnery and the old Abbey of St. Alban forming most interesting objects in the landscape. Unusually fine specimens of *Cardamine pratensis* were here gathered by the botanists, while the attention of the geologists was directed to a heap of stones by the roadside a little further on, in which were seen pieces of the Hertfordshire conglomerate, and fragments of quartzite and other rocks ice-borne from a distance; and after inspecting a gravel-pit in the lane leading towards Napsbury Farm, the members passed, by permission, through Mrs. Worley's Park to a wooded dell formed by an old chalk-pit. The little moschatel (*Adoxa Moschatellina*) with its pale-green leaves, stems, and flowers, especially attracted attention here, and in the copse a little further on in the direction of Hedges Farm several patches of the strange-looking downy flesh-coloured parasite, *Lathræa squamaria*, and the equally striking and scarcely more attractive looking honey-combed fungus, the morel, were seen.

Ascending the hill, Hedges Farm was soon reached, and here the party were courteously received and entertained at tea by Mrs. Silvester and her family, after which Mr. Evans gave a brief *resumé* of the afternoon's proceedings and a description of the geological features of the country traversed. The members then returned to Watford and elsewhere from Park Street station.

The following plants in the Meteorological Society's list were observed in flower in the course of the walk :—

No.
1. *Anemone nemorosa* (wood anemone).
2. *Ranunculus Ficaria* (pilewort).
4. *Caltha palustris* (marsh marigold).
7. *Cardamine pratensis* (cuckoo flower).
12. *Stellaria Holostea* (greater stitchwort).
16. *Geranium Robertianum* (herb Robert).
20. *Vicia sepium* (bush vetch).
30. *Anthriscus sylvestris* (wild chervil).
53. *Veronica hederifolia* (ivy-leaved speedwell).
57. *Nepeta Glechoma* (ground ivy).
60. *Ajuga reptans* (creeping bugle).
61. *Primula veris* (cowslip).
62. *Plantago lanceolata* (ribwort plantain).
63. *Mercurialis perennis* (dog's mercury).
71. *Endymion nutans* (blue bell).

ORDINARY MEETING, 11TH MAY, 1876.

JOHN EVANS, Esq., F.R.S., etc., President, in the Chair.

Mr. John Marnham, The Hollies, Boxmoor; Mr. Charles W. Nunn, Hertford; and Miss H. M. King Smith, The Hawthorns, Watford, were elected Members of the Society.

Dr. F. V. Hayden, Director of the United States Geological and Geographical Survey of the Territories, Washington, U.S.A., was elected an Honorary Member.

The following paper was read :—
" The Geology and Water Supply of the Neighbourhood of Watford." By the Rev. James C. Clutterbuck, M.A. Communicated by Dr. A. T. Brett, Vice-President (*Vide* p. 125).

Mr. G. J. Symons (Hon. Member) referred to the extreme rapidity with which the wells in the Chalk of the South Downs responded to the rainfall—the rainwater sinking 200 or 250 feet in a few hours. With regard to the streams of water in the Chalk, he had heard wondrous accounts of the rivers running through the Chalk at Grays, where water was found to such an extent that the level could not be reduced by pumping with engines, and the Chalk could not therefore be excavated. It was a question whether it might not be that the water of the Thames found its way into the Chalk there. We had, he said, been told that we were not to drink Thames water, nor mountain water, nor rain water, but only water out of wells. If we must depend entirely upon well water, we should have to be very economical, for the level of the water below

London had already been lowered; and if the water were withdrawn more rapidly, it might disappear altogether.

Mr. John Hopkinson mentioned that Mr. Wailes had told him that at the London Orphan Asylum (at Watford), when the pump was worked beyond a certain speed, the level of the water was reduced to below the suction pipe. With regard to Otterspool he thought it very remarkable that the springs which had been known to run a million gallons a day should at any time be so diminished that the water ceased to flow out of the pool.

The President said that in all probability the connexion between the springs at Otterspool and the water in the swallow-holes would some day be established. One of the most interesting points in the paper was, he considered, that by measuring the wells Mr. Clutterbuck had been able to give experimentally the level of the surface of the water in the subterranean reservoir. So accurate was this calculation that, on one occasion, when levelling up the valley to ascertain what would be the level of the water in a well, he took the recognized calculation and found that it came within a foot of the level ascertained by measurement. The question of the supply of water to be derived from the Chalk was one of such magnitude that he refrained from entering into it. He had entered at considerable length into the question of the supply of water to London in his recent Address to the Geological Society, and any one who wished to see what the probable effect of carrying out the suggestions of the Royal Commission would be, could see it in that Address. In years when the rainfall did not exceed twenty-three or twenty-four inches, the area from which the drainage would be required in order to supply London would exceed that of a great many English counties. He should like to see the use of Dalton's gauge extended, as he considered that the experiments which had been made required supplementing to a considerable extent. He did not agree with Mr. Symons as to the rapidity of the percolation, unless possibly when the whole body of the Chalk was saturated.

Mr. Clutterbuck, in reply, said that he had visited Grays to look into the question of deriving a supply of water from the Chalk there, and had come to the conclusion that when the water was reduced to a certain level, it was drawn in from the Thames, and the Thames there was very foul. A friend of his, an engineer having the direction of a Water Company, had also made an experiment at Grays, and found that the water did come in from the Thames. In making the lake in St. James's Park it was found that the level of the water was affected by the tide. So it would be with the well at the Colne Valley Water Works. The water would come from the river, and as to trying to keep it out, they might as well try to sweep back the Atlantic with a broom.

FIELD MEETING, 13TH MAY, 1876.

HATFIELD PARK.

On this occasion the Society, for the second time, met the Geologists' Association of London, and at the place of meeting, the principal entrance to Hatfield Park, at 3 o'clock, a party of at least 130 ladies and gentlemen assembled,—the two Societies being about equally represented. Permission to see over Hatfield House, and to visit the Hatfield Park Kiln, had been kindly granted by the noble owner, the Marquess of Salisbury, and to this the presence of a larger number of members than usual was no doubt due.

Hatfield House, which was first visited, is necessarily of greater interest to the antiquary than the naturalist. It is built on the site of the palace of Bishop Morton, which was erected about the end of the fifteenth century, and of which a fragment—examined with much interest by some of the party—still remains;

and on its site again, from the commencement of the twelfth
century, an episcopal residence had existed. The present mansion
was commenced in 1607, and the geologist may be interested in
knowing that the materials used in its construction, by its builder
and architect, Robert Cecil, the first Earl of Salisbury, consisted
chiefly of Caen stone, with stone from Tattenhall in Staffordshire,
Worksop in Nottinghamshire, and the quarries of Northampton-
shire, and bricks and flints also from the old palace which had
fallen into decay.

After spending a considerable time in the house and grounds,
the party proceeded across the park to the brick-fields, noticing on
the way Queen Elizabeth's favourite oak, under which she was
sitting when the news was brought to her that she was Queen of
England, and the fine less-decayed oaks and other trees for which
this park is so justly famed.

In the pits here, the Upper Chalk, and all the beds present
at the northern outcrop of the London Tertiaries, are exposed,
and are overlaid by the high-level gravel of Post-Pliocene age,
the outline of which is well defined by the moistness of the surface
of the ground around it. The section was described by Mr.
Hopkinson, and compared with the sections of the same beds seen
in the neighbourhood of Watford and elsewhere, both north and
south of the Thames, and the position of the fossiliferous beds was
pointed out. As, however, a detailed description of the section,
drawn up by Mr. Whitaker, has already been given by Professor
Morris in the Transactions of the Society (vol. i. p. 98), the observations that were made need not here be repeated. For information on the geology of the immediate neighbourhood reference may
also be made to a report of an excursion of the Geologists' Association to Hatfield, in 1873, given by Mr. Lobley in the
Proceedings of the Association (vol. iii. p. 241).

In the "basement-bed" of the London Clay a few fossils were
collected, and the members of the two Societies then returned
to Hatfield across the park in detached parties, and thence, after
partaking of tea at the Salisbury Arms, to their respective destinations—London, Watford, and various parts of Hertfordshire—by
rail or road, having spent a very enjoyable afternoon in one of the
most beautiful parks of Hertfordshire, and, for its historical asso-
ciations, the most interesting in the County.

To convey the members residing in the neighbourhood of
Watford a special train was engaged from St. Albans to Hatfield
and back, the ordinary trains not running at convenient times.

FIELD MEETING, 3RD JUNE, 1876.

BRICKET WOOD AND COMMON.

When a field meeting is chiefly devoted to the collection of
microscopic objects, there is little to record of its results, and still
less to be said in the field, for it is impossible to determine on the

spot the objects collected, and as each microscopist studies as a rule a particular class of objects—a special department of the animal or vegetable kingdom—it is not an easy matter for the Secretary of a Society to ascertain afterwards what has been found. This is the case with this afternoon's meeting, which took place in conjunction with the Quekett Microscopical Club.

The members of the two Societies met at Bricket Wood Station, and formed at once two or three detached parties. One section searched the wood in quest of plants; another, with butterfly nets and collecting boxes, made acquaintance with its insect-inhabitants; while a third—and by far the largest party—started off for the common, to collect, for after-study with the miscroscope, the minute organisms with which its stagnant pools are peopled.

After some time spent in collecting these various objects, the members of the two societies again united, and took a south-easterly course across the low meadows through which flow the rivers Ver and Colne, to the Nether Wyld Farm, where they were hospitably entertained at tea by Mr. and Mrs. Waghorn, and Mr. C. F. Hollingsworth, after which they returned by different routes to the Bricket Wood Station.

ORDINARY MEETING, 8TH JUNE, 1876.

JOHN EVANS, Esq., F.R.S., etc., President, in the Chair.

The Rev. F. W. Goadby, M.A., St. Albans Road, Watford, was elected a Member of the Society.

The following communications were read:—

1. "Meteorological Observations taken at Oaklands, Hempstead Road, from 1871 to 1875." By Edward Harrison.*

2. "On the Advantage of observing Phenological Phenomena." By Lieut. Richard B. Croft, R.N., F.L.S., F.R.M.S.

The Author urged upon the members the advantage, to themselves and to the Society, of observing periodical natural phenomena, pointing out that the position and even the existence of the Society depended upon the work done by it in the cause of Science, and that there could be but few members who could not do some work for the Society by noting at least one or two occurrences in each month and forwarding their notes to the Secretary. In fact, he said, we all do notice these occurrences, though we may not record them. Who does not listen for the first note of the nightingale? Who does not look out for the first swallow? Who can help saying, once a year at least, "There's the cuckoo!" And it is the same with flowers—the cowslip, the sweet violet, the blackthorn, and many others. It is impossible for the most unobservant person not to notice these on their first flowering, and if noticed, why not noted?

In concluding his remarks, the Author suggested that children should be trained to observe the blossoming of wild flowers, and to look out for the arrival of birds, etc., which observations might be recorded by their parents and sent to the Society.

3. "The Hertfordshire Bourne." By the President (*Vide* p. 137).

---

* A copy of Mr. Harrison's observations is deposited in the Society's Library.

In reply to a question by Dr. Brett, the President said that there were two methods of ascertaining the amount of water flowing in a river. One had been tried at Watford, and was by the number of millstones the river was able to drive; but the ordinary method was for the water to be penned back and only allowed to flow over an orifice of a certain width. The amount of water passing in a minute was taken, and from that it was calculated what the volume of water was. It was in this manner that Telford gauged the Gade some fifty years ago.

4. "Section of the Strata passed through in boring at the Colne Valley Water Works." By William Verini (*Vide* p. 135).

5. "The Ermine Street traced by its Vegetation." By Lieut. R. B. Croft, R.N., F.L.S. (*Vide* p. 135).

The President said that this very interesting Note combined archæology with botany. He had not before known buttercups brought in as indices of Roman roads. Such indications were generally seen in the height of summer, for the soil above the road being only of a moderate thickness, the vegetation then dried up. Stukeley noticed these appearances, and called them *umbras strati*—the shadows of a street.

Mr. R. A. Pryor having mentioned that buried foundations gave rise to similar appearances, the President said that the theatre at St. Albans was discovered by such appearances.

6. "Note on the Larvæ of the Goat Moth." By J. Henry James (*Vide* p. 135).

7. " Notes on the Cuckoo." By Alfred T. Brett, M.D. (*Vide* p. 136).

Mr. R. A. Pryor said that he had known a cuckoo lay its eggs for two consecutive years in the nests which a water wagtail had been for some years in the habit of building in an out-house.

Lieut. Croft mentioned that he had seen both robins and greenfinches bring a cuckoo food.

8. Cuttings from 'The Field,' being two Notes on the Ornithology of Herts.

The first of these related to the appearance of the gannet and the little auk in Herts. They had both been picked up alive, but in an exhausted condition, near Baldock, during the latter part of November, 1875.

The second extract referred to the destruction of fish by a heron. For several weeks at about the end of the year 1875, a large heron had been seen flying over Bengeo towards Waterford Marsh, near Hertford, and returning towards Ware. On one occasion it had been seen to dart into the river that runs near Waterford Hall, and kill a very fine trout.

9. "Description of a new Field-Naturalist's Microscope." By Lieut. Croft, R.N., F.L.S.

Lieut. Croft said that he believed this little instrument, which he exhibited, would be found useful not only for work in the field, for which he had specially designed it, but also at other times when it was impossible to use a large microscope, or when it might be inconvenient to take such an instrument out of its case; for although in theory our microscopes ought always to be set up ready for use, yet in practice this seldom was possible.

The instrument consisted of a telescopic body sliding in a case to which a stage and mirror were attached, the whole when packed, together with a live-box, fitting into a small leather case which could be carried in the pocket or slung on the shoulder. It was fitted with a 3-inch object-glass, as being the most useful power for out-door work, but he also carried in his waistcoat pocket a low-angle half-inch, for which, or even with care for a quarter-inch object-glass, he found the sliding adjustment all that was needed.

FIELD MEETING, 17TH JUNE, 1876.

BOXMOOR, BENNET'S END, AND NASH MILLS.

Meeting at Boxmoor station at about half-past two, the members, under the guidance of their President, Mr. John Evans, went direct to the Chalk-pit on Rough Down, where there is an exposure of the band of hard, cream-coloured chalk known as the "chalk-rock," which here forms the highest bed of the Lower Chalk, and divides it distinctly from the overlying Upper Chalk or "chalk-with-flints"

This chalk-rock is well known, through the researches of Mr. Evans, as the principal fossiliferous bed of the Chalk in this area. It crops out near the highest part of the pit, which is a hollow cut out of the hill-side. Its thickness is here about 18 inches,—the upper portion, for three or four inches, consisting almost entirely of nodules which contain about 10 per cent. of phosphate of lime.

To get at this bed the steep face of the pit had to be scaled, and the bed when reached was found to have so suffered from the repeated attacks of geologists, that, instead of projecting, as from its hardness it would naturally have done, it was sunk back from the face of the pit, rendering it no easy matter to work at it. A number of fossils were however found, including an *Inoceramus*, a *Trochus*, a *Rhynchonella*, *Terebratula cornea* and *semi-globosa*, *Ananchytes ovatus*, *Spatangus cor-anguinum*, and two species of *Ventriculites*. In addition to these there have been found in the chalk-rock in this pit, almost entirely by Mr. Evans, undetermined species of *Baculites*, *Nautilus*, *Turrilites*, *Inoceramus* (two species), *Micraster*, *Parasmilia*, *Ocellaria*, etc., and the following named species :—

Ammonites prosperianus.	*Spondylus spinosus.*
Scaphites æqualis.	*Rhynchonella Mantelliana.*
Spondylus latus.	*Terebratula biplicata.*

After botanising a little on Rough Down, the members, some walking and others driving, proceeded to the Bennet's End brick-field, noticing on the way the Boxmoor thistle, and other interesting plants pointed out by Mr. Pryor, and a well-marked "pipe" near Bennet's End, to which attention was directed by the President, who explained its formation by the percolation through the Chalk of water with carbonic acid in solution. At the brick-fields Mr. Evans also gave an interesting account of the beds exposed, the conditions of deposition of which, and the fossil contents, are known chiefly through his researches. These brick-fields are in an outlier of the Lower Tertiaries, which are supposed to have been saved from denudation, partly, by a slight change of dip in the underlying Chalk—a cause to which several *lines* of similar outliers in this and other Chalk districts are most probably due—but chiefly by a fault in the Chalk, running north and south, against the face of which the London Clay with its basement-bed, and the plastic clay of the Woolwich and Reading Series, abut, and towards which they dip at a slight angle. There are also other minor faults, one of which throws the London Clay against its basement-bed, and another the London Clay and underlying Reading Beds against a

xlii PROCEEDINGS OF THE

mass of brick-earth, for which one of the pits is mostly worked. In the basement-bed of the London Clay a mammal's bone, sharks' teeth, an annelide (*Ditrupa plana*), wood, impressions of leaves, and the following species of Mollusca, have been found :*—

Fusus, sp.	*Cytherea orbicularis.*
Natica, sp.	*Nucula*, sp.
Cardium Laytoni.	*Ostrea Bellovacina.*
Cyprina Morrisii.	*Panopæa intermedia.*
Cytherea obliqua.	*Solen*, sp.

The meeting terminated at the residence of the President, at Nash Mills, about a mile and a half south of the brick-fields; and on their arrival here the members were hospitably entertained at tea by Mr. and Mrs. Evans, and for the second time had the advantage of examining a number of carefully-selected examples of the extensive collection of pre-historic implements, and more recent ornaments, coins, and other interesting and valuable objects, which Mr. Evans has formed.

FIELD MEETING, 1st JULY, 1876.

ELSTREE RESERVOIR AND STANMORE COMMON.

To meet again the Quekett Microscopical Club, and to collect microscopic objects, as on the 3rd of June, a few members only of the Watford Natural History Society assembled at Elstree Reservoir on the bridge at its upper end.

At first a little collecting was done in the reservoir itself; but no objects of special interest finding their way into the nets and bottles, some small pools near were tried, and here the most interesting object obtained was the *Volvox globator*, a free-swimming microscopic plant, which has been referred as often to the animal as to the vegetable kingdom, but seems now to be generally regarded as one of the confervoid algæ. It is a delicate green globe, which, moving gracefully through the water, revolving as it goes, is just visible to the naked eye, and under the microscope is seen to contain within its transparent membrane other smaller globes, the miniatures of itself, and these again sometimes even a third generation in embryo.

By the side of the reservoir several plants of larger dimensions and more steadfast habits were collected; and in their botanical researches the members of the two societies had the advantage of the presence of two good botanists—Mr. Leo Grindon, author of the well-known 'Field and Garden Botany,' and Mr. W. W. Reeves, Assistant Secretary of the Royal Microscopical Society. Mr. Grindon's poetical yet truly philosophical expositions of the structure and uses of the different organs of various plants met with formed, indeed, a distinctive feature in the meeting; and when the party arrived at Stanmore Common, it was found that

* This and the list of fossils of the chalk-rock are from Mr. Whitaker's 'Geology of the London Basin,' part i., in which further particulars of the Boxmoor and Bennet's End pits are given.

so much time had been expended in listening to his discourses on the wonderful adaptations of means to ends in the works of the Creator that there was no time to spare to botanise on the Common or to search its pools for their microscopic inhabitants.

The two societies here therefore separated, the members of the Quekett Club returning to London by way of Stanmore, and the members of the Watford Society dispersing in various directions.

ORDINARY MEETING, 12TH OCTOBER, 1876.

ALFRED T. BRETT, Esq., M.D., Vice-President, in the Chair.

Mrs. Arnold, Redbourne Bury, St. Albans; Dr. William Henry Hobson, Berkhampstead; Mr. George Lambert, F.S.A., Coventry Street, Haymarket, London; Mr. Oliver Lemon, Langley Hill House, East Langley; Dr. Charles Edward Saunders, 21, Lower Seymour Street, London; and Mrs. George Tidcombe, Chalk Hill, Bushey, were elected Members of the Society.

A letter was read from Dr. F. V. Hayden, thanking the Society for his election as an Honorary Member.

The following lecture was delivered:—
"The Polarisation of Light." By James U. Harford (*Vide* p. 152).

The lecture was illustrated by a series of diagrams, and by various experiments with polarising apparatus.*

ORDINARY MEETING, 9TH NOVEMBER, 1876.

JOHN EVANS, Esq., F.R.S., etc., President, in the Chair.

Mr. Robert Marcus Carew, Carpenders Park, Watford, was elected a Member of the Society.

The following communications were read:—

1. "The Hertfordshire Ordnance Bench Marks, from the 'Abstracts of Levelling' of the Ordnance Survey." By John Hopkinson, Hon. Sec. (*Vide* p. 141).

2. "On some Boulders in the Neighbourhood of Buntingford, Herts." By Robert Philips Greg, F.G.S. (*Vide* p. 172).

3. "On the Earth Pyramids near Botzen in the Tyrol." By the President, John Evans, F.R.S., etc.

Mr. Evans stated that these pyramids, of which he exhibited a photograph, were in a valley in the neighbourhood of Klobenstein, a few miles from Botzen, and at an elevation of 3000 feet above the sea-level. They had been already described by Sir Charles Lyell in his 'Principles of Geology,' and by other authors; but as they were such striking instances of the effects of sub-aerial denudation, he thought that a few words about them might not be unacceptable to the Society.

The pyramids, as might be seen from the photograph, were obelisks of soil thickly clustered together, some of them fifty or sixty feet high, and by far the

---

* The subject was brought before the Society by Mr. Harford for the second time by special request, on account of the small attendance owing to the great storm on the first occasion (13th April).

greater number of them having a large block of stone upon the top. The question as to the manner in which they were formed had already been solved by geologists, but its solution might probably be unknown to many of the members of the Society.

The valley in which the pyramids stand is an old valley, probably excavated by a glacier at a time when the temperature of that part of Europe was somewhat colder than it now is, and was partly filled with a thick deposit of moraine matter, consisting in the main of a micaceous sand with a small amount of clay intermixed, derived from the grinding away of red porphyry and granite, with pebbles and large blocks of which, the sand was interspersed.

The stream which now runs along the bottom of the valley must, when the glacier first retreated and left the moraine matter, have flowed at a much higher level. As it worked its way down through the hard sand, side streams would run in during the heavy rains, which are not unfrequent. The course of these would be guided partly by cracks formed during the heat of summer, and partly by certain portions of the sand being protected from the action of the rain by the large blocks of stone lying on the surface, or laid bare by the sand above them having been washed away. These side streams in course of time formed deep lateral ravines opening into the main valley ; but as the ridges between each of these lateral ravines were only in places protected from the effects of the rain by the large blocks of stone, they also got cut into so as to form a second series of lateral ravines opening into the first, and thus these irregular lines of columns were left.

Although the stones, which acted like umbrellas for the columns, preserved them for a long time, so long indeed that the columns might gradually be developed so as to become fifty or sixty feet high, yet eventually the power of the weather was too great for them, and their supports were weakened so that they fell. The columns having lost their covering, gradually became pointed like church spires, but eventually were washed away, as the bottom of the valley to the height of 100 or 200 feet above the stream was now free from columns, which now are only found higher up the slope.

The essentials for the formation of such columns, which have been noticed in several parts of the world, seem to be

1. A soil readily acted on by water, but sufficiently hard and compact to carry a great weight, and through which a valley has been cut.

2. An admixture in the soil of large blocks to protect it from the rain in certain places only.

3. Occasional rains sufficient to cut deep gullies.

4. A main torrent at the bottom of the valley capable of removing all the sand and blocks washed into it, and of keeping the sides of the valley in which it runs inclined at a high angle.

4. "On the Supposed Recent Extinction of *Cyclostoma elegans* in North Herts." By H. George Fordham, F.G.S. (*Vide* p. 172).

5. "On the *Anacharis alsinastrum* in the River Colne, near Watford." By Alfred T. Brett, M.D. (*Vide* p. 173).

6. A letter from Mr. R. A. Pryor, B.A., F.L S , giving a list of plants he has recently discovered in new stations in the neighbourhood of Watford, and notes on the blossoming of certain spring wild-flowers during the last few weeks (*Vide* p. 173).

7. A letter from Mr. Clarence E. Fry on the recent capture of the oleander hawk-moth *(Chaerocampa Nerii)* at Hemel Hempstead (*Vide* p. 174).

The Secretary recorded the discovery, near St. Albans, by Miss Willshin, of *Campanula latifolia*, a species of which the only previous record of the occurrence near St. Albans, many years ago, by Miss Henslow, had been considered doubtful ; and of a new thistle which Mr. Pryor considered to be a hybrid between *Carduus palustris* and *C. pratensis*, and of which he had placed a specimen in the Herbarium of the British Museum.

Dr. Brett recorded the fact of an unusual number of squirrels having been seen in the neighbourhood of Watford this year.

The following objects were exhibited:—Small pieces of the boulders found near Buntingford, by Mr. R. P. Greg; Photograph of the Earth-pyramids near Botzen, by the President; Shells of *Cyclostoma elegans* from Highley Hill Tumulus, by Mr. H. George Fordham; *Anacharis alsinastrum* from the Colne, by Dr. Brett; and, under their microscopes, Diatoms, by Mr. Arthur Cottam, and living Sertularian Hydroids, from Tenby, South Wales, by the Secretary.

ORDINARY MEETING, 14TH DECEMBER, 1876.

JOHN EVANS, Esq., F.R.S., etc., President, in the Chair.

The following lecture was delivered:—
"The Eocenes of England and their Extension in Hertfordshire."
By J. Logan Lobley, F.G.S., F.R.G.S. (*Vide* p. 161).

A discussion ensued in which the President, the Secretary, and Dr. Brett took part.

Fossils from the London Clay were exhibited by Mr. Lobley in illustration of his lecture; and Eocene Fossils from the London and Hampshire Basins, by the Secretary.

The Greenough Geological Map of England was also kindly lent for the occasion by the Geological Society of London.

DONATIONS TO THE LIBRARY IN 1876.

TITLE.	DONOR.
ANON. Minstrelsy of the Woods. 8vo. London, 1832.	*Mr. J. Hopkinson.*
———— Physiognomy. 2 vols. 8vo. . . .	*Miss Scholz.*
ARAGO, FRANÇOIS. Meteorological Essays. 8vo. London, 1855	„
BRANDE, Prof. W. T. Manual of Chemistry. 2nd Edition. 3 vols. 8vo. London, 1821 . . .	*Lieut. R. B. Croft.*
CHITTENHAM, G. B. Meteorological Observations . . . . in Colorado and Montana Territories. 8vo. Washington, 1874	*Dr. F. V. Hayden.*
CONYBEARE, Rev. W. D., and WILLIAM PHILLIPS. Outlines of the Geology of England and Wales. 8vo. London, 1822 . . .	*Mr. J. Hopkinson.*
COOKE, M. C. A Plain and Easy Account of the British Fungi. 8vo. London, 1866.	„
COPE, E. D. The Vertebrata of the Cretaceous Formations of the West. (*U.S. Geol. Surv.*) 4to. Washington, 1876	*Dr. F. V. Hayden.*
COUES, ELLIOTT. Birds of the Northwest. (*U.S. Geol. Surv.*) 8vo. Washington, 1874	„

TITLE.	DONOR.
CROLL, Dr. JAMES. The 'Challenger's' Crucial Test of the Wind and Gravitation Theories of Oceanic Circulation. (*Phil. Mag.* 1875.)	*The Author.*
—— On the Mechanics of Glaciers. (*Geol. Mag.* 1876.)	
CURTIS, JOHN. Farm Insects. 4to. London, 1867	*Mr. Chippindale.*
CUVIER, BARON. Discours sur les Révolutions de la Surface du Globe. 8vo.	*Lieut. R. B. Croft.*
DENNIS, Rev. J. B. P. The Existence of Birds during the deposition of the Stonesfield Slate proved . . . . (*Quart. Journ. Micr. Science.*)	*Mr. J. Hopkinson.*
DRUMMOND, Dr. JAMES L. First Steps to Botany. 3rd Edition. 12mo. London, 1831	,,
EVANS, JOHN. Address delivered at the Anniversary Meeting of the Geological Society of London, on the 19th of February, 1875. (*Quart. Journ. Geol. Soc.* 1875.)	*The Author.*
—— —— 18th of February, 1876. (*ib.* 1876.)	.,
FERGUSSON, Dr. ROBERT M. Electricity. 8vo. London and Edinburgh, 1868	*Lieut. R. B. Croft.*
FORDHAM, H. GEORGE. On the Section of the Chloritic Marl and Upper Greensand on the Northern Side of Swanage Bay, Dorset. (*Proc. Geol. Assoc.* 1876.)	*The Author.*
GANNETT, HENRY. Meteorological Observations . . . . in Utah, Idaho, and Montana. 8vo. Washington, 1873	*Dr. Hayden.*
—— List of Elevations . . . . west of the Mississippi River. 3rd Edition. *ib.* 1875	,,
GEOGRAPHICAL MAGAZINE. Vols. ii, iii. 4to. London, 1875-76.	*Lieut. R. B. Croft.*
GLAISHER, JAMES. On the Meteorological and Physical Effects of the Solar Eclipse of March 15, 1858. 8vo.	*Dr. A T. Brett.*
—— On the Meteorology of England during the Year ending December 31st, 1861	*Mr. J. Hopkinson.*
GOSSE, P. H. Fishes. 8vo. London, 1851	*Lieut. R. B. Croft.*
GREG, R. P., and W. G. LETTSOM. Manual of the Mineralogy of Great Britain and Ireland. 8vo. London, 1858	*Mr. R. P. Greg.*
HAYDEN, Dr. F. V. First, Second, and Third Annual Reports of the United States Geological Survey of the Territories, for the Years 1867, 1868, and 1869. (*Reprint.*) 8vo. Washington, 1873	*The Author.*
—— Fourth Report, for 1870. (Wyoming.) *ib.* 1872	,,
—— Fifth Report, for 1871. (Montana) *ib.* 1872	,,
—— Sixth Report, for 1872. *ib.* 1873	,,
—— Seventh Report, for 1873. (Colorado.) *ib.* 1875	,,
—— Final Report of the United States Geological Survey of Nebraska. *ib.* 1872	,,
HERSCHEL, Sir JOHN F. W. Discourse on the Study of Natural Philosophy. 8vo. London, 1830	*Mr. J. Hopkinson.*
—— Manual of Scientific Enquiry. 2nd Edition. 8vo. London, 1851	*Lieut. R. B. Croft.*
—— Familiar Letters on Scientific Subjects. 8vo. London, 1866	,,
HICKS, HENRY. On the Succession of the Ancient Rocks in the Vicinity of St. David's, Pembrokeshire. (*Quart. Journ. Geol. Soc.* 1875.)	*The Author.*

TITLE.	DONOR.
HICKS, H. On the Northern Palæozoic Rocks. (*Geol. Mag.* 1876.)	*The Author.*
HOPKINSON, JOHN, and C. LAPWORTH. Descriptions of the Graptolites of the Arenig and Llandeilo Rocks of St. David's. (*Quart. Journ. Geol. Soc.* 1875.)	*The Authors.*
JOHNS, Dr. WILLIAM. Practical Botany. 8vo. London, 1840	*Mr. J. Hopkinson.*
JUKES, J. BEETE. The Students' Manual of Geology. 2nd edition. 8vo. Edinburgh, 1862	*Mr. C. E. Fry.*
LEIDY, JOSEPH. Contributions to the Extinct Vertebrate Fauna of the Western Territories. (*U.S. Geol. Surv.*) 4to. Washington, 1873	*Dr. F. V. Hayden.*
LESQUEREUX, LEO. Contributions to the Fossil Flora of the Western Territories. Part 1. The Cretaceous Flora. (*U.S. Geol. Surv.*) 4to. Washington, 1874	,,
LIEBIG, JUSTUS VON. Letters on Modern Agriculture. 8vo. London, 1859	*Lieut. R. B. Croft.*
———— Natural Laws of Husbandry. 8vo. London, 1863	,,
LINNEAN SOCIETY. Transactions. Vol. xxiv, Part 3. Vol. xxviii, Part 1. 4to. London, 1864–71	*Mr. J. Hopkinson.*
LOBLEY, J. L. Two days in a Mining District. (*Proc. Geol. Assoc.* 1871.)	*The Author.*
———— On the Stratigraphical Distribution of the British Fossil Brachiopoda. (*ib.* 1871)	,,
———— On the Stratigraphical Distribution of the British Fossil Lamellibranchiata. (*Quart. Journ. Geol. Soc.* 1871.)	,,
———— Excursion of the Geologists' Association to Malvern. (*Proc. Geol. Assoc.* 1874.)	,,
MARLBOROUGH COLLEGE NATURAL HISTORY SOCIETY. Reports for 1869 to 1874. 8vo. Marlborough, 1869–1875	*Rev. T. A. Preston.*
MAWE, J. Woodarch's Introduction to the Study of Conchology. 3rd ed. 8vo. London, 1825	*Mr. J. Hopkinson.*
MEEK, F. B. Report on the Invertebrate Cretaceous and Tertiary Fossils of the Upper Missouri Country. (*U. S. Geol. Surv.*) 4to. Washington, 1876	*Dr. F. V. Hayden.*
METEOROLOGICAL SOCIETY. Report of the Council for 1857-58. 8vo. London, 1859	*Dr. A. T. Brett.*
MIALL, L. C. Remains of Labyrinthodonta from the Keuper Sandstone of Warwick. (*Quart. Journ. Geol. Soc.* 1874.)	*Mr. J. H. Kirshaw.*
MUDIE, ROBERT. The Feathered Tribes of the British Islands. 2 vols. 8vo. London, 1834	*Mr. J. Hopkinson.*
NEWMAN, E. A History of British Ferns. 8vo. London. 1840	,,
PACKARD, Dr. A. S. A Monograph of the Geometrid Moths or Phalænidæ of the United States. (*U. S. Geol. Surv.*) 4to. Washington, 1876	*Dr. F. V. Hayden.*
PHILLIPS, Prof. JOHN. Treatise on Geology. 2 vols. 12mo. London, 1837–39	*Mr. J. Hopkinson.*
———— Notices of Rocks and Fossils in the University Museum, Oxford. 8vo. Oxford, 1863	,,
PHILLIPS, WILLIAM. Elementary Introduction to the Knowledge of Mineralogy. 12mo. London, 1816	,,
PORTER, T. C., and J. M. COULTER. Synopsis of the Flora of Colorado. 8vo. Washington, 1874	*Dr. F. V. Hayden.*

TITLE.	DONOR.
POWELL, Rev. Prof. BADEN. History of Natural Philosophy. 8vo. London, 1834	*Mr. J. Hopkinson.*
PRESTON, Rev. T. A. Flora of Marlborough. Parts 1–3. 8vo. Marlborough, 1871—75 . . .	*The Author.*
———— Observations on the Flowering of Plants. (*Rep. Marlb. Col. Nat. Hist. Soc.* 1873.) . .	,,
———— Meteorological Observations, 1865—72. (*ib.* 1874)	,,
PRYOR, R. A. On the Occurrence of *Medicago lappacea*, Lamk., in Bedfordshire . . . . . (*Journ. of Botany,* 1876.)	,,
RAMSAY, Prof. A. C. The Physical Geology and Geography of Great Britain. 8vo. London, 1863 .	*Mr. J. Hopkinson.*
REDGRAVE, GILBERT R. A Short Account of Mountsorrel, and the Working of its Granite Quarries. 8vo. Leicester, 1870	,,
RICHARDSON, RALPH. The Ice Age in Britain. 8vo. Edinburgh, 1876	*The Author.*
RICKETTS, CHARLES. The Cause of the Glacial Period with reference to the British Isles. (*Geol. Mag.* 1875.)	,,
SMITH, Sir J. E. Introduction to Physiological and Systematic Botany. 6th Edition. 8vo. London, 1827	*Lieut. R. B. Croft.*
SOMERVILLE, MARY. The Connexion of the Physical Sciences. 5th Edition. 8vo. London, 1840. .	*Mr. J. Hopkinson.*
SYMONS, G. J. On the Fall of Rain in the British Isles in the Years 1860—63. (*Rep. Brit. Assoc. for* 1862 *and* 1864.)	*Dr. A. T. Brett.*
———— British Rainfall, 1860—64. 8vo. London. 1862—65	,,
———— Tables of the Total Depth of Rain in 1866. 8vo. London. 1867	,,
———— On the Distribution of Rain over the British Isles during the Years 1867, 68. 8vo. *ib.* 1868-69	,,
———— Rules for Rainfall Observers, and Total Amount of Rain recorded during the Year 1870. 8vo. *ib.* 1871	,,
———— British Rainfall, 1875. 8vo. London, 1876	*The Author.*
———— Monthly Meteorological Magazine. Vol xi, Nos. 121-131. 8vo. London, 1876 . .	,,
THOMAS, Dr. CYRUS. Synopsis of the Acrididæ of North America. (*U. S. Geol. Surv.*) 4to. Washington, 1873	*Dr. F. V. Hayden.*
UNITED STATES GEOLOGICAL AND GEOGRAPHICAL SURVEY OF THE TERRITORIES. Catalogue of the Publications. 8vo. Washington, 1874 . .	,,
———— Bulletin. No. 2. Second Series—No. 2 and No. 4. 8vo. *ib.* 1874—75	,,
URE, Dr. ANDREW. Dictionary of Chemistry. 8vo. London, 1821	*Lieut. R. B. Croft.*
WOODWARD, HENRY. On a new Species of Rostellaria from the Gray Chalk, Folkestone. (*Geol. Mag.* 1872.)	*Mr. J. Hopkinson.*
———— Further Remarks on the Xiphosura. (*Quart. Journ. Geol. Soc.* 1872.)	,,

PUBLICATIONS OF SOCIETIES RECEIVED IN EXCHANGE.

BATH NATURAL HISTORY AND ANTIQUARIAN FIELD CLUB. Proceedings. Vol. iii, Nos. 1-3. 8vo. Bath, 1874-76.

BELFAST NATURALISTS' FIELD CLUB. Proceedings. Series 2, Vol. i, Parts 1-3. 8vo. Belfast, 1874-76.

BOSTON (U.S.A.) SOCIETY OF NATURAL HISTORY. Proceedings. Vol. xvii, Parts 3 and 4. Vol. xviii, Parts 1 and 2. 8vo. Boston, 1875-76.

BRIGHTON AND SUSSEX NATURAL HISTORY SOCIETY. Proceedings for 1874-75. 8vo. Brighton, 1875.

BRISTOL NATURALISTS' SOCIETY. Proceedings. New Series. Vol. i, Part 3. 8vo. Bristol, 1876.

———— Annual Report for 1875-6. 8vo. ib. 1876.

EASTBOURNE NATURAL HISTORY SOCIETY. Papers. Session 1873-4, and 1875-6. 4to. Eastbourne, 1874-76.

EDINBURGH BOTANICAL SOCIETY. Transactions. Vol. xii, Part 3. 8vo. Edinburgh, 1876.

EDINBURGH GEOLOGICAL SOCIETY. Transactions. Vol. ii, Part 3. 8vo. Edinburgh, 1874.

GEOLOGICAL SOCIETY. Abstracts of the Proceedings. Session 1875-76. 8vo. London, 1876.

GEOLOGISTS' ASSOCIATION. Proceedings. Vol. iv, Nos. 5-8. 8vo. London, 1876.

———— Annual Report for 1875. 8vo. ib. 1876.

GLASGOW, GEOLOGICAL SOCIETY OF. Transactions. Vol. v, Part 1. 8vo. Glasgow, 1875.

GLASGOW, NATURAL HISTORY SOCIETY OF. Proceedings. Vol. i, and Vol. ii, Part 1. 8vo. Glasgow, 1869-76.

GLASGOW, PHILOSOPHICAL SOCIETY OF. Proceedings. Vol. ix, and Vol. x, No. 1. 8vo. Glasgow, 1875-6.

IRELAND, ROYAL GEOLOGICAL SOCIETY OF. Journal. New Series. Vols. i-iii, and Vol. iv, Parts 1 and 2. 8vo. Dublin, 1867-75.

LEEDS NATURALISTS' CLUB AND SCIENTIFIC ASSOCIATION. Annual Report for 1875-76. 8vo. Leeds, 1876.

MANCHESTER FIELD NATURALISTS' AND ARCHÆOLOGISTS' SOCIETY. Report for 1875. 8vo. Manchester, 1876.

MANCHESTER GEOLOGICAL SOCIETY. Transactions. Vol. xiv, Parts 1-5. 8vo. Manchester, 1876.

MANCHESTER, LITERARY AND PHILOSOPHICAL SOCIETY OF. Memoirs. Third Series. Vols. i-v. 8vo. Manchester, 1862-76.

———— Proceedings. Vols. iii-xv. 8vo. ib. 1864-76.

MARLBOROUGH COLLEGE NATURAL HISTORY SOCIETY. Report for the half-year ending Christmas, 1875; and Midsummer, 1876. 8vo. Marlborough, 1876.

METEOROLOGICAL SOCIETY. Quarterly Journal. New Series. Vol. iii, Nos. 17-19. 8vo. London, 1876.

———— Catalogue of the Library. 8vo. ib. 1876.

———— List of the Fellows. 8vo. ib. 1876.

NORFOLK AND NORWICH NATURALISTS' SOCIETY. Transactions. Vol. ii, Parts 1 and 2. 8vo. Norwich, 1875-76.

QUEKETT MICROSCOPICAL CLUB. Journal. Nos. 30-32. 8vo. London, 1876.

SMITHSONIAN INSTITUTION. Annual Report of the Board of Regents for 1874. 8vo. Washington, 1875.

SOMERSETSHIRE ARCHÆOLOGICAL AND NATURAL HISTORY SOCIETY. Proceedings. New Series. Vol. i. 8vo. Taunton, 1876.

WARWICKSHIRE NATURAL HISTORY AND ARCHÆOLOGICAL SOCIETY. Annual Reports for 1874 and 1875. 8vo. Warwick, 1875-76.

WEST LONDON SCIENTIFIC ASSOCIATION AND FIELD CLUB. Proceedings. Vol. i, Parts 1-3. 8vo. London, 1876.

———— Annual Report for 1875-76. 8vo. ib. 1876.

WILTSHIRE ARCHÆOLOGICAL AND NATURAL HISTORY SOCIETY. Magazine. Vol. xvi, Nos. 46 and 47. 8vo. Devizes, 1876.

ORDINARY MEETING, 11TH JANUARY, 1877.

JOHN EVANS, Esq., F.R.S., etc., President, in the Chair.

Dr. John Attfield, F.C.S., Professor of Practical Chemistry to the Pharmaceutical Society of Great Britain, Ashlands, Watford, and Mr. Sydney Humbert, Little Nascot, Watford, were elected Members of the Society.

The following papers were read :—

1. "Fish-hatching and Fish-culture in Hertfordshire." By Alfred T. Brett, M.D. With "Notes on Pisciculture" by Peter Hood, M.D. (*Vide* p. 179).

2. "Notes and Queries on the River Colne, Watford." By A. T. Brett, M.D. (*Vide* p. 175).

Mr. John E. Littleboy gave an account of an attempt he made to rear trout, and stated that only a few out of 300 young fish grew to be of any considerable size. Crayfish, he said, abounded in the stream at Hunton Bridge, and he had often eaten them at tea.

Mr. Humbert remarked with regard to the scarcity of fish that men came from London and caught with a net perhaps a bushel of fish in a day. He thought they supplied the shops where live bait was sold. The scarcity of fish at Mr. King's might be owing to Wiggenhall being below the Watford Gas Works.

The President spoke at some length upon the origin of the word "Colne," which he thought was most probably derived from the Breton word *colen*, signifying "small," as so many small rivers in this country were called "Colne." The elevation of the banks of the Colne, alluded to by Mr. Clutterbuck in his letter, seemed to show that the mill at Watford was a very ancient one, like many others in the neighbourhood, which date back seven or eight hundred years. The disease among the fish at Cassiobury he considered to be parasitical, and he thought that the absence of trout in the river could be best accounted for by the accumulation of mud at the bottom of the river, trout requiring a gravelly bottom upon which to deposit their ova. Jack he said were very destructive to trout.

The following objects were exhibited:—A fish-hatching apparatus, and fish-ova, by Mr. Jonathan King; sketches of trout caught in the Colne, by Mr. King and Mr. H. Howard; a pike, stuffed, weighing 18 lbs., caught by Mr. W. Rogers, and another weighing 14½ lbs., caught at Aldenham Abbey, by Mr. Durham; and salmon, hybrids of salmon and trout, the sey or golden trout from Germany, Swiss trout, pike, roach, dace, bream, and minnows, living, from the Fish Museum, South Kensington, by Mr. Frank Buckland. Dr. Brett, Mr. Jonathan Chater, and the Honorary Secretary, also exhibited fish scales under their microscopes.

Mr. James U. Harford and Mr. C. F. Hollingsworth were appointed Auditors of the Accounts for 1876.

ANNUAL MEETING, 9TH FEBRUARY, 1877.

JOHN EVANS, Esq., F.R.S., etc., President in the Chair.

Mr. F. J. Marnham, The Hollies, Boxmoor, and Miss Wilson, Nutfield, Watford, were elected Members of the Society.

Charles Darwin, M.A., F.R.S., F.R.S.E., F.L.S., F.G.S., Down, Beckenham, Kent, and the Rev. George Henslow, M.A., F.L.S., F.G.S., Lecturer on Botany at St. Bartholomew's Hospital, 7, Bentinck Terrace, Regent's Park, London, were elected Honorary Members.

The Report of the Council for 1876, and the Treasurer's Account of Income and Expenditure, were read and adopted.

The President delivered an Address (*Vide* p. 187).

The Balloting-glass having been removed, and the lists examined by the Scrutineers, the following gentlemen were declared to have been duly elected as the Officers and Council for the ensuing year :—

President.—Alfred T. Brett, M.D.

Vice-Presidents.—Arthur Cottam, F.R.A.S.; the Right Honourable the Earl of Essex; John Evans, F.R.S., V.P.S.A., V.P.G.S., F.M.S., etc.; J. Logan Lobley, F.G.S., F.R.G.S.

Treasurer.—Charles F. Humbert, F.G.S.

Honorary Secretary and Librarian.—John Hopkinson, F.L.S., F.G.S., F.R.M.S., F.M.S.

Honorary Curator.—W. Lepard Smith.

Other Members of the Council.—R. Russell Carew, F.R.G.S., F.C.S.; E. M. Chater; George Chippindale; Lieut. Richard B. Croft, R.N., F.L.S., F.R.M.S.; James U. Harford; J. E. Harting, F.L.S., F.Z.S.; Thomas Heather; J. Gwyn Jeffreys, LL.D., F.R.S., F.L.S., F.G.S., etc.; John E. Littleboy; the Rev. C. M. Perkins, M.A.; R. A. Pryor, B.A., F.L.S.; Frank W. Silvester.

It was then resolved—

That the thanks of the Society be given to Mr. John Evans, F.R.S., retiring from the office of President; to Dr. A. T. Brett and Mr. C. F. Humbert, retiring from the office of Vice-President; to Mr Arthur Cottam, retiring from the office of Treasurer; and to Mr. W. M. Fawcett, Mr. George Rooper, and Mr. John Sedgwick, retiring from the Council.

The thanks of the Society were also accorded to the Honorary Secretary.

REPORT OF THE COUNCIL FOR 1876.

In presenting this, their second Annual Report, the Council of the Watford Natural History Society and Hertfordshire Field Club may again congratulate the members on the prosperity of the Society, both with regard to the state of its finances and the position it continues to hold as a Society doing work of permanent value in the investigation of the Natural History of its county.

During the year 27 Ordinary Members and three Honorary Members have been elected; ten members have compounded for their annual subscription (raising the number of life members from five to fifteen); and nineteen members—twelve of whom have removed from the neighbourhood of Watford—have resigned.

The Council have again, with much regret, to record the loss of one member by death. The Countess of Essex, who was elected a member of the Society at its first meeting, died on the 5th of May, beloved and esteemed by all who knew her.

The census of the Society at the end of the years 1875 and 1876 was as follows:—

	1875	1876
Honorary Members	5	8
Life Members	5	15
Annual Subscribers	140	137
Total	150	160

Three parts of the first volume of the Society's 'Transactions' have been printed and distributed to the members during the year, making in all five parts; and a sixth is now in the press and will shortly be issued. Arrangements have been made for this and future parts to be published in London, by Messrs. Hardwicke and Bogue, 192, Piccadilly, from whom also any of the parts previously published may now be obtained. They will still be kept on sale as before at the Watford Public Library, and at the printers', Messrs. Stephen Austin & Sons, Hertford.

The following are the principal papers and lectures that have been read or delivered during the year 1876:—

Jan. 13.—Meteorological Observations taken at Cassiobury House from May to December, 1875; by the Right Honourable the Earl of Essex.

—— . On the Construction, Adjustment, and Use of Meteorological Instruments; by Thomas Heather.

—— . On the supposed Chalybeate Spring at Watford, and on other Medicinal Waters in Herts; by R. A. Pryor, B.A., F.L.S.

Feb. 10.—Anniversary Address; by the President, John Evans, F.R.S., F.S.A., F.G.S., etc.

March 9.—On some of the simpler methods of Microscopical Mounting; by Arthur Cottam, F.R.A.S.

April 13.—The Polarisation of Light; by James U. Harford. (First lecture.)

May 11.—The Geology and Water Supply of the Neighbourhood of Watford; by the Rev. James C. Clutterbuck, M.A.

June 8.—Meteorological Observations taken at Oaklands, Hempstead-road, Watford, from 1871 to 1875; by Edward Harrison.

—— . On the Advantage of observing Phenological Phenomena; by Lieut. Richard B. Croft, R.N., F.L.S., F.R.M.S.

—— . The Hertfordshire Bourne; by John Evans, F.R.S., etc., President.

Oct. 12.—The Polarisation of Light; by James U. Harford. (Second lecture.)

Nov. 9.—The Hertfordshire Ordnance Bench Marks, from the 'Abstracts of Levelling' of the Ordnance Survey; by John Hopkinson, F.L.S., F.G.S., Hon. Sec.

Dec. 14.—The Eocenes of England and their extension in Hertfordshire; by J. Logan Lobley, F.G.S., F.R.G.S.

In addition to these papers, several shorter communications, relating principally to the Geology and Botany of the county, have been read, and the Council would urge upon the members never to allow any observation, however trivial it might appear, that may in any way add to our knowledge of the Natural History of Hertfordshire, to pass unrecorded. That an observation of a certain occurrence has been previously made and recorded is not a sufficient reason for it to pass unnoticed when it again occurs. The visit of a rare bird, the unusual abundance of certain insects, the blossoming "out of season" of a common wild flower—which has happened to several this autumn and winter—and many other phenomena, are worth noticing and recording every time they occur ; and the time of flowering of certain plants, of first appearance of certain insects, and of arrival and departure, etc., of certain birds, should be recorded every year.

A report on the observations of the periodical phenomena to which allusion is here made, that have already been communicated to your Secretary, will shortly be presented to the Society; but the Council cannot but regret that only two members—one at Watford and the other at Ware—have so far carried on these observations.

Reports on the rainfall, which were communicated quarterly in 1875, have been discontinued, it being thought that a more comprehensive annual report would be of greater value. Such a report, embracing returns from about 20 stations in the county, will be presented at the first opportunity; and the Council desire here to express their thanks to your honorary member, Mr. G. J. Symons, for the facilities he has afforded for these reports to be obtained from observers who are co-operating with him in his system of rainfall registration, and who have forwarded their returns on the application of your Secretary. The Society has already been the means of increasing the number of these observers, one member having started a new gauge at Watford, and another at Odsey. A set of standard meteorological instruments, sufficiently complete for all the usual observations, and verified at the Kew Observatory, has also been obtained by your Secretary, whose daily observations are carried out in accordance with the regulations of the Meteorological Society, to which they are forwarded monthly. A summary of these observations will also be given annually in your 'Transactions.'

The Field Meetings that have taken place during the year must now be alluded to. They have been more uniformly successful than they were the previous year, the weather having been much more favourable. Of the five meetings arranged the programme announced was in every case but one fully carried out, and this exception relates merely to mode of conveyance. At these Field Meetings the following localities were visited :—

April 29.—Bernard's Heath and Hedges, St. Albans.
May 13.—Hatfield Park.
June 3.—Bricket Wood and Common, and the Wylde, St. Albans.
—— 17.—Boxmoor, Bennet's End, and Nash Mills.
July 1.—Elstree Reservoir and Stanmore Common.

Of these meetings, that at Hatfield Park requires special mention. It is the one alluded to above as having been carried out differently from the announcement, which was that conveyances would be hired from St. Albans to Hatfield, the trains not running at convenient times. A greater number of members than could be thus provided for having signified their intention of taking part in this meeting, it was decided to engage a special train from St. Albans to Hatfield and back. The Great Northern Railway Company ran this train for the sum of £2 beyond the ordinary fares—an expenditure the Council are gratified to state was fully warranted by the large number of members who took advantage of the arrangement. Including a few who arrived by different routes, the Society was represented at Hatfield by a party of from 60 to 70 ; and the Geologists' Association, in conjunction with which the meeting had been arranged, was represented by about the same number, making altogether a party of fully 130, to whom Hatfield House and Park, and the Hatfield Park brick-fields, were thrown open by the kind permission of the Marquess of Salisbury. At the other meetings, of which the third and fifth took place in conjunction with the Quekett Microscopical Club, from about twenty to thirty members were present.

For hospitality kindly afforded at the field meetings the Society is indebted to three of its members—Mr. Silvester, Mr. Hollingsworth, and your President. To Mr. Evans the thanks of the Society are also especially due for his invaluable assistance in other ways. He has rendered the field meetings the medium of imparting a knowledge of the geological structure and features of the country traversed ; and at the evening meetings, whatever has been the subject of discussion, and a very wide range has been traversed during the year, he has thrown some new light upon it, or added information which has considerably increased the interest of the meeting and enhanced its value. It is with much regret that the Council have to announce the expiration of the term of his Presidency in accordance with your laws—a regret which they feel assured will be equally felt by all the members of the Society.

The Council have also to regret that your Treasurer has tendered his resignation, owing to his numerous engagements preventing his regular attendance at the meetings and rendering it impossible for him to devote the time to the affairs of the Society that he would wish. To Mr. Cottam, as one of the three who took the first steps towards the formation of the Society, as well as for his valuable services as Treasurer during the first two years of its existence, the Society is greatly indebted.

The Society continues to be in a satisfactory financial condition, the balance in hand being considerably larger than at the end of the previous year. The capital account, consisting of the amounts received for life compositions, having increased from £25 to £75, it has been decided to invest it in the purchase of Consols, and the Council have appointed three life members—Dr. Brett, Mr. John Hopkinson, and Mr. W. Lepard Smith—Trustees, and in their names the funded and other property of the Society will be held.

Numerous donations to the Society's library have been received during the year, including some very valuable works, of which the publications of the United States Geological and Geographical Survey of the Territories, presented by your Honorary Member,

Dr. F. V. Hayden, Director of the Survey, are the most important. Several of the scientific societies with which exchange of publications is made, have presented entire volumes, and a few have most liberally given complete sets of volumes of their publications. A considerable number of books and pamphlets has also been received from authors and others, both members and non-members of the Society. The books, maps, etc., belonging to the Society in the Watford Public Library have been insured, in the names of the Trustees, in the Liverpool and London and Globe Fire Insurance Office to the amount of £50.

A cabinet for microscopic slides has been purchased, and the Council invite donations of slides, which will be gladly received by your Curator. When a sufficient number has accumulated, it is intended to let them circulate amongst the members, and those who may desire to borrow the slides are recommended to procure, for their safe conveyance, small cases such as are used by the members of the Quekett Microscopical Club for this purpose.

In conclusion the Council have again to express their thanks to the Committee of the Watford Public Library, for the facilities afforded for the holding of the evening meetings of the Society; and more especially also to their Chairman, Dr. Iles, for his kindness in inviting the members of the Society to his conversazione on the 27th of October.

INCOME AND EXPENDITURE DURING THE YEAR ENDING 31ST DECEMBER, 1876.

DR.	£	s.	d.	CR.	£	s.	d.
Balance	0	16	6	Books and Stationery	2	3	9
Subscriptions for 1875	6	0	0	Advertising	0	8	0
„ „ 1876	69	0	0	Printing ' Transactions '	32	9	11
Entrance Fees	11	10	0	Miscellaneous Printing	8	18	1
Life Compositions	50	0	0	Reporting	2	2	0
Sale of ' Transactions '	0	16	0	Rent — Watford Public			
Interest on Deposit (£25)	0	6	10	Library	5	0	0
				Attendance at ditto	1	2	6
				Expenses of Hatfield Meeting	2	10	6
				Library	5	7	6
				Microscopical Cabinet	1	15	0
				Postages	7	4	2
				Sundry small expenses	0	18	3
				Amount transferred to Capital Account	50	0	0
				Balance	18	9	8
	£138	9	4		£138	9	4

Subscriptions received for 1877 .... 6 0 0

The foregoing account was audited and found correct by us, and we find that the amount of £75 is to the credit of the Society at the London and County Bank, Watford, in addition to the above balance.

JAMES U. HARFORD,
C. F. HOLLINGSWORTH, } AUDITORS.

3rd February, 1877.

ORDINARY MEETING, 8TH MARCH, 1877.

ALFRED T. BRETT, Esq., M.D., President, in the Chair.

Mr. G. P. Bernard, Marlowes, Hemel Hempstead; Mr. Henry Haynes, Langley Road, Watford; Mr. Henry Marnham, Beech Lodge, Watford; Miss S. Pugh, High Street, Watford; and Mr. H. Demain-Saunders, Brickendon Grange, Hertford, were elected Members of the Society.

Letters were read from Mr. Charles Darwin, F.R.S., and the Rev. George Henslow, thanking the Society for their election as Honorary Members.

The following lecture was delivered:—
"The Fertilisation of Plants." By the Rev. George Henslow, M.A., F.L.S., F.G.S. (*Vide* p. 201).

A discussion ensued, in which Mr. E. M. Chater, Mr. Arthur Cottam, and the President, took part.

Specimens of plants, with drawings of their organs of fructification, and diagrams, were exhibited by Mr. Henslow in illustration of his lecture.

ORDINARY MEETING, 12TH APRIL, 1877.

ALFRED T. BRETT, Esq., M.D., President, in the Chair.

Mr. J. E. Cussans, 179, Junction Road, Upper Holloway, London, was elected a Member of the Society.

The following communications were read:—
1. "Instructions for taking Meteorological Observations." By William Marriott, F.M.S., Assistant Secretary of the Meteorological Society. Communicated by the Honorary Secretary (*Vide* p. 211).
2. "Meteorological Observations taken at Holly Bank, Watford, during the year ending 28th February, 1877." By John Hopkinson, F.L.S., F.M.S., etc., Hon. Sec. (*Vide* p. 217).
3. "Report on the Rainfall in Hertfordshire in 1876." By the Honorary Secretary.
4. "Notes on a Remarkable Storm in Hertfordshire on the 4th April, 1877." By Lieut. Richard B. Croft, R.N., F.L.S., etc.

Meteorological Instruments were exhibited, in illustration of these papers, by the President, the Secretary, and Mr. Marriott.

Mr. J. J. Hicks, of Hatton Garden, London, also exhibited some new meteorological instruments, amongst which was a solar-radiation thermometer mounted with a radiometer to test the vacuum in its outer jacket,—an invention of considerable interest, being the first application of the radiometer to a practical purpose.

FIELD MEETING, 5TH MAY, 1877.

STANMORE COMMON.

This meeting having been arranged to enable members to collect microscopic objects for exhibition at the succeeding evening meeting (10th May), there is but little to record. The place of meeting was at the corner of the Common, at the junction of the road from Watford to Stanmore with that to Harrow. Some members arrived here from London, walking from Harrow station by Harrow Weald and Bentley Priory, and others came direct from Watford and from the more immediate neighbourhood.

The meeting was under the direction of Mr. Arthur Cottam, and under his guidance the various pools on the Common were searched with more or less success, the most beautiful object found (when viewed under the microscope) being the Rotifer, *Conochilus volvox*.

After spending some time in collecting microscopic and other plants and animals—for several botanists and entomologists were among the party—the members left the Common, the majority walking to Watford, not however without a rest on the way, for at his residence on Bushey Heath Mr. William Verini most kindly provided tea. Although the weather was cold for the time of the year, the air was dry and the road dusty, making the rest and refreshment especially acceptable.

ORDINARY MEETING, 10TH MAY, 1877.

ALFRED T. BRETT, Esq., M.D., President, in the Chair.

Miss Lucy A. Gaubert, Chalk Hill, Bushey, and Mr. W. R. Woolrych, Croxley Green, Rickmansworth, were elected Members of the Society.

The following papers were read :—

1. "On Microscopic Fungi." By E. M. Chater (*Vide* p. 231).

The President said that microscopic fungi were most important agents in the great laboratory of nature. They were the innocent cause of more misery and crime, and of more disease of body and of mind in the human race than any other agent; for fermentation, and therefore the production of alcohol, was their entire work. Fermentation had been well called by Pasteur "life without air." The *Torula*, if deprived of air, would live by extracting oxygen from sugar in solution, and it thus caused a set of changes one result of which was the production of wine or alcohol; and the *Penicillium*, if allowed to grow on the surface of a fluid where it could obtain oxygen from the air, would grow rapidly and not produce alcohol, but forcibly submerge the little plant—push it down deep into the liquid where the quantity of free oxygen was insufficient for its needs—it immediately began to act as a ferment, supplying itself with oxygen by the decomposition of the sugar, and producing alcohol as one of the products of decomposition. Other microscopic plants also acted in a similar manner.

2. "Notes on some Hertfordshire Plants." By R. A. Pryor B.A., F.L.S.*

* The publication of this paper is unavoidably postponed.

In illustration of these papers microscopic fungi were exhibited by Mr. Chater and other members under their microscopes, and Hertfordshire plants by Mr. Pryor.

Various living objects, collected at the Field Meeting on Stanmore Common, were also exhibited by the members under their microscopes, and Mr. Arthur Cottam described the structure of *Conochilus volvox*, of which he and the Honorary Secretary exhibited specimens under different powers and different methods of illumination in order to illustrate it in various aspects.

FIELD MEETING, 26TH MAY, 1877.

PINNER.

Leaving Pinner Station at about three p.m. on the arrival of trains from Watford and Euston, the members proceeded first to the lime-kiln and sand-pit between Wood Hall and Pinner Green, known as "The Dingles," where the northern margin of the "Pinner Inlier" of the Woolwich and Reading Beds is exposed, and a shaft is sunk through them to the Chalk.

Here the director of the meeting, Mr. J. Logan Lobley, F.G.S., gave an account of the geology of the neighbourhood, more especially explanatory of this inlier. Outliers, he said, are portions of a formation detached from the main mass and surrounded by lower beds, of which we have an example in the "Harrow Outlier" of the Bagshot Sands. Inliers, on the other hand, are exposures of underlying beds laid bare by the removal of higher ones by which they are surrounded. This Pinner inlier is in the London Clay area, the boundary of which is about three miles to the north, and the Woolwich and Reading Series here seen— surrounded on all sides by the London Clay—has been brought up by an upheaval, and the same upheaval to which we are indebted for the hill on which stands Windsor Castle, which is an inlier of the Chalk surrounded by Tertiary beds, and is in a line with the inliers at Ruislip Reservoir, Northaw, and here. The London Clay is a few feet to the north of us, so that we are just on the northern margin of the inlier, which includes the village of Pinner and runs west to Ercot. The outlier of the Bagshot Sands at Harrow, he concluded, is the most northern patch of these sands in existence, not only in England, but in the world.

After examining the section of the Reading Beds, and noticing the shaft which is sunk forty feet through them to the Chalk, here got at to burn for lime, the members left the pit, and a little to the north, a dyke, known as Gryme's Dyke, was pointed out by Mr. William A. Tooke, who then conducted the party to his residence, Pinner Hill, where tea was kindly provided, after which most of the party ascended a clock tower which he has recently built.

From the summit of the tower, which is fifty-five feet high, a good view of the surrounding country was obtained, and Mr.

Lobley pointed out how different formations are characterised by the physical features and vegetation of the country,—the Chalk usually forming rounded hills without trees, and frequently sheep walks called "Downs"; the London Clay, broad valleys and gently rising hills with oaks and elms as its principal trees; and the Bagshot Sands, broad heaths and barren plains.

A very fine lime tree, about 100 feet high, was seen from this tower, and it was noticed that while beeches were growing on the gravels capping the hill, most of the trees around—situated on the underlying London Clay—were oaks and elms.

On leaving Mr. Tooke's grounds, a gravel-pit, on the opposite side of the road from Pinner to Watford, was visited, and the gravel was seen to be of glacial age. Some of the pebbles, but not all, were rounded, and they were mostly of flint, but some were quartzite and pebbles from the older rocks. Mr. Lobley stated that there was none of this glacial gravel south of the Thames; the gravels in the Thames Valley being river-gravels—newer than these—and that between the age of the gravels here and those on Harrow Hill the Alps, Pyrenees, and Himalayas were formed.

Here the party took leave of Mr. and Mrs. Tooke, and soon entered the Oxhey Woods, and in walking through the woods, in several places pools of water were seen, some of considerable size, showing that, retaining the water, there was clay under the bed of pebble-gravel on which these woods are situated.

The woods were gay with wild flowers, but there was little time to devote to botany, and it was late in the day when Bushey Station, where the party separated, was reached.

ORDINARY MEETING, 14TH JUNE, 1877.

ALFRED T. BRETT, Esq., M.D., President, in the Chair.

Mrs. George Brightwen, The Grove, Great Stanmore, was elected a Member of the Society.

The following communications were read:—

1. A Letter from Mr. Robert Clutterbuck, F.G.S., to the President, on the Coprolite Beds at Hinxworth, North Herts (*Vide* p. 238).

Mr. J. E. Littleboy said that he supposed every one knew there were extensive coprolite beds near Chittenden. The quantity of coprolites got from them was very considerable indeed, and the value was something like £60 per acre. A little further on, in the hamlet of Standbridge, between Leighton and Dunstable, there was a tract of land belonging to his brother, and he let it out for working at £30 per acre. The value of the coprolite beds entirely depended on the depth at which the coprolites were found. At Chittenden they were six or seven feet deep, and at Standbridge rather deeper, and therefore the beds were not so valuable. He should be very much interested to hear a few hypotheses as to their origin.

The President said that he must refer the matter to the Secretary.

Mr. Hopkinson said that this was a difficult question to give an opinion upon. Geologists were not agreed as to the origin of these beds of phosphate of lime — whether their nodules were partially or entirely coprolitic, or were merely concretions formed round decaying sponges and other decomposing animal matter.

2. Notes on the Size and Growth of Trees at Watford. By the President.

The following trees were mentioned by Dr. Brett:—1. The Grimston or Oxhey Oak, supposed to have been planted about the year 1750, on the 28th November, 1876, measured 20 feet in circumference at the base, 15 ft. 4 ins. at 3 feet from the ground, and 12 ft. 10 ins. at 6 feet from the ground. 2. An Oak at Wiggenhall from an acorn of the Panshanger Oak sown in 1826, on the 28th November, 1876, measured 7 ft. 11 ins. in circumference at the base, 5 ft. 5 ins. at 3 feet from the ground, and 5 ft. 2 ins. at 6 feet from the ground. 3. "The Royal Oak," planted at Wiggenhall on the 9th November, 1841, 3 inches high when planted, had attained the height of 33 feet on the 9th November, 1876, and measured 4 ft. 9 ins. in circumference at the base, 3 ft. 6 ins. at 3 feet from the ground, and 3 ft. 4 ins. at 6 feet from the ground. 4. A *Wellingtonia gigantea* at the Stanboroughs, planted by Mr. Cottrell on the 9th February, 1859, then under 2 feet high, grew 4 inches in 1859, 12 in 1860, 16 in 1861, and 27 in 1862, and on the 27th March, 1877, had attained the height of 32 ft. 6 ins. 5. A *Wellingtonia gigantea*, planted at Cliff Villa by Mr. Savill on the day the Prince of Wales was married—10th March, 1863—then 3 feet high, on the 8th December, 1876, was 32 ft. 6 ins. in height, and 4 ft. 10 ins. in circumference at the base, 3 ft. 3 ins. at 3 feet from the ground, and 2 ft. 4 ins. at 6 feet from the ground.

3. A Letter from the Rev. R. H. Webb, M.A., to the Secretary, on the Fertilisation of *Aucuba Japonica* (*Vide* p. 239).

4. Note on the Appearance of the Clouded Yellow Butterfly (*Colias Edusa*). By Arthur Cottam, F.R.A.S. (*Vide* p. 239).

The Secretary said that he had heard of another of these butterflies having been seen. The Rev. C. M. Perkins, whom he met at St. Albans last Sunday, told him that he had seen one that afternoon.

5. Notes on the Owl. By the President (*Vide* p. 240).

6. Notes on the Otter and Badger in Hertfordshire. By the President (*Vide* p. 236).

The Secretary read, from the 'Zoologist'—the number for the current month—a note, by Mr. George Rooper, F.Z.S., on a cuckoo laying in a swallow's nest, and remarked that although it was mentioned there as being the first known occurrence of the kind, this Society had previously published in its 'Transactions' a note by Dr. Brett, read last year at the June meeting, in which he recorded the hatching of a cuckoo in a swallow's nest at Wiggenhall in 1874.

Numerous interesting objects, illustrative of the Natural History of the neighbourhood, were exhibited, including the following:— An old worn-out watering-pot with the nest of a robin built in it, in which four young ones were hatched; the nest of a chaffinch; the nest of a gold-crested wren which was found suspended from the bough of a cedar tree; the nest of a wren which was built in an elder; the nest of a long-tailed tit injured by the brown owl; a gold-crested wren (called here the "bee bird"); a white owl; and a long-eared owl, exhibited by Mr. Jonathan King. Two green woodpeckers—called in Hertfordshire "whetiles" from the nature of their cry—shot at Edge Grove, Aldenham, 30 years ago; a black woodpecker; a black tern shot at Elstree Reservoir; a waxwing, shot in Mrs. Bailey Smith's garden, Watford Fields; the large snowy owl; an otter killed at Munden; and a badger killed at the Grove, lent by their owners to Dr. Brett for exhibition.

FIELD MEETING, 16TH JUNE, 1877.

HITCHIN.

Having received a kind and pressing invitation from Mr. William Ransom, of Hitchin, to visit that locality, about 30 of the members of the Society and their friends assembled at the Hitchin railway station on the arrival of the 11·46 a.m. train from Hatfield. They were met on their arrival by Mr. William and Mr. Alfred Ransom, and at once proceeded to the chalk-pits, near the station, from which the chalk is derived to supply the lime works belonging to the latter gentleman.

These extensive excavations are in the upper part of the Lower Chalk, of which they have yielded numerous characteristic fossils. At the top of the section the junction of the Chalk at different places with the beds above afforded material for considerable discussion; and the nature and origin of a large "pipe" of sand and gravel—which measures about six feet in diameter, and which penetrates the Chalk perpendicularly in the form of a well, being readily observable for a distance of about 60 feet from the top of the pit—was lucidly explained by Dr. John Evans, F.R.S The beds of clay and gravel which were seen to overlie the Chalk were next alluded to by Dr. Evans, who considered them to have been formed during the Glacial period, and to be most probably due to marine conditions, a large block of chalk in a bed of boulder-clay at the highest part of the pit having, for instance, with little doubt, been brought there and deposited on the spot by an iceberg.

The party then wended its way, single file, up some rather steep steps cut out in the Chalk, to the summit of the pit, and thence adjourned to Fairfield, the residence of Mr. William Ransom.

Here a number of flint implements, recently discovered in a bed of clay or "brick-earth" a few miles from Hitchin, at once attracted the attention of Dr. Evans, who determined them to be celts of the Palæolithic Age occurring under conditions which seemed to afford conclusive proof of an almost inconceivable antiquity. They were, he said, the earliest traces of the handiwork of intelligent beings which this country had so far afforded. From the top of the bed in which these were found a flint implement of the Neolithic Period was shown, together with some Roman urns, coins, and culinary utensils, which were carefully examined by the party. A few minutes were pleasantly spent in this manner, and the company was then summoned to the dining-room, where a sumptuous cold luncheon was most hospitably provided. The table was elegantly decorated with wild flowers, amongst which the bee, the fly, the bird's-nest, and the butterfly orchis, the white helleborine, and a beautiful little vetch (*Lathyrus Nissolia*), were specially noticeable. At the conclusion of the repast a few words of hearty thanks were expressed, on behalf of the Society, by the President, Dr. Brett, and were acknowledged in a most cordial manner by the host.

Eight carriages were then placed at the disposal of the company, and a drive was taken in the direction of Lilley Hoo, a distance of about five miles. In the course of the drive some remarkable box trees in the Hermitage Road, believed to be of a very great age, attracted general attention; and the "Icknield Way," an old Roman road, was observed with much interest. In the neighbourhood of Lilley Hoo the geological structure of the district is readily seen, and the Chalk here presents a splendid escarpment, extending several miles across the country. At the foot of this escarpment the Chalk Marl was seen to present an almost level plain, and just beyond it coprolite works indicated the position of the outcrop of the underlying Chloritic Marl, beyond which again dense woods showed the line of the Gault Clay, while in the extreme distance the lowest formation here seen—the Lower Greensand, or Neocomian—bounded the horizon, its comparative hardness, by better withstanding denudation, causing it to rise above the level of the Gault and to shut out from view more distant formations.

At Pegsdon Barns a "combe" or "dyke" in the Chalk again afforded Dr. Evans the text for a very interesting address; and a small torrent afterwards visited, which issues from the base of a picturesque ravine in the grounds of Captain Young, and rejoices in the soubriquet of "Roaring Meg," illustrated in a striking manner the correctness of his views regarding the formation of the adjacent dyke. Some banks profusely abounding with choice orchids, amongst which *Orchis ustulata*, *Orchis pyramidalis*, *Gymnadenia conopsea*, and *Ophrys apifera*, were conspicuous, were next visited. Two "barrows" or "tumuli," of Saxon or Roman origin, were noticed at a short distance from the road, but time forbade the possibility of a nearer inspection.

After driving through sundry meadows and skirting a wood which from its carpet of flowers and delightful shade tempted a closer acquaintance, the party alighted at High Down, the residence of Mr. Joseph Pollard, a member of the Society. Mr. Pollard was unavoidably away from home, but the members and their friends were welcomed by Mrs. Pollard in a most kind and hospitable manner. The house, an excellent specimen of architecture of the reign of James the First, was carefully inspected by those interested in the architecture of that period, and after partaking of tea, a most agreeable surprise after the exertion and heat of the day, the members again resorted to their several conveyances, and arrived at the Hitchin railway station in time for the 5·30 p.m. train to London and Watford.

Thus ended a very charming day,—the beauty of the scenery, the interesting and instructive geological illustrations, the lovely wild-flowers, and, in an especial manner, the profuse hospitality of the host and hostess of the day, will long be remembered by all who constituted the party.

The arrangements were under the direction of Mr. John E. Littleboy, through whom Mr. Ransom's invitation had been received.*

FIELD MEETING, 30TH JUNE, 1877.

CASSIOBURY PARK.

The members, amongst whom was a large proportion of ladies, assembled at about half-past three at the private entrance to Cassiobury Park, nearly opposite Nascot House. They were here joined by a few members of the Quekett Microscopical Club, and, availing themselves of the kind permission of the Earl of Essex, at once proceeded, along the charming wood-walks that lead by the outskirts of the park, to the house and gardens.

A group of magnificent silver firs soon arrested special attention. They are noble trees of unusual girth and height, and are fortunately sufficiently isolated to allow of their full proportions being observed. The gardens were next visited, and under the guidance of Dr. Brett the fine conifers and other rare or remarkable trees were successively examined. Dr. Brett stated, on the authority of Lord Essex, that the splendid cedar, which is so conspicuous on approaching the house, was planted in 1683, by Arthur, Earl of Essex, and was one of the earliest cedars introduced into England. It now measures at its base 22 feet in circumference. The ash-leaved beech (a very rare variety), the *Abies Douglassi*, planted in 1842, the *Taxodium sempervirens*, planted in 1854, and several other ornamental trees, of which particulars of the date of planting and rate of growth, etc., were contributed by Lord Essex, were also observed with much interest.

The party then visited Cassiobury House, and were conducted through the splendid suite of reception rooms that constitute the greater portion of the ground floor. The numerous family portraits, some of them painted by Vandyke, and several possessing considerable historical interest, were carefully noticed; three landscapes by Turner attracted a large share of attention; and the curious in old china found a rich treat awaiting them. It was stated by Dr. Brett that Lord Essex had most kindly proposed personally to conduct the party over the house and grounds, but, greatly to the regret of all present, an attack of indisposition rendered such a course impossible.

The picturesque old mill on the Gade near Cassiobury Lock was the next halting-place, and here, through the kindness of Dr.

* For a considerable portion of this and the following report I am indebted to Mr. Littleboy.—ED.

Brett, a welcome refreshment, in the form of delicious ices, awaited the party. Had it been possible to carry out the programme proposed, the fine avenue of limes in the second park, which was stated to have been planted in 1683, by Le Notre, gardener to Louis the Fourteenth, Rouse Barn Lane, and Rickmansworth Common Moor, would now have been visited; but unfortunately a heavy shower forbade the attempt, and as soon as the rain permitted, an adjournment to the Swiss Cottage was proposed. The clouds quickly vanished, sunshine again prevailed, and this lovely retreat was well seen in all the perfection of its quiet and secluded beauty. The picturesque chalet, the woodland walks, the clear water of the Gade, and "now and then a lusty trout" as it darted rapidly by the observer, were all objects of special interest. By and by, thanks again to the President, the tables on the lawn were plentifully spread with a most acceptable and refreshing tea, at the conclusion of which a vote of thanks to Lord Essex was moved in highly appreciative terms, by the Rev. Canon Gee, and was warmly responded to. A vote of thanks to Dr. Brett, for his kind attention and hospitality, was then moved by Mr. Littleboy and carried by acclamation.

At about half-past six the party separated, a few of the members exploring the botany of Rouse Barn Lane, others fishing for microscopic objects in the water-cress beds that nearly adjoin the grounds of the Cottage, and some of the more zealous microscopists and botanists proceeding to Rickmansworth Common Moor.

The party numbered at least 80, of whom about 10 or 12 were members of the Quekett Microscopical Club.

TRANSACTIONS

OF THE

WATFORD NATURAL HISTORY SOCIETY.

VOL. I.

1.—THE CRETACEOUS ROCKS OF ENGLAND.

By J. LOGAN LOBLEY, F.G.S., F.R.G.S.

[A Lecture delivered 11th March, 1875.]

GEOLOGY is one of the sciences for the promotion of the study of which this Society has been founded; and the investigation of the geological features of Hertfordshire will doubtless engage a large share of your attention. As a preparation for the due observation of the geological phenomena of the district, I have been requested to bring before your notice the outlines of what is known respecting that most interesting group of rocks of which the Chalk, so familiar to the inhabitants of this neighbourhood, is the principal member.

Not more than half a century since, the rocks of the earth were thought to be without order or arrangement; but about this time, William Smith, the uncle of a most worthy successor, who died only last year, Professor Phillips, published to the world the great discovery that a certain order of superposition prevailed, and that strata might be identified by the organic remains which they contained. From that time to the present geologists have assiduously explored the rocks in this and other countries, and have carefully studied the fossils which their researches have brought to light. These investigations have revealed the order and method of the formation of the rocks composing the crust of the globe. The most important results of the researches of geologists in our own country are shown by the diagrams and maps now exhibited. Though the geological scale or table of the sedimentary rocks represents a very definite order of arrangement, it must not be supposed that all the steps of the ladder, so to speak, are to be found in all places. Denudation, or the action of the atmosphere, rain, rivers, and ice, through long periods of time, has so worn and removed the uppermost portions of the rocks, and so many movements consequent upon subterranean forces have occurred, that any one of the rocks named in the scale may be found at the surface. Nay more, so many and so great changes have taken place, that a rock may be wanting though those usually found next below and above it are present. The geological scale, however, tells us without doubt the order of superposition of those rocks which we may find at any place. Thus we may certainly predicate the absence at any locality of the rocks which the scale indicates to be above those there exposed.

The whole of the sedimentary rocks, or those formed by the consolidation of sediment at the bottom of water, are divided, in accordance with their relative age, into three great groups, commonly called Primary, Secondary, and Tertiary, or, as they are now more philosophically named, Palæozoic, Mesozoic, and Cainozoic; but in this lecture scientific words will be used sparingly. The Cretaceous rocks are the uppermost and the newest of the second of the three great divisions (see Fig. 1), and hence it will be at once seen that enormous thicknesses of rocks had been deposited, and vast periods of time had elapsed, before the Chalk was formed: and when it is remembered that the Chalk itself has been found to have a maximum thickness of 1000 feet, and to consist of material extracted by microscopic animals from clear sea-water, the vastness of the period during which the rocks have been in course of formation must be forcibly impressed upon the mind.

As will be seen from the accompanying map (Fig. 2), the Cretaceous rocks of England extend in a roughly fan-shaped or diverging manner from the coast of Dorsetshire to the north-east of the county of Norfolk, with a further extension forming the Wolds of Yorkshire and terminating at Flamborough Head. West of Weymouth there are merely a few detached outlying beds of Cretaceous age, the remnants of deposits the greater portion of which have been removed by Nature's destroying forces.

The Chalk forms by far the most conspicuous member of the Cretaceous group as exhibited in England, and the geographical extension of the Chalk coincides generally with the extension of the Cretaceous rocks considered as a whole, the other members of the system fringing or lying within those great lines, and for the most part roll-like extensions of Chalk called Downs and Wolds, which form so marked a feature of the physiography of the southern and eastern parts of our island.

Three great ribs, as it were, of Chalk can be clearly traced. One, the southernmost, extending along the coast, forms the coast hills of Dorsetshire, the ridge of high land running through the Isle of Wight from the "Needles" to Culver Cliff, and further still to the east, the well-known South Downs terminating in Beechy Head. The second branches from the one just described in Hampshire, and though also running east, extends along the northern side of the Weald of Surrey, Sussex, and Kent, and so forms the North Downs, which, like the South Downs, terminate only when the sea is reached. The cliffs from Margate to Ramsgate, and those bold headlands, Dover Cliffs, are the extremities of the second rib. The third great line of Chalk gives to England Salisbury Plain, the

Fig. 1.—*Section showing the approximate relative thickness of the British Sedimentary Rocks.*

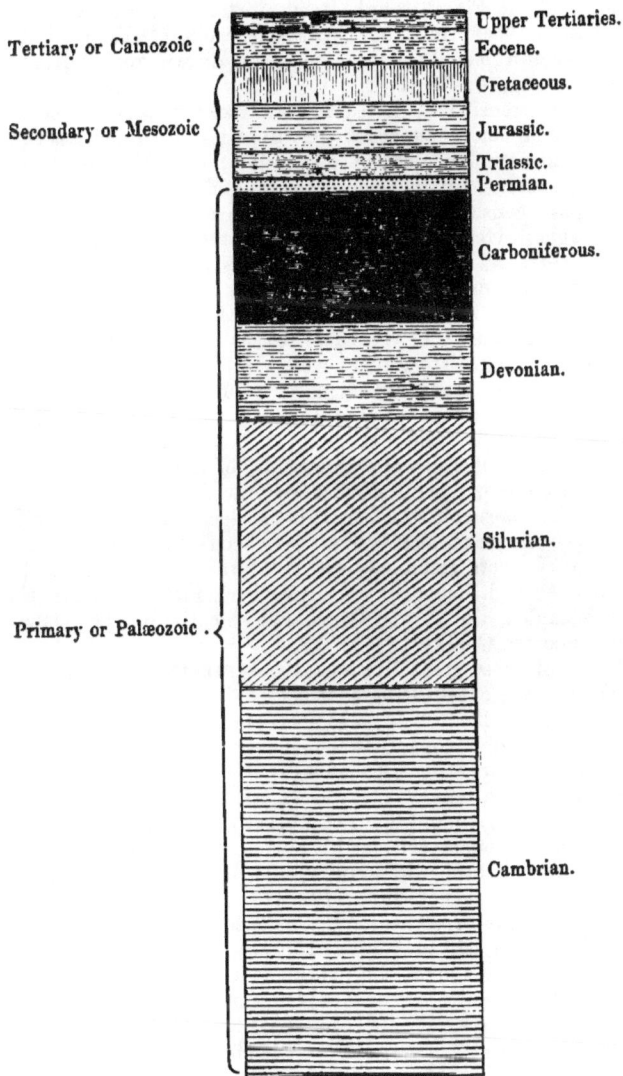

Marlborough Downs, and the Chiltern Hills, and then extends to the north-east through this county, Cambridgeshire, Suffolk, and Norfolk, to the North Sea. The Norfolk Chalk, however, gives off, as it were, a branch, which, after running through Lincolnshire, widens into the Wolds of the eastern part of Yorkshire, then contracts, until, at Flamborough Head, it terminates in a point. Thus it will be seen that the Cretaceous rocks of England lie almost wholly on the south-east side of a line drawn from Portland Bill to Scarborough Castle Rock.

Though the extension of the Cretaceous rocks is thus limited in England, it must not be supposed that deposits of Cretaceous age are nowhere else to be found. In North America they occur in New Jersey, as stated by Sir Charles Lyell; and in South America, Charles Darwin considers that they are to be met with in various parts of a region extending from Columbia north of the Equator as far south as Terra del Fuego, and in the Andes, at very considerable elevations, while beds of Cretaceous age are found so far to the East as Pondicherry in India. Deposits of the same epoch were not, however, necessarily of the same sea or ocean; for at every period of the earth's history there were doubtless large and small seas, as at present, and during each geological epoch a distribution of land and sea prevailed, which was peculiar to that period, and markedly different from that of the preceding or succeeding epoch. The physical geography of the earth varied as the ages rolled on, and became what we now find it only after a succession of changes co-extensive with the age of the earth itself.

The Cretaceous rocks, as a system, have been divided into several minor groups of strata commonly called "formations," and named chiefly from their lithological or physical characters. Thus we have the Wealden, the Lower Greensand, the Gault, the Upper Greensand, and the Chalk.

The lowest of these great divisions, the WEALDEN, is a formation of peculiar interest, constituting as it does a distinct portion of our island, and suggesting to the geologist a distribution of land and sea strikingly different from that which now obtains. Though of great thickness, variously estimated at 1300, 1600, and 2000 feet, the Wealden group of rocks is of freshwater and estuarine origin, being, in fact, an old delta of a great river which must have flowed over a portion of the earth's surface now covered by the sea. In England it forms the country lying between the North and South Downs, but it is not confined to what is called the Wealden area. The most westerly locality where Wealden beds are seen is Brook Point, in the Isle of Wight; the most northerly, Shotover Hill, near Oxford; while on the Continent it is found constituting the country near Boulogne; and as far south as Vassy, deposits assigned to the Wealden occur. So great a delta as must have existed to leave these wide-spreading remains would be the accumulated detritus brought down by a great river, and many are therefore led to the conclusion that a continent existed where is now the Atlantic Ocean, and that from this ancient land came

FIG. 2.—*Map showing the extension of the Cretaceous Rocks in England.*

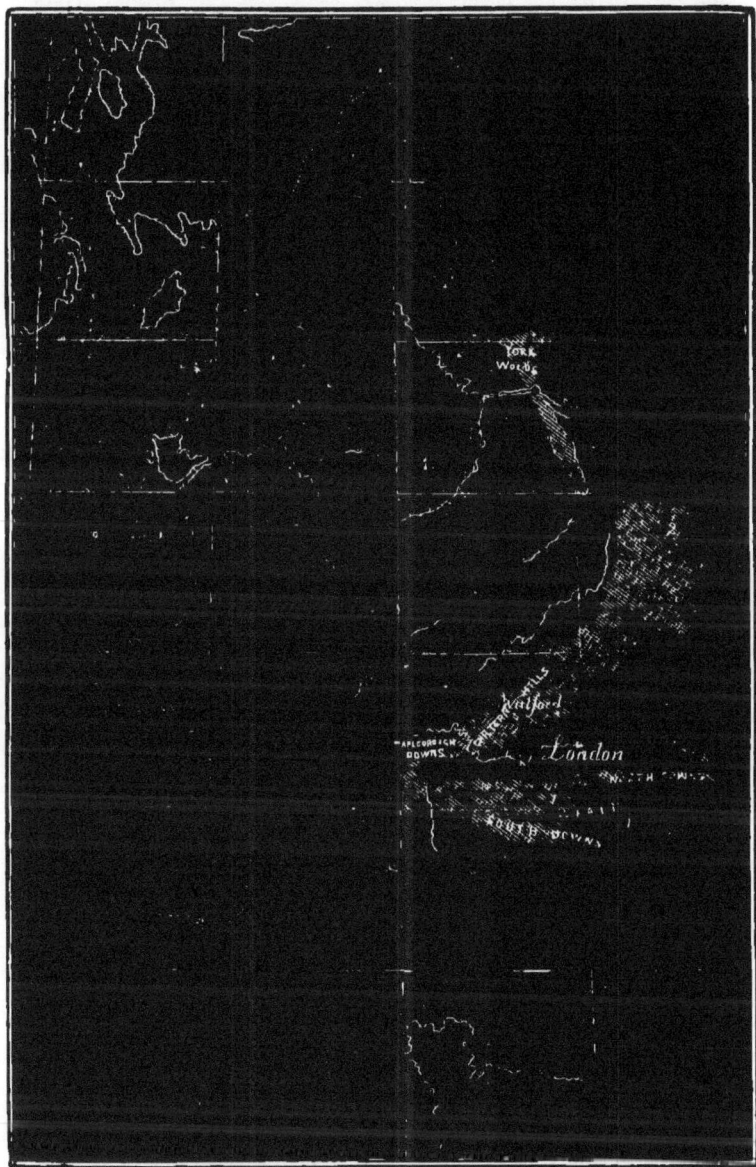

The distribution of the Cretaceous Rocks is shown by the shaded portion of the Map, the darker shading (the lines uncrossed) indicating the Wealden.

the flood of waters which deposited at its mouth the Wealden formation. It has been, however, suggested that several rivers of moderate or even of small size may have given origin to the Wealden deposits, even as off the coast of the island of New Guinea a mass of sediment is now being formed by rivers, by no means great, flowing from Papua, which, though a large island, can make no pretensions to continental dimensions.

Remarkable in origin, the Wealden is remarkable also as a feature of the England of to-day, since it forms the great valley, elevated in the centre, bounded north and south and east by the North and South Downs, and opening out to the sea between Beechy Head and Dover Cliffs. This great vale, of old covered with wood, as its name indicates, is the tract of country known as the Weald, and proverbial for picturesque beauty and exuberant fertility. The dip of the Chalk forming the ranges of hills north and south is so uniformly north and south respectively, and the underlying beds crop out so regularly, that geologists can come to no other conclusion than that the entire area has been covered by Chalk of great thickness, by Upper Greensand, by Gault, and by Lower Greensand, also of great thickness, all of which groups of strata have been swept away during successive ages by rain and rivers, or by the sea, and that the North and South Downs are but the remnants of what was once a vast sheet of Chalk continuous from the one range to the other. The dome-like centre of this "valley of elevation" plainly speaks of a great uprise, producing fractures of sufficient magnitude to greatly facilitate the subsequent denudation of the surface rocks. The Wealden formation also possesses considerable interest from the character of the organic remains found entombed in its beds. The great reptiles (*Iguanodon*), forty or fifty feet in length, the bones of which have been disinterred, doubtless lived on the banks of the Wealden river or rivers, and gave after death their skeletons to the stream, by the side of which they had probably tranquilly died. At Brook Point, in the Isle of Wight, a mass of fossil timber, once a raft of inland trees brought down to the Wealden estuary and there stranded or sunk, strikingly illustrates the conditions prevailing during the Wealden epoch.

Lying upon the Wealden beds we find a great thickness of sands containing a large amount of iron, with local beds of limestones and clays, to which the name of LOWER GREENSAND was given, but now frequently called the NEOCOMIAN. The name *Greensand* is so far a misnomer that the beds of sand usually present to the eye a reddish-brown colour. Sometimes, however, the green grains, from the occurrence of which the beds obtained the name of Greensand, are plainly observable. These green grains have been found from microscopical examination to be the casts of minute creatures, of which more will be said when the origin of the Chalk is spoken of. Though green, these grains contain a large amount of iron, but in the form of silicate, while the reddish-brown sands owe their colour to the oxide of the metal. The Lower Greensand, though immediately succeeding the Wealden, has had a markedly different origin.

It is a marine deposit, the fossils shells abundantly found in it being the remains of genera living only in salt water, as, for instance, the *Trigonia* and the *Terebratula*, both of which now flourish in Australian seas. It will be seen from this illustration how important for the right reading of the history of the formation of the earth revealed by the rocks is a knowledge of their fossils, which can tell us whether the water in which a rock was deposited was fresh, or salt, or brackish, or, in other words, whether the deposition took place at the bottom of a lake, a sea, or an estuary. The Lower Greensand is especially well seen in the Isle of Wight, the sea-cliffs east and west of Shanklin presenting a fine section, while the cliffs west of Black Gang Chine exhibit the many beds into which the whole series has been divided, each characterized by peculiar species of fossils.

The third great division of the Cretaceous rocks in ascending order is the GAULT, an important bed of stiff blue clay that may be studied to advantage at Folkestone, and is also well seen near Cambridge. The thickness of the Gault is perhaps 200 feet, some beds, especially near Folkestone, containing abundant and generally beautifully preserved fossils. Amongst these the *Ammonites* are conspicuous. Ordinary univalve shells, or Gasteropoda, are numerous and varied, and the remains of what may be said to be the progenitors of our crabs and lobsters are frequently met with.

To the beds of sands succeeding the Gault the name of the UPPER GREENSAND has been given. These sands are generally characterized by the green grains previously mentioned, and seldom display those rich brown colours usually exhibited by the Lower Greensand. These Upper beds are of much less importance than the Lower, being by some considered to be a mere basement bed of the Chalk, and vary greatly in thickness, diminishing northwards from about 140 feet in Wiltshire to not more than two feet near Cambridge, where they form the famous "Coprolite" beds that yield so abundantly those remarkable phosphatic nodules, the high agricultural value of which was discovered by the late Professor Henslow. In addition to the phosphatic bodies, these thin beds contain many fossils, including the remains of most extraordinary creatures which were neither birds nor reptiles, but possessing characters common to both, being in fact flying lizards, and of no inconsiderable size, some having had an expanse of wing of 20 feet.

We now approach the most conspicuous, the most important, and in every respect the most remarkable member of the Cretaceous group of rocks, the CHALK, a rock specially interesting to the members of this Society, since the Chalk forms nearly the whole of Hertfordshire, and is the formation underlying the town of Watford. This soft white rock, so welcome to the eye of the returning traveller when he sees it forming the sentinel-like "Needles," or the towering bulwarks of the Cliffs of Dover, is as remarkable in its origin as in its aspect, and tells a tale to those who can read the records of the rocks aright of marvellous interest and value.

Probably no geological formation so conspicuously affects the scenery, the agriculture, and the general character of a district as the Chalk, forming as it does those softly-rounded Downs, treeless for the most part, and covered with a springy velvety turf, which give to England her great sheep-grounds of the southern counties. No formation affords so striking an example of the importance of the study of the geological structure of a district as a preparation for the proper consideration of its Natural History. An illustration of this is at hand. In the beautiful park of Cassiobury, adjoining Watford, beeches famed for their beauty abound ; while these trees are not found to flourish nearer London. Geology supplies the reason, for it tells us that though at Cassiobury we have the Chalk, with a thin covering of superficial deposits, the London Clay under-lies the country to the south, and supports elms and oaks rather than beeches, which grow most luxuriantly over the Chalk. Many other facts might be stated to show that Naturalists generally, whether Botanists, Entomologists, or Meteorologists, will be mate-rially assisted in their studies by making themselves acquainted with the geological structure of the district which is to become the field of their investigations.

The origin of the Chalk must now engage our attention. The aqueous or sedimentary rocks have all been formed by the accu-mulation of sediment deposited at the bottom of water. But the deposition of the sediment which has produced these rocks has been of a threefold character. Sediment may accumulate at the bottom of water from (1) simple mechanical action, or the sinking of particles of solid matter previously held *in suspension* by the water ; from (2) chemical action, or the precipitation of solid matter pre-viously held *in solution* by the water ; or (3) from organic action, or the formation of solid matter in the form of shell, bone, wood, etc., by animals or plants. The Chalk has been produced by the third of these processes, and is therefore, as geologists say, an organically formed rock.

One of the lowest Classes of the Animal Kingdom, called the Foraminifera or hole-bearing animals, comprises creatures so small that to see them the aid of the microscope is required. These minute animals, although themselves consisting merely of a jelly-like substance called *sarcode*, have the power of extracting from the sea-water carbonate of lime, and of secreting this in a solid form, and so encasing themselves with a thin shell. This shell is perforated by minute canals, through which fine threads of sarcode are protruded, to expand and form other little shells, and so continue growth. Sometimes the compound animal takes the form of a spiral, while sometimes it is elongated, and various modifications of the spiral and of the linear forms constitute the several genera and species which have been described. Of these microscopic shells the Chalk consists. What an expanded view of time, and of the operations of Nature, must be given to any one who learns for the first time that the great South Coast Cliffs, which impressed our Roman invaders and gave the name Albion to our island ; that the great masses of white rock forming the Downs and Wolds of England, and composing whole counties, consist almost altogether of the shells of animals so minute that thousands would be required to form a cubic inch. Yet such is the fact, and not only so, but these humble workers are still at work, and have been working ever since the summit of the highest down in England was a portion of the bed of a deep sea.

We are indebted, however, for this knowledge to researches of but a few years ago. Science produces inventions, and gives to the useful arts most nourishing food. The arts again give rise to research and exploration, which yield to Science its only suitable food—facts. Science has given us the Electric Telegraph, and the Electric Telegraph has required for its due development the exploration of the bed of the ocean. The exploration of the bed of the Atlantic Ocean gave to Science the great fact that there is now forming a deposit precisely analogous to our English Chalk, —that, in short, at the bottom of the Atlantic is a mass of white mud

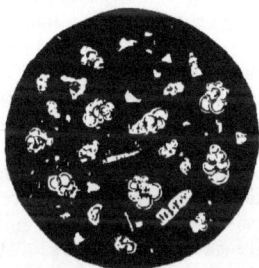

FIG. 3.—Foraminifera from the Chalk, magnified 50 diameters.

FIG. 4.—Foraminifera from the Atlantic ooze, magnified 25 dia.*

or ooze, of which 95 per cent. consists of shells of the same genus, nay, even of the same species of animal which formed the Chalk in the Cretaceous epoch. This mud or ooze is none other, therefore, than Chalk in process of formation, and we are, by the soundings for the Atlantic Telegraph Cable, shown the origin of our English, our Hertfordshire Chalk. The name of the prevailing species of the modern deposits is *Globigerina bulloides*, which closely resembles the most common form in the Chalk, but many others occur, such as those shown in the diagrams on the walls.†

The recent investigations of the CHALLENGER expedition have revealed other facts of a deeply interesting character. The white calcareous ooze, composed of the shells of Foraminifera, though covering an immense area at the bottom of the Atlantic, does not extend the whole length of the Atlantic canal, which at its northern and southern extremities rests on a bed composed of siliceous matter, the accumulated cases of another Class, the *Polycistina*.

* The Foraminifera in these figures are copied from illustrations in Professor Geikie's ' Primer of Geology.'

† Some of the forms here alluded to are represented in Figs. 3 and 4.

which inhabit northern and southern latitudes, leaving the intermediate ocean as the habitat of the calcareous covered *Foraminifera*.
Those siliceous nodules, the flints, so abundant in the Chalk, remind us that in the ancient waters there was in like manner a large
amount of silica. It was formerly supposed that these marine
animals lived and died at the bottom. There now appears good
evidence for believing that they live near the surface, and that the
ooze is formed by the raining down as it were of the shells of the
dead animals from the upper stratum of the oceanic waters. This
is a fact of great importance in connexion with another now to be
mentioned.

It has been ascertained that not merely is the calcareous white
ooze confined to certain latitudes, but it is confined to certain
depths also, and beyond those depths the white ooze is not to be
found. Between Africa and South America there is a sub-marine
valley of enormous depth, and at the bottom of this valley, instead
of the white calcareous deposit, there is a red argillaceous mud.
Now it has been found that about two per cent. of the material of
the white ooze is argillaceous or clayey matter, and it is hence inferred that this red mud is the argillaceous portion of the Foraminiferal remains which have rained down over this portion of the
Atlantic bed, but of which the calcareous portion has not reached
these exceptionally great depths, possibly in consequence of some
solvent agency in existence at certain depths. We thus learn that
even argillaceous deposits, clays and slates, may be produced by
organic agency, and the bold hypothesis of clay rocks generally, as
well as calcareous and siliceous, the limestones and the sandstones,
being of organic origin, has been enunciated by Professor Huxley.

Judging of the past from what we know of the present, as is the
wont of geologists, we conclude that a wide-spreading and deep
sea has deposited the Chalk of England, and that its present extension by no means marks out the area over which it once spread.
The Wealden area has already been mentioned as having been at
one time covered by the Chalk, and over districts now occupied by
sub-Cretaceous formations the great sheet of Chalk once extended,
but, yielding to the various wasting, or, to speak more correctly,
changing forces of Nature, it gradually diminished and ultimately
disappeared, leaving uncovered the rocks on which it had before
reposed. Lyell says, " Pure Chalk, of nearly uniform aspect and
composition, is met with in a north-west and south-east direction,
from the north of Ireland to the Crimea, a distance of about 1,140
geographical miles, and in an opposite direction it extends from the
south of Sweden to the south of Bordeaux, a distance of about
840 geographical miles." That the great Chalk bed continues
under districts where less ancient deposits occur, is abundantly
proved by well-sinking, and thus we know that though we do
not find the Chalk at the surface between Watford and London, it
extends southwards from Watford under the great bed of London
Clay forming the Thames Valley, and rises again to the surface
near Croydon, in Surrey (see Fig. 5). Watford is, therefore, on

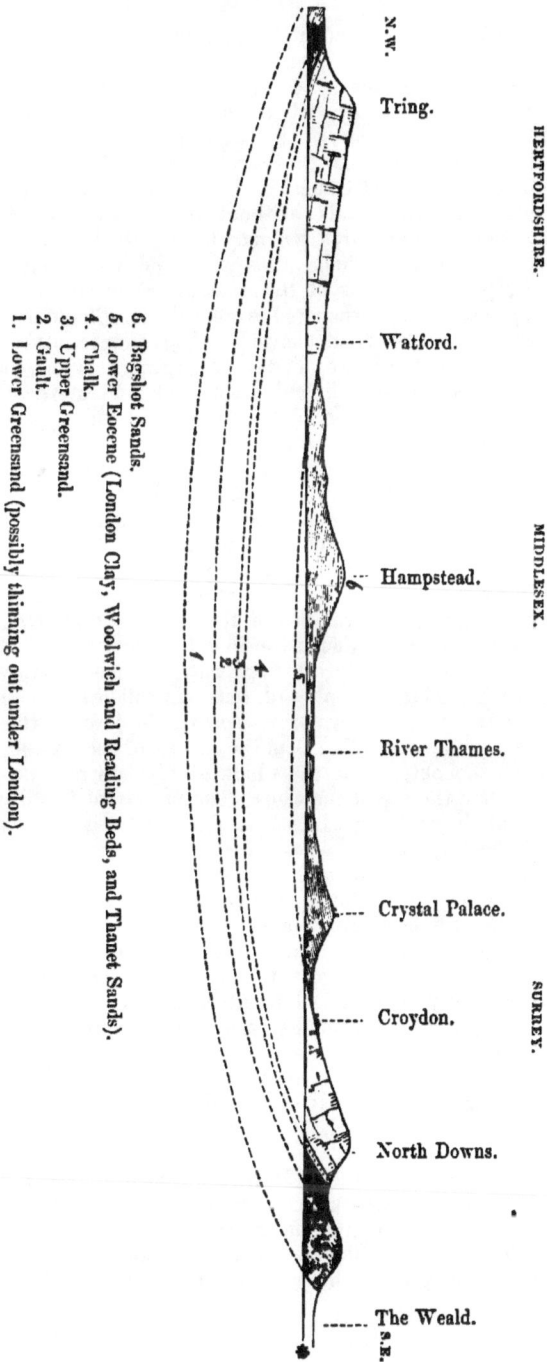

Fig. 5.—*Section across the London Tertiary Basin.*

N.W.

Tring.

HERTFORDSHIRE.

Watford.

MIDDLESEX.

Hampstead.

River Thames.

Crystal Palace.

Croydon.

SURREY.

North Downs.

The Weald.

S.E.

6. Bagshot Sands.
5. Lower Eocene (London Clay, Woolwich and Reading Beds, and Thanet Sands).
4. Chalk.
3. Upper Greensand.
2. Gault.
1. Lower Greensand (possibly thinning out under London).

* Sea-level.

the northern edge of the London Tertiary Basin, and the geology of this neighbourhood is consequently very interesting.

Sections showing the Lower Eocene beds reposing on the Chalk are to be found near Bushey, where the Tertiary Woolwich and Reading Series, and the lowest or Basement Bed of the London Clay, may be seen lying on the Secondary Chalk; and nearer Watford, Glacial and Post-Glacial beds of gravels and sands are displayed, covering the Chalk without any intermediate Lower Tertiaries. In these exposures, too, may be seen sections of curious lengthened sinkings in the Chalk, filled with sand, which have been called sand-pipes, telling us of the gradual subterranean erosion or dissolving away by carbonated water of the Chalk at those points where the water from above has had more ready access. From the sections of the Lower Tertiaries, organic remains, chiefly fish teeth, may be without difficulty obtained, and in the Chalk will be found the more common of the echinoderms which the Upper Chalk everywhere contains.

The great bed of the Chalk and Upper Greensand underlying the London area forms a vast reservoir for the holding of water, since, lying as it does between the London Clay above and the Gault below, it holds the water which falls where the Chalk or Upper Greensand forms the surface rock south and north of the Thames Valley. This great reservoir is tapped whenever a well is sunk in the London area to the lower bed of the Chalk. Such wells are numerous, and give to London a considerable portion of its water supply, since most of the great breweries and manufactories of London obtain their large supplies of water in this manner. These wells are *artesian*, since the water rises above the level of the rock which yields it, and even higher than the surface of the ground, consequent upon the outcrop of the Chalk at Watford and Croydon being higher than the top of the wells. The rainfall of this district, therefore, contributes in no inconsiderable degree to the water supply of the metropolis.

To the south-west, north, and north-east the Chalk constitutes the whole of the country for a long distance from Watford, and forms nearly the whole of the County of Hertford, covered, however, in many places by superficial gravels and sands of glacial and post-glacial age, which diversify the vegetation and contribute greatly to the richly wooded and beautiful aspect of this county. The Chalk has been so repeatedly spoken of as a whole, that it may be thought to be unvaried in character throughout. This is not the case, however, several divisions having been described, three of which are conspicuously observable. The Chalk is usually divided into the Chalk Marl, the Lower Chalk, and the Upper Chalk.

The lowest division, the Chalk Marl, is a transition bed from the Upper Greensand to the Chalk, and contains those green glauconitic or chloritic grains which give the name to the underlying beds. Sometimes these lower strata assume an indurated character, and varying lithologically yield the well-known Firestone of Godstone, in Surrey, and the Tottornhoe Stone of Buckinghamshire and Hertfordshire.

The Lower Chalk is generally described as the Chalk without flints, though these curious siliceous nodules do occasionally occur in the Lower Chalk, and are occasionally wanting in beds of the Upper Chalk. This division is less brilliantly white than the Upper Chalk, and contains fossils not found in the higher beds. Between the Lower Chalk and the Upper Chalk a hard bed is found at several localities, and has been called by Mr. Whitaker the Chalk Rock.

The Upper Chalk or the Chalk with flints, is characterized by its softness, its brilliant whiteness, by its numerous bands of flints, and by its fossils, which are numerous and interesting. This is the Watford Chalk, though it is probable that the Chalk of Norfolk is a higher bed of the same division. The fossils of the Chalk confirm the teaching of the Foraminiferal character of the rock itself, and proclaim the formation to be purely marine. Sponges are numerous, many being inclosed in the flint nodules. Sea-urchins (Echinoderms) —*Micraster, Ananchytes, Galerites, Marsupites*, abound; and bivalve shells—*Terebratula, Rhynchonella, Spondylus, Pecten, Inoceramus,* etc., are common. The discoidal chambered shells called *Ammonites*, allied to the recent *Nautilus*, sometimes attain very large dimensions, and are especially interesting since none have since lived in the seas of the earth so far as we know; while vertebrate animals are represented by the fishes which are frequently found both in the Lower and in the Upper divisions. On the Continent of Europe, Cretaceous beds higher than the Chalk, and containing reptilian remains, are found; but these deposits, called the Maestricht beds, are wanting in England, and nothing but a band of green-coated flints, telling of beds dissolved away, separates the Chalk from the Tertiary beds above.

The Cretaceous rocks of England, it will be seen, possess an interest to the student of Nature of no mean order. Various in lithological character, possessing rich stores of organic remains which tell a wondrous story, contributing striking features to the landscape, affecting greatly the botany and zoology of extensive districts, and all easily accessible from this neighbourhood, they strongly invite your attention and study. The Field Meetings of this Society will give you opportunities of obtaining a personal acquaintance with the rocks and the phenomena they exhibit, and of prosecuting the study of geological science in the most agreeable and at the same time most advantageous manner. The knowledge of the Cretaceous rocks will induce the investigation of other groups of strata, older and newer, and you will, I trust, be led on step by step in the great field of geological investigation until you become possessed of a large amount of geological knowledge.

2.—Notes on the Flora of the Watford District.

By Arthur Cottam, F.R.A.S.

[Read 8th April, 1875.]

The following list contains some of the plants which in two years' not very careful or continuous collecting I have come across in this District. Many others more common are, of course, omitted. I have added in parentheses a few that I believe are, or at least ought, to be found here, but which have escaped my notice.

There are some few genera that require careful examination—*Viola*, for instance. *V. hirta* grows in the middle of Cassiobury Park; *V. canina*, and one or two of its sub-species would, I believe, be found in our woods and lanes, but it is a matter of some difficulty to separate them.

Our District does not contain any of those parts of the County in which Chalk is at the surface, and therefore the exclusively chalk plants, of which many and some very rare ones are included in the Hertfordshire Flora, are not found here.

The number preceding each plant is its number in the 'London Catalogue,' seventh edition, 1874.

6. *Thalictrum flavum.*—Bushey Mill.

11. *Myosurus minimus.*—Corn-fields, Watford Heath; and behind the Orphan Asylum.

22. *Ranunculus sceleratus.*—Edge of Haydon Hill Pond, Bushey.

24. *R. Flammula.*—Bricket Wood; abundant.

27. *R. auricomus.*—Copse at the beginning of Rouse Barn Lane; and many other places; unusually fine.

34. *R. arvensis*; occasionally.—Corn-fields; occasionally.

36. *Caltha palustris.*—Very common in wet fields.

40. *Helleborus viridis.*—Mr. Eley's (private) wood, Oxhey; and in a copse between Watford and Leavesden.

57. *Chelidonium majus.*—Hedge banks; abundant.

82. *Diplotaxis muralis.*—Railway banks.

92. *Dentaria bulbifera.*—Woods at Red Heath.

98. *Arabis thaliana.*—Arable fields and roadsides.

110. *Nasturtium officinale.*

112. *N. palustre.*—River banks.

128. *Thlaspi arvense.*—Fields and roadsides; occasionally.

205. *Stellaria aquatica.*

206. *S. nemorum.*

207. *S. media.*

208. *S. holostea.*

210. *S. graminea.*

262. *Malva moschata.*—Roadsides; not uncommon.

271. *Linum angustifolium.*—One plant near Haydon Hill, Bushey.

Geranium.—Of the twelve species of this genus, we have six, and probably a seventh.

277. *G. pyrenaicum.*—Common; by the Workhouse; in Hagden Lane; and by the Railway Arch in Water Lane.

278. *G. molle.*—Abundant.

279. (*G. pusillum.*—This species ought to be found here, and careful examination would probably be rewarded.)

281. *G. dissectum.*

282. *G. columbinum.*—Gravel-pit by the Workhouse.

283. *G. lucidum.*—Hagden Lane; and in a lane between Watford and Hamper Mill; abundant in both stations.

284. *G. Robertianum.*

295. *Euonymus europæus.*—Not uncommon in the hedges.

318. *Melilotus officinalis.*—Railway banks between Bushey and Pinner.

392. *Alchemilla arvensis.*

393. *A. vulgaris.*—Near Bushey Mill and Chandler's Cross.

520. *Sedum Telephium.*—Oxhey.

540. *Saxifraga tridactylites.*—Tops of old walls; Loates Lane and elsewhere.

543. *S. granulata.*—Fields near Hamper Mill.

589. (*Silaus pratensis.*—Ought to be found.)

596. *Pastinaca sativa.*—Railway banks.

609. *Scandix Pecten-Veneris.*—Occasionally as a weed of cultivation.

610. *Conium maculatum.*—Gravel-pit by the Workhouse.

618. *Adoxa moschatellina.*—Woods and banks near Hamper Mill, etc.

621. *Viburnum Opulus.*

622. *V. Lantana.*—Bricket Wood.

630. *Galium verum.*

632. *G. Mollugo.*

633. *G. saxatile.*

635. *G. palustre.*

636. *G. uliginosum.*

639. *G. Aparine.*

641. *Asperula odorata.*—Abundant in Whippingdale and other woods.

645. *Valeriana dioica.*—Cassio Bridge; Grove Park, by the Canal; and Bricket Wood.

646. *V. officinalis.*—Near Bushey Mill.

695. *Achillea Ptarmica.*—Bricket Wood.

725. *Bidens cernua.*—Haydon Hill Pond.

726. *B. tripartita.*—Pond on Watford Heath.

736. *Erigeron acris.*—Railway banks near the High Street Station; very abundant.

742. *Petasites vulgaris.*—Cassio Bridge; and Bushey Mill.

743. *Eupatorium cannabinum.*—Cassio Bridge.

761. *Lactuca muralis.*—Road to Cassio Bridge.

846. (*Monotropa Hypopitys.*—Said to grow, and likely, at Red Heath.)

850. *Vinca minor.*—Rouse Barn Lane.

872. *Cuscuta Trifolii.*—Clover-fields at Bushey.

875. *Atropa belladonna.*—Near Chandler's Cross.

880. *Verbascum nigrum.*—Beyond the Workhouse; and elsewhere.

900. *Limosella aquatica.*—Bricket Wood.

Veronica.—Ten species, of which

917. *V. montana* is the rarest. It grows abundantly in the Copse at the beginning of Rouse Barn Lane.

918. *V. scutellata.*—Bricket Wood.

932. *Lathræa squamaria.*—Hunton Bridge.

943. *Lycopus europæus.*—Haydon Hill Pond, Bushey.

Mentha.—Several species probably.

973. *Scutellaria galericulata.*—Haydon Hill Pond, Bushey.

989. *Lamium amplexicaule.*—Near Wiggenhall.

991. *L. incisum.*—Ditto.

995. *L. Galeobdolon.*—Not uncommon.

1047. *Lysimachia Nummularia.*—Bricket Wood.

1048. *L. nemorum.*—Bricket Wood, Red Heath, etc.

1134. *Euphorbia Helioscopia.*

1138. *E. amygdaloides.*—Woods; abundant.

1144. *E. exigua.*—Corn-fields.

1252. *Sagittaria sagittifolia.*—River Colne, near Wiggenhall, etc.

1257. *Butomus umbellatus.*—Bank of the Colne near Wiggenhall, and at Cassio Bridge.

1268. *Orchis Morio.*—Oxhey.

1269. *O. mascula.*—Oxhey, etc.

1273. *O. maculata.*—Bricket Wood.

1278. *Habenaria chlorantha.*—Bricket Wood; and Red Heath Wood.

1289. *Listera ovata.*—Bricket Wood.

1290. *Neottia Nidus-avis.*—Bricket Wood.

1311. *Narcissus Pseudo-narcissus.*—Cassio Bridge; and elsewhere in meadows.

3.—Notes on a proposed re-issue of the Flora of Hertfordshire, with Supplementary Remarks on the Botany of
the Watford District.

By R. A. Pryor, B.A., F.L.S.

[Read 8th April, 1875.]

More than five-and-twenty years have elapsed since the publication of the 'Flora Hertfordiensis.' In the mean time Botanical
Science has been continually advancing ; changes have been made
alike in nomenclature and arrangement ; and many new forms have
been brought into notice.

Nor has it been otherwise with our knowledge of the Local Flora.

The fresh material that has accumulated during the same period
has been in part collected in the various Supplements that have
been issued at intervals—an inconvenient arrangement on account
of the increased difficulty of reference ; other particulars have from
time to time appeared in different scientific periodicals ; but a large
proportion, the result of the investigations of the last few years,
remains altogether unpublished.

The gradual changes that are being effected in the surface of the
country through the extended operations and improved methods of
the agriculturist, together with the spread of population and great
increase in building, have almost, if not altogether, extirpated
several of our choicer rarities ; while the same causes have led to
the introduction of a considerable number of exotics, for the most
part of but very ephemeral duration, but in some cases likely to
become permanently established.

Questions as to the nativity and distribution of British plants
have of late years, owing in a great measure to the writings of Mr.
Watson, risen into more prominence ; and all botanists, however
much they may differ in their views of specific limitation, will
acknowledge the importance of ascertaining precisely what forms
are included under the aggregate names of the older catalogues.

Unequalled as was perhaps the 'Flora Hertfordiensis' at the date
of its original publication, and excellent as it still remains, there is
yet room for addition and improvement.

To this end, the surviving editor, the Rev. R. H. Webb, has, in
the most generous manner, allowed me the use of his manuscript
material ; and I am in addition indebted already to the kindness of
several correspondents for information of interest ; indeed the last
few months have added several novelties to our list.

I shall be very grateful for any communications bearing upon
the subject ; however few in number, or unimportant they may
appear by themselves, in combination with other facts of a similar
character they have their own value, and may supply the key to
some hitherto insoluble problem in our local botany.

To make the nature of my especial requirements more plain, I
have put together the following lists :

No. I.—Comprises the segregate forms, of whatever rank, which are known or thought likely to occur within the county, and which are included under the aggregate names of the Flora. It is very desirable to ascertain the distribution of these as completely as possible.

No. II.—Consists of those plants which are possibly or very probably extinct. To these have been added a few others, originally recorded for but a very small number of localities, and of which nothing has been heard for many years.

No. III.—Contains those which have been introduced into the Flora upon untrustworthy authority, or are on various grounds open to more or less doubt. Some additional species have been inserted, which have been undoubtedly met with at no great distance from our borders, although not actually within the county.

It will be seen that in some few instances the same names occur in more than one of the lists. This has been done intentionally: a given plant may, for instance, have become extinct in a locality where it was once truly found, and have been recorded subsequently by error from another station.

It is much wished that a fresh specimen should, if possible, in every case accompany any communication.

Notes upon the physical geography, or the peculiarities of the general vegetation of a district, will be always acceptable.

Any information also as to the vernacular names that are actually in use in the county will be of interest.

I.

Thalictrum " minus."
,,   flavum, varr.
Ranunculus fluitans.
,,   ,,   var. Bachii.
,,   truncatus.
,,   floribundus.
,,   penicillatus.
,,   pseudo-fluitans.
,,   submersus.
,,   radians.
,,   Drouetii.
,,   trichophyllus.
,,   confusus.
,,   intermedius.
,,   Lenormandi.
,,   hederaceus.
,,   ,,   v. homœophyllus.
,,   Flammula, v. pseudo-reptans.
,,   auricomus,v.depauperatus.
,,   acris, v. tomophyllus.
,,   Ficaria, v. incumbens.
Caltha palustris, v. Guerangerii.
Papaver somniferum, v. hispidum.
,,   ,,   v. glabrum.
,,   (dubium) Lamottei.
,,   ,,   Lecoqii.
,,   Rhœas, v. strigosum.

Fumaria "capreolata."
Cardamine hirsuta.
,,   sylvatica.
Draba verna, v. brachycarpa.
Brassica sp.?
Camelina sativa, v. fœtida.
,,   ,,   v. sylvestris.
Viola sylvatica, v. Riviniana.
,,   ,,   v. Reichenbachiana.
,,   canina (vera).
,,   tricolor.
,,   ,,   v. arvensis.
Polygala vulgaris.
,,   oxyptera.
,,   depressa.
,,   calcarea.
Silene inflata, v. puberula.
Stellaria media, varr.
Arenaria serpyllifolia, v. leptoclados.
Sagina apetala (vera).
,,   ciliata.
Spergula arvensis.
,,   ,,   v. vulgaris.
Montia fontana, v. rivularis.
Erodium cicutarium, varr.
Ulex nanus (verus).
,,   Gallii.
Trifolium pratense, v. sylvestre.

Vicia angustifolia, v. segetalis.
„   „   v. Bobartii.
Alchemilla vulgaris, v. montana.
Rubus fruticosus, subspp.
Geum intermedium.
Rosa tomentosa, varr.
„   " inodora."
„   canina, varr.
„   arvensis, v. bibracteata.
„   stylosa, varr.
CratægusOxyacantha,v.oxyacanthoides.
„   „   v. monogyna.
Pyrus " Aria."
„   communis, varr.
„   Malus, v. acerba.
„   „   v. mitis.
Epilobium angustifolium, v. brachy-
    carpum.
Epilobium parviflorum, varr.
„   tetragonum (verum).
„   obscurum.
Callitriche vernalis.
„   stagnalis.
„   platycarpa.
„   hamulata.
„   pedunculata.
Ribes rubrum, v. sativum.
„   „   v. sylvestre.
Sedum Telephium, v. purpurascens.
„   „   v. Fabaria.
Helosciadium nodiflorum, v. pseudo-
    repens.
Galium erectum.
„   palustre, v. elongatum.
„   „   v. Witheringii.
Valeriana officinalis, v. Mikanii.
„   „   v. sambucifolia.
Carduus crispus, varr.
„   (hybrids).
Arctium majus.
„   minus.
„   intermedium.
„   nemorosum.
Centaurea nigra, v. decipiens.
Filago apiculata.
„   spathulata.
Bidens cernua, v. radiata.
Solidago Virga-aurea, varr.
Tragopogon pratensis (verus).
Taraxacum officinale,v.erythrospermum.
„   „   v. lævigatum.
Hieracium " maculatum."
„   tridentatum.
Verbascum (hybrids).
Euphrasia officinalis, v. gracilis.
Bartsia odontites, varr.
Mentha sylvestris, varr.
„   piperita, varr.
„   pubescens, varr.
„   hirsuta, varr.
„   sativa, varr.

Mentha gentilis, varr.
„   arvensis.
„   „   v. agrestis, etc.
Thymus Serpyllum.
„   Chamædrys.
Calamintha Nepeta.
„   menthifolia.
Nepeta Glechoma, varr.
Galeopsis Ladanum, v. canescens.
„   Tetrahit, v. bifida.
Lamium purpureum, v. decipiens.
Stachys ambigua, etc.
Myosotis palustris, v. strigulosa.
„   arvensis, v. umbrosa.
Symphytum officinale, v. patens.
Primula (hybrids, etc.).
Plantago lanceolata, v. Timbali.
Chenopodium polyspermum,v.spicatum.
„   „   v.cymosum.
„   album, v. candicans.
„   „   v. viride.
„   „   v. paganum.
„   urbicum.
„   „   v. intermedium.
„   rubrum, v. pseudo-
        botryodes.
Atriplex " erecta."
„   deltoidea.
„   hastata.
Rumex nemorosus, v. sanguineus.
„   obtusifolius, v. sylvestris.
„   maximus.
Polygonum Convolvulus, v. pseudo-
    dumetorum.
Polygonum aviculare, varr.
„   Persicaria, v. elatum.
„   lapathifolium, varr.
„   maculatum, varr.
„   amphibium, v. terrestre.
Ceratophyllum aquaticum, v. sub-
    mersum.
Parietaria diffusa, varr.
Quercus Robur, v. intermedia.
Betula alba, v. glutinosa.
„   „   v. pubescens.
Salix fragilis, varr.
„   viridis.
„   triandra, varr.
„   purpurea, varr.
„   cinerea, varr.
„   repens, varr.
„   (hybrids).
Potamogeton natans (verus).
„   polygonifolius, v. erice-
        torum.
„   „   „   v. pseudo-
            fluitans.
„   lucens, v. acuminatus.
„   flabellatus.
Zannichellia palustris (vera).
„   pedicillata.

Orchis incarnata.
„ latifolia (vera).
Epipactis latifolia.
„ violacea.
Iris pseud-acorus, varr.
Allium vineale, v. bulbiferum.
„ „ v. compactum.
Luzula multiflora.
„ „ v. congesta.
Juncus supinus, varr.
„ bufonius, v. fasciculatus.
Carex muricata, v. pseudo-divulsa.
„ divulsa.
„ acuta, varr.
„ fulva, v. speirostachya.
„ flava (vera).
„ „ v. lepidocarpa.
„ Œderi.
Agrostis interrupta.

Agrostis pumila.
Aira uliginosa.
Molinia cœrulea, v. depauperata.
Poa subcœrulea.
Glyceria fluitans, v. pedicillata.
„ plicata.
Bromus racemosus.
„ commutatus.
Triticum repens, v. nemorale.
„ „ v. littorale.
Athyrium Filix-fœmina, varr.
Aspidium lobatum.
„ aculeatum.
„ angulare.
Nephrodium Filix-mas, varr.
„ dilatatum, varr.
Equisetum palustre, v. subnudum.
„ „ v. polystachion.
„ limosum, v. fluviatile.

II.

Ranunculus Lingua.
„ hirsutus.
Dentaria bulbifera.
Cardamine amara.
Nasturtium sylvestre.
Teesdalia nudicaulis.
Drosera rotundifolia.
Stellaria glauca.
Radiola Millegrana.
Medicago falcata.
Trigonella ornithopodioides.
Trifolium subterraneum.
Astragalus hypoglottis.
„ glycyphyllus.
Vicia gracilis.
Lathyrus Aphaca.
Sanguisorba officinalis.
Comarum palustre.
Geum rivale.
Lythrum Hyssopifolia.
Sedum dasyphyllum.
Cicuta virosa.
Apium graveolens.
Petroselinum segetum.
Sium latifolium.
Caucalis latifolia.
Smyrnium Olusatrum.
Sambucus Ebulus.
Lonicera Xylosteum.
Valerianella auricula.
Carduus pratensis.
Filago gallica.
Senecio campestris.
Hypochœris glabra.
Taraxacum palustre.
Hieracium murorum.
Vaccinium Myrtillus.
Erica cinerea.

Erythræa pulchella.
Gentiana germanica.
„ campestris.
Cuscuta Epithymum.
Verbascum Lychnitis.
Limosella aquatica.
Melampyrum arvense.
Orobanche cœrulea.
Mentha piperita.
„ pubescens.
„ rubra.
„ gracilis.
Scutellaria minor.
Myosotis repens.
Anchusa sempervirens.
Cynoglossum montanum.
Pinguicula vulgaris.
Utricularia vulgaris.
Anagallis tenella.
Centunculus minimus.
Littorella lacustris.
Chenopodium olidum.
„ murale.
„ urbicum.
Rumex palustris.
Polygonum minus.
Thesium humifusum.
Asarum Europæum.
Aristolochia Clematitis.
Euphorbia Lathyris.
Sparganium " natans."
Acorus Calamus.
Potamogeton plantagineus.
„ rufescens.
„ heterophyllus.
„ acutifolius.
„ obtusifolius.
Alisma ranunculoides.

Actinocarpus Damasonium.
Aceras anthropophora.
Orchis militaris.
Herminium Monorchis.
Epipactis palustris.
Cephalanthera ensifolia.
Polygonatum multiflorum.
Muscari racemosum.
Allium oleraceum.
Luzula Forsteri.
„ sylvatica.
Juncus diffusus.
„ squarrosus.
Schœnus nigricans.
Scirpus acicularis.
„ multicaulis.
„ pauciflorus.

Scirpus fluitans.
„ sylvaticus.
Eriophorum latifolium.
Carex dioica.
„ teretiuscula.
„ Bœnninghauseniana.
„ stricta.
„ acuta.
„ "distans."
Phleum Bœhmeri.
Agrostis spica-venti.
Calamagrostis lanceolata.
Aira flexuosa.
Lycopodium clavatum.
Pilularia globulifera.
Equisetum sylvaticum.

III.

Adonis autumnalis.
Ranunculus "fluitans," "with ternate
floating leaves, with wedge-shaped
segments."
Ranunculus heterophyllus.
Fumaria "capreolata."
Arabis hirsuta.
Barbarea stricta.
Dianthus plumarius.
Silene anglica.
Sagina maritima.
Hypericum montanum.
Geranium rotundifolium.
Sanguisorba officinalis.
Rosa "inodora."
Myriophyllum alterniflorum.
Œnanthe crocata.
Hypochœris maculata.

Tragopogon "pratensis."
Hieracium murorum.
„ "maculatum."
„ "sabaudum."
Pyrola media.
Scrophularia Ehrharti.
Myosotis sylvatica.
Primula elatior.
Polygonum mite.
Daphne Mezereum.
Ulmus "glabra."
"Hertfordshire Elm."
"Wormley Grange or Byford Elm."
Salix "Helix."
Sparganium "natans."
Polygonatum multiflorum.
Carex lævigata.
„ "distans."

I do not think that it will be necessary to go through the
general lists, which refer rather to the County at large; but, as an
application of the same principle to local requirements, I have
drawn up a catalogue of all the more important plants of the
Watford district, which, under one or other of the three heads above
mentioned, are liable to any degree of uncertainty; and to facilitate
their investigation I have added the localities, where such have
been specially given.

The remarks that I have to submit to you will be thus mainly
interrogatory in their scope, and are designed not so much to give
—and indeed this would be beyond my power—as to be the means
of eliciting information, and of inviting the attention of botanists
in this neighbourhood to some of those points which require
elucidation, before we can claim to possess an accurate knowledge
of the Flora.

While thus limited in their purpose, these notes can offer but
little that is original. I have, however, availed myself, I believe.

of all sources of information that were at my disposal, and I am especially indebted to the excellent 'Flora of Middlesex' for a considerable portion of my material : at present but very little is known of the Botany of the adjacent districts of Buckinghamshire. I will now proceed with my enumeration.

Anemone Apennina.—Berry Wood, Aldenham. I have seen during the past fortnight the young leaves and buds of this pretty Anemone in the Vicarage garden at Aldenham ; into which the roots were introduced from Berry Wood more than thirty years ago by the late Lady Rendlesham. Although I was unsuccessful in finding the Anemone in the wood itself, probably owing to the backwardness of the season, I am assured that it still grows there, although less plentifully than in former years. It would appear to be well naturalized.

Anemone ranunculoides. — Both the herbarium specimens that I have seen and the book records are about equally divided between King's and Abbot's Langley ; nor can the locality, " in a field a quarter of a mile south of Abbot's Langley " very well be the same with that more usually given, " under a tree on a lawn." It is curious that there should be so much uncertainty about the precise station of a plant which has long enjoyed a perhaps unmerited degree of notoriety.

Ranunculus aquatilis.— Very little is known about the Batrachian Ranunculi of the Watford district. There is a specimen of *R. submersus* gathered about ten years back at Cashiobury in Professor Babington's herbarium, and the same plant is recorded from Harefield, under the name of *R. Drouetii,* in the ' Flora of Middlesex.' *R. fluitans* and *R. pseudofluitans* both occur in the same neighbourhood, and this last is not improbably, judging from Mr. Coleman's specimens, which have a hispid receptacle and long stamens, the *R. fluitans* of the ' Flora Hertfordiensis.' *R. pantothrix* of the same work, in the absence of the original specimens, must remain quite a doubtful plant. Subject to this uncertainty, they have each been recorded for the district. Both *R. truncatus* and *floribundus* will doubtless, as in Middlesex, be found to occur.

Ranunculus hederaceus.—Bacher Heath ; and between Scott's Bridge and Rickmansworth. One or both of these localities may perhaps produce the floating form, *R. Homœophllyus* of Mr. Hiern's paper.

Papaver dubium.—Watford ? ; wall of Aldenham Churchyard. *P. Lecoqii* has perhaps occurred at Pinner, but *P. Lamottei* is the usual Middlesex plant.

Dentaria bulbifera.—Loudwater Wood ; near High Wood, Rickmansworth ; Red Heath ; Garret Wood ; and probably in other woods in the neighbourhood. Blackstone first discovered the Coral-wort about Harefield in 1734, but Parkinson had previously met with it in Sussex. *Lunaria rediviva,* "the second kind of Bolbonac or White Sattin," according to Gerarde, "groweth about Watford." Is it altogether impossible that the mistake should have arisen from some confused account of the occurrence of *Dentaria* in the district ?

Cardamine amara.—Riverside between Harefield and Rickmansworth. First observed by Blackstone, and not noticed since 1822. Specimens from this locality gathered by the late Mr. Cory, in the herbarium of the Rev. A. Bloxam of Twycross, establish the correctness of the name. It might still be re-found.

Nasturtium amphibium.—Cashio Bridge Waters. Requires confirmation.

Viola sylvatica.—*V. Riviniana* is the Middlesex plant ; *V. Reichenbachiana*, however, which is not uncommon in Herts, will almost certainly be found. It flowers earlier than the other form.

Polygala vulgaris.—*P. eu-vulgaris* has been noticed at Harefield, but *P. depressa* is the usual plant of Middlesex. It occurs on Stanmore Heath, and Harrow Weald Common.

Drosera rotundifolia.—The Bushey Heath station given in the Supplement to the 'Flora Hertfordiensis' is perhaps really on Harrow Weald Common, and in Middlesex.

Cerastium semidecandrum.—Walls near Watford. *Cerastium arvense.*—In the chalk cutting near the Watford station. Both these observations should perhaps be received with some degree of reserve. A form of *C. triviale*, with unusually large flowers, occurs in several places on the newly constructed embankment in the same neighbourhood, and something of the kind may perhaps have been mistaken for *C. arvense.*

Arenaria serpyllifolia.—*A. serpyllifolia* and *leptoclados* are probably equally common, as in Middlesex ; the latter occurs at Harefield.

" *Alsine montana minima, Acini effigie, rotundifolia.*"—" In montosis comitatus Hartfordiæ ad confinia Bucks propè vicum Chalfont D. Petri dictum. D. Plukenet." Ray, Synopsis, ii. 210. Dillenius conjectured that this was *Centunculus minimus*, but it seems more probable that it was a variety of some *Arenaria.* The connexion of Plukenet, one of the most eminent of the botanists of the seventeenth century, with this neighbourhood, through his farm at Horn Hill, will not be altogether without interest to the members of our Society. He has left notes of several other plants that he observed, and his name, with that of Blackstone, will always be associated with the botanical history of the district.

Sagina nodosa.—Wall of Rickmansworth Churchyard. Blackstone, Specimen Bot. 3. Blackstone could hardly have been mistaken in this plant, but the station seems improbable.

Spergula arvensis.—Watford and Rickmansworth. *S. vulgaris,* with papillose seeds, is the plant of North Middlesex.

Scleranthus annuus.—Watford. " The Harefield plant seems to be *S. biennis*," with shorter stems, internodes, and calyx-lobes.

Montia fontana.—Bacher Heath ; Bushey Heath. This last is perhaps in Middlesex, where *M. minor* is the commoner form, and occurs on Harrow Weald Common. *M. rivularis* has, however, been noticed on Stanmore Heath, and both varieties will not improbably be found in Herts.

Erodium cicutarium.—Near Sherard's Wood, Watford Heath. This seems to be scarce in the district, as it is also in Middlesex.

Ulex nanus.—Bucher Heath; Abbot's Langley; Chorley Wood Common; Watford Road, St. Albans. There seems to be some doubt about the Chorley Wood plant, and I fear that a weak form of *Europæus* was mistaken for this near St. Albans. Professor Babington appeared to consider that our plant was *U. Gallii*, but I have seen only *nanus* proper in the County.

Ononis spinosa.—Watford Heath; Rickmansworth Common. Both require confirmation.

Medicago falcata.—Between Watford and Bushey Hill. This rests on the authority of the accurate Doody, and there can be little doubt as to the correctness of the original record. It has probably, however, long since become extinct.

Melilotus alba.—Railway banks north of Watford.

Trifolium ochroleucum.—Field by West Wood, Grove Park, near Watford.

Trifolium filiforme.—Watford. All three standing in need of confirmation, and the last perhaps only *T. minus.*

Lotus tenuis.—Near Watford Heath. This also requires confirmation.

Vicia angustifolia.—Watford Road, St. Albans; and, apparently, a second station, near Watford.

Lathyrus Aphaca.—Near a chalk-pit in a wood at Grove Park. Still there?

Prunus domestica.—There is a specimen in the Kew Herbarium, gathered by Mr. Bentham near the farm at Cashiobury in 1834.

Alchemilla vulgaris.—Rickmansworth Common Moor, and near Bushey. The variety *subsericea* or *montana* is perhaps the commoner form.

Comarum palustre.—Rickmansworth Common Moor. I have no recent notice of this, and it is to be feared that it has perished through drainage.

For the last five-and-twenty years but little attention has been paid to the fruticose Rubi in Herts, and I have unfortunately been unable to meet with any of the specimens collected in the County by the late Rev. W. H. Coleman, to whose exertions almost all that is known about them is owing. Professor Babington has kindly gone through those in his herbarium, but I am quite uncertain how far the names now given can be correctly transferred from the individuals there preserved to those others that had been associated with them in the pages of the 'Flora Hertfordiensis.' The Rev. W. M. Hind, who has contributed much valuable information on this subject to the 'Flora of Harrow,' is, as far as I am aware, the only other person who has attempted any examination of the Brambles of this neighbourhood. Much, therefore, remains to be accomplished before we can consider ourselves out of the wood; and the vicinity of Watford appears to be so rich in these troublesome but instructive forms, that the labour of investigation is likely to be amply repaid. I will now give the *names* that have, rightly or otherwise, been hitherto put on record for the district.

Rubus Lindleianus.—On Harrow Weald Common, just beyond our boundary.

R. rhamnifolius.—With the last.

R. leucostachys.—Rickmansworth.

R. villicaulis.—Pinner Wood; should probably be added to the list.

R. umbrosus.—Woods by Pinner Lane. The *carpinifolius* of Bloxam and the 'Flora Hertfordiensis.'

R. Schlectendalii and *R. Hystrix.*—In company with *umbrosus.*

R. rosaceus.—Pinner Hill.

R. pygmæus.—Oxhey Wood; edge of Pinner Wood; and, perhaps, in other "hedges about Watford."

R. rudis.

R. Radula.

R. Kœhleri.—All in woods by Pinner Lane.

R. pallidus.—Harrow Weald Common.

R. "fuscus."—Woods by Pinner Lane. This may be either *pallidus, humifusus,* or *hirtus,* and a Middlesex plant in the herbarium of the British Museum named *fuscus* by Bloxam belongs to *macrophyllus.*

R. diversifolius.—Woods by Pinner Lane. From a specimen in Babington's Herbarium the *fusco-ater* of 'Flora Hertfordiensis,' but *Balfourianus* may also be included under this name. This last has occurred at Pinner.

R. Lejeunii.—Edge of wood, Oxhey.

R. Guntheri.—Woods near Pinner Lane.

R. corylifolius.—Rickmansworth.

R. althæifolius.—Pinner.

Rosa "inodora."—Oxhey Lane. The *R. inodora* of the Herts Flora is probably a mere variety of *canina.*

R. Monsoniæ.—Near Watford. A low bush distinguished from the other forms of *R. stylosa* by its very large red flowers, and scarcely protruded styles. I have never seen a wild specimen.

Cratægus oxyacanthoides.—Is abundant at Pinner, and will probably be found, when looked for, in Herts. I have seen it already in several of the districts, and although nowhere very common, it is perhaps generally distributed throughout the county. I have noticed several intermediates or hybrids.

Pyrus malus.—Both forms occur about Harefield, and should be looked for in the district.

Epilobium angustifolium.—Copse by the Watford railway tunnel.

E. palustre.—Bacher Heath.

E. tetragonum.—Near Little Bushey. I have myself seen *eutetragonum* near the Watford station, and it occurs also on Harrow Weald Common. *E. obscurum* has also been noticed close to our boundary on Stanmore Heath.

Sedum dasyphyllum.—On a wall at Rickmansworth.

Pimpinella magna.—Bricket Wood Common, and apparently not

uncommon in the St. Albans district. The form with the leaflets cut into linear segments occurs in the eastern division of the county, as also in Bedfordshire. It was distinguished by Morison and Sherard, but until recently had dropped out of notice. The narrow-leaved form of *Heracleum* also has been observed in several places about Harefield. This is, however, no permanent variety, and has even been seen growing from the same root as the usual form.

Sium latifolium.—In several parts of the Harefield River. Black-stone, the sole authority, 1746.

Œnanthe crocata.—An immature specimen gathered by the Rev. R. H. Webb near Rickmansworth is the only representative in the county of this poisonous umbellifer, which is so conspicuous in many places by the Thames. It appears, however, to be rightly named, and deserves some further investigation.

Valerianella auricula.—Otterspool (Alchorne MS.); and near Berry Wood, Aldenham; probably the same station.

Carduus pratensis.—Rickmansworth Common Moor; and on Stanmore Heath; but this last must, I suppose, be in Middlesex.

Arctium majus.

A. minus.

A. intermedium.

A. nemorosum.—All four have been noticed at Harefield, and will almost certainly be found in the adjoining district of Herts.

Gnaphalium sylvaticum.—Bushey Heath. Possibly in Middlesex.

Solidago virgaurea.—A composite, supposed to be this, has been recorded from Pinner Lane, under the name of *Erigeron Canadense.* The station may, perhaps, be the same as that at Eastbury, where the true *Solidago* has been since noticed.

Petasites vulgaris.—Specimens of the female plant are in the Kew Herbarium, collected at Munden, near Aldenham, by Mr. Borrer in 1844.

Hieracium murorum.—Reported to grow on St. Alban's Abbey in company with *H. vulgatum.* Something else also has been recorded from walls at St. Albans as *H. maculatum.*

"*Hieracii seu Pilosellæ majoris species humilis, foliis longioribus rarius dentatis plurimis simul, flore singulari nostras.*—On a dry bank at the edge of a wood in a lane leading from Horn Hill to Reickmeersworth in Hartfordsh. D. Plukenet." Ray, Synopsis, ii. 75. From Plukenet's figure (Phytographia, t. 37). This has been identified with *H. boreale,* of which it is rather a dwarf single-headed monstrosity, with crowded leaves, than a variety properly so called. The recorded stations for *H. boreale* and *sylvaticum* (about Rickmansworth; Bricket Wood Common; and Woods by Pinner Lane) deserve further examination. *H. tridentatum* may not impossibly be found to occur.

Campanula rotundifolia.—The var. *montana* of Syme, with oblong-lanceolate lower leaves, and subsolitary flowers, was found by Plukenet "about Reickmeersworth in a dry gravel-pit." Ray, Syn. ii. 158.

Campanula Rapunculus.—Croxley Green Lane; between Patchetts Green and the Four Ways, Aldenham.

Vaccinium Myrtillus.—Oxhey Woods.

Erica tetralix.—Bacher Heath; Bushey Heath. This last is perhaps the same as Harrow Weald Common, of the 'Flora of Middlesex.' It occurs also on Stanmore Heath, and at Harefield.

Pyrola minor.—Woods at Red Heath; also in considerable quantity at the Grove, Stanmore Heath, just beyond our borders.

Cuscuta trifolii.—Garston.

"*Scrophularia major caulibus foliis et floribus viridibus; Figwort with green Leaves and Flowers.*—In the shady woods between Harefield and Chalfont St. Peters." Blackstone, Sp. Bot. 91. This, which is Bobart's plant, has been generally identified with *Scrophularia Ehrharti.* Blackstone remarks that "its Leaves are of a pale green, and the whole plant is much smaller than the common Figwort," and Ray (Synopsis, ii. 161) observes that "Common Figwort is called Brownwort from its remarkable brown colour. This hath nothing of brownness in it." The station may very well have been in Herts.

Orobanche elatior?—Long Valley Wood, near Rickmansworth. There is some doubt about the specific name.

O. minor.—At Brightwells and Cole Kings. This is entered as *O. major* in the Supplement to the 'Flora Hertfordiensis,' but a specimen from "near Brightwell's Farm," collected by Mr. Pidcock, is rightly named *minor* in the herbarium of the Rev. R. H. Webb.

Mentha rotundifolia, sylvestris, piperita, and *sativa,* have all been reported for Watford, but in each case there is reason to suspect some mistake. The last has however occurred by the canal north of Harefield, a station that is perhaps in Herts. Specimens from the same neighbourhood are in Hill's herbarium. *M. rotundifolia* also grew formerly in Harefield churchyard, and might be looked for in similar situations in this county.

Thymus Serpyllum and *Chamædrys.*—Both sub-species occur just beyond our boundary in Middlesex.

Scutellaria minor.—Bacher Heath; occurs also abundantly on Harrow Weald Common.

Galeopsis canescens.—I have gathered this on the railway embankment at Watford, and the Harefield plant seems to be the same thing.

Cynoglossum montanum.—In a damp wood by the river at Cashiobury, near the Swiss Cottage.

Pinguicula vulgaris.—Watford Common Moor.

Lysimachia vulgaris.—With double flowers; near King's Langley (How.).

Centunculus minimus.—Moor Park.

Euphorbia platyphylla.—Near Otterspool. Doody, 1700. This locality, taken from Doody's MS. notes in his interleaved copy of the second edition of Ray's Synopsis, has been erroneously referred by Dillenius to *E. hiberna;* but, as observed in the 'Flora of

Middlesex,' the writer evidently intended his note to refer to the species opposite to which he wrote it, *Tithymalus segetum longifolius*, —*E. platyphylla* of modern writers.

Salix purpurea.—Rickmansworth.

S. Lambertiana occurs north of Harefield, and not improbably in Herts.

S. rugosa.—Near Pinchfield; between Moor Hall and Hamper Mill.

S. repens. — Bacher Heath; Rickmansworth Common Moor; Bricket Wood Common; and in the adjoining district of Middlesex, seemingly *S. fusca.*

Sparganium, sp.—I am informed that a floating Sparganium has been noticed just on our side of the county boundary near Pinner Hill.

Potamogeton polygonifolius. — Bacher Heath. The usual heath form is the var. *ericetorum* of Syme, but the deep water plant occurs in a ditch on Harrow Weald Common; either or both may be found in Herts.

P. rufescens.—Ditches by the Colne between Rickmansworth and Harefield Mill.

P. pusillus.—Rickmansworth Common Moor. Something under the name of *compressus* has been recorded from streams at Harrow Weald in Mr. Melvill's 'Flora of Harrow.' *P. mucronatus* of Schrader, with which *P. compressus* of Smith has been generally identified, is arranged by Dr. Hooker and others as a variety of *pusillus*, and our plant may possibly be found to come under the same form.

P. pectinatus.—Rickmansworth; and in the Grand Junction Canal to the north of Harefield. *P. flabellatus* occurs in the same waters in the neighbourhood of Tring, and will perhaps be found to accompany *pectinatus* in this district also. But the great increase of *Anacharis* has been very unfavourable to the existence of our rarer pond weeds.

Zannichellia palustris.—Rickmansworth. Where is this station?

Hydrocharis Morsus-ranæ.—Near Watford; and long ago observed by Blackstone as abundant at Harefield, where however it has not, I believe, been met with lately. The Watford locality requires some more precise definition.

Orchis militaris.—In a chalky thicket near Corner Hall. This is in the extreme south-western angle of the county, and at no great distance from, if, as I cannot help suspecting, it is not the same place as, "the old chalk-pit near the paper-mill at Harefield," where *O. militaris* was observed by Blackstone in company with *O. purpurea* and *ustulata*, and *Ophrys apifera* and *muscifera*. A large chalk-pit is marked in the Ordnance Map in the immediate neighbourhood. There is however a specimen of *O. militaris* in the Banksian herbarium from a second station near Harefield, which is undoubtedly in Middlesex.

O. latifolia.—On the Common Moor, and other low meadows near Rickmansworth. This will probably turn out to be *O. incarnata.*

Gymnadenia Conopsea.—Bushey Heath; Cashio Bridge. There is some doubt about the former of these stations, and it may not improbably prove to be in Middlesex.

Epipactis latifolia.—High Wood, Rickmansworth; Cashiobury Park. Both these are perhaps the same as the *E. purpurata* of Nansfot Wood. Another form, that is perhaps *palustris*, has been gathered just beyond our boundary at Pinner Wood.

Cephalanthera grandiflora.—Wood near Buck's Hill.

Convallaria maialis.—Bushey Heath, and near Cashiobury. No recent authority. It occurs however just within our county, near Pinner.

Fritillaria meleagris.—In a moist pasture near the Watford railway arches. Field near Bushey Heath.

Luzula Forsteri.—Woods by Pinner Lane.

Juncus diffusus.—Oxhey Lane.

J. supinus.—Bacher Heath.

J. squarrosus.—Bushey Heath. Perhaps on Harrow Weald Common and in Middlesex.

Scirpus setaceus.—Bacher Heath.

Eriophorum angustifolium.—Rickmansworth Common Moor.

Carex pulicaris.—Bushey Heath. Recorded also from Harrow Weald Common, and perhaps the same station.

C. stellulata.—Newland's Wood; Bacher Heath; Bushey Heath. This last perhaps in Middlesex.

C. ovalis.—Bacher Heath; Bushey Heath.

C. pilulifera.—Bacher Heath; and in other places just beyond our boundary.

C. pallescens.—Woods by Pinner Lane; Newland's Wood.

C. pendula.—With the last in the former station.

C. binervis.—Bacher Heath. Grows also on Harrow Weald Common and on Stanmore Heath, and as *C. lævigata* has been noticed in the same neighbourhood, that sedge also may be found to occur within our limits.

C. flava.—Rickmansworth Common Moor.

C. Œderi.—Bricket Wood Common; Bacher Heath; Bushey Heath. One or other of these may possibly be *C. lepidocarpa*, but typical *flava* certainly occurs in the north of the county. The Bushey Heath station may possibly be the same as the Harrow Weald Common of the 'Flora of Middlesex,' where, however, it is named *flava*. They all require further examination.

C. ampullacea.—Rickmansworth Common Moor. I do not believe that this is so common in the county as the Flora would lead one to expect. I have no other station on record for the district.

Setaria viridis.—I have noticed this near the Watford station in company with *Amaranthus retroflexus, Camelina, Raphanus caudatus, Barbarea præcox, Lepidium sativum,* and *Trifolium hybridum,* with an abundance of *Diplotaxis muralis.* This last seems to be now thoroughly established, and the *Amaranthus* is not unlikely to obtain a permanent footing, if not destroyed by the recent alterations.

Calamagrostis Epigeios.—Copse by the south entrance of the Watford Railway Tunnel.

Agrostis canina.—Chorley Wood Common; and just beyond our limits on Stanmore Heath; also on Harrow Weald Common in company with *A. pumila.*

Aira flexuosa.—Woods by Pinner Lane; Newland's Wood; as also in the adjoining district of Middlesex.

Molinia cœrulea.—With the last in Newland's Wood.

Catabrosa aquatica.—By the Colne, near Bricket Wood.

Glyceria plicata.—North of Harefield. Perhaps in Herts, but the plant is probably *pedicillata.* It has been suggested that *G. fluitans (eu-fluitans)* will probably turn out to be less common in the county than either *plicata* or *pedicillata,* and the three forms deserve a careful examination.

Festuca sciuroides.—Watford. The station requires more precise definition.

F. ovina.—Chorley Wood Common. This and *F. duriuscula* stand in need of further observation; both however occur in the neighbouring district of Middlesex.

F. elatior.—Rickmansworth. In the original record, however, Mr. Coleman has added a MS. note, " Probably large *pratensis.*" The two species are not always easy to discriminate.

Bromus erectus.—Under Stocker's Wood, Rickmansworth.

B. commutatus.—Rickmansworth. This and *racemosus* require further examination in all the recorded stations.

Triticum caninum.—Rickmansworth. This is not, in my experience, so common in the county as the Flora would lead one to suppose, and I suspect that a variety of *T. repens,* with longer awns, has been in some cases mistaken for it. The true plant occurs near Harefield.

Hordeum sylvaticum.—Long Spring, Watford; Hill Wood; and near Stocker's Farm, Rickmansworth.

Nardus stricta.—Bacher Heath.

Lomaria Spicant.—Newland's Wood; Bacher Heath. Recorded also from Bushey Heath, but the station has been ascertained to be in Middlesex.

Asplenium Ruta-muraria.—Wall by Moor Park. The only station known to me in the district.

Athyrium Filix-fœmina.—Berry Grove, Aldenham; Cashiobury Park, near Rouse Barn. *A. rhæticum* will probably turn out to be the commoner form, but I have seen *incisum* in the county.

Scolopendrium vulgare.—Gerarde describes "a kind of ferne," probably a young state of this species, which is " called likewise *Hemionitis sterilis,* which is a very small and base herbe, not above a finger high, having fower or five small leaves of the same substance and colour, spotted on the back part, and in taste like Harts toong; but the leaves beare the shape of them of Tota Bona, or good Henrie, which many of our Apothecaries do abusively take for Mercury. The roots are very smooth, black, and threddie, having neither stalk, flower, nor seede. This plant my very good friend Master Nicholas Belson founde in a gravellie lane in the way leading to Oxey Park, neare unto Watford, fifteene miles from London." I have no other notice of the existence of *Scolopendrium* in the district, where, however, it will almost certainly be met with. To the observations of the same old herbalist we owe, I believe, the earliest record of the occurrence of *Malva moschata*, *Alchemilla vulgaris*, *Campanula Trachelium*, *Lamium Galeobdolon*, *Butomus umbellatus*, and *Convallaria maialis* in Hertfordshire; all of which were remarked by Gerarde in the neighbourhood of Bushey and Watford.

Aspidium aculeatum.—Near Bacher Heath. This is called *lobatum* in the ' Flora Hertfordiensis,' but the plant of the immediately adjoining districts of Middlesex appears to be *aculeatum*, and the two forms were confused by the authors of the Flora. *A. angulare*, for which I have no stations in the Watford district, may, perhaps, also be occasionally included with it.

Nephrodium spinulosum.—Oxhey Woods; Aldenham Wood.

N. dilatatum. — Berry Wood, Aldenham; Newland's Wood. These two are often confounded together, and the Aldenham plant at least requires further examination, as it is possible that the two names may represent one and the same thing. *N. dilatatum* was also recorded by Blackstone from a bog near Moor Hall, in company with *Saxifraga granulata* and *Dipsacus pilosus*. This may have been at Harefield, but Moor Park was occasionally called by that name, and so Edward Forster seems to have understood it.

N. oreopteris.—With the last in Aldenham Wood. Recorded also from Bushey Heath, but it has been ascertained that the station is in Middlesex.

Equisetum maximum.—Rickmansworth, by the road to Denham. The only station, and not known to occur anywhere in the neighbourhood.

APPENDIX.

I have put together, as an Appendix, a list of those plants which have been observed in the immediately adjoining portion of Middlesex, but which have not yet been recorded for the Watford district. Some of these, however, rest upon the testimony of the older authors only, and have not been noticed for many years. They are principally from the neighbourhood of Harefield, Pinner and Harrow Weald, and Stanmore Heath.

Ranunculus parviflorus.	Sagina ciliata.
Papaver Argemone.	Radiola Millegrana.
P. hybridum.	Oxalis corniculata.
Brassica Rapa (var. sylvestris).	Impatiens fulva.
Sisymbrium Sophia.	Medicago maculata.
Cardamine hirsuta.	M. denticulata.
Nasturtium sylvestre.	Melilotus arvensis.
Lepidium campestre.	Trifolium subterraneum.
Viola canina (vera).	T. fragiferum.
Moenchia erecta.	T. hybridum.

Vicia lathyroides.
Prunus Cerasus.
Potentilla argentea.
Fragaria elatior.
Rosa systyla.
Pyrus communis.
P. Aucuparia.
Myriophyllum alterniflorum.
Carum Carui.
Bupleurum rotundifoliun.
Chærophyllum Anthriscus.
Sambucus Ebulus.
Galium saxatile.
G. uliginosum.
G. Witheringii.
Silybum Marianum.
Onopordum Acanthium.
Serratula tinctoria.
Centaurea Cyanus.
C. Calcitrapa.
Filago minima.
Inula Helenium.
Lactuca Scariola.
Erica cinerea.
Solanum nigrum.
Verbascum Blattaria.
Limosella aquatica.
Mentha rubra.
M. gracilis.
Salvia Verbenaca.
Lithospermum officinale.
Myosotis repens.
Anagallis tenella.
Plantago Coronopus.
Littorella lacustris.
Chenopodium polyspermum.
C. olidum.

Chenopodium viride.
C. ficifolium.
Rumex nemorosus (v. sanguineus).
R. pratensis.
Populus nigra.
Salix pentandra.
S. vitellina.
S. Smithiana.
Betula glutinosa.
Taxus baccata.
Typha angustifolia.
Acorus Calamus.
Potamogeton crispus.
Alisma lanceolata.
A. ranunculoides.
Actinocarpus Damasonium.
Habenaria viridis.
Narcissus poeticus.
Tulipa sylvestris.
Juncus compressus.
Luzula sylvatica.
Blysmus compressus.
Scirpus acicularis.
S. cœspitosus.
S. fluitans.
Carex disticha.
C. acuta.
C. strigosa.
C. paludosa.
Alopecurus fulvus.
Polypogon monspeliensis.
Agrostis Spica-venti.
Bromus velutinus.
Lolium italicum.
Cystopteris fragilis.
Lycopodium inundatum.
Equisetum sylvaticum.

Including casuals, and a few doubtful plants, not far short of one hundred species—a number that should be some stimulus to further exertion.

4.—On the Observation of Periodical Natural Phenomena.

By John Hopkinson, F.L.S., F.G.S.

[Read 13th May, 1875.]

Introductory Remarks.

Attention has at various times been drawn to the importance of obtaining a record of observations of certain periodical natural phenomena, conducted universally upon some uniform plan. Meteorologists have agreed upon an uniform system of registration of periodical atmospheric changes, as recorded by the barometer, thermometer, and other instruments; but hitherto, in this country, only here and there, and without concert, has the naturalist assisted the meteorologist in climatological investigations by the aid of a mechanism infinitely more refined and more sensitive to atmospheric influences than any instruments man can construct.

Such a mechanism we have in the delicate structure of plants and animals. With the periodical return of the seasons a series of phenomena takes place, differing in the time of occurrence year by year, but in the same place and under similar conditions usually in the same order. In plants the leaf unfolds, the flower opens, the fruit ripens, and finally the leaf falls. Amongst animals, insects one by one appear, birds arrive and depart, commence and leave off their song, and amphibians, reptiles, and mammals appear and disappear.

From observations of these and other similar phenomena several Naturalist's Calendars, as they are called, have been compiled, the best known being perhaps the "Calendarium Floræ" of Linnæus, in the 'Amœnitates Academicæ,' 1756; the calendar drawn up by Aikin from the manuscripts of the Rev. Gilbert White, first published, with other observations in Natural History, in 1795, and usually appended afterwards to the 'Natural History of Selborne;' Markwick's calendar of observations made at Catsfield, near Battle, first published in the 1802 edition of this work; and that given by Jenyns in his 'Observations in Natural History,' the record of notes which he made at Swaffham Bulbeck, a village a few miles beyond Cambridge.

The work of which this carefully compiled calendar forms a part was published in 1846. At the meeting of the British Association for the Advancement of Science held at Cambridge in the previous year, a report of a Committee, "Appointed for the purpose of Reporting on the Registration of Periodical Phenomena of Animals and Vegetables," was presented, the Report consisting mainly of a translation (revised and enlarged by the Rev. L. Jenyns and M. de Selys-Longchamps) of a series of 'Instructions for the Observation of Periodical Phenomena,' previously prepared at Brussels by M. Quetelet and other Continental naturalists.

This report was a most valuable contribution to the subject, but it is only now, after a lapse of thirty years, that it seems likely to

bear fruit in the general adoption of its leading principles, and in
the uniform carrying out of investigations to the importance of
which attention was then for the first time in this country systematically drawn.

For this recent attempt to re-awaken an interest in the periodical
phenomena of nature we are indebted to the Meteorological Society
of London. This Society has within the last few months issued a
list of plants, insects, and birds recommended to be observed, and a
code of Instructions to observers.* This list I propose to adopt
without alteration at present, leaving the question of any extension
or modification that may be thought desirable to meet the special
requirements of our district to future consideration. In the list
as published by the Meteorological Society there are seventy-one
species of plants recommended for observation of the time of
flowering, this being the most important point to observe and
record. Observations on the time of leafing, fruiting, and shedding
of the leaves of trees are also considered useful, provided the same
trees are observed every year. Of insects there are eight species of
which the first appearance is recommended for registration. Of
birds there are seventeen species recommended for notice of their
arrival, commencement of song, etc. ; and the last entry we have
is that of frog spawn, the first appearance of which should be
noted.†

From these and other similar observations, valuable information,
of immediate practical application, as well as of a theoretical nature,
may in time be gained. Alone, such observations may furnish
climatological data of importance in the operations of the farmer
and gardener. The most favourable time for sowing seed, for
instance, may be determined by the flowering of some plant, or
even by the appearance of some insect; for, as Quetelet has observed, "the phases of the existence of the minutest plant-aphis,
of the paltriest insect, are connected with the phases of the existence of the plant which nourishes it, and this plant itself, in its
gradual development, is in some measure the product of all the
anterior modifications of the soil and atmosphere." The germi-
nation of seed, and the safety of the young shoot afterwards, are as
dependent upon these modifications as upon the time of the year
at which it is sown and the state of the weather.

Combined with meteorological observations those we are considering may afford valuable assistance in investigations on climate ;

* 'Instructions for the Observation of Phenological Phenomena, prepared at
the request of the Council of the Meteorological Society by a Conference con-
sisting of Delegates from the following Societies, viz.:—Royal Agricultural
Society, Royal Botanic Society, Royal Dublin Society, Royal Horticultural
Society, Marlborough College Natural History Society, Meteorological Society.'
London : Williams and Strahan. 1875.

† It may here be mentioned that it is not intended that these observations
should be limited to the species which will be enumerated, nor that observations
should be limited to the points alluded to. Notes of observations in any department of Natural History will be welcome, and however brief may be of value as
contributions to the Natural History of our county.

for these periodical phenomena, both of plants and animals, are all more or less regulated by the laws of climate and the varying influences of the seasons. It is here that union is required, for it is only by the combination of the records of many observers scattered over a wide area that results of importance can be obtained. That the Naturalists' Calendar for the County of Hertford, which I hope in time will be compiled from the observations of the members of our Society, may be of value in this respect, the list of the Meteorological Society is adhered to. This list is founded upon the more extensive list of Quetelet adopted by Continental observers, and any species it may in time be deemed advisable to add to our list should be selected from this, for by so doing the results we may obtain can be compared with the results arrived at on the Continent of Europe and in other countries. As an example of the information that may be derived from these calendars, it may be mentioned that by comparing the various records of similar observations, made simultaneously upon the species selected at a number of stations in this and other countries, we may distinguish those localities at which the same phenomena occur at the same time, and by drawing lines through these localities we may indicate with clearness the *isochronism* of the phenomena, and therefore of the climatal conditions upon which they are dependent.

It is, however, only by observations extending over a number of years that the *mean date* of these occurrences for any locality can be determined.* This is what is required. The average range of variation is about a month, and it has been found to be greater with the phenomena that occur early in the year than with such as occur later. The long and severe winter we have had this year will therefore make the earlier and later phenomena occur nearer together than they usually do, and we may expect the summer to be not nearly so backward as the spring now is, while the autumnal phenomena may not even be appreciably affected.

It may be *many* years before the mean date of each phenomenon for Watford and elsewhere in our county can be determined with any degree of accuracy. Let us then at once commence to record our observations on the species selected, and not be deterred by the thought that it may not be in our time that inferences of high scientific value may be drawn from them. Moreover, without considering the ulterior object we have in view, every accurate observation, carefully and faithfully recorded, is at once of value, and available for comparison with others. The cultivation of habits of observing is also in many ways beneficial to ourselves. The more we observe, the more we find to observe, and the more we are capable of observing;—our senses are sharpened and we see and hear things which, had we not cultivated this habit, would never have been noticed. As Edward Forbes has remarked, " It is surprising how little we see until we are taught to observe."

* The true mean is not the mean of the *extremes*, but the mean of *all* the dates, found by adding them together and dividing by their number.

LIST OF THE SPECIES RECOMMENDED TO BE OBSERVED.

When all the Plants in the list cannot be observed, special attention should be given to those of which the names are printed in capitals.

PLANTS.

1. ANEMONE NEMOROSA (Wood Anemone).
2. RANUNCULUS FICARIA (Pilewort—Lesser Celandine).
3. *Ranunculus acris* (Upright Crowfoot).
4. CALTHA PALUSTRIS (Marsh Marigold).
5. *Papaver Rhœas* (Red Poppy).
6. *Cardamine hirsuta* (Hairy Bittercress).
7. *Cardamine pratensis* (Cuckooflower—Lady's Smock).
8. *Draba verna* (Whitlow-grass).
9. *Viola odorata* (Sweet Violet).
10. *Polygala vulgaris* (Milkwort).
11. *Lychnis Flos-cuculi* (Ragged Robin)
12. *Stellaria Holostea* (Greater Stitchwort).
13. MALVA SYLVESTRIS (Common Mallow).
14. *Hypericum tetrapterum* (Square St. John's Wort).
15. *Hypericum pulchrum* (Upright St. John's Wort).
16. GERANIUM ROBERTIANUM (Herb Robert—Stinking Cranesbill).
17. TRIFOLIUM REPENS (DutchClover).
18. *Lotus corniculatus* (Bird's-foot Trefoil).
19. *Vicia Cracca* (Tufted Vetch).
20. „ *sepium* (Bush Vetch).
21. *Lathyrus pratensis* (MeadowVetchling—Meadow Pea).
22. PRUNUS SPINOSA (Sloe—Blackthorn).
23. *Spiræa Ulmaria* (Meadow-sweet).
24. *Potentilla anserina* (Silver-weed).
25. „ *Fragariastrum* (Barren Strawberry).
26. *Rosa canina* (Dog Rose).
27. *Epilobium hirsutum* (Great Hairy Willow-herb).
28. *Epilobium montanum* (Broad Willow-herb).
29. *Angelica sylvestris* (Wild Angelica).
30. *Anthriscus sylvestris* (Wild Chervil—Cow Parsley).
31. HEDERA HELIX (Ivy).
32. *Galium Aparine* (Cleavers—Goosegrass).
33. *Galium verum* (Yellow Bedstraw).
34. *Dipsacus sylvestris*(Common Teasel)
35. *Scabiosa succisa* (Devil's-bit).
36. *Petasites vulgaris* (Butter-bur).
37. TUSSILAGO FARFARA (Coltsfoot).
38. ACHILLEA MILLEFOLIUM (Milfoil—Yarrow).
39. *Chrysanthemum Leucanthemum* (Ox-eye Daisy—Dog Daisy).
40. *Artemisia vulgaris* (Mugwort).
41. *Senecio Jacobæa* (Ragwort).
42. CENTAUREA NIGRA (Black Knapweed—Hardheads).
43. *Carduus lanceolatus*(Spear Thistle).
44. „ *arvensis* (Field Thistle).
45. *Sonchus arvensis*(Corn Sow-thistle)
46. *Hieracium Pilosella* (Mouse-ear Hawkweed).
47. CAMPANULA ROTUNDIFOLIA (Hairbell).
48. *Gentiana campestris* (Field Gentian).
49. CONVOLVULUS SEPIUM (Greater Bindweed).
50. *Symphytum officinale* (Comfrey).
51. *Pedicularis sylvatica* (Red Rattle).
52. *Veronica Chamædrys* (Germander Speedwell).
53. *Veronica hederifolia* (Ivy-leaved Speedwell).
54. *Mentha aquatica* (Water Mint).
55. *Thymus Serpyllum* (Wild Thyme).
56. *Prunella vulgaris* (Self-heal).
57. *Nepeta Glechoma* (Ground Ivy).
58. *Galeopsis Tetrahit* (Hemp-nettle).
59. *Stachys sylvatica* (Hedge Woundwort).
60. *Ajuga reptans* (Creeping Bugle).
61. PRIMULA VERIS (Cowslip).
62. *Plantago lanceolata* (Ribwort Plantain).
63. *Mercurialis perennis* (Dog's Mercury).
64. *Ulmus montana* (Wych Elm).
65. *Salix caprea* (Great Sallow—English Palm).
66. *Corylus Avellana* (Hazel).
67. *Orchis maculata* (Spotted Orchis).
68. *Iris Pseudacorus* (Yellow Iris—Flag).
69. *Narcissus Pseudo-narcissus* (Daffodil).
70. *Galanthus nivalis* (Snowdrop).
71. *Endymion nutans* (Blue-bell).

INSECTS.

72. *Melolontha vulgaris* (Cock-chafer).
73. *Rhizotrogus solstitialis* (Fern-chafer).
74. *Apis mellifica* (Honey Bee).
75. *Pieris Brassicæ* (Large White Cabbage Butterfly).

76. *Pieris Rapæ* (Small White Cabbage Butterfly).
77. *Epinephile Janira* (Meadow-brown Butterfly).
78. *Bibio Marci* (St. Mark's Fly).
79. *Trichocera hiemalis* (Winter Gnat).

BIRDS.

80. *Strix Aluco* (Brown, or Tawny Owl).
81. *Muscicapa grisola* (Flycatcher).
82. *Turdus musicus* (Song Thrush).
83.   „   *pilaris* (Fieldfare).
84. *Daulias Luscinia* (Nightingale).
85. *Saxicola Œnanthe* (Wheatear).
86. *Phylloscopus Trochilus* (Willow Wren).
87. *Phylloscopus collybita* (Chiff-chaff).

88. *Alauda arvensis* (Sky-lark).
89. *Fringilla cœlebs* (Chaffinch).
90. *Corvus frugilegus* (Rook).
91. *Cuculus canorus* (Cuckoo).
92. *Hirundo rustica* (Swallow).
93. *Cypselus Apus* (Swift).
94. *Columba Turtur* (Turtle-dove).
95. *Perdix cinerea* (Partridge).
96. *Scolopax Rusticola* (Woodcock).

AMPHIBIAN.

97. *Rana temporaria* (Common Frog).

REGISTRATION OF OBSERVATIONS.

For recording the phenomena—the "Phenological* Phenomena" of the Meteorological Society—recommended for observation in the above species, blank forms, each to contain the record of a single month, will be forwarded to any of our members who may inform me of their intention to undertake observations, whether on the whole of the species, or on either the plants, the insects, or the birds. These forms should be returned at the expiration of each month, for transmission (after their contents have been registered, for publication in the Transactions of our Society) to the Secretary of the Meteorological Society; and the actual specimens of the plants and if possible also of the insects observed should be forwarded at the same time.† Specimens of the plants are required "for obtaining a notion of the *phase* of vegetation which each observer would look upon as *flowering*," as well as for identification and comparison.

In the 'Instructions' of the Meteorological Society it is recommended that "in the case of plants the *aspect* of the locality in which the specimen grew should be stated, and a general notion given of the kind of weather (whether unusually warm or dry) during the fortnight previous to its being gathered;" and that "it would be well to record the dates of the first two or three specimens gathered, unless the species comes into flower very rapidly after the first notice;" and in respect to insects, that "*the state of the weather* at the time of observation should be recorded, as well as any other circumstances which may be deemed

---

* From φαίνω, *phaino*, I show, or manifest; and λόγος, *logos*, a discourse.

† The forms, when filled up, may for the present be sent to me, and at any future time to the *then* Secretary of our Society, and the insects and plants to Mr. Arthur Cottam, who has kindly consented to undertake their examination.

necessary or interesting." In observing any fact connected with birds, the most important point insisted upon is that the observer " should set down the exact locality at which it occurred, even if it be but a few miles distance from his own station, and if possible again record the fact when it recurs there, or *vice versâ*."

There are many valuable suggestions, in addition to the above, in the excellent code of Instructions to which reference has so frequently been made.

CALENDAR OF PHENOMENA TO BE OBSERVED.

The accompanying Calendar may be found useful as indicating the phenomena which should be observed in the species enumerated, and the probable dates of their occurrence. It is compiled from the record of ten years' observations at Marlborough, given in the 'Instructions' of the Meteorological Society, and of twelve years' (1820–1831) at Swaffham Bulbeck, near Cambridge, from the Rev. L. Jenyns' 'Observations in Natural History.'

This double record may be instructive as showing the difference between two localities, one of which is about the same distance to the south-west of Watford as the other is to the north-east; but in comparing them it should be borne in mind that the Cambridge calendar is of a period forty years before that of the Marlborough calendar. It may also be mentioned that the former is not uniformly a continuous record, some of the phenomena having been only occasionally observed during the twelve years, while others have been observed every year during that period. The number of years each observation was made is given in the original calendar, which is prefaced by some very valuable remarks on the subject of this inquiry.

It may be noticed that the order adopted in our calendar is not exactly in accordance with the mean dates of either the Marlborough or the Cambridge calendar. In compiling it, both these records have been taken into consideration, and in some cases the calendars of White and Markwick have also been consulted. Extended observation may possibly clear up such discrepancies as are shown (taking two of the earlier occurrences as examples) in the recorded times of flowering of the hazel and the ivy-leaved speedwell, of which the mean date of coming into flower is about the same at Marlborough, and yet differs by six weeks at Cambridge. Although a greater irregularity than is even here shown *may* be introduced by observations in this neighbourhood, there are doubtless various causes, affecting different species in different ways, to the discovery of which these apparent discrepancies may eventually lead.

CALENDAR OF PERIODICAL NATURAL PHENOMENA RECOMMENDED FOR OBSERVATION.

FROM THE REV. T. A. PRESTON'S RECORD AT MARLBOROUGH, AND THE REV. L. JENYNS' AT SWAFFHAM BULBECK, NEAR CAMBRIDGE.

Abbreviations:—fl.—flowers open; ap.—first appears; sg.—song commences.

No. in List	Phenomena	MARLBOROUGH			CAMBRIDGE		
		Mean	Earliest	Latest	Mean	Earliest	Latest
	JANUARY.						
74	Honey Bee (*Apis mellifica*) ap.	....	....	....	Jan. 29	By Jan. 1	Feb. 25
88	Skylark (*Alauda arvensis*) sg.	Feb. 1	Jan. 11	....	Jan. 23	Jan. 13	Feb. 21
70	Snowdrop (*Galanthus nivalis*) fl.	....	....	Feb. 20	Jan. 30	Jan. 21	Feb. 16
82	Song Thrush (*Turdus musicus*) sg.	Feb. 8	Jan. 17	Mar. 10	Jan. 31	By Jan. 1	Feb. 23
66	Hazel (*Corylus Avellana*) fl.	....	....	....	Jan. 25	By Jan. 1	Feb. 20
	FEBRUARY.						
63	Ivy-leaved Speedwell (*Veronica hederifolia*) fl.	Feb. 7	By Jan. 1	Feb. 20	Mar. 11	Feb. 1	Apl. 3
89	Chaffinch (*Fringilla coelebs*) sg.	....	....	....	Feb. 1	Jan. 7	Feb. 14
80	Tawny Owl (*Strix Aluco*) hoots	....	....	....	Feb. 2	Jan. 24	Feb. 14
2	Pilewort (*Ranunculus Ficaria*) fl.	Feb. 14	Jan. 26	Mar. 6	Mar. 2	Jan. 21	Mar. 28
63	Dog's Mercury (*Mercurialis perennis*) fl.	Feb. 21	Feb. 1	Mar. 27	Mar. 26	Feb. 15	Apl. 10
6	Hairy Bittercress (*Cardamine hirsuta*) fl.	Feb. 27	Feb. 6	Apl. 8	....	....	....
37	Coltsfoot (*Tussilago Farfara*) fl.	Feb. 27	Feb. 11	Apl. 1	Mar. 13	Feb. 24	Apl. 1
25	Barren Strawberry (*Potentilla Fragariastrum*) fl.	Mar. 1	Jan. 18	Apl. 7	....	....	....
	MARCH.						
90	Rook (*Corvus frugilegus*) builds	Mar. 4	Feb. 16	Mar. 25	Mar. 3	Feb. 12	Mar. 13
9	Sweet Violet (*Viola odorata*) fl.	Mar. 4	Feb. 16	Apl. 3	Mar. 7	Jan. 25	Mar. 26
65	Great Sallow (*Salix caprea*) fl.	Mar. 9	Feb. 26	Apl. 6	....	....	....
8	Whitlow Grass (*Draba verna*) fl.	....	....	....	Mar. 5	Jan. 21	Apl. 10

No. in List	Phenomena	Marlborough Mean	Marlborough Earliest	Marlborough Latest	Cambridge Mean	Cambridge Earliest	Cambridge Latest
	MARCH—continued.						
4	Marsh Marigold (*Caltha palustris*) fl.	Mar. 15	Feb. 14	Apl. 13	Mar. 4	Feb. 9	Mar. 29
69	Daffodil (*Narcissus Pseudo-narcissus*) fl.	Mar. 6	Feb. 12	Apl. 3	Mar. 13	Feb. 28	Mar. 21
97	Common Frog (*Rana temporaria*) spawns				Mar. 16	Mar. 4	Mar. 25
64	Wych Elm (*Ulmus montana*) fl.	Mar. 7	Feb. 5	Apl. 1	Apl. 1	Mar. 23	Apl. 10
87	Chiff-chaff (*Phylloscopus collybita*) sg.				Apl. 3	Mar. 15	Apl. 14
1	Wood Anemone (*Anemone nemorosa*) fl.	Mar. 11	Feb. 27	Apl. 6	Apl. 10		
36	Butter-bur (*Petasites vulgaris*) fl.	Mar. 13	Feb. 18	Apl. 10	Apl. 24	Apl. 19	Apl. 29
67	Ground Ivy (*Nepeta Glechoma*) fl.	Mar. 20	Mar. 3	Apl. 9	Apl. 3	Mar. 9	Apl. 23
86	Willow Wren (*Phylloscopus Trochilus*) sg.						
61	Cowslip (*Primula veris*) fl.	Mar. 30	Mar. 19	Apl. 7	Mar. 30	Feb. 5	Apl. 20
22	Blackthorn (*Prunus spinosa*) fl.	Mar. 29	Feb. 20	Apl. 16	Apl. 7	Mar. 15	Apl. 20
76	Small White Butterfly (*Pieris Rapæ*) ap.				Apl. 11	Mar. 14	May 9
	APRIL.						
30	Wild Chervil (*Anthriscus sylvestris*) fl.	Apl. 1	Mar. 16	Apl. 21	Apl. 18	Mar. 29	May 1
7	Cuckoo Flower (*Cardamine pratensis*) fl.	Apl. 6	Mar. 12	Apl. 22	Apl. 18	Mar. 21	May 7
12	Greater Stitchwort (*Stellaria Holostea*) fl.	Apl. 9	Mar. 25	Apl. 24			
92	Swallow (*Hirundo rustica*) first seen				Apl. 19	Apl. 9	Apl. 26
84	Nightingale (*Daulias Luscinia*) sg.				Apl. 21	Apl. 8	Apl. 28
75	Large White Butterfly (*Pieris Brassicæ*) ap.				Apl. 23	Mar. 26	May 11
71	Blue Bell (*Endymion nutans*) fl.	Apl. 11	Mar. 31	Apl. 22	Apl. 25	Apl. 11	May 10
52	Germander Speedwell (*Veronica Chamædrys*) fl.	Apl. 15	Mar. 12	May 4	Apl. 29	Apl. 19	May 13
62	Ribwort Plantain (*Plantago lanceolata*) fl.	Apl. 18	Apl. 3	Apl. 28	Apl. 27	Apl. 15	May 13
91	Cuckoo (*Cuculus canorus*) first heard				Apl. 27	Apl. 21	May 7
3	Upright Crowfoot (*Ranunculus acris*) fl.	Apl. 19	Apl. 5	May 15	May 16	May 4	May 30
20	Bush Vetch (*Vicia sepium*) fl.	Apl. 22	Apl. 11	May 5			
50	Comfrey (*Symphytum officinale*) fl.	Apl. 24	Apl. 16	Apl. 30	May 12	May 5	May 22
78	St. Mark's Fly (*Bibio Marci*) ap.						
60	Creeping Bugle (*Ajuga reptans*) fl.	Apl. 28	Apl. 15	May 6	May 3	Apl. 2	May 15
16	Herb Robert (*Geranium Robertianum*) fl.	Apl. 30	Apl. 27	May 4	May 4	Mar. 23	May 18
10	Milkwort (*Polygala vulgaris*) fl.	Apl. 28	Apl. 18	May 7	May 12	Apl. 20	May 28

MAY.

#		C1	C2	C3	C4	C5	C6
94	Turtle Dove (*Columba Turtur*) first seen	May 16	Apl. 27	May 8	May 31	Apl. 18	May 5
51	Red Rattle (*Pedicularis sylvatica*) fl.	May 30	May 6	May 13		Apl. 28	May 6
93	Swift (*Cypselus Apus*) first seen	June 7	Apl. 14	May 15		May 6	May 12
72	Cock-chafer (*Melolontha vulgaris*) ap.	May 24	Apl. 12	May 16		Apl. 30	May 12
81	Flycatcher (*Muscicapa grisola*) first seen	July 1	May 9	May 29	May 17	May 1	May 13
32	Cleavers (*Galium Aparine*) fl.	May 31	May 13	May 22	May 21	May 5	May 16
24	Silver-weed (*Potentilla anserina*) fl.	June 9	May 3	May 18	May 23	May 9	May 16
17	Dutch Clover (*Trifolium repens*) fl.	June 7	May 16	May 24	May 28	May 7	May 13
18	Bird's-foot Trefoil (*Lotus corniculatus*) fl.	June 11	May 17	May 27	May 22	May 5	May 31
46	Mouse-ear Hawkweed (*Hieracium Pilosella*) fl.	June 9	May 10	May 19	June 8	May 1	May 16
39	Ox-eye Daisy (*Chrysanthemum Leucanthemum*) fl.	June 16	May 22	May 31	May 22	May 9	June 1
11	Ragged Robin (*Lychnis Flos-cuculi*) fl.		May 10	May 16	May 19	May 7	May 2
5	Red Poppy (*Papaver Rhoeas*) fl.		May 22	June 11	June 3	May 20	June 8
67	Spotted Orchis (*Orchis maculata*) fl.	July 3	May 30	June 16	June 11	May 15	May 26
68	Yellow Iris (*Iris Pseudacorus*) fl.	June 30	June 9	June 12	June 21	May 21	May 31
77	Meadow-brown Butterfly (*Epinephile Janira*) ap.	July 8	June 12				
21	Meadow Vetchling (*Lathyrus pratensis*) fl.		June 23	June 11	June 11	May 15	May 29
38	Milfoil (*Achillea Millefolium*) fl.	July 18	June 1	June 21	June 30	May 21	May 31

JUNE.

#		C1	C2	C3	C4	C5	C6
26	Dog Rose (*Rosa canina*) fl.	June 22	May 31	June 13	June 9	May 22	June 1
65	Wild Thyme (*Thymus Serpyllum*) fl.	June 27	May 23	June 8	June 11	May 26	June 2
13	Common Mallow (*Malva sylvestris*) fl.	June 18	June 7	June 19	June 11	May 13	June 3
59	Hedge Woundwort (*Stachys sylvatica*) fl.	June 29	June 1	June 14	June 11	May 31	June 7
73	Fern-chafer (*Rhizotrogus solstitialis*) ap.						
42	Black Knap-weed (*Centaurea nigra*) fl.	June 29	May 22	June 24	June 15	June 7	June 16
56	Self-heal (*Prunella vulgaris*) fl.	June 28	June 9	June 22 (?)	June 20	June 6	June 16
95	Partridge (*Perdix cinerea*) hatches				June 21		
28	Broad Willow-herb (*Epilobium montanum*) fl.	July 25	June 16	June 17	July 2	June 4	June 10
91	Cuckoo (*Cuculus canorus*) changes its note						
23	Meadow-sweet (*Spiraea Ulmaria*) fl.	July 15	June 14	June 25	June 30	June 2	June 16
41	Ragwort (*Senecio Jacobaea*) fl.	July 9	June 24	June 30 (?)	July 3	May 17	June 11
19	Tufted Vetch (*Vicia Cracca*) fl.	July 20	June 15	July 1	July 3	June 8	June 18
33	Yellow Bedstraw (*Galium verum*) fl.	July 18	June 22	June 30 (?)	July 6	May 26	June 20
44	Field Thistle (*Carduus arvensis*) fl.	July 17	July 1	July 10	July 8	June 10	June 30

No. in List	Phenomena	Marlborough * Mean	Earliest	Latest	Cambridge Mean	Earliest	Latest
	JULY.						
49	Greater Bindweed (*Convolvulus sepium*) fl.	....	....	....	July 8	June 28	July 20
47	Hair-bell (*Campanula rotundifolia*) fl.	....	....	....	July 3	......	July 18
45	Corn Sow-thistle (*Sonchus arvensis*) fl.	....	....	....	July 15	June 21	July 29
58	Hemp-nettle (*Galeopsis Tetrahit*) fl.	....	....	....	July 16	July 8	July 30
27	Great Hairy Willow-herb (*Epilobium hirsutum*) fl.	....	....	....		June 28	
85	Wheatear (*Saxicola Œnanthe*) returns....	....	....	....			
14	Square St. John's Wort (*Hypericum tetrapterum*) fl.	....	....	....	July 19	July 9	Aug. 4
15	Upright St. John's Wort (*Hypericum pulchrum*) fl.	....	....	....			
43	Spear Thistle (*Carduus lanceolatus*) fl.	....	....	....	July 19	July 10	Aug. 2
34	Wild Teasel (*Dipsacus sylvestris*) fl.	....	....	....	July 27	July 8	Aug. 13
	AUGUST.						
29	Wild Angelica (*Angelica sylvestris*) fl.	....	....	....	July 31	July 25	Aug. 11
40	Mugwort (*Artemisia vulgaris*) fl.	....	....	....	Aug. 4	July 26	Aug. 8
92	Swallow (*Hirundo rustica*) begins to flock	....	....	....	Aug. 12	July 23	Aug. 25
35	Devil's-bit (*Scabiosa succisa*) fl.	....	....	....	Aug. 18	Aug. 5	Aug. 31
48	Field Gentian (*Gentiana campestris*) fl.	....	....	....			
54	Water Mint (*Mentha aquatica*) fl.	....	....	....		......	......
	SEPTEMBER.						
87	Chiff-chaff (*Phylloscopus collybita*) last heard	....	....		Sept. 20	Sept. 9	Sept. 29
31	Ivy (*Hedera Helix*) fl.	....	....	....	Sept. 26	Sept. 5	Oct. 22
	OCTOBER—DECEMBER.						
96	Woodcock (*Scolopax Rusticola*) first seen	....	....	....	Oct. 30	Oct. 18	Nov. 18
83	Fieldfare (*Turdus pilaris*) arrives	....	....	....	Nov. 21	Oct. 26	Dec. 21
79	Winter Gnat (*Trichocera hiemalis*) ap......		....	....		......	

* No record has been made of the time of first flowering of plants at Marlborough after the month of June.

43

5.—NOTES ON THE PLANTS ON WHICH THE METEOROLOGICAL SOCIETY
INVITES OBSERVATIONS AS TO THEIR TIME OF FLOWERING.

By the Rev. W. MARSDEN HIND, LL.D.

[Read 13th May, 1875.]

As I have never made special observations on the season of
flowering of plants, I am not in a position to give any trustworthy information on this subject to the members of this Society. I purpose,
therefore, saying but little on this point, and must content myself
with making a few general remarks on the plants contained in the
Meteorological Society's list with respect to which observations are
invited.

As all the plants contained in that list, with the exception of
three, viz. *Senecio Jacobæa*, common ragwort ; *Gentiana campestris*,
field gentian ; and *Galanthus nivalis*, the snowdrop, are natives
either of Harrow or Pinner, it may confidently be expected that
all will be found in the County of Hertford.

Plants 1 to 4 in the list belong to the Ranunculus family.* Of
these, *Ranunculus Ficaria*, pilewort, and *Caltha palustris*, marsh
marigold, closely resemble each other in their glossy heart-shaped
leaves, yet are vastly different in size and habit, as well as in the
flowers, which in the former are pale yellow, generally of from
eight to ten narrow petals ; but in the latter are of a rich golden
yellow, the broad petals forming a well-rounded, and occasionally
a deep cup. This plant in the North of England and Ireland does
not come into flower until the latter end of April, fully a month
later than at Marlborough, and in Co. Antrim is usually known as
the May flower.

Plants 6 to 8 belong to the Crucifers. Of these the *Cardamine
pratensis*, cuckoo flower, or lady's smock of the meadows, must be
known to all. The *Cardamine hirsuta*, hairy bittercress, with
small white flowers, is frequent in damp places and about gardens
throughout the spring. It is now distinguished from a larger
plant common in shady places, with larger and more angular leaves
and with a taller and more zigzag stem, and which has been
separated under the name *Cardamine sylvatica*, or *flexuosa*. The
Draba verna, whitlow-grass, is a very modest plant, often not more
than an inch high. Its minute stem rises from a tiny rosette of
leaves, and bears a few small white flowers, which develope into
short oval seed-pods.

10, *Polygala vulgaris*, milk-wort, is a pretty trailing plant with
woody stem, affecting hilly pastures, and exhibiting a considerable
variety of colour in its blossoms. The normal tinge appears to be
dark blue or purple, from which it varies through pink to pure
white. The blossoms are peculiar in form, approaching those
somewhat of a small vetch. It may be found in flower the greater
part of the summer and occasionally far on in the autumn.

* The numbers here given refer to the list at page 36.

11 and 12 belong to the Pink family. *Lychnis Flos-cuculi*, or ragged Robin, may be seen in our damp meadows in May and June, and occasionally as late as September, with its pink blossoms cut into narrow filaments crowning its purple-ribbed calyx. The *Stellaria Holostea*, or stitchwort, is one of the earliest ornaments of our hedges, repaying the thorns and brambles to which its weak stem clings for support by a luxuriance of white star-like blossoms.

13, *Malva sylvestris*, common mallow, is a somewhat coarse plant found on waysides and waste ground, with roundish lobed leaves and striped mauve flowers. It is easily distinguishable from the dwarf mallow by the small and paler flowers of the latter, and from the musk mallow by the cut and hairy leaves of the last-named plant.

14 and 15, *Hypericum tetrapterum* and *pulchrum*, square and upright St. John's-wort, may be distinguished from each other, and from the other small flowered St. John's-worts, by the square winged stalk, the compact panicle, the oval ribbed leaves, and moist habitat of the former, and the somewhat heart-shaped, stem-clasping leaves, and the loose axillary and terminal panicles of the latter.

16, *Geranium Robertianum*, herb Robert, is the most common of our native geraniums, growing in nearly every hedge, with its deeply cut hemlock-like leaves, frequently blotched with purple, and its pretty pink slightly pencilled flowers. The plant may be known by its peculiar and somewhat offensive smell.

17 to 21, Leguminous plants. Of these, *Trifolium repens*, white or Dutch clover, is known to every one. *Lotus corniculatus*, bird's foot trefoil, the yellow and sometimes ruddy blossoms of which so frequently adorn and perfume our pastures, is almost as familiarly known. *Vicia Cracca* and *sepium*, tufted and bush vetch, are easily distinguished in our hedges; the former by its leaves of about ten pairs of narrow leaflets, and its closely packed racemes of many small bluish flowers; the latter by its soft leaves of four to eight pairs of ovate leaflets, and its compact cluster of four to six purplish flowers. *Lathyrus pratensis*, meadow vetchling, occasionally found in hedges, is a meadow plant, and is at once distinguished from the above by its leaves of two lance-shaped leaflets, and its drooping bunches of bright yellow flowers.

22 to 26 are plants of the Rose tribe. Passing over the others, I direct your attention to *Spiræa Ulmaria*, or meadow sweet. This plant you will readily recognise in the meadows, ditches, etc., by its luxuriant panicle of cream-coloured blossoms and its sweet almond-like perfume. There are two other plants of this genus in our native Flora. *S. Filipendula* is a smaller plant with a large rosette of multifid root-leaves, but with blossoms not unlike the plant in our list. The third plant is a good-sized shrub very different in its appearance from the above-named, and not likely to be found in Herts. *Potentilla anserina*, or silver-weed, is the plant so common by every wayside, with silvery interruptedly pinnate leaves and large yellow blossoms. *Rosa canina*, dog-rose, is the

common wild briar of our hedges, and may be distinguished with ease from the not uncommon *Rosa arvensis*, trailing rose, by its coarser and more robust habit, its stronger prickles, and its more loosely compacted flowers, which are either rose-coloured or shim-white, not cream-white, as in *Rosa arvensis*. Any other rose which is likely to occur will have glandulose leaves, and either a sweet or resinous scent; or will approach *Rosa arvensis* in character.

27 and 28, *Epilobium hirsutum* and *montanum*, the great hairy and broad willow-herbs. The former is a large plant with soft downy leaves and large purplish flowers, growing usually in streams and ditches, and from its size not likely to be confounded with any other plants of the same family. *E. angustifolium*, it is true, equals it in size, but its firm well-cut leaves and cruciform flowers do not allow it to be mistaken for the other. The broad willow-herb is a much smaller plant than either of the above, common on banks, with broad ovate leaves, and a round slightly downy stem; the flowers are small, pale purple, and the stigma is four-cleft. It may be easily distinguished from *E. roseum*, which somewhat resembles it, by the longer leaf-stalks and uncleft stigma of the latter plant.

29 and 30 are the only representatives in the list of a large British family, the Umbellifers. *Angelica sylvestris*, wild angelica, is a tall plant, common in moist woods and by the sides of streams, with a round, hollow, jointed stem, and handsome bi- or tri-pinnate leaves. The umbel is generally compact and symmetrical, and the flowers have frequently a slight pinkish tinge. *Anthriscus sylvestris*, the wild chervil or cow parsley, so common in all our hedges, may be known from somewhat similar plants by its larger, more glossy, and rather coarser cut leaves, and by its coming into flower a month earlier than its congeners.

32 and 33 represent the Madder tribe, which is known by whorled leaves, and which are often armed. *Galium Aparine*, goose grass or cleavers, can be no stranger to any of you. *Galium verum*, yellow bedstraw, is abundant in dry pastures and on banks. Its leaves are linear with revolute edges. The plant bears a profuse panicle of tiny yellow flowers.

34, *Dipsacus sylvestris*, wild teasel, is a plant not to be mistaken. It has some resemblance to some of the thistles, and is, like them, armed with spines; its flowers are also gathered together in heads, but each flower is enveloped in a separate sheath and inserted in the axil of a spinous bract and arranged round a central column.

35, *Scabiosa succisa*, devil's-bit scabious, is found towards the end of summer, or in early autumn, in moist pastures. Its flowers are collected in a hemispherical head, and are usually darkish blue, or violet, in colour. This plant is noted for its premorse root, appearing as if bitten off, which is attributed to the great enemy of mankind, who was fearful that its virtues should become known to men, and therefore maliciously destroyed it.

36 to 46 are the representatives of our largest family of British flowering plants, the Composites. *Petasites vulgaris*, butter-bur, our largest-leaved British plant, is found in moist ground, generally

near streams. The flowers appear in early spring, before the
leaves; they are of a pale purplish colour, and are borne on, what
is technically called, a thyrsus. The male and female flowers
are produced by different plants. *Tussilago Farfara*, coltsfoot,
is a still earlier plant; its bright yellow blossoms decking our
pastures and ploughed fields even before the first breath of spring
is felt. *Achillea Millefolium*, milfoil or yarrow, may be known by
its tufted finely-cut leaves, justifying its name (thousand leaves), and
by its dense corymbs of white, occasionally purplish-red, blossoms.
It is common in our pastures, and not infrequent by the waysides.
Chrysanthemum Leucanthemum, ox-eye, is frequent in our meadows
and pastures, and is well known as horse or dog daisy. *Artemisia vulgaris*, mugwort, is a large and somewhat coarsish plant,
occurring on banks and waste places. Its leaves resemble those
of the hawthorn in shape, but are more fleshy and softer in their
texture, and are woolly and white beneath. The flowers are
racemose, brownish-yellow, and altogether unattractive. *Senecio
Jacobæa*, ragwort, does not occur in the Harrow Flora. Its
place is supplied by the *Senecio aquaticus* and *erucifolius*. It is a
coarse inelegant plant, with raggedly-cut leaves, and a corymb of
coarse yellow flowers, which not infrequently are defective, having
no ray, or strap-shaped florets which encircle the tubular florets of
the disk in Composite flowers. *Carduus lanceolatus* and *arvensis* are
our two most common thistles—the former the large coarse thistle
of our roadsides; and the latter, the common pest of our pastures,
growing in masses and increasing by running roots or underground
stems. *Sonchus arvensis*, corn sow-thistle, frequent in our corn-
fields, is a tall plant with large rich yellow flowers, which in hot
sunshine give out a perceptible almond scent. *Hieracium Pilosella*,
mouse-ear hawkweed, is a frequent plant on dry banks, with
lemon-coloured flowers and oblong hairy leaves. It spreads by
creeping scions, and is easily distinguished from other hawkweeds
and other Composite plants by these marks.

47, *Campanula rotundifolia*, harebell, a plant affecting dry banks,
heaths, and mountain pastures, is easily recognised by its light blue,
nodding, bell flowers. Its trivial name, round-leaved, belongs to
it only in its early state. As the plant advances, its rounded or
kidney-shaped leaves die off, and leave only the lanceolate leaves
on the stem.

48, *Gentiana campestris*, field gentian, is an autumn plant; it
may be found in flower in August, and occasionally as late in the
year as October. The corolla is salver-shaped, four-cleft, with a
long, slightly swollen tube. The colour is pale or blotched purple.
The books set it down as a limestone plant, but I have found it on
at least half-a-dozen different formations. It loves a thin soil
where its roots can reach the rock below.

49, *Convolvulus sepium*, greater bindweed, the white convolvulus
of our hedges, is too well known to require further notice. It
blooms in the end of summer and throughout the autumn.

50, *Symphytum officinale*, comfrey, is a coarse plant growing at the edge of pools and streams; it has large hairy leaves, which taper at both ends; the flowers are borne in double racemes, which gradually unfold like the fronds of a fern; they are drooping in habit, cream-coloured; or, in the variety *patens*, pale purple.

51 to 53, *Pedicularis sylvatica*, red rattle, *Veronica Chamædrys* and *hederifolia*, Germander and ivy-leaved speedwell, belong to the Scrophularia family. The rattle is found in wet pastures, growing close to the ground; the leaves, with the exception of those close to the ground, are pinnate and lobed, usually pale green; the flowers are rose-coloured, protruding from a five-lobed calyx. There is a larger plant growing in the marshes, with a stem 6 to 12 inches high, leaves frequently tinged with brown, and having crimson flowers. This is the *Pedicularis palustris*, or marsh lousewort. The Germander speedwell is one of the most attractive of our spring plants, decking our hedgerows and the borders of our fields with its racemes of bright blue blossoms. The leaves are broad, nearly heart-shaped, saw-edged, and strongly veined; the stem has a line of soft hairs running up each side of it. The ivy-leaved speedwell generally occurs as a weed of cultivation in gardens, fields, and on banks. It grows close to the ground, and its pale blue stalked flowers grow in the axils of the leaves. It is easily distinguished from the other speedwells by the shape of its leaves.

54 to 60 belong to the Labiates. *Mentha aquatica*, water mint, may be discerned from the other mints by the fact that it bears its flowers in a terminal blunt head, as well as in axillary clusters. This separates it from one-half of the British species. It differs from the remaining species in its stalked ovate leaves. The triangular teeth of the calyx, and its coarser perfume, further distinguish it from *M. piperita*, peppermint, to which it is the nearest. *Thymus Serpyllum*, wild thyme, will be known by its trailing habit, its tiny fringed leaves, its perfume, and its whorls and heads of red gaping flowers. It is however believed that our British plant has been wrongly named; it ought to be set down as *T. Chamædrys*. *Prunella vulgaris*, self-heal, may be easily known by its short, blunt, somewhat quadrangular spike of purplish blossoms. *Nepeta Glechoma*, ground ivy, is a trailing plant of our woods and hedgerow bottoms. It comes into flower early in spring, and bears three or four flowers in a cluster. Its leaves are roundish kidney-shaped, with crenate or scolloped edges. The whole plant has a strong, peculiar, and not unpleasant perfume. *Galeopsis Tetrahit*, hemp-nettle, is a coarse plant of our corn-fields, with a square bristly stem, swollen at the joints, and having small purplish flowers flecked with white. *Stachys sylvatica*, hedge woundwort, is a still larger plant with large cordate leaves, and frequent whorls of reddish-purple flowers; it grows in woods and waste places. *Ajuga reptans*, bugle, is a spring flower, appearing in our moist meadows and woods. Its shoots spread on the ground, and its blue flowers are borne in a short, stiff, pyramidal spike.

62, *Plantago lanceolata*, ribwort plantain, is common in all meadows and pastures. Its short cylindrical spike of unattractive flowers is borne on a long furrowed scape.

63, *Mercurialis perennis*, dog's mercury, is one of the earliest plants of our hedgerows and woods. It bears its green flowers in lax spikes; the male and female on different plants. Its fresh green leaves form the first furnishing of our hedgerows.

64, *Ulmus montana*, wych elm, is of rare occurrence in this neighbourhood. It is of more branching habit than the *Ulmus suberosa*, common, or cork-bark elm. It has also larger, rougher, and more acuminate leaves, and its fruit grows in hop-like clusters.

65, *Salix caprea*, great sallow, may be known from the other members of this large genus by its large, broad oval, or rounded leaves. As it bears its catkins before its leaves, it is not so easily recognised when in flower.

69, *Narcissus Pseudo-narcissus*, daffodil, locally called Lent-lily. I need not point out any distinguishing features of this well-known gay flower. Though it occurs so plentifully in this neighbourhood, I fear that in none of the places where I have found it, it can prefer a claim to be considered indigenous.

71, *Endymion nutans*, bluebell, is one of the best known plants of our country, coming into flower with the advancing spring, just as our primroses and earlier flowers are beginning to wane, and adorning our copses and hedge banks with its nodding spikes of bright blue blossoms.

This closes the list. Scientific botanists will, I trust, excuse me for having added nothing to their previous knowledge. Learners and non-botanists will, I hope, kindly accept the few meagre hints which I have given them to enable them to recognise the plants with respect to which their observations are invited. There is no part of our published Floras that I so much distrust as the recorded times of flowering; and it is at least desirable that these should be stated as exactly as possible. It is obvious, however, that this gain would not satisfy the Meteorological Society. In ascertaining and recording the local phenomena of the vegetable and animal kingdom throughout this country, and the differences of the same from year to year, they are laying the foundation of a more accurate knowledge of the climate of this country, and of its relation to animal and vegetable life. This is a matter in which all are directly interested, and in carrying out which all should be ready to lend a hand. Surely the Watford Natural History Society will not be the last to help on so good a work !

APPENDIX.

In the Instructions of the Meteorological Society the following remarks are contributed by the Rev. T. A. Preston, M.A., and as the species of which he treats are not referred to above, are here appended.

1, *Anemone nemorosa*. When it first comes up the flower is bent downwards, and the stamens are visible long before the plant can be fairly said to be in flower. Perhaps no specimen should be considered to be in flower till the flower is turned upwards.

3, *Ranunculus acris*. There are three plants very similar to one another as regards the flowers. This species is known at once by its *round* flower-stalks (the other two have them channelled).

5, *Papaver Rhœas.* Known by the hairs on the flower-stalk spreading at right-angles to it, not pressed close. It is not the first poppy in flower, and hence care must be taken to observe whether any particular specimen belongs to this species or not.

9, *Viola odorata.* Care must be taken to observe truly wild specimens, as it is in flower, when under cultivation, long before its wild brethren.

20, *Vicia sepium.* Not to be confounded with *Vicia sativa*, which has the flowers solitary, or rarely two together, whilst *V. sepium* has the flowers three or four together.

22, *Prunus spinosa.* There are three species, united by some persons into one under the name of *P. communis.* As a general rule *P. spinosa* flowers before the expansion of the leaves. It has not unfrequently been confounded with the hawthorn *(Cratægus Oxyacantha)*, and it will be well for intending observers to understand the numerous and obvious differences between the two.

25, *Potentilla Fragariastrum* bears some resemblance to the strawberry *(Fragaria vesca)*. It flowers very much earlier (though some specimens of *F. vesca* are occasionally found at the same time). The most obvious characteristic between the two is the fact that the sepals of *P. Fragariastrum* close over the fruit after flowering, whilst they remain expanded in *F. vesca;* it is also a much more delicate plant than *F. vesca*, but a comparison of the actual specimens will alone enable beginners to discriminate between the two.

42, *Centaurea nigra.* Large specimens are not, at first sight, very dissimilar from those of *C. scabiosa: C. nigra* has the leaves lanceolate; *C. scabiosa* has them deeply divided in a pinnate manner.

63, *Mercurialis perennis;* 65, *Salix caprea;* 66, *Corylus Avellana.* The opening of both the barren and the fertile flowers of these three should be noted.

67, *Orchis maculata.* Not to be confounded with *O. mascula*, the early purple orchis. This species has pale lilac flowers, and comes into flower when *O. mascula* is very nearly over.

70, *Galanthus nivalis.* In warm gardens this comes out early; hence *locality* must be noted, as well as the fact whether plants are generally coming into bloom elsewhere. It may be considered to be in flower when the *heads hang down.*

6.—NOTES ON THE OBSERVATION OF INSECTS IN CONNEXION WITH INVESTIGATIONS ON SEASONAL PHENOMENA.

By ARTHUR COTTAM, F.R.A.S.

[Read 13th May, 1875.]

THE Report prepared by Mr. R. McLachlan, F.L.S., for the Meteorological Society, as to insects proper to be observed in connexion with seasonal phenomena, temperature, etc., is so excellent that there is but little I can add to it. The selection of insects made by Mr. McLachlan as suitable for the purpose appears to me a very judicious one, and although the number is small—eight only—I believe these will be found to be amply sufficient. They are all insects that will be known to most persons who are at all in the habit of observing natural objects, or which can, at all events, be readily identified by any one desirous to make them out. There is just a possibility, but hardly a probability, of making a mistake between the two white cabbage butterflies. It is not always safe to trust to the difference in size, as I have often seen specimens of the large one as small as, or even smaller than, normal specimens of the small white cabbage butterfly. There is a greater likelihood of mistaking the green-veined white for the smaller cabbage white, unless the markings on the underside are carefully examined. The colour and markings of the two cabbage butterflies are somewhat similar, but the underside of the green-veined white is quite distinct. The green-veined white often appears quite as early as the small cabbage, is as nearly as possible the same size, and it also feeds upon one of the cabbage tribe—*Brassica Napus*, after which it is called *Pieris Napi*.

The meadow-brown butterfly is at the time it makes its appearance, towards the end of June, very much the commonest of all the brown butterflies. There are one or two other species out at the same time, but they have to be sought for in woods, or, at all events, are not to be found in every meadow, and in fact everywhere, as the meadow-brown usually is.

Mr. McLachlan suggests that occasional appearances in unusual numbers of any insects should be noted. These occasional appearances are one of the greatest puzzles to entomologists, and at present are not in any way satisfactorily accounted for. One of the butterflies referred to, the pale clouded yellow, was very abundant in 1846, and scarce from that year till 1868, when it was positively commoner than almost any other butterfly all along the south coast. At Margate and Westgate I saw it flying twenty or thirty at a time, and I could without difficulty have taken a couple of hundred in the course of a week. Probably not one in twenty of all that there were, were taken, and yet hardly a specimen has been seen since. *Vanessa Cardui* was also common that year; and in 1872, *Vanessa Antiopa*, the rare Camberwell beauty, was tolerably abundant, but only one or two stray specimens have been seen or taken since.

The Entomology of Watford and its neighbourhood has never, that I am aware of, been worked, or if it has, there is no record of our fauna, so that there is an excellent field for work here ; and I would ask the lady members of our Society to help us in this matter, for so many insects are entirely day-fliers, and can only be observed or taken in the mid-day sunshine, when comparatively few gentlemen have leisure or opportunity to be out in the country, that, with the butterflies especially, we shall have to trust very much to our lady friends to look out for their appearance.

I append the remarks of Mr. McLachlan, given in the Meteorological Society's ' Instructions.'

The time of first appearance of any particular species should be carefully noted, as also the time when it becomes common. This is especially necessary with the two white butterflies, for, as certain larvæ of these often enter houses and other buildings in order to undergo their transformations, it follows that these will necessarily be developed before the main body of individuals that pass through their transformations out of doors.

Notes on the species here follow :—*

72. The appearance of the cock-chafer may be taken as an indication of the near approach of summer.

73. The fern-chafer is a beetle much like the cock-chafer in appearance, but very much smaller. It flies in swarms in the evening round any object (trees, the observer, etc.), and indicates that summer has fairly set in.

74. The honey-bee need not be observed after the end of March in spring, or before the end of October in autumn.

75, 76. The two white cabbage-butterflies need only be noticed in their vernal broods. *P. Rapæ* always appears before *P. Brassicæ*, and care must be taken to avoid mistaking for the latter, hybernated females of *Gonopteryx Rhamni* (the brimstone butterfly), which appear in fine sunny weather from the earliest advent of spring or the end of winter. [Records of the first appearance of this butterfly will, however, be useful.]

77. The meadow-brown butterfly may be taken as indicating summer.

78. St. Mark's fly is a large intensely black hairy dipterous insect with rather long legs, appearing generally about St. Mark's Day (April 25th), and lasting for a very short time.

79. The winter-gnat dances in the air (singly or in little swarms) throughout the winter, excepting during the hardest frosts. A continuous record of its appearance should be kept from Christmas to the end of March.

Occasional appearances in unusual numbers.—It is well known that certain insects appear occasionally in enormous numbers, and then are comparatively rare, or disappear altogether, for a series of years. *Vanessa Cardui* (the painted lady butterfly), *Colias Edusa* and *Hyale* (the clouded-yellow butterflies), *Sphinx Convolvuli* (the convolvulus hawk-moth), are familiar examples. Such exceptional occurrences should be carefully noticed. Meteorologists may thus possibly throw light upon phenomena that have never been satisfactorily accounted for by naturalists.

* The numbers prefixed to these notes refer to the list of the species, which will be found at page 37.

7.—On the Pleasures and Advantages to be Derived from a Study of Natural History, and more particularly from the Observation of Birds.

By J. E. Harting, F.L.S., F.Z.S.

[Read 13th May, 1875.]

There are few studies better calculated to expand the mind and gratify our natural thirst for knowledge than the study of Natural History. The relation between organized beings and the circumstances by which they are surrounded; the structure of certain organs which necessitate a modification of others, and fix the mode of existence; the varieties produced by accident, and the species designedly preserved distinct; in fine, the astonishing results of that mysterious cause termed instinct; all these are surely subjects of the highest interest, and constitute the peculiar charm of Zoology. And yet, how few there are, comparatively, who perceive any interest in the study!

When conversing with persons who have resided in the country all their lives, it has frequently been a matter of surprise to me to observe how little information they possess, even as regards the commonest objects which surround them, and which contribute so much, either directly or indirectly, to their happiness. The most ordinary plants which grow in the hedgerows, the commonest birds and insects which cross their path, are daily passed unheeded and uncared for, and are scarcely even known by their proper names. Should you venture to point out to them that a particular plant is of use as a medicine, that another produces a beautiful dye, or that a third, which is very troublesome as a weed, forms the chief food of certain small birds which they thoughtlessly destroy, they appear quite astonished. Should you call their attention to a beetle, and inform them that its larva, or grub, is one of the farmer's worst enemies, while another, to be seen further on, is of great service in burying decayed animal substances, and in preying upon refuse of all kinds, they express surprise that they should never have made that discovery before. It is to be regretted that these persons make so little use of their eyes, and profit so little of the advantages by which they are surrounded.

With many, probably, this proceeds from a misapprehension of the term "Zoology," or "Natural History." They consider the subject, as they say, "too scientific for them," and imagine that it necessitates a great amount of what is called "book learning." But this is a mistake. All that is required is a correct eye, a good memory, and a method of study, all of which can be wonderfully improved by practice. It is simply the want of attention which makes the discrimination of objects appear difficult; for no sooner do we become acquainted with the trivial distinctions, than we are surprised to find how easy it is to recollect them; and things which appeared wrapt in mystery then become obvious and familiar to us.

Or possibly their indifference may proceed from a contemptuous opinion of what they are pleased to term a childish pursuit. But here again how mistaken is their idea. It surely cannot be childish to labour at acquiring knowledge, and we know from experience that the application of knowledge is power.

The author of that pleasant little book, ' Glaucus; or, the Wonders of the Shore,' says:—" Let no one think that Natural History is a pursuit fitted only for effeminate or pedantic men. We should say rather that the qualifications required for a perfect naturalist are as many and as lofty as were required by old chivalrous writers for the perfect knight-errant of the middle ages; for our perfect naturalist should be strong in body, able to haul a dredge, climb a rock, turn a boulder, walk all day, uncertain where he shall eat or rest; ready to face sun and rain, wind and frost, and eat or drink thankfully anything, however coarse or meagre; he should know how to swim for his life, to pull an oar, sail a boat, and ride the first horse which comes to hand; and, finally, he should be a good shot and a skilful fisherman, and if he go far abroad, be able on occasion to fight for his life.

" For his moral character he must, like a knight of old, be first of all gentle and courteous, ready and able to ingratiate himself with the poor, the ignorant, and the savage; not only because foreign travel will be often otherwise impossible, but because he knows how much invaluable local information can be only obtained from fishermen, miners, hunters, and tillers of the soil. Next, he should be brave and enterprising, and withal patient and undaunted—not merely in travel, but in investigation. He must be of a reverent turn of mind also; not rashly discrediting any reports, however vague and fragmentary; giving man credit always for some germ of truth, and giving Nature credit for an inexhaustible fertility and variety, which will keep him his life long always reverent, yet never superstitious, wondering at the commonest, but not surprised by the most strange.

" Moreover, he must keep himself free from all those perturbations of mind, which not only weaken energy, but darken and confuse the inductive faculty; from haste, and laziness; from melancholy, testiness, pride, and all the passions which make men see only what they wish to see. Of solemn and scrupulous reverence for truth; for without truthfulness, science would be as impossible now as chivalry would have been of old. And last, but not least, the perfect naturalist should have in him the very essence of true chivalry, namely, self-devotion; the desire to advance, not himself and his own fame or wealth, but knowledge and mankind. The spirit which gives freely, because it knows that it has received freely; which communicates knowledge without hope of reward, without jealousy and mean rivalry, to fellow-students and to the world."

This is but an ideal sketch, but nevertheless one worthy of serious consideration; for although it be impossible and absurd to wish that every one should grow up a naturalist by profession, yet this age offers no more wholesome training, both moral and intellectual, than that which is given by a taste for outdoor physical science.

Having learnt, then, what are the requirements of a naturalist, let us proceed to consider the pleasures and advantages which proceed from such a profession.

How many there are who take a walk as they would take a draught or a pill, merely for the benefit of health ; and how many others there are who refrain from walking altogether, because, as they say, "there is nothing to go out for—nothing to see!" Truly, a walk without an object, unless in the most lovely and novel of scenery, is a poor exercise, and as a recreation utterly nil ; but having once an object in view, as those have who take up any particular branch of Natural History, they derive a positive pleasure from their walks, and a gain in mind as well as in body. Anon, when viewing new scenes, and new objects which compose them, comes *the pleasure of discovery*, the pleasure of finding something which they have never seen before—a pleasure which is so delightful, and yet so difficult to define, but one which leaves a lasting impression upon the memory. Then, too, may be considered that pleasure which results from a feeling of complete rest, when the mind is diverted for a time from the more serious duties and cares of life, and we experience a benefit as regards the mind analogous to that resulting from change of air to the body.

Who is there who has not experienced the delightful sensation of having left for a while the City and its tumult, to see the country and inhale its purer air? Many of you will, no doubt, remember those beautiful lines of Longfellow :—

> " If thou art worn and hard beset
> With sorrows that thou would'st forget,
> If thou would'st read a lesson that will keep
> Thy heart from fainting and thy soul from sleep,
> Go to the woods and hills! No tears
> Dim the sweet look that Nature wears."

Tennyson, also, in his 'Two Voices,' alludes to the elevation of soul which follows from a contemplation of Nature :—

> " I wonder'd while I paced along :
> The woods were filled so full with song,
> There seem'd no room for sense of wrong,
> So variously seem'd all things wrought
> I marvel'd how the mind was brought
> To anchor by one gloomy thought."

In close attendance upon this last-named pleasure is that feeling of reverence and inward satisfaction, arising from a conviction of the superintendence exercised by the Creator over all His creatures, and of His goodness and bounty in our regard. Surely these are pleasures sufficient to tempt the most indifferent to investigate His marvellous works! Linnæus tells us that he who does not make himself acquainted with God from a consideration of Nature, will scarcely acquire a knowledge of Him from any other source ; for if we have no faith in the things which are seen, how shall we believe those things which are not seen ?

As we come to understand the relations and mode of existence in the various organisms by which we are surrounded, and observe the wonderful adaptation of structure to habits, we are compelled to admit that one of the chief advantages of the study is our great gain in knowledge. The number of new facts which may be daily acquired by practical outdoor observation is almost incredible.

Consider for a moment the extent of the Animal, the Vegetable, or the Mineral Kingdom. Consider what a world in itself is each of these, and what a multitude of facts may be gathered concerning a single class in any one of them; nay, concerning even a single species.

An eminent statesman,* in a speech delivered some time since at the opening of a School of Science, aptly showed that amongst the advantages resulting from a contemplation of natural objects were the triumphs of science which had been effected by the application of experience thereby gained. "The shell of the lobster suggested the strong tube to Watt; the earthworm the tunnel to Brunel; the bird's wing produced the oar; the gyrations of a hawk the wheel; while the plough was founded on intelligent observation of certain practices of the pig." Be this as it may, there can be no doubt that a correct knowledge of natural objects is of very great assistance to us when endeavouring to delineate them, and many of the improvements observable in painting, sculpture, and other arts, is, in a great measure, attributable to a more truthful representation of Nature.

The occupation which a study of Natural History gives to the mind is a further advantage, not only to ourselves, but to others, and cannot be too highly estimated; for while it diverts the mind from what is sensual and degrading, and induces a greater tone of reverence, it at the same time suggests practical results beneficial to our fellow-creatures.

It only remains for us to consider, then, in what way we may gain the object in view, and derive the pleasures and advantages of which I have spoken. In the first place, the *art of seeing* is indispensable, and this, coupled with a good memory and a method of study, will form the basis of operations.

It is chiefly because people neither use their eyes sufficiently, nor exercise their memory, that they remain so long in ignorance of important truths. It is wonderful how sharp the sight may become by practice, and the close observer of Nature will detect the most beautiful though minute objects, which a casual observer would pass unnoticed.

To all of us this faculty is a natural gift, but how few, alas! exercise it. It is true, with some it is ever active, and increases in proportion as it is called forth. With others it lies dormant, and is only aroused when they are convinced that some advantage will follow from its exercise.

* The Right Hon. W. E. Gladstone, Speech delivered at the opening of the School of Science, Liverpool, October, 1861.

It is to the latter class that I propose chiefly to address myself, and to point out to them certain land-marks, as it were, in the wide field of Ornithology, which may guide them to a discovery of pleasures as yet unknown, and enable them to reap the advantages of which I have spoken.

Our first difficulty in commencing the study of Ornithology, and, indeed, any branch of Natural History, is the vastness of the subject, and hence, to avoid confusion, and to reduce our daily observations to order, some method of study is absolutely necessary.

It is desirable in the onset to make oneself acquainted with certain general, well-defined characters, which in every Order of Birds are found to connect all the families, genera, and species in that Order. When we are able to state from an examination of any particular species to what Order it belongs, we have already made a step in advance. The consideration of other characteristics will enable us to point to a particular *family* in the *Order* to which the species in question must be referred; and as we become acquainted with more minute details of form and structure, we can at length fix with tolerable certainty even the *genus* to which the individual belongs. Having thus narrowed the limits of our inquiry, it is not difficult at length to identify the species itself. And then the real pleasure in the study begins. So soon as we have acquired a knowledge of the outward form and appearance of a species, we are in a position to observe and appreciate its modification of structure in accordance with its habits, its peculiarities of carriage and gait, its mode of flight, method of nesting, number and colour of its eggs, its manner of feeding, the nature of its food, the character of its song or cry, and many other interesting details concerning it.

Let me illustrate my meaning by pointing out that in the Order *Raptores*, or Birds of Prey, all the species are characterized by their possession of a strong hooked bill, the edges of the upper mandible being notched or indented and very sharp, to enable them to kill and cut up the living animals upon which they feed. The legs and feet are strong, the latter armed with long, curved, and sharp claws to grasp and firmly hold the resisting prey. The legs are bare as in the hawks, or feathered as in the owls. The wings are long and pointed as in the true falcons, or short and rounded as in the owls. The flight is rapid and capable of being long sustained.

In the Order *Insessores*, or Perching Birds, the bill is short and comparatively straight, and either conical or wedge-shaped for splitting seeds, nuts, and other hard food, or weak and slender where the food consists of insects or tender shoots and buds of various kinds. The legs are short, with toes and claws well formed for grasping and securing a hold amongst the branches, where most of their time is spent. The wings are short, rounded, and comparatively feeble, not being required for such active employment or speed as in the Birds of Prey.

In the Order *Rasores*, or Scrapers, amongst which are included the pigeons and game birds, the bill is short, robust, and specially adapted for seizing grain and culling the tops and shoots of various plants upon which these birds subsist. The legs and toes are short, admirably adapted for walking and running upon a plane surface, the claws reduced to mere nails, which are useful in scraping and clearing away the surface soil in a search after fallen seeds or lurking insects. The wings, comparatively short and rounded, are capable of moderate and tolerably well-sustained flight.

In the Order *Grallatores*, or Wading Birds, the long and slender legs enable their owners to wade in shallow water and marshy places, where they seek the food which their long bills enable them to seize below the surface, while their long toes, which in many species are semi-palmated or partially webbed, support them with ease upon the yielding mud or ooze upon which they walk. In most species the bill is longitudinally grooved for a considerable portion of its length, and in some, as in the true snipes, the extremity is dilated and sensitive.

The *Natatores*, or Swimming Birds, are characterized by their webbed feet, and in most cases by having the bill compressed vertically instead of laterally, without any of the longitudinal grooves or furrows in it which are observable in the bills of the Grallatorial Birds. The feet, as a rule, are placed far back, which gives the owners a somewhat awkward appearance and waddling gait on land, although their actions are graceful enough when in the water, their natural element.

On observing a species for the first time, there ought to be no great difficulty in assigning it a position in one or other of these large groups, or Orders as they are termed; and the process of narrowing the limits of this position is, as I have pointed out, gradually effected as we become acquainted with the various modifications of structure upon which families and genera have, for the sake of convenience, been based.

"A good ornithologist," says Gilbert White, "should be able to distinguish birds by their air as well as by their colours and shape ; on the ground, as well as on the wing ; and in the bush, as well as in the hand. For though it must not be said that every species of bird has a manner peculiar to itself, yet there is somewhat, in most genera at least, that at first sight discriminates them, and enables a judicious observer to pronounce upon them with some certainty. Put a bird in motion,

'——et vera incessu patuit——.'

"Thus kites and buzzards sail round in circles with wings expanded and motionless ; and it is from their gliding manner that the former are still called in the north of England 'gleads,' from the Saxon verb *glidan*, to glide. The kestrel or wind-hover has a peculiar mode of hanging in the air in one place, his wings all the while being briskly agitated. Hen-harriers fly low over heaths or fields of corn, and beat the ground regularly like a pointer or setting dog.

"Owls move in a buoyant manner, as if lighter than the air ; they seem to want ballast. There is a peculiarity belonging to ravens that must draw the attention even of the most incurious. They spend all their leisure time in striking and cuffing each other on the wing in a kind of playful skirmish ; and when they move from one place to another, frequently turn on their backs with a loud croak, and seem to be falling to the ground. When this odd gesture betides them, they are scratching themselves with one foot, and thus lose the centre of gravity. Rooks sometimes dive and tumble in a froliesome manner ; crows and daws swagger in their walk ; woodpeckers fly *volatu undoso*, opening and closing their wings at every stroke, and so are always rising or falling in curves. All of this genus use their tails, which incline downward, as a support while they run up trees. Parrots, like all other hooked-clawed birds, walk awkwardly, and make use of their bills as a third foot, climbing and descending with ridiculous caution.

" All the *Gallinæ* parade and walk gracefully, and run nimbly, but fly with difficulty, with an impetuous whirring, and in a straight line. Magpies and jays flutter with powerless wings, and make no dispatch ; herons seem encumbered with too much sail for their light bodies ; but these vast hollow wings are necessary in carrying burdens, such as large fishes and the like ; pigeons, and particularly the sort called smiters, have a way of clashing their wings the one against the other over their backs with a loud snap ; another variety, called tumblers, turn themselves over in the air. Some birds have movements peculiar to the seasons : thus ring-doves, though strong and rapid at other times, yet in the spring hang about on the wing in a playful manner ; thus the cock snipe, forgetting his former flight, fans the air like the wind-hover ; and the greenfinch, in particular, exhibits such languishing and faltering gestures, as to appear like a wounded and dying bird ; the king-fisher darts along like an arrow ; fern-owls, or goat-suckers, glance in the dusk over the tops of trees like a meteor ; starlings, as it were, swim along ; while missel-thrushes use a wild and desultory flight ; swallows sweep over the surface of the ground and water, and distinguish themselves by rapid turns and quick evolutions ; swifts dash round in circles ; and the bank-martin moves with frequent vacillations like a butterfly. Most of the small birds fly by jerks, rising and falling as they advance. Most small birds hop ; but wagtails and larks walk, moving their legs alternately. Skylarks rise and fall perpendicularly as they sing ; woodlarks hang poised in the air ; and titlarks rise and fall in large curves, singing in their descent. The whitethroat uses odd jerks and gesticulations over the tops of hedges and bushes. All the duck kind waddle ; divers and auks walk as if fettered, and stand erect on their tails ; these are the *compedes* of Linnæus. Geese and cranes, and most wild fowls, move in figured flights, often changing their position. Dab-chicks, moorhens, and coots fly erect, with their legs hanging down, and hardly make any dispatch ; the reason is plain, their wings are placed too forward out of the true centre of gravity, as the legs of auks and divers are situated too backward.

" From the motion of birds, the transition is natural enough to their notes and language. . . . . The notes of the eagle kind are

shrill and piercing, and about the season of nidification much
diversified. . . . . The notes of our hawks much resemble those of
the king of birds. Owls have very expressive notes; they hoot in
a fine vocal sound, much resembling the *vox humana*, and reducible
by a pitch pipe to a musical key. This note seems to express complacency and rivalry among the males; they use also a quick call
and a horrible scream, and can snore and hiss when they mean to
menace. Ravens, besides their loud croak, can exert a deep and
solemn note that makes the woods to echo; the sound of a crow
is strange and ridiculous; rooks, in the hatching season, attempt
sometimes, in the gaiety of their hearts, to sing, but with no great
success; the parrot kind have many modulations of voice, as appears
by their aptitude to learn human sounds; doves coo in a mournful
manner, and are emblems of despairing lovers; the woodpecker
sets up a sort of loud and hearty laugh; the fern-owl, or goat-
sucker, from the dusk till daybreak, serenades his mate with the
clattering of castanets. All the tuneful *Passeres* express their
complacency by sweet modulations, and a variety of melody. The
swallow, ... by a shrill alarm, bespeaks the attention of the
other *Hirundines*, and bids them be aware that the hawk is at hand.
Aquatic and gregarious birds, especially the nocturnal, that shift
their quarters in the dark, are very noisy and loquacious, as cranes,
wild-geese, wild-ducks, and the like; their perpetual clamour
prevents them from dispersing and losing their companions."

In so extensive a subject, as Gilbert White says, sketches and
outlines are as much as can be expected, for it would be endless to
instance all the infinite variety of the feathered nation.

The number of species which have more or less claim to be included in a list of British Birds is 395. Of these, in round numbers,
130 are Residents; 100 Periodical Migrants; and 30 Annual Visitants; the remainder being Rare and Accidental Visitants.

By *Residents* I mean those species which rear their young annually in the British Islands, and are to be found in some part or
other of the United Kingdom throughout the year. Of these many,
like the kestrel, song thrush, linnet, and pied wagtail, are partially migratory. Nevertheless, as specimens of all may be obtained
in some locality or other during every month in the year, they may
be regarded for all practical purposes as residents.

Periodical Migrants are those which visit us annually and regularly at particular seasons, and whose advent and departure may be
dated in advance with considerable precision. Of these we have
familiar examples in the swallow and nightingale, which come
here for the summer, and the redwing and fieldfare, which spend
the winter with us; whilst others, like most of the sandpipers,
perform a double migration, and pass through the country twice a
year, viz. in spring and autumn.

The *Annual Visitants* comprise those which occur in some part
of the British Islands annually, but comparatively in very limited
numbers, and at irregular and uncertain intervals. The month in
which some or one of them may be expected may be named; but

the uncertainty of their arrival in any particular county precludes their being placed with the Periodical Migrants. Amongst these may be mentioned the golden oriole, the hoopoe, the waxwing, the Lapland bunting, and others.

The *Rare and Accidental Visitants* form a large proportion of the total number of species in the British list, being at present 135 out of 395, or rather more than one-third of the whole. If from these we exclude the gulls, terns, and petrels, many of which are almost cosmopolitan in their distribution, it will be found that of the remainder 48 are European, 14 Asiatic, 11 African, and 42 American in their origin.

I need not dwell longer upon this portion of the subject, although of considerable interest, for I have discussed it at some length in the Introduction to my ' Handbook of British Birds,' which may be found in the Library of this Society.

You are no doubt aware of the steps which have been taken by the Meteorological Society to obtain a record of periodical natural phenomena ; and you have probably already perused the published observations by Professor Newton addressed to that Society, and entitled, " Suggestions as to the Acts of Birds most proper to be observed by Meteorologists."

These suggestions are excellent in their way, and I do not know that I can do better than enumerate the species of birds which he recommends to be observed, and refer you to his remarks under the head of each.

The birds named by him are the Tawny Owl, Spotted Flycatcher, Song Thrush, Fieldfare, Nightingale, Wheatear, Willow Wren, Chiff Chaff, Skylark, Chaffinch, Rook, Cuckoo, Swallow, Swift, Turtle Dove, Partridge, Woodcock.

The connexion between the habits of birds and meteorological conditions has been insisted on by many authors, but few have brought forward any facts in support of their assertions. The subject is one which members of a Society like this may well investigate ; and, indeed, it is desirable that as many as can do so should co-operate with the Meteorological Society in carrying out the object in view. The birds recommended to be observed are all of well-known species, and are either pretty widely distributed in these islands, or excite pretty general interest ; while the peculiarities recommended to be observed in them are of a kind that may be readily noticed by persons who possess no special knowledge of ornithology, but are nevertheless accustomed to walk about with their eyes and ears open.

The class of birds, however, to which, at this season of the year, I would especially direct your attention are the *Periodical Migrants*. All our summer birds have by this time arrived, and when I state that they belong to some thirty different species at least, it will be readily understood how much their presence or absence must add to, or detract from, the appearance and beauty of a landscape.

There is something almost mysterious in the way in which we find numbers of these small and delicately formed birds scattered in one day over a parish where, on the previous day, not one was to be seen; and the manner of their arrival is scarcely more remarkable than the regularity with which they annually make their appearance.

The subject of migration, as I have elsewhere pointed out, is a curious one, and the laws which govern it are yet imperfectly understood; but to advance here all that might be said in regard to it would be beyond the limits of the present paper. It appears highly probable from their constitution that most birds incline to remain as much as possible *in the same temperature throughout the year*, and hence their gradual movements north and south as they feel the effects of heat and cold. If a sudden change comes, like a sharp frost, we find birds lying dead under the hedges. This is a proof of their sensitiveness. Some species, better able to endure cold, but still averse to it, if they do not die, disappear suddenly, and we are often surprised at the extraordinary scarcity of a species one day which on the previous day was plentiful. I have always attributed the cause to sudden change of weather. No doubt the abundance or scarcity of food has some influence upon birds in their migration, but not to the same extent, I conceive, as change of temperature.

By wonderful instinct birds will follow cultivation, and make themselves denizens of new regions. The crossbill has followed the introduction of the apple into England. Glenco, in the Highlands of Scotland, never knew the partridge till its farmers of late years introduced corn into their lands; nor did the sparrow appear in Siberia until the Russians had made arable the vast wastes of that part of their dominions.

For those who reside in the country, and have both taste and leisure to observe the movements and habits of birds, I do not know a more entertaining occupation than that of noting the earliest arrival of the migratory species, the haunts which they select, and the proportions in which they are distributed.

In 1872, through the medium of the Natural History columns of 'The Field,' I distributed a number of copies of a 'Calendar of Ornithology,' and invited the co-operation of naturalists in different parts of the country in collecting and arranging statistics, from which I hoped to derive some very interesting results. Referring to the utilization of such observations, I remarked that upon various points some addition to our knowledge seemed desirable. Amongst other interesting facts, for example, might be ascertained the precise line of direction in which various species migrate ; the causes which necessitate a divergence from this line ; the relative proportions in which different species visit us ; the causes which influence the abundance or scarcity of a species in particular localities ; the result of too great a preponderance of one species over another, whether beneficial or otherwise to man as a cultivator of the soil; the simultaneity or otherwise of their departure from this country in autumn ; the causes operating to retard such departure, and so forth. All these are matters of interest, especially to those who reside in the country and have leisure to inquire into the subject.

Of the calendars which I distributed, twenty-six were filled up in different parts of the country and returned to me ; and I thereupon prepared a report upon the results obtained, which was published in the Natural History columns of ' The Field,' and subsequently reprinted at my request for private distribution.   It seems to me that this Society may assist very materially in carrying out such a scheme, and I have accordingly handed copies of the ' Calendar' and of the ' Report' to our Secretary for the Library, and I shall be happy to distribute further copies to such of our members as may feel disposed to take up the subject.   To those who, like our-selves, reside in the country, and have leisure to observe and to note their observations, the practice of keeping an annual record or register especially commends itself ; for besides being an agreeable occupation, it sooner or later furnishes the means for drawing important conclusions from trustworthy data.   Nor need it be con-sidered a selfish gratification, when we remember that one of the most delightful books ever published upon Natural History owed its origin to the author's habit of systematically noting every natural occurrence or phenomenon which seemed worthy of future consider-ation.   So important did such a practice appear to him that he remarked : " If stationary men would pay some attention to the districts in which they reside, and would publish their thoughts respecting the objects that surround them, from such materials might be drawn the most complete county histories, which are still wanting in many parts of the kingdom."   In this respect the historian of Selborne set an excellent example in his own district, which we in ours would do well to follow, though we can scarcely expect to do so with a like result.

The secret of success consists in knowing " how, when, and where to observe,"—a knowledge which all may attain, but which can be acquired only by method and by practice.

If the foregoing remarks should tend to remove some of the difficulties which seem at starting to beset the path of would-be observers (but which difficulties indeed are more apparent than real), it will be a gratification to me to have acquiesced in the request of our Secretary by submitting them for your consideration.

8.—MISCELLANEOUS NOTES AND OBSERVATIONS.

[Read 10th June, 1875.]

METEOROLOGY.

Rainfall at Watford and Hemel Hempstead.—The following reports of the rainfall at Watford House, Cassiobury, and Nash Mills, Hemel Hempstead, for the first quarter of the present year, have been received:—

LOCALITIES.	Watford House.	Cassiobury.	Nash Mills.
OBSERVERS.	Dr. Brett.	Mr. Swanston.	John Evans, Esq.
	In.	In.	In.
January	3·68	3·90	3·13
February	0·62	0·56	1·03
March	1·05	1·19	0·68
TOTALS......	5·35	5·65	4·84

From the 1873 Report of the Rainfall Committee of the British Association we are enabled to compute the monthly fall of rain at Nash Mills in the decade 1860-1869, the mean annual fall for this period, and the monthly per-centage of the annual fall, being given in this report. It will be found to be as follows:—January, 2·88; February, 1·58; March, 2·03; giving a total for the quarter of 6·49 inches. The rainfall (at Nash Mills) in the first three months of this year was, therefore, rather more than an inch and a half less than the average in the ten years referred to, the difference being due to the small amount of rain that fell in March.—ED.

GEOLOGY.

Mineral Spring at Watford.—In the ' National Gazetteer of Great Britain and Ireland,' under the head of Watford, in vol. xi., I read, " In 1689 a mineral spring was discovered here, the water of which becomes as black as ink when mixed with nut-galls." I should be glad if you would inquire of the members of the Watford Natural History Society if such a spring now exists, and where, and its properties, and the analysis of the water. If the spring no longer exists, what is the history of it ?—*A. T. Brett, M.D.*

BOTANY.

Botany of Hertfordshire.—During a short excursion in East Herts, in company with Mr. Britten, of the British Museum, I have found the true *Myosotis sylvatica* in profusion in several localities. This is as good as new to our list, as a former record could not be relied on. *Poterium muricatum*, another novelty, *Alopecurus fulvus*, and other good things, were met with. I have also been able to expunge a good many species from my list of extincts, nearly all of which I have seen growing myself. *Lepidium Draba* and *Silene conica* have both occurred as casuals, but the former will, as elsewhere, in all probability become established.

I have been able to extend the range of *Carum Bulbo-castanum* considerably to the westward, and am not without hope that it may yet be found in the Tring district.—*R. A. Pryor, B.A., Hatfield.*

ENTOMOLOGY.

Destruction of an Oak-tree by the Larvæ of the Goat Moth.—For the last three years I have observed with vexation that a fine oak-tree upon my farm, fit to square twenty or twenty-two inches and to live another century or two, has shown strange signs of premature decay. Knowing that there was no reason to suppose that the roots could have tapped any substrata calculated to injure the vitality of the timber, I recently made a careful examination of the trunk. The bark was withered and split in three or four places, as if the tree had been struck by lightning, but as the splits were not vertical or continuous, I could not look on lightning as the real cause. Careful search led to my noticing some small round holes, two at the base and one nearly up at the fork, about the size of a moderate bullet, round the orifices of which was a kind of black fetid oil, as if a greased and rusty auger had been driven in. From the appearance I assumed that the larvæ of the goat moth (*Cossus ligniperda*) had taken possession of the tree, and that its days were numbered. Accordingly, on Wednesday the 21st [April] I had it felled, and found that the east side of the bole was riddled by innumerable families of larvæ. Many dozens were killed on the spot, more withdrew into the trunk and cannot now be reached until the timber is broken up, and I have captured a number which I shall endeavour to rear through the pupa stage to the perfect moth. I fear that nearly all of them, however, are too young for successful operations; but should I succeed, I will send some specimens properly set up to the Society. It may not be generally known that this insect remains an exceptionally long period (three years) in the larva state, and that only three year olds are easily reared artificially. In this tree there must have been contemporaneously three generations, some specimens being less than half-an-inch long, and of the diameter of the smallest wire, others upwards of two inches, and as substantial as my little finger. The west side of the tree seems curiously free from the honey-combing operations of the grub. Can any members of the Society give me a reason for this?—*J. H. James, Kingswood, Watford.*

The Death's Head Moth at Watford.—The neighbourhood of Watford is singularly prolific of that fine insect the death's head moth (*Acherontia Atropos*), and search in any large potato field towards the end of July will probably be successful. With perhaps the exception of the poplar hawk moth (*Smerinthus Populi*), none of the larger of our indigenous moths are so easily reared from the larvæ as the death's head.—*J. H. James.*

CAMBRIDGESHIRE

A MAP OF

HERTFORDSHIRE

Showing the Districts into which is proposed to
divide the County for the illustration of its

BOTANICAL GEOGRAPHY.

R. A. Pryor B. A. F. L. S. 1875.

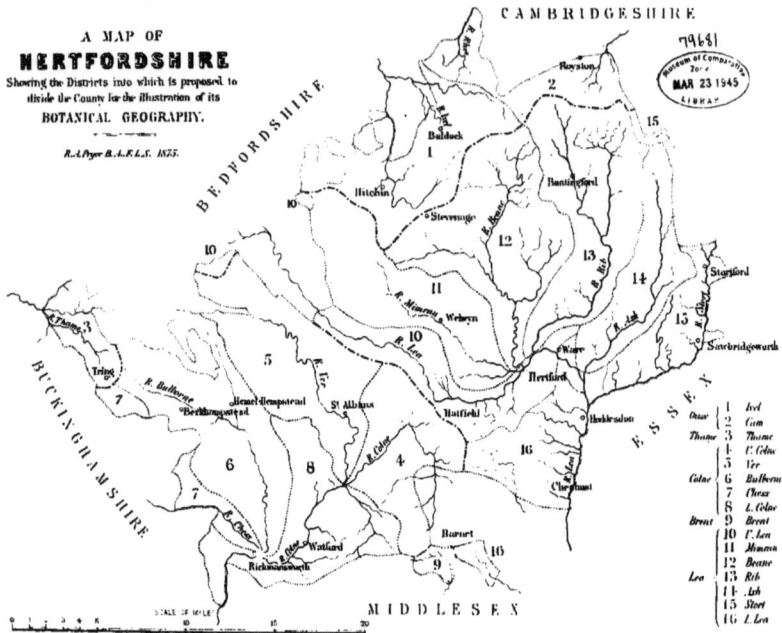

BEDFORDSHIRE

BUCKINGHAMSHIRE

ESSEX

MIDDLESEX

Royston
2
15
Baldock
1
Hitchin
10
Stevenage 5
12
13
14 Stortford
11
10
R. Minerva Welwyn
13
Tring 3
5
Ware
Sawbridgeworth
Berkhampstead 7
Hemel Hempstead
St Albans
Hertford
Hatfield
Hoddesdon
6
8
4
16
Cheshunt
Watford
Barnet
Rickmansworth
9
16

Draw | 1 *Ivel*
Thame | 2 *Cam*
 | 3 *Thame*
 | 4 *U. Colne*
 | 5 *Ver*
Colne | 6 *Bulborn*
 | 7 *Chess*
 | 8 *L. Colne*
Brent | 9 *Brent*
 | 10 *U. Lea*
 | 11 *Mimms*
 | 12 *Beane*
Lea | 13 *Rib*
 | 14 *Ash*
 | 15 *Stort*
 | 16 *L. Lea*

SCALE OF MILES
0 1 2 3 4 5   10   15   20

9.—ON THE BOTANICAL WORK OF THE PAST SEASON.

By R. A. PRYOR, B.A., F.L.S.

[Read 11th November, 1875.]

(PLATE I.)

AFTER a good deal of consideration I have found it necessary to make some material alteration alike in the number and limits of the botanical districts into which Hertfordshire has been divided, and to extend the system of river-basins, originally proposed by the late Mr. Coleman, to its fullest and most legitimate development, by adhering strictly to the natural drainage, and by making the tract of country drained by each stream a separate and independent division.

The number of districts thus arrived at will perhaps be considered too large; but although at first sight the arrangement may appear somewhat cumbersome, it will be found that the practical results more than counterbalance any seeming inconvenience; nor can there be any real disadvantage in carrying out what is believed to be a sound principle, to its furthest application.

The primary separation of the county is, of course, into the two basins of the Ouse and Thames—districts which, in the Floras of the future, will probably be entirely dissociated from each other, and united respectively to those portions of the same river-system with which they are naturally connected, but which are now scattered among the southern and eastern shires.

Beginning with that part of the basin of the Ouse which is included in Herts, and which, however, comprises little more than one-eighth of the county at large, we shall find that its western and larger portion is drained by several small streams, which combine to form the Ivel, and "move slowly together to *Biglesrade*, thence to *Temsford*, and there are united to the great *Owse*,"* a short distance below Bedford. The drainage of the other and smaller portion of this division, from Ashwell to Royston, is received by the feeders of the Cam, the principal of which, the Rhee,† "comes from a Source of Springs, which spin from small Veins out of a Rock of stone, on the East side of *Ashwell*, and joyning together in the space of two Furlongs, make a Torrent that drives a Mill, and on the sudden swells to a fair River, and overtaking the *Cam* leadeth to *Cambridge*,"‡ and is soon after-

* Chauncy, Hist. Antiq. Herts, pp. 2, 3.

† The names Rhee or Rhe, and Cam, seem to be applied indifferently to the Ashwell and Quendon streams, the two principal of those which unite to form the Graunt, as the Cambridge river is perhaps most properly called. The name Rhee is also, I believe, sometimes given locally to the stream which rises at Baldock, which is generally supposed to be the true Ivel. The words are said to mean in the Celtic respectively "swift" (Rhe) and "crooked or meandering" (Cam). If any weight is to be attached to this etymology, the Ashwell stream should be the true Cam. Cf. Babington, 'Flora of Cambridgeshire,' p. xxii.

‡ Chauncy, l.c.

wards lost in the ancient channel of the Ouse at a spot formerly called Harrimere, a little to the south of Ely.

It will be seen that the two districts thus defined do not correspond precisely with those of Messrs. Webb and Coleman. Their floras should be compared with those of Bedfordshire and Cambridge respectively.*

By far the larger portion of the county, however, belongs to the basin of the Thames, and is drained entirely by four of its affluents —the Thame, the Colne, the Brent, and the Lea.

Our connexion with the first of these is but slight. The waters of a small district to the north of Tring, which are mostly intercepted by the reservoirs that supply the Grand Junction Canal, unite in the Thistle Brook, in its present state an insignificant tributary of the Thame, but at one time perhaps a stream of greater importance. Prompted no doubt by some sort of patriotic enthusiasm, our great county historian saw in this petty streamlet one of the principal sources of the Thames itself. "The *Thame*," he says, "the most famous River of *England*, issues from three Heads in the Parish of *Tring*; the First rises in an Orchard, near the Parsonage house, the second in a place called *Dundell*, and the other proceeds from a spring named *Bulbourne*; which last Stream joyns the other Waters at a place called *New Mill*, whence all gliding together in one Current thro' *Puttenham* in this County, pass by *Ailesbury* . . . . to *Thame* . . (which borrowed its name from this River), hastneth away to *Dorchester* . . and then congratulates the *Isis*; but both emulating each other for the Name, and neither yielding, they are complicated into that of *Thamisis*."†

Apart from the direction of the drainage, the physical and geological features of this outlying tract confer upon it an interest quite disproportionate to its actual extent. Its botanical importance may be readily anticipated.

The Colne, which receives the drainage of the whole of the western division of the county, with the exception of the Tring peninsula, divides in the lower part of its course into numerous irregularly anastomosing channels, and "serving the Town of Uxbridge, it denominates that of Colnbrook, and . . disembogues itself into the Thames"‡ by several outlets in the neighbourhood of Staines.

---

* Of several interesting plants which are peculiar to the Ouse division, three —*Œnanthe Lachenalii*, Gmel, *Samolus Valerandi*, L., and *Carex distans*, L.— are especially deserving of notice, as being the only representatives in the county of that type of vegetation which is most at home in the neighbourhood of the sea, although not always necessarily exposed to its immediate influence, and which may be conveniently called semi-maritime. It would perhaps hardly be safe to conclude that their presence in this instance was connected with some former submergence of the fens. *Carex distans* has been doubted as a Hertfordshire plant, but Mr. Coleman's original specimens, which have been kindly placed at my disposal, have been submitted to re-examination by a competent authority, and are undoubtedly correctly named. It is to be feared, however, that it has become extinct in the only known locality, as Ashwell Common has been some years since drained, and entirely brought under cultivation.

† Chauncy, l.c.   ‡ *ib.*

A very small portion of Hertfordshire, about Totteridge, comes into the basin of the Brent,* and is thus especially connected with Middlesex. This is one of those rivers "which rise in the several Borders of this County, and immediately leave the same."† It eventually terminates at Brentford.

Finally, the Lea, "the greatest River" of those "which run thro' the Body of the County," of which it drains the central and eastern districts, fully half of its entire extent, after "severing the Counties of Essex and Middlesex, ... loses her name in her confluence with the Thames "‡ at Bow Creek, a little east of Blackwall.

We have thus six natural districts; but, leaving out of question the great inequality of their size, so large an amount of valuable work would be lost by their adoption as they stand (the carefully prepared lists of desiderata in the 'Flora Hertfordiensis' having been drawn up for double the number), that it seems at once the most logical and convenient course to break up the two largest, those of the Colne and Lea, and to take the basins of their several tributaries as ultimate divisions in their stead.

The complete scheme will then stand as follows:—

A. OUSE.	I. IVEL. . . .	1. IVEL.
	II. CAM	2. CAM.
B. THAMES.	III. THAME . .	3. THAME.
	IV. COLNE.	4. UPPER COLNE.
		5. VER.
		6. BULBORNE AND GADE.
		7. CHESS.
		8. LOWER COLNE.
	V. BRENT . .	9. BRENT.
	VI. LEA.	10. UPPER LEA.
		11. MIMRAM.
		12. BEANE.
		13. RIB.
		14. ASH.
		15. STORT.
		16. LOWER LEA.

The area of each district averages a little less than forty square miles.§

For the present purpose it will not be necessary to enter into any

* Although by far the smallest of our divisions, the flora is not the least characteristic, and is probably of a more southern type than that of the county generally. *Rumex palustris*, Sm., *Chenopodium glaucum*, L., *Actinocarpus Damasonium*, R. Br., with the naturalized *Lilium Martagon*, L., and *Acorus Calamus*, L. (with the exception of the *Lilium*, all Middlesex plants), are peculiar to this district.

† Chauncy, l.c.   ‡ *ib.*

§ Of generally recognised species, which are indubitably native, forty are at present known to occur in one only of the districts. It is worth noticing that twenty-two of these, or fifty-five per cent., are aquatic or palustral in their character, a ratio almost double of that which prevails in the flora as a whole; and that of a still larger number the localities are confined to quite the confines of the county.

further detail with regard to the county generally : it will suffice if I indicate roughly the circumscription of the district with which we are here more immediately concerned.

No. 8, Lower Colne, comprises the basin of the Colne and Ver, from their junction near Park Street, where " tho' the Verlume is much the greater" river, "yet the Colne usurps the Glory of her own name,"* to the point where the united stream leaves the county near Harefield ; *including* the country drained by the Elstree and Radlets brook, which belongs naturally to this division, and has no real connexion with the North Mimms district, whose waters flow in quite a different direction, and are mostly lost in swallow-holes in the Chalk, which thus absorbs the drainage of some twenty square miles of country ; † and *excluding* the valley of the Chess, and the lower part of that of the Gade, which were formerly combined with it to make up the Rickmansworth district.

The re-arrangement of the boundary-line will entail a certain amount of trouble, since it will be impossible to make use of the lists of common plants that have hitherto been recorded for " Rickmansworth," as it must remain uncertain whether they have been actually observed in the basin of the Lower Colne, or in one of its conterminous districts. Nor is this altogether to be regretted. A good knowledge of the general flora of one's own neighbourhood is of far more value than any possible success in the mere hunting after rarities. It is only by the careful study of the plants of every-day occurrence that we can hope to discriminate those that are less common with any degree of certainty. Thus, too, only shall we realize the force of Linnæus' maxim, " *Genus dabit characterem, non character genus*," by learning to know a plant as a whole, with a real existence, a vitality of its own, and not as a bare dead formality, depending solely on the technicalities of book descriptions, important as *their* study is at first ; for the broadest views can only be held with safety when they are founded upon a previous knowledge that will often lie under the imputation of narrowness from its faithful attention to minute accuracy of detail.

A wide, and I hope not uninteresting, field is thus open to your exertions. Of the botany of the valley of the Chess, with the exception of a few of the scarcer plants, nothing whatever is known.

After all, it may perhaps be objected that I have rather begged the question of the importance of river-basins as the foundations of botanical districts. But in truth no other method was available. Apart from the scientific objection on the score of their representing nothing in nature, there was no system of purely artificial lines that could be drawn, so as to present either any inherent convenience of their own, or to be in any way readily recognisable upon the surface of the country.

Nor are the hills any more likely to furnish useful divisions.

* Chauncy, l.c.
† Whitaker, Geology of the London Basin, part i. p. 224.

" In general," indeed, " the apparent hills of Hertfordshire are not ridges elevated above the general level of the surface ; but appear to be such only when viewed from the valleys of the rivers, whose waters have cut and furrowed deeply below the general level," * " for the wash of rain digs down where the ground is soft, and leaves hills or ridges where it is hard. And as a stream cuts through a hard stratum, the wash of rain is scooping out lateral valleys behind it," † as in the neighbourhood of Hitchin. " Now and then," to use Mr. Geikie's words, " a valley has been cut completely across the watershed, so as to draw its waters from the other side." ‡ Thus the Lea has cut a channel through the gorge of the chalk hills at Luton, and now draws its head-waters from the Bedfordshire levels. Thus, too, the Bulborne receives the drainage of the north-western face of the Aldbury Nowers, and were it not for the disturbing influence of the Grand Junction Canal, would probably encroach still further upon the country now drained by the Thame. For it must be confessed that the exact boundaries of our districts are not altogether permanently fixed, but change with the slow changes of the configuration of the earth's surface ; as from inequality of denudation owing to the greater hardness or softness of the soil, the basin of one river eats back into that of another, and gradually interferes with the drainage of an entire district. The ridges, then, " instead of being considered as barriers to the river, have been actually *formed* by the river by the abstraction of intervening masses," § and, except in that connexion, they cannot claim with us any importance as limiting lines.

Neither will a consideration of the geology of the county help us to any convenient method of division. For as, with the exception of a very limited tract on our northern borders, " the Chalk either forms the surface of all the county, or underlies it at no great depth," ‖ it would be necessary to fall back upon the superficial beds, an arrangement that it would be almost impossible to work out in practice.

It is not intended, however, for a moment, to undervalue the geological side of the question. M. Thurmann has pointed out, in his ' Essai de Phytostatique,' ¶ that the distribution of plants is influenced to a great extent by the mechanical properties of the subjacent rocks, and to a much less degree by their chemical composition. The Cretaceous rocks of England belong to his dysgeogenous series: they are very permeable to fluids, and but slightly absorbent, thus forming a dry shallow soil, whose chemical condition however, it can hardly be doubted, is the cause of at least some of the peculiarities of their flora. On the other hand, a deep open soil with moisture at no great distance from the surface is owing to the disintegration of eugeogenous rocks, which, as they are very absorbent, and but slightly permeable, are readily

* Coleman, Flora Hertfordiensis, p. xxxi.
† Greenwood, Rain and Rivers, p. 58. ‡ Nature, vol. xiii. p. 2.
§ Rain and Rivers, p. 59. ‖ Coleman, Flora Hertfordiensis, p. xxx.
¶ Cf. Flora of Middlesex, p. 357.

affected by atmospheric influences. Among them are included the
gravels and sands, and, in a still finer state of subdivision, the pure
loams and clays, these differences also resulting ultimately from
their chemical—siliceous or aluminous—composition. Our own
county affords examples of all of these, and the specialities of their
floras might be advantageously compared with those shown by M.
Thurmann's lists of characteristic plants.

Mr. Watson's opinion—and none can in a question of this kind
be deserving of greater weight—coincides to a certain extent with
that of M. Thurmann. "I doubt," he observes, "whether pre-
sently living plants can be properly said to have any geologic
relationships except indirectly through mineralogy; that is, through
the mechanical and chemical peculiarities of the ground on which
they grow." *   The same writer had already warned us of some of
the difficulties "which attend any attempts to draw up tabular
lists with a view to show the distribution of plants in connexion
with geologic strata." †   It requires indeed a very accurate knowledge of the botany of some considerable tract of country before we
can pronounce with certainty that a particular plant has any real
relation with a given subsurface. And if difficulties arise from
the occurrence of plants through some natural causes on formations
to which they do not strictly or truly belong, but on which they
chance only to be growing, they are still further complicated when
the introduction is owing, although unintentionally, to the operations of man. Thus when gravel or clay has been imported with
railway ballast into a chalk district, or *vice versâ*, the adventitious
plants may be noted, and, what is worse, recorded by an incurious
observer, as if equally native with the legitimate children of the
soil, side by side with which they are for the first time growing
—a confusion that has before now been the source of much error.

But I have detained you too long already from the professed
object of my paper.

With our actual progress botanically during the past season I
do not think we have much reason to be discontented.

I have first to put on record a few additions to the flora of the
county generally.

Perhaps the most noteworthy of these is the discovery of
Galium erectum, Huds., near Hitchin, where, however, as far as is
at present known, it grows but very sparingly. As it has been
reported for Bedfordshire, and has certainly been found in Cambridgeshire and Essex, its occurrence in the Ouse division of
Hertfordshire might perhaps have been fairly anticipated, and fits
in with its recorded distribution. It is a plant of considerable
critical interest, and is quite rare as a native in England. The
Hitchin specimens were unusually luxuriant.

Myosotis sylvatica, Hoffm., has been already brought before our
Society as one of the good things of the year, but, apart from the
beauty of its flowers, is of sufficient importance to merit a few

* Topographical Botany, p. 651.   † *ib.* p. 649.

words on the present occasion. It seems to be confined to the basin of the Ash, where, however, it occurs in profusion in several localities, and is undoubtedly native. This has often been confused with the large-flowered woodland variety of *M. arvensis*, Hoffm., and a previous record for another part of the county is on that account altogether untrustworthy. It has long been known as a plant of Essex, but has not been observed in any other of the adjacent counties.

Potamogeton mucronatus, Schrad. Specimens from Marsworth Reservoir, in the Thame district, have been submitted to Dr. Boswell (late Syme), who has confirmed the correctness of the name. This is the *P. compressus*, L., of Smith, and British botanists generally, but not of the last edition of Babington's 'Manual,' or of the 'Student's Flora.' It is a difficult species, and has been greatly confused with *P. pusillus* on the one hand, and *P. acutifolius*, Link., or *obtusifolius*, Koch., on the other. It has only hitherto been known, with any degree of certainty, to have occurred in six counties (Dorset, Surrey, Norfolk, Warwick, Salop, and Notts, cf. 'Top. Bot.' ii. p. 400), and the ripe fruit, which I have not yet been able to obtain, is a great desideratum. *P. lucens*, L., *perfoliatus*, L., *crispus*, L., *obtusifolius*, Koch., *pusillus*, L., *pectinatus*, L., *flabellatus*, Bab., and *Zannichellia palustris*, L., are all to be found in the same neighbourhood, with many other interesting aquatics, and some good Carices and other marsh plants: the whole district is worthy of more careful examination than it has yet received.*

Impatiens fulva, Nutt. Grand Junction Canal (near Hunton Bridge). Mr. J. E. Littleboy. I do not suppose the *Impatiens* at Hunton Bridge has originated directly from American seed, but rather that its appearance in our waters is closely connected with the whole history of the first introduction of the plant into Britain, and its gradual extension throughout the Thames basin. It will be found to afford an excellent "example of the interdependence of the parts of a river-system with reference to their floras."† I have borrowed the following particulars principally from the 'Flora of Middlesex.' A North American species, which is "now so thoroughly and perfectly naturalized as to give no suspicion of its exotic origin, it almost certainly originated in the gardens of Albury Park, Surrey. A small stream, the Tillingbourne, flows through these gardens, and runs into the Wey above Guildford; and this in turn flows into the Thames a little above Shepperton. In this way the seeds have been carried by the water-current, and by barges, etc., throughout the Thames Valley district."‡

---

* There is a specimen of *Cardamine amara* labelled from Tring, and collected about forty years back, in the herbarium of Professor Babington at Cambridge.

† Flora of Middlesex, p. xix.

‡ *ib.* p. 71. This kind of naturalization is not confined to the vegetable kingdom. *Dreissena polymorpha*, Van Ben., a byssiferous freshwater mussel, which is supposed to have been originally introduced from Russia on logs of timber, has now spread itself through many of the navigable waters of England, and may

It is thought to have been first noticed in the neighbourhood of Albury, in 1822, by the late Mr. John Stuart Mill, the celebrated logician and metaphysician, who was in early life an enthusiastic field botanist and had devoted considerable attention to the flora especially of Surrey. In 1838 it had already become established on the banks of the Thames,* and soon extended itself along those of its Middlesex tributaries. It has been noticed for some years past (before 1869),† by the side of the Grand Junction Canal at Harefield ; and I do not doubt but that it was conveyed thence to the locality in which we owe its detection to the acuteness of Mr. Littleboy. It has been recorded for Wilts, Sussex, Surrey, Middlesex, and Bucks,‡ and we may now add Hertfordshire to the list. It is said to be naturalized also in Scotland, on the banks of the Clyde.§ I do not know anything of its continental distribution;‖ but its application, both internally and externally, has recently been suggested in India, by Dr. Reid, as a sovereign cure for spider and snake bites (' Report on Sanitary Measures in India in 1873-4,' lately issued from the India Office), and in default of further information, it is perhaps not altogether unreasonable to conclude that it may have found its way also into some of our Asiatic dependencies.¶ The dispersive power of the seeds in *Impatiens fulra* is shared by the whole genus to which it belongs, and by many of its more immediate allies; the brown-leaved oxalis, *O. corniculata rubra*, so common in gardens, will afford a familiar instance, and the separation of the carpels from the axis in our native geraniums, belonging to the same natural family, will furnish a second example of a somewhat similar kind. There is another species of the same genus, *Impatiens parviflora*, DC., a native of Russia, which has recently made its appearance in several parts of the country, and is likely to become an established weed. It has been noticed in our county, at Essendon, by Mr. R. T. Andrews, of Hertford. It is not improbable, indeed, in the opinion of many botanists, that *I. Noli-me-tangere*, L., although so long reckoned among our indigenous plants, has no more real claim to be held a genuine native than its American congener; if anywhere, "it must be so very locally ; say in North Wales and Westmoreland."**

Among other more or less naturalized species, *Poterium muricatum*, Spach, which is not uncommon amongst sown sainfoin, has

---

often be found adhering to lock gates. It was first noticed by Mr. J. C. Sowerby in the Commercial Docks in 1824, and has been found, I believe, even in the supply pipes of the London water companies. I do not know whether we have it in Herts.

* Irvine, Lond. Flora, p. 171.   † Fl. Middlesex, p. 71.
‡ Watson, Top. Bot. i. p. 112.   § Student's Flora, p. 80.
‖ De Candolle (Géog. Bot.) does not give it as occurring on the Continent.
¶ It seems more probable that it was proposed to make use of the imported plant.
** Watson, Top. Bot. ii. p. 608.

seemingly established itself in the borders of fields, where it has been formerly introduced with the crop, and on railway banks. It is strange that so conspicuous a plant should not have been noticed before the present season. It is often accompanied by *Bromus arvensis*, L., and *B. commutatus*, Schrad.—the latter has usually been held a native, the former as a mere casual; but both, I think, occupy an intermediate position between the truly indigenous *B. mollis*, L. (almost ubiquitous in dry situations), or *B. racemosus*, L. (confined with us to damp meadows in the lowlands), and a grass of but a season's duration like their congener *B. secalinus*, L., which seems quite unable to obtain any permanent footing in the soil. *Bromus arvensis*, of which a single stray specimen only had previously been noticed in the county, I have seen quite naturalised, to all appearance, by hedge-banks and on the sides of fields, and that too in our own district. It is probably of much more recent introduction than *B. commutatus*, but both are likely to make good their claim to the title of colonist. *Plantago Timbali*, Jord., is perhaps not very uncommon amongst clover, but occurs only where sown. *Barkhausia taraxacifolia*, DC., however, originally introduced with grass seeds, will probably be more permanent : it has been remarked in increasing quantity for the last three or four years at Rush Green, near Hertford. *Lepidium Draba*, L., has also been observed in two widely separated localities, and, from the great depth to which the roots run, is not unlikely to become a troublesome weed, as it is almost impossible to eradicate it. Both these last appear to be spreading rapidly in many parts of the South of England. *Lepidium ruderale*, L., is another plant in the same category.

But it would be alike tedious and unprofitable to attempt any complete account of the numerous exotics that have recently made their appearance in the county. The following list of introduced plants growing during the past summer on a siding by the railway at Hatfield, where manure had been unloaded, will give some idea of their number and variety.

Fumaria densiflora, DC.	*Panicum miliaceum*, L.
Sinapis nigra, L.	„ *capillare*, L.
Camelina sativa, Crantz.	*Setaria viridis*, P.B.
Linum usitatissimum, L.	„ *glauca*, P.B.
Centaurea Cyanus, L.	*Phalaris canariensis*, L.
Echinospermum Lappula, Lehm.	*Agrostis Spica-Venti*, L.
Solanum Lycopersicum, L.	*Bromus secalinus*, L.
Galeopsis latifolia, Hoffm.	„ *arvensis*, L.
Polygonum lapathifolium, L.	*Hordeum pratense*, L.
„ *maculatum*, Dyer.	*Secale cereale*, L.
Panicum Crus-Galli, L.	*Lolium italicum*, A.Br.

Amongst these, however, several usually indigenous species are included. There is one point of view, indeed, from which some importance is attaching to the first notice of these aliens: some of them may very possibly become so far established, that in the future they will be not readily distinguishable from the real constituents of the flora. Thus a record of their present occurrence as *casuals* will be hereafter available towards clearing up this obscurity.

Carduus tenuiflorus, Curt. (*C. pycnocephalus*, Jacq., of Hooker's 'Student's Flora'). In profusion and perfectly established at Boxmoor, extending for some distance by the roadside, and on ditchbanks in many places, having quite the air of an indigenous plant. Strangely enough, however, it is quite absent from the railway embankment, and its introduction is apparently owing to the traffic on the Grand Junction Canal.

Mentha citrata, Ehrh., has been noticed at Northaw, growing abundantly in and about a pond on the village green. This seems to be very rare in England in a quasi-wild state, and is not, I believe, common in cultivation; at least, I have never so seen it myself. It is a distinct-looking plant, with a strong odour of bergamot, very different from the scent of any other mint.*

It would take up too much time were I to go through the subspecies and varieties enumerated in the paper that I had the honour to read to you during our last session; but I may mention that I have been able to strike off from the roll of possibly extinct plants given in the second part of that paper the following species, most of which I have seen myself in a growing state: where this has not been the case, I am indebted for fresh specimens to the kindness of several correspondents, including some of our own members.

Ranunculus hirsutus, Curt.	*Limosella aquatica*, L.
Dentaria bulbifera, L.	*Scutellaria minor*, L.
Teesdalia nudicaulis, R.Br.	*Myosotis repens*, Don.
Stellaria glauca, With.	*Pinguicula vulgaris*, L.
Astragalus hypoglottis, L.	*Anagallis tenella*, L.
„ *glycyphyllus*, L.	*Polygonum minus*, Huds.
Potentilla Comarum, Nestl.	*Thesium humifusum*, DC.
Geum rivale, L.	*Potamogeton rufescens*, Schrad.
Sedum dasyphyllum, L.	„ *obtusifolius*, Koch.
Smyrnium Olusatrum, L.	*Juncus diffusus*, Hoppe.
Valerianella Auricula, DC.	*Eleocharis acicularis*, R. Br.
Filago gallica, L.	*Scirpus sylvaticus*, L.
Senecio campestris, DC.	*Carex acuta*, L.
Gentiana campestris, L.	*Aira flexuosa*, L.

Myriophyllum alterniflorum, DC., was inserted in the list of doubtful plants on account of its having been queried in 'Topographical Botany.' I have observed it this year in many of the localities assigned to it in the 'Flora Hertfordiensis,' and there can be no doubt that the name was correctly given.

So much for the county at large.

With regard to our own district, as limited above, the follow-

* This is, however, in all probability "*M. Aquatica* γ. *glabrata*, Koch," of Fl. Hts. p. 220, if the specimen was correctly referred to Koch's plant. Cf. 'Synops. Flo. Germ.' p. 550 (ed. i.).

ing species, sub-species, or varieties have not previously been put on record:—

Ranunculus floribundus, Bab.	*Cratægus oxyacanthoides*, Thuill.
„ *peltatus*, Fries.	*Sedum Fabaria*, Koch.
„ *pseudo-fluitans*, Syme.	*Callitriche pedunculata*, DC.
Papaver Lamottei, Bor.	*Epilobium obscurum*, Schreb.
Cardamine hirsuta, L.	*Galium elongatum*, Presl.
Lepidium ruderale, L.	*Valeriana sambucifolia*, Mikan.
„ *campestre*, L.	*Arctium majus*, Schk.
Viola Riviniana, Reich.	„ *minus*, Schk.
Silene puberula, Jord.	*Nardosmia fragrans*, Reich.
Arenaria leptoclados, Guss.	*Filago spathulata*, Presl.
Sagina ciliata, Fr.	*Lactuca virosa*, L.
Spergula arvensis, L.	*Rumex pulcher*, L.
„ *vulgaris*, Bœnn.	„ *pratensis*, M. & K.
Scleranthus biennis, Reut.	*Atriplex deltoidea*, Bab.
Rubus rhamnifolius, W. & N.	*Salix Woolgariana*, Borr.
„ *Lindleianus*, Lees.	*Potamogeton flabellatus*, Bab.
„ *corylifolius*, Sm.	*Carex acuta*, L.
„ *pallidus*, Weihe.	„ *paludosa*, Good.
Poterium muricatum, Spach.	*Glyceria pedicellata*, Towns.
Rosa dumalis, Bechst.	„ *plicata*, Fries.
„ *urbica*, Leman.	*Bromus racemosus*, L.
„ *tomentella*, Leman.	

Among the Rickmansworth plants that were mentioned in my previous paper as requiring examination—

Potentilla Comarum, Nestl, is still to be found on the Common Moor in some plenty.

Rubus leucostachys, Sm., the true plant, occurs at Rickmansworth.

Limosella aquatica, L., is still to be found at Elstree, besides the new station at Bricket Wood given in Mr. Cottam's paper in the first part of our 'Transactions.' In the former locality it is accompanied by *Eleocharis acicularis*, R. Br., and *Alopecurus fulvus*, Sm.

Festuca elatior, L. The Rickmansworth plant is correctly named. Very characteristic specimens occur by the side of the railway on the Common Moor.

While we may thus perhaps congratulate ourselves on the results of the work of the past season, some of which I have endeavoured, however imperfectly, to lay before you, it will be seen that much more remains to be accomplished.

I venture therefore earnestly to invite your co-operation, in the hope that amidst the various claims upon your attention, the investigation of which is amongst the objects of this Society, the Botany of the Watford District may not be forgotten. I have now only, in concluding, to apologize for having so long trespassed upon your kindness, and to express a regret that I have not had anything more worthy to place before you.

APPENDIX.

Considerable progress has been made in working out the distribution of the more recent segregates (*vide* 'Transactions,' vol. i. pt. i.

p. 18). Since the date of the Rev. R. H. Webb's concluding paper on " Additional Species and Localities," originally published in the 'Herts Mercury,' but reprinted in the 'Journal of Botany' for June, 1872 (vol. i. N.s. p. 182), the following sub-species, varieties, etc., which were not previously on record for Hertfordshire, have been noticed by different observers in the county. Some few have appeared in subsequent numbers of the same Journal, but the majority are now published for the first time.

Ranunculus peltatus, Fr.
  „ *radians*, Rev.
  „ *submersus*, Godr.
  „ *pseudo-fluitans*, Syme.
  „ *trichophyllus*, Chaix.
  „ *Drouetii*, Schultz.
  „ *hederaceus*, L., v. *homœophyllus*, Ten.
  „ *Ficaria*, L., v. *incumbens*, F. Schultz.
Caltha Guerangerii, Bor.
Papaver Lamottei, Bor.
Fumaria Borœi, Jord.
Erophila brachycarpa, Jord.
Viola hirta, L., v. *calcarea*, Bab.
  „ *permixta*, Jord.
  „ *sepincola*, Jord.
  „ *Riviniana*, Reich.
  „ *Reichenbachiana*, Jord.
Polygala vulgaris, L. (vera).
  „ *oxyptera*, Reich.
  „ *depressa*, Wend.
Arenaria sphærocarpa, Ten.
  „ *leptoclados*, Guss.
Spergula arvensis, L.
  „ *vulgaris*, Bœnng.
Scleranthus biennis, Reut.
Erodium commixtum, Jord.
  „ *triviale*, Jord.
Rosa canina, L., v. *lutetiana*, Leman.
  „ „ *dumalis*, Beckst.
  „ „ *tomentella*, Leman.
Cratægus oxyacanthoides, Thuill.
  „ *laciniata*, Ster.
Callitriche hamulata, Kuetz.
Epilobium tetragonum, L. (verum).
  „ *obscurum*, Schreb.
Apium nodiflorum, Reich., v. *longipedunculatum*, Schultz.
Galium palustre, L. (verum).
  „ *elongatum*, Presl.
  „ *Witheringii*, Sm.
Valeriana Mikanii, Syme.
  „ *sambucifolia*, Mikan.
Arctium majus, Schk.
  „ *nemorosum*, Lej.

Arctium intermedium, Lange.
  „ *minus*, Schk.
Taraxacum erythrospermum, Audrz.
Crepis agrestis, W. K.
Symphytum officinale, L., v. *patens*, Sibth.
Odontites verna, Reich.
  „ *serotina*, Reich.
Thymus Serpyllum, L. (verus).
  „ *Chamædrys*, Fries.
Galeopsis canescens, Schultz.
  „ *bifida*, Bœnn.
Polygonum amphibium, L., v. *terrestre*, Auct.
  „ *biforme*, Wahl.
  „ *aviculare*, L. (verum).
  „ *arenastrum*, Bor.
  „ *microspermum*, Jord.
  „ *rurivagum*, Jord.
  „ *Convolvulus*, L., v. *pseudodumetorum*, Wats.
Chenopodium polyspermum, L., v. *acutifolium*, Sm.
  „ *rubrum*, L., v. *pseudobotryodes*, Wats.
Atriplex hastata, Huds. (vera).
  „ *deltoidea*, Bab.
Salix purpurea, L., v. *ramulosa*, Borr.
Orchis latifolia, L. (vera).
  „ *incarnata*, L.
Epipactis latifolia, Auct.
  „ *media*, Auct.
  „ *Violacea*, Dur.
Iris Bastardi, Bor.
Alisma lanceolatum, With.
Potamogeton lucens, L., v. *acuminatus*, Schum.
Carex flava, L. (vera).
  „ *lepidocarpa*, Tausch.
Phleum præcox, Jord.
Agrostis pumila, Lightft.
Glyceria pedicillata, Towns.
Asplenium Filix-fœmina, Bernh. (verum).
  „ *rhæticum*, Roth.

The following introduced plants, aliens, casuals, waifs from cultivation, etc., which have been observed for the most part during the same period, are also new to the county list.

Adonis autumnalis, L.
Eruca sativa, Lamk.
Lunaria biennis, Mœnch.
Camelina sylvestris, Wallr.
Lepidium ruderale, L.
   „   sativum, L.
   „   Draba, L.
Neslia paniculata, Desv.
Raphanus sativus, L.
   „   caudatus, L. (?).
Erucaria latifolia, DC.
Rapistrum rugosum, All.
Silene conica, L.
   „   dichotoma, Ehrh.
   „   quinque-vulnera, L.
Hypericum elatum, Ait.
Malva parviflora, L.
Geranium striatum, L.
Impatiens fulva, Nutt.
   „   parviflora, DC.
Ulex Gallii, Planch.
Medicago maculata, Sibth.
   „   denticulata, Willd.
   „   apiculata, Willd.
Melilotus parviflora, Desf.
Trifolium incarnatum, L.
   „   hybridum, L.
Lathyrus sphæricus, Retz.
   „   latifolius, L.
Poterium muricatum, Spach.
Epilobium brachycarpum, Leight.

Chærophyllum sativum, Lamk.
Coriandrum sativum, L.
Centranthus ruber, DC.
Valerianella eriocarpa, Desv.
Dipsacus Fullonum, L.
Carduus tenuiflorus, Curt.
Nardosmia fragrans, Reich.
Helianthus annuus, L.
Anthemis tinctoria, L.
Doronicum plantagineum, L.
Senecio viscosus, L.
Barkhausia taraxacifolia, DC.
Campanula Medium, L.
   „   rapunculoides, L.
   „   patula, L.
Symphytum, sp.
Asperugo procumbens, L.
Omphalodes verna, Mœnch.
Plantago Timbali, Jord.
Linaria purpurea, L.
Salvia sylvestris, L.
   „   verticillata, L.
Galeopsis latifolia, Hoffm.
Cyclamen hederæfolium, Willd.
Rumex sylvestris, Wallr.
Salsola Kali, L.
Spinacia spinosa, Mœnch.
Mercurialis annua, L.
Cannabis sativa, L.
Panicum miliaceum, L.
   „   capillare, L.

There are a few other species which have been observed by different botanists in the county, and of which specimens are preserved in the public herbaria, or which have been mentioned as Hertfordshire plants by some standard authority on British botany, but which are unnoticed in the writings of Messrs. Webb and Coleman. Such are—

Papaver Lecoqii, Lamot.
Rubus pygmæus, Weihe.
Galium approximatum, Gr. & Godr.
Picris stricta, Jord.
Xanthium spinosum, L.

Cuscuta hassiaca, Pfeiff.
Mentha pubescens, Willd.
Amaranthus retroflexus, L.
Chenopodium glaucum, L.

Papaver Lecoqii is not uncommon in the chalky parts of the county. The others are mostly rare and critical forms, or have no claim to be reckoned as natives.

10.—List of Works on the Geology of Hertfordshire.

By William Whitaker, B.A., F.G.S.,

Of the Geological Survey of England, Editor of the 'Geological Record.'

Communicated by J. Hopkinson, Hon. Sec.

[Read 9th December, 1875.]

The following list is one of a series, the corresponding lists for Cambridgeshire, Cornwall, Devonshire, the Hampshire Basin, Warwickshire, and Wiltshire having already been published by local societies, besides some others in Geological Survey Memoirs. etc. It is for the greater part selected from that in vol. iv. of the 'Memoirs of the Geological Survey,' which refers to a much larger area. There may be other works named in the latter, however, which refer in some measure to Hertfordshire, besides those here given, but which could not be fairly entered without a re-examination of their contents, a task involving great labour. Some additions have been made to the older list, bringing it up to the end of 1873, after which year the newly established 'Geological Record' will give full information of works on English Geology, rendering needless any further efforts of my own.

Although a small county, and with a small range of formations, yet a good deal has been written on the Geology of Hertfordshire. The chief interest perhaps is centred in the Lower Tertiary beds, for our detailed knowledge of which we are so largely indebted to the papers of Professor Prestwich, published in the 'Quarterly Journal of the Geological Society.' The Geological Survey in its progress through the London Basin has indeed, as far as general conclusions are concerned, done little more than register the accuracy of Prof. Prestwich's observations and the soundness of his views, filling in of course a vast amount of detail and correcting some doubtful points.

The Glacial Drift is another interesting feature of the county, and all who have studied that wonderful and varying series must bear witness to the good work done in its minute investigation over the whole East of England by Mr. Searles V. Wood, jun.

Having been to a great extent brought up in Hertfordshire, at the St. Albans Grammar School, it has always been a pleasure to me to have had a share in the Geological Survey of the county, and this pleasure is increased when I am able in any way to help the study of my science therein.

1756.

1. Parsons, Dr. J. Remarks upon a petrified Echinus . . . found at Bunnan's Land in the parish of Bovingdon in Hertfordshire. *Phil. Trans.* vol. xlix. p. 155.

1804.

2. Young, A. General View of the Agriculture of Hertfordshire. (With a Map and an Account of the Soils.) 8vo. *Lond.*

1819.

3. SMITH, W. Geological View and Section in Essex and Hertfordshire, and of the Country between London and Cambridgeshire.

1822.

4. SOWERBY, J. On a Fossil Shell of a fibrous structure, the fragments of which occur abundantly in the Chalk Strata and in the flints accompanying it. (Royston.) *Trans. Linn. Soc.* vol. xiii. p. 453.

1836.

5. MITCHELL, Dr. J. On the Beds immediately above the Chalk in the Counties near London. *Phil. Mag.* ser. 3, vol. ix. p. 356.

1837.

6. MITCHELL, Dr. J. An Account of a Well at Beaumont Green in the County of Hertford. *Proc. Geol. Soc.* vol. ii. p. 551.

7. MORRIS, J. On the Strata usually termed Plaistic Clay. (Section at Northaw.) *Proc. Geol. Soc.* vol. ii. p. 450.

1838.

8. MITCHELL, Dr. J. On the Drift from the Chalk and the Strata below the Chalk in the Counties of Norfolk, Suffolk, Essex, Cambridge, Huntingdon, Bedford, Hertford, and Middlesex. *Proc. Geol. Soc.* vol. iii. p. 3.

1840.

9. STEPHENSON, R. London and Westminster Water Company. Report (Watford, etc.). 8vo. *London.*

1841.

10. CLUTTERBUCK, Rev. J. C. A Letter to Sir J. Sebright on the injurious consequences likely to accrue to a portion of the County of Hertford if the London and Westminster Water Company should carry into effect their project of supplying the Metropolis with water from the valley of the River Colne. 8vo. *Watford and London.*

11. STEPHENSON, R. London, Westminster, and Metropolitan Water Company. Second Report (Watford, etc.). 8vo. *London.*

1842.

12. CLUTTERBUCK, Rev. J. C. Observations on the Periodical Drainage and Replenishment of the Subterraneous Reservoir in the Chalk Basin of London. *Proc. Inst. Civ. Eng.* vol. i. p. 155.

13. CLUTTERBUCK, Rev. J. C. Supply of Water to the Metropolis from the Valley of the Colne. A few words in answer to Mr. Stephenson's Second Report. 8vo. *Watford.*

1843.

14. CLUTTERBUCK, Rev. J. C. Continuation of the paper of the year before (No. 12). *Proc. Inst. Civ Eng.* vol. ii. p. 156.

15. STOCKEN, W. On Drifted Remains found in Gravel, near Radwell, Herts (N. of Baldock). *Geologist,* p. 64.

1847.

16. IBBETSON, Capt. L. L. B.   Sections shown by the cuttings on the London and Birmingham Railway. No. 10, Cheddington to Northchurch; No. 11, Northchurch to Watford. *MS. Drawings in the Mining Record Office.*

1850.

17. CLUTTERBUCK, Rev. J. C.   On the Periodical Alternations and Progressive Permanent Depression of the Chalk Water-level under London. *Proc. Inst. Civ. Eng.* vol. ix. p. 151.

18. PATEN, R.   Appendix on the Bushey Well in Mr. S. C. Homersham's 'Report to the Directors of the London (Watford) Spring-water Company.' Ed. 3. 8vo. *London.*

19. PRESTWICH, J.   On the Structure of the Strata between the London Clay and the Chalk. Part I. The Basement-bed of the London Clay. *Quart. Journ. Geol. Soc.* vol. vi. p. 252.

20. PRESTWICH, J.   On the Geological Conditions which determine the Relative Value of the Water-bearing Strata of the Tertiary and Cretaceous Series, and on the Probability of finding in the Lower Members of the Latter, beneath London, Fresh and Large Sources of Water-supply, etc. *Trans. Roy. Inst. Brit. Architects.* 4to.

1851.

21. PRESTWICH, J.   A Geological Inquiry respecting the Water-bearing Strata of the Country around London, etc. 8vo. *Lond.*

22. TRIMMER, J.   On the Agricultural Geology of England and Wales. *Journ. Roy. Agric. Soc.* vol. xii. p. 445.

1854.

23. PRESTWICH, J.   On the Structure of the Strata between the London Clay and the Chalk. Part II. The Woolwich and Reading Series. *Quart. Journ. Geol. Soc.* vol. x. p. 75.

1855.

24. BARLOW, P. W.   On some peculiar features of the Water-bearing Strata of the London Basin. *Proc. Inst. Civ. Eng.* vol. xiv. p. 42.

25. HOMERSHAM, S. C.   The Chalk Strata considered as a source for the supply of Water to the Metropolis. *Journ. Soc. Arts,* vol. iii. No. 115, p. 168.

26. PRESTWICH, J.   On the Origin of the Sand- and Gravel-Pipes in the Chalk of the London Tertiary District. (With a Section from the Hills south of High Wycombe to the Chalk-pit at Harefield Copper-mills, near Rickmansworth.) *Quart. Journ. Geol. Soc.* vol. xi. p. 64.

1856.

27. HUGHES, S.   A Treatise on Waterworks for the supply of Cities and Towns, with a Description of the principal Geological Formations of England as influencing the supplies of Water. 8vo. *London.*

1858.

28. DENTON, J. B.   Hinxworth Drainage. (Analyses of Soils.) *Journ. Roy. Agric. Soc.* vol. xx. p. 273.

29. PRESTWICH, J.　On the Occurrence of the Boulder Clay, or Northern Clay Drift, at Bricket Wood, near Watford.　*Geologist*, vol. i. p. 241.

1861.

30. SEELEY, H.　Notes on Cambridge Palæontology.　1. Some new Upper Greensand Bivalves.　*Ann. and Mag. Nat. Hist.* ser. 3, vol. vii. p. 116.　[Ashwell, pp. 118, 119, 121, 122.]　2. Some new Gasteropods from the Upper Greensand.　*Ibid.* p. 281.　[Ashwell, p. 282.]　3. Some new Upper Greensand Echinoderms. *Ibid.* vol. viii. p. 16.　[Ashwell, pp. 17, 20, 23.]

31. WHITAKER, W.　On the "Chalk-rock," the Topmost Bed of the Lower Chalk, in Berkshire, Oxfordshire, Buckinghamshire, etc.　*Quart. Journ. Geol. Soc.* vol. xvii. p. 166.

32. WHITAKER, W., and R. TRENCH.　The N.E. part of Sheet 7 of the Map of the Geological Survey of England; scale one inch to a mile.　(Berkhampstead, Watford, St. Albans.)　New Edition, with Drifts added, by H. W. BRISTOW, W. WHITAKER, H. B. WOODWARD, F. J. BENNETT, W. A. E. USSHER, and J. H. BLAKE, in 1872, but dated 1871.

1862.

33. WHITAKER, W.　On the Westerly End of the London Basin ; on the Westerly Thinning of the Lower Eocene Beds in that Basin ; and on the Greywethers of Wiltshire.　*Quart. Journ. Geol. Soc.* vol. xviii. p. 258.　[Herts, pp. 269, 271, 272.]

1864.

34. CLUTTERBUCK, Rev. J. C.　Agricultural Notes on Hertfordshire.　(Physical Geography, Swallow-holes, the Water-level in the Chalk, etc.)　*Journ. Roy. Agric. Soc.* vol. xxv. p. 302.

35. EVERSHED, H.　Agriculture of Hertfordshire.　(Sketch Geological Map and Account of Soils.)　*Journ. Roy. Agric. Soc.* vol. xxv. p. 269.

36. WHITAKER, W.　The Geology of Parts of Middlesex, Hertfordshire, etc.　Memoir on Sheet 7 of the Geological Survey Map.

1865.

37. BAUERMAN, H., and W. WHITAKER.　The S.E. part of Sheet 46, S.W. of the Map of the Geological Survey of England.　Scale, one inch to a mile.　(Tring.)

38. CLUTTERBUCK, Rev. J. C.　Water Supply.　(Notes of wells, etc.)　*Journ. Roy. Agric. Soc.* ser. 2, vol. i. p. 271.

39. LATHAM, B.　On the Supply of Water to Towns.　(Well-sections.)　*Trans. Soc. Eng.* vol. iii. p. 199.

40. PRESTWICH, J.　Part of the South-eastern Sheet of the "Greenough Map."　*Geol. Soc.*

41. SEELEY, H.　On Ammonites from the Cambridge Greensand. *Ann. and Mag. Nat. Hist.* ser. 3, vol. xvi. p. 225.　[Ashwell.]

42. WOOD, S. V., jun.　A Map of the Upper Tertiaries in the Counties of Norfolk, Suffolk, Essex, Middlesex, Hertford, Cambridge, Huntingdon, and Bedford (with Sections and Remarks in 8vo.).　*Privately printed.*

1866.

43. GREEN, A. H. On Supposed Faults in the Drift-gravel at Hitchin. *Geol. Mag.* vol. iii. p. 572.

44. SALTER, J. W. On the Faults in the Drift-gravel at Hitchin. Herts. *Quart. Journ. Geol. Soc.* vol. xxii. p. 565.

1867.

45. SALTER, J. W. (Letter on) Faults in the Drift at Hitchin. *Geol. Mag.* vol. iv. p. 40.

46. WHITAKER, W. On Subaërial Denudation, and on Cliffs and Escarpments of the Chalk and the Lower Tertiary Beds. (Part 2.) *Geol. Mag.* vol. iv. p. 483. [Tertiary Escarpment, etc., in Herts, pp. 486, 487.]

47. WHITAKER, W., and F. J. BENNETT. Part of Sheet 46, N.E. of the Map of the Geological Survey of England. Scale, one inch to a mile. (Baldock, Hitchin.)

48. WHITAKER, W., T. McK. HUGHES, A. H. GREEN, W. TOPLEY, and R. H. TIDDEMAN. Sheet 46, S.E. (all but N.W corner) of the Map of the Geological Survey of England. Scale, one inch to a mile. (Hatfield, Hertford, Stevenage.)

49. WOOD, S. V., jun. On the Structure of the Post-Glacial Deposits of the South-east of England. *Quart. Journ. Geol. Soc.* vol. xxiii. p. 394.

50. WOOD, S. V., jun. (Letter on) the Faults in the Drift at Hitchin, etc. *Geol. Mag.* vol. iv. p. 37.

1868.

51. HUGHES, T. McK, On the Two Plains of Hertfordshire and their Gravels. *Quart. Journ. Geol. Soc.* vol. xxiv. p. 283.

52. WHITAKER, W. The N.W. corner of Sheet 1, N.W. of the Map of the Geological Survey. Scale, one inch to a mile. (Hoddesdon.)

53. WHITAKER, W. Sheet 79 of the Horizontal Sections of the Geological Survey of England. Scale, 6 inches to a mile. Across the London Basin from Beddington . . . to near Hemel Hempstead.

54. WOOD, S. V., jun. On the Pebble-beds of Middlesex, Essex, and Herts. *Quart. Journ. Geol. Soc.* vol. xxiv. p. 464.

1871.

55. HOPKINSON, J. Excursion to Watford, June 23rd, 1870. *Proc. Geol. Assoc.* vol. ii. No. 2, p. 43.

1872.

56. WALKER, H. On the Glacial Drifts of North London. *Proc. Geol. Assoc.* vol. ii. No. 7, p. 289.

57. WHITAKER, W. The Geology of the London Basin. Part 1. The Chalk and the Eocene Beds of the Southern and Western Tracts. *Mem. Geol. Survey,* vol. iv.

1873.

58. HOPKINSON, J. Excursion to Watford, April 13th, 1872. *Proc. Geol. Assoc.* vol. iii. No. 2, p. 65.

11.—A Few Words about our Local Ferns.

By John E. Littleboy.

[Read 11th November, 1875.]

Of late years no branch of Botany has been more popular, I might almost say fashionable, than the study of Ferns. I do not know that the Fern mania rages quite so determinately at present as it did some ten years ago, but it is yet impossible to visit either Wales or Scotland without meeting, at almost every turn, enterprising ladies, trowel in hand, laden with baskets containing their favourites, intent, no doubt, on the creation of charming little ferneries in certain garden corners far off in England. It is rather amusing to notice how carefully the very commonest varieties are not unfrequently bought from the fern-women at Llandudno and other popular Welsh watering-places, and brought home with considerable trouble, to be planted in garden ferneries, when they might have been procured far more readily, and certainly at considerably less expense, in the nearest lane or hedgerow.

After all, it matters but little. To those who are unable to distinguish the different varieties, the commonest fern that grows is just as beautiful as the rarest, and when once a taste for the cultivation of ferns is thoroughly acquired, a knowledge, more or less perfect, of the different species is almost certain to follow.

I am sorry that I can lay but slight claim to the name of "Botanist," so far as its scientific attributes are concerned, but I have been a collector of ferns from my school-days to the present time, and it is impossible for me to exaggerate the pleasure that I have derived from the pursuit. There is scarcely an English fern that is not intimately associated with some pleasant episode in my past life,—some mountain scramble, some walking tour, some rugged sea-girt rock, or possibly some companionship ever to be remembered with pleasure.

I shall only attempt to notice this evening those varieties of our ferns that I have, at different times, collected on this side of Hertfordshire.

There are, in all, between forty and fifty pretty distinct species of British ferns. I have had about thirty-eight of these growing successfully under cultivation; but as far as I am aware, only about eighteen are indigenous in Hertfordshire. I will briefly notice each species and variety that I have met with *seriatim*.

1. *Asplenium Adiantum-nigrum.*—This ornamental little fern, tolerably common in Hertfordshire, is one of the species eagerly collected by amateurs. It is to be found generally in dry sheltered lanes; it springs up very frequently from under some old stump, or from between stones slightly separated by loamy soil; it requires considerable shade, and the size of its fronds is principally dependent on the conditions under which it grows. Under favour-

able circumstances the frond itself will measure six to eight inches, and its almost black stipes nearly as much. The *Asplenium Adiantum-nigrum* is extremely abundant wherever the sandstones of the Coal-measures, or the rocks of the Silurian formation, are prevalent, and it hangs in graceful sprays on the northern side of old stone walls or ruins.

2. *Asplenium Ruta-muraria.*—This is the smallest of our local ferns, and might readily be mistaken by the uninitiated for a moss. In this district it grows, as far as I am aware, exclusively from among the mortar in old walls. I have found it in several localities, and I am inclined to think that it is more generally distributed than it is frequently supposed to be. It finds its most congenial home among the rocky hills of Wales and Scotland: its tiny fronds peep out from the fissures of the rocks, and often defy the most determined efforts of the collector to remove them. It is commonly known as the "rue" fern, from the great similarity of its fronds to the leaves of that plant.

3. *Asplenium Trichomanes.*—The maidenhair spleenwort, as this beautiful little fern is frequently called, is found but rarely in our district; it has, however, its established habitats, and is unquestionably indigenous. Like the two preceding species, it thrives most luxuriantly on the rocks of the Coal-measures. It festoons with its ornamental clusters the sides of most of the stone walls that prevail so universally in the Coal-districts, and lends not unfrequently a pleasing charm to many a forsaken building or otherwise unsightly engine-house.

4. *Athyrium Filix-fœmina.*—The beautiful "lady-fern" may fairly be considered the Queen of British Ferns. It is perfectly distinct, and readily distinguishable from all others by the veriest novice in fern-culture. Its peculiarly graceful and feathery fronds, always of the palest green, spring up in charming clusters and in profuse abundance beside the hill-sides and rivulets of many of our English counties. On this side of Herts it occurs but rarely, but it grows in tolerable abundance in the neighbourhood of Wigginton Common. There is a deserted lane crossing the table-land between Tring and Chesham, which is peculiarly rich in the production of ferns. Not only are two varieties of the lady-fern to be found, in close proximity, in this favoured spot, but *Blechnum Spicant, Lastrea spinulosa, Lastrea dilatata,* and *Lastrea Oreopteris,* are all more or less abundant. The soil is of rich loam, and I believe that most of the varieties mentioned will only be found where a loamy soil prevails. Like most of its family, the lady-fern delights in a damp shady situation.

> " Where the morning dew lies longest,
>   There the Lady Fern grows strongest."

5. *Athyrium Filix-fœmina,* var. *convexum.*—This is a distinct variety of the lady-fern, with purple stipes, and generally of more rigid appearance, that is tolerably common. and which, as I have already stated, is to be found near Wigginton Common.

6. *Lastrea Filix-mas.*—The *L. Filix-mas* is the commonest of all our ferns; scarcely a hedgerow can be found where its strong vigorous fronds are not discernible. It flourishes alike in shady woods or on open heaths. Its fronds often attain to the height of three or even four feet. Its colour is of a darker green than that of the species last described, and the lower portion of its stipes or stalk is profusely clothed with dark shaggy scales.

7. *Lastrea Filix-mas,* var. *Borreri.*—This variety is distinguished by its yellow hue, and also by the fact that its rachis is more or less scaly throughout its entire length. It is exceedingly abundant in some parts of Scotland, where it imparts a rich golden colour to many a mountain side, and is readily observable by the passing tourist. I have gathered it near Wigginton Common.

8. *Lastrea dilatata.*—This is one of the largest of our British species. On this side of Hertfordshire it is uncommon, but it grows very luxuriantly in moist sheltered woods throughout many of our English counties, and still more so in Wales. The crown of the caudex, or root, is densely covered with large brown scales. Its fronds are of a rich dark green, and under favourable circumstances they will attain to a length of four or perhaps five feet. Its growth is graceful in the extreme, and it constitutes one of the most ornamental species for garden culture. I have already mentioned one of its local habitats.

9. *Lastrea spinulosa.*—I need say but very little of this species. It is closely allied to *L. dilatata,* but is much smaller, and its colour is a dull light green. It grows, I believe, almost exclusively in moist woods, and often by the side of stagnant pools when completely surrounded by trees. It succeeds well under cultivation, and is by no means uncommon.

10. *Lastrea Oreopteris.*—I have no reason to suppose that the heath or mountain fern, as this is frequently styled, is particularly scarce in Herts, but I have only been successful in finding it in two localities. It will only flourish on our higher table-lands, and prefers a loamy soil. I have again and again transplanted it, in its own soil, to my fernery at Hunton Bridge, but it will not survive beyond one or two seasons.

11. *Polystichum angulare.*—12. *Polystichum aculeatum.*—I will take these two species together. They are closely allied, and yet readily distinguishable the one from the other. Both are evergreen. The *P. angulare* is a large and peculiarly handsome fern. It vies in graceful beauty with the lady-fern, and is most effective in cultivation. Its fronds are soft and drooping, are generally of a dull green, and vary from two to four feet in length. The beauty of this fern in the early spring, when first unfolding its young fronds, is very remarkable, and cannot fail to attract the attention of those who watch its growth. All the fronds are symmetrically arranged round the crown of the caudex, and are literally covered with silvery brown scales.

The *P. aculeatum* may be distinguished by its thick leathery

dark green fronds; they are more or less rigid, and are not nearly
so large and handsome as are those of *P. angulare*. Its pinnæ
are packed much closer together, and it possesses a bright burnished
appearance peculiarly its own.

There is said to be an intermediate species, sometimes described
as *P. lobatum*. Mr. Newman considers that it does not differ
sufficiently from the two last mentioned to claim distinctive notice,
and as far as I have been able to judge I concur in his opinion.
I have frequently planted specimens apparently perfectly distinct,
but in the course of a few years they have varied so considerably
under cultivation as to be hardly distinguishable from each other.

13. *Scolopendrium vulgare.*—No fern is more universally known
or more readily distinguished than the hart's-tongue. Its long
ribbon-like fronds, so strikingly different from those of every other
species, are eagerly sought after by all who attempt the formation
of garden ferneries. It is very generally distributed over this side
of Hertfordshire. It grows, for the most part, on damp banks, by
the side of streams and deep ditches; not unfrequently around the
upper portion of wells or pits, and on the underside of arches or
culverts through which water passes. It is extremely ornamental,
and when found in profusion, especially on old walls or ruins,
cannot fail to excite general admiration.

14. *Polypodium vulgare.*—This, like the preceding, is a perfectly
distinct species. It abounds in every lane and copse throughout
our district. Mr. Newman remarks—"Just as the common brake
seems to shun man and to seek the forests and the wilds and
heaths, where his implements of husbandry offer it no disturbance;
so does the polypody appear to affect the companionship of man, to
shun the waste, and to claim the shelter of the hedgerow; it for-
sakes the common and establishes itself on the church-tower or the
church-yard wall."* I have seen the thatched roofs of cottages
completely covered with it, its roots creeping along the surface in
entangled horizontal masses. It is emphatically a parasite, and
appears to flourish just in proportion as decay progresses. Its
bright green fronds, on the back of which a beautiful golden fructification is very conspicuous, crown with a profusion of beauty a
large proportion of the decaying stumps and old timbers so common
in our country lanes.

15. *Blechnum Spicant.*—The only habitat for this fern with
which I am acquainted, throughout this district, is the deserted
lane near Wigginton Common, to which I have already several
times alluded. Formerly it was to be found here in considerable
abundance, but when last I visited the locality the operations of
of the spade were very apparent, and many clumps had evidently
been carried away. It generally abounds on heaths and along the
sides of damp woods. Its fertile and barren fronds are entirely
distinct, and display a pleasing contrast: the fertile fronds always
rise from the centre of the plant, and the barren ones form a rich

* British Ferns (1854), p. 43.

border of green foliage all round them; it is nearly, if not quite, an evergreen.

16. *Ceterach officinarum.*—I do not feel quite certain that this comparatively rare fern is thoroughly naturalized in this district. I have met with it in two perfectly distinct localities; one of them being the outside ledge of a garden wall about half a mile from Hunton Bridge, and the other an old wall forming a portion of a terrace in some grounds near Rickmansworth. I have recently been informed that it has also been found in the neighbourhood of Hemel Hempstead. It is a charming little fern, possessing, during the early summer, a soft downy appearance. It grows freely and without difficulty under cultivation, if supplied with a sufficiency of leaf-mould.

17. *Pteris aquilina.*—The common brake is probably well known to every individual present, and needs but little notice from pen of mine. It abounds in our parks and commons; it forms a ready shelter for the deer, and adds a picturesque beauty to our woodland landscapes. Under favourable circumstances it will attain the height of six or eight feet, but, more generally, it varies from two to five. Its long dark roots, or rhizomes, are about the thickness of one's finger, and penetrate the soil for several feet; when cut transversely, they display with extraordinary exactness the appearance of an oak tree. This freak of nature has been described as follows:—

> " Have ye to learn, how the Eagle fern
>   Doth in its heart enshrine
> An oak tree like that which the hunter Hearne
>   Haunted in days " lang syne " ?
> An oak tree small is repeated all
>   Complete in branch and root,
> Like the tree whereunto King Charles did flee
>   When pressed by hot pursuit."

18. *Ophioglossum vulgatum.*—The curious little plant, well known as the "adder's-tongue," is found in great abundance in many of our damp pastures. It abounds in the Grove Park, and may be gathered in almost every meadow in the valley extending from Berkhampstead to Cassio Bridge. The frond of the adder's-tongue is first observable in May; it is composed of a long pale-coloured stipes and a deep green leaf, from the base of which an erect spike issues. This spike is distinctly stalked, its upper portion being composed of two series of crowded capsules: when ripe, these capsules burst open and discharge their contents on the turf around.

The appearance of the adder's-tongue is very peculiar; in shape and style it somewhat resembles the *Arum maculatum*—the lords and ladies of our hedges—but is infinitely smaller.

I believe that I have now mentioned the leading characteristics of most, if not all, of our local ferns. I feel very certain that no phase of botanical research will be found more replete with gratification to those who follow it than is the study and cultivation of this delightful group of cryptogamic plants.

To lovers of the graceful and beautiful in nature they present varied and manifold attractions, and I warmly commend them to the careful attention and study of all our members.

Perhaps I may be allowed to conclude by quoting a few quaint lines, in the sentiment of which I entirely and heartily concur, although I cannot vouch for their antiquity.

> " The greene and gracefull Ferne,
> How beautifull it is!
> There's not a leafe in all the lande
> So wonderfull I wis—
> Have ye ever watch'd it budding,
> With eche stemme and leafe wrapp'd smalle,
> Coyl'd up within eche other
> Like a rownd and hairie balle?
> Have ye watch'd y^t balle unfolding
> Eche closelie nestling curle,
> And its fayre and featherie lenfeletts
> Their spreading formes unfurle?
> Oh y^n most gracefullie they wave
> In ye forrest like a sea;
> And deare as they are beautifull
> Are those Ferne-leaves to me."

12.—The Physical Structure of the London Basin, considered in its Relation to the Geology of the Neighbourhood of Watford.

By John Morris, F.G.S.,

Professor of Geology and Mineralogy in University College, London.

[A Lecture delivered 14th October, 1875.]

I have been requested by your Secretary to give to the Society, in the form of a short lecture, some general observations on the physical features of the London Basin, and I hope this evening to lay before you some of those conditions under which the various strata which constitute that basin were deposited, with the view of attempting to explain the formations existing in the neighbourhood of Watford, and the adjacent parts of Hertfordshire. It is well known that when the physical structure of any district has been carefully worked out, as this has been by the assiduous and ardent labours of Mr. Whitaker and Mr. Prestwich, it is comparatively easy for an ordinary geologist to say under what conditions the various strata were formed and modified.

In entering on the consideration of the physical structure of the London Basin, we should regard it in several different aspects:

Firstly—Its general physical features.

Secondly—The nature of the materials of which it is composed.

Thirdly—The conditions under which these materials were probably accumulated.

Fourthly—The evidence afforded by the fossil remains as to the climatal character of its several periods.

Lastly—The successive and subsequent changes by which the physical features of the district have been produced.

Already you have had laid before you, in the perspicuous and very interesting lecture by Mr. Lobley, the subject of the Chalk formation. He has pointed out the conditions under which that remarkable deposit of the British Islands was accumulated, and informed you that that White Chalk, so marked a feature in British geology, formed the last great group of the Secondary period. It is true that the Upper White Chalk, as known in England, is on the Continent overlain by a somewhat higher series than is represented in this country, as the Maestricht beds, Faxoe limestone, and probably the pisolitic limestone of France; for these strata represent certain deposits towards the close of the Cretaceous era not fairly represented in the British Islands.

It will be well, however, to take our basis from the Chalk formation, described by Mr. Lobley; and, commencing from that, we have a series of formations which constitute that third group in British Geology known as the Tertiary series, or Caenozoic period. This is subdivided into three or four groups, dependent partly upon the nature of their fossil contents—in ascending order, the Eocene, Miocene, Pliocene, and Pleistocene. They were long ago worked out by Sir Charles Lyell and M. Deshayes, and constitute an important feature in the physical structure of modern Europe. In the area of the London Basin we find two or three of these divisions more or less regularly developed. In the immediate neighbourhood of Watford there are only two representatives of these divisions, the Eocene and Pleistocene,—one belonging to the lower and older portion of the Tertiary series; and the other to the far higher and more modern one. In the lower formation the rocks follow each other in stratified order and regular sequence. The other, or upper, is part of a widespread group, the Boulder-clay and Glacial beds, without any regular stratification, covering, without order, all preceding formations. It is these latter I shall mention in referring to the Glacial Period.

The lower period, or the Eocene, supplies some of the most marked features of the London Basin. It is divided into a series of groups somewhat remarkable, and variable in their lithological and palæontological character. These are, in descending order:—

Upper	Bembridge beds ....Fluvio-marine. *	
	Osborne and Headon series... ....Fluvio-marine.	

Middle	Upper Bagshot Sands ....Marine.
	Barton beds ....Marine.
	Bracklesham beds....................................Marine.
	Lower Bagshot Sands and pebble-beds ....Marine.

Lower	London Clay ....Marine and Estuarine.
	Oldhaven and Blackheath beds ....Marine and Estuarine.
	Woolwich and Reading beds ....Estuarine.
	Thanet Sands ....Marine.

All the above divisions are not represented in the London Basin, but only those belonging to the middle and lower divisions, with the exception of the Barton clay,—the Upper Bagshot Sands lying directly on the Bracklesham beds, as near Chobham. The upper, or fluvio-marine series, is fully developed in Hampshire and the Isle of Wight, and is well represented in the Paris Basin. The celebrated gypsum beds of Montmartre with their rich mammalian fauna belong to this division.

The so-called London Basin constitutes a somewhat triangular area, which is bounded north and south by the Chalk treated of in the previous lecture, and shown in the figure ('Trans.' vol. i. p. 11); therefore it looks like a basin-shaped arrangement in which the later materials of the Tertiary beds were deposited. That these are posterior to the Chalk there is no doubt, but they do not really assume the basin-shaped form known popularly as a basin. The Chalk, although much eroded, was not scooped out before the

* The Hempstead beds of the Isle of Wight overlying the Bembridge, sometimes classed with the Eocene (Jukes, 1872), are considered to belong to the Lower Miocene, and are represented by the Rupelmonde and Tongrian beds of Belgium, and the *Calcaire de la Beauce* and *Grès de Fontainebleau* in France.

Tertiary series was laid down upon it, but the latter extended over a large portion of the Chalk, and was subsequently let down by the same disturbance which affected the Chalk formation. I mention this that you may get a clear idea of the term "basin"; because, if it were simply a basin scooped out of the Chalk, in which the strata were successively deposited, we should naturally imagine that the oldest groups, as this basin was filled up, would have gradually succeeded each other in a more or less horizontal order, so that the newest, or last formed, would occur in the centre as well as on the margins of the basin. This is not the case. When we examine a geological diagram, as the one above alluded to, we find, in proceeding from the margins on each side towards the centre, a series of beds of similar kinds successively cropping out or exposed on each side, except where concealed by superficial gravels, thus showing that they are continuous beneath, and are limited within the basin. Hence you see that the trough-shaped arrangement was formed, not by the deposition of successive strata in a basin of the Chalk previously cut out, but that the newer beds were deposited over a broad and level surface, and have partaken of the movements to which the Chalk has been subjected.

This we know from the study of the general geology of southern England. If we made a traverse from this district or the Hertfordshire Chalk hills over the London Basin to the North Downs, and again across the Valley of the Weald to the South Downs, we should find the Wealden area a raised dome, occupying part of a great vault or anticlinal fold, the London Basin lying in what is called a synclinal trough to the north. If we continued the section across the Channel into the French area, it would be seen that the Chalk re-appears both north and south of Paris, forming another trough, in which are inclosed Eocene strata similar to those of the Isle of Wight, and thus forming the so-called Paris Basin. Hence the Paris and London Basins with their Eocene strata occupy two synclinal folds, the result of one or more movements by which the anticlinal axis of the Wealden area, and similar parallel ones in the south of England and part of France, have been produced.[*] In fact, the general teaching is, that after the

* M. Ch. Barrois has published some interesting papers ('Ann. Soc. Géol. du Nord,' tome ii. p. 85; 'Revue Scientifique,' 1875, pp. 1070, 1192) on the undulations of the Chalk in the south of England, and their probable continuation with similar folds and faults in the north of France. M. Barrois recognises three great anticlinal lines or axes of elevation:—1. The axis of Kingsclere, in an east and west direction, has separated the basin of London from that of Hampshire, and the movement which determined it took place between the Chalk with *Marsupites* and that with *Belemnitella*, and more slowly towards the end of the Eocene period. The axis of Artois is considered to be a continuation of that of Kingsclere. 2. The axis of Winchester. This axis is parallel to the preceding, was formed during the same period, and is thought to be a prolongation of the axis of the Bresle. It is probable, however, that this axis, as well as that of Artois, underwent the last movement during the Upper Eocene. 3. The axis of the Isle of Wight and Purbeck. This axis is parallel to the two preceding, and its elevation and that of Kingsclere has given the basin-shaped arrangement to the Chalk of Hampshire. Its last movement was about the period of the Barton

deposition of the Cretaceous and certain overlying strata, the beds
underwent plications and foldings, in consequence of subterranean movements, by which they partly received their present
configuration; since, however, considerably modified by denuding
agency, which has swept off the beds from the anticlinal folds,
and allowed their edges to be exposed at the margin of the basin,
the older strata occurring at the margin, and the younger successively appearing towards the centre.

The Tertiary strata of the London Basin are but partially represented in the vicinity of Watford. After the close of the Chalk
period a limited area was probably submerged beneath the waters
of the ocean. Not improbably this district of Hertfordshire was not
so much submerged as to be covered by the earliest Tertiary stratum,
or the Chalk was not subjected to much erosion and destruction;
for, as shown by Prestwich and others, by comparing the thickness of the Chalk strata in Kent and Surrey with that of
Hertfordshire, we find that the Chalk in the latter district attains
a far greater thickness—about 1000 feet—than in the area to the
south of London, where it is in some places but 300 or 400 feet
thick.* Hence, therefore, it is not improbable that, through the
physical changes which caused so marked a feature between the
Secondary and Tertiary periods, there was at the commencement
of the Tertiary period a movement of the water which scooped out
and destroyed the Chalk bed in one district more than in another.

Upon the Chalk was deposited the first of the series of the
Tertiary strata.† These are called by Mr. Prestwich the THANET
SANDS, from their constituting an important feature in the physical
geology of the Isle of Thanet and its neighbourhood. They have

beds, and it is considered to be a continuation of the axis of the Pays de Bray.
But, as M. Barrois remarks, it is very difficult to follow these lines of elevation
with exactitude, as the forces which produced them have acted with varying
intensity from one point to another, and with different effects.—See also papers
by MM. Hébert and Mercey, in the 'Bull. Géol. Soc. France,' ser. 2, tome xx.
pp. 615, 643.

* " But in Suffolk and Norfolk, the upper part of the Chalk is, like the lower
part, nearly destitute of flints. This portion of it I believe to have been denuded
at London, and consequently the thickness of the mass has been much diminished.
This may have arisen from a greater relative elevation of the bed of the sea to the
south at the conclusion of the Cretaceous period, in consequence of which the
earlier Tertiary seas planed down its more exposed and elevated surface; and
thus the upper beds of the Chalk, which to the northward, owing to their greater
depth from the surface, escaped this denudation, may have been removed by it in
proportion as they trended southward. Hence there would result a gradual
decrease in the thickness of the chalk as it ranges from north to south."—
Prestwich, 'The Water-bearing Strata,' 1851, p. 139. See also 'Quart. Journ.
Geol. Soc.,' vol. viii. p. 257.

† Overlying the Chalk, however, and separating it from the Thanet Sand
above, there occurs a bed of green-coated flints, known as the Bull's-head Bed:
these unrolled and unmoved flints formed one of the original zones of flint in
the Chalk, from which the latter has been removed by chemical action either
before, but more probably subsequently to, the deposition of the Thanet Sand,
during which they also acquired the green coating of silicate of iron. This bed
is well seen at Grays, Erith, Charlton, and Croydon.

a somewhat limited extension, for we find them apparently deposited in an area scooped out of the Chalk. They are of marine origin. They extend from a little westward of London to the Isle of Thanet, where they are largely developed; but they do not terminate there, for we find in the old Tertiary times, when the Straits of Dover did not exist, that the seas which deposited the sands in the Kentish and Surrey area extended over the Paris Basin and over part of Belgium. Similar strata, or strata of the same age, occur both in the Belgian and Parisian areas, and are known by different names according to the district in which they are found. In Belgium they are termed the *Système Landénien*, and in the Paris Basin are represented by the sands of Bracheux and Abbecourt.

These Thanet Sands thicken eastwards, and thin out westwards, and partly extend under London, but do not reach this district, although found north of the Thames at Purfleet and Grays, in Essex. They are (or were) the means by which London is partly supplied with deep and pure well water from what are known as artesian wells. It is the permeable nature of the sands, allowing them at their outcrop to receive the rain, kept in by the impervious nature of the London Clay above, and the saturated Chalk below, which causes them to form part of the stores of the deep well supply of the London area.[*]

The Thanet Sands indicate moderate climatal conditions, and, according to Mr. Prestwich, were formed in a sea of a somewhat temperate climate, inasmuch as the nature of the shells found in them *(Astarte, Cyprina, Trophon)* would scarcely indicate a sea of a tropical character.[†]

---

[*] "The Chalk is the chief source of water-supply for the deep wells in the London district. Not very many years ago the overlying Thanet Sand was the great water-bearing bed, but its limited outcrop and small thickness soon caused it to be unable to bear the greatly increasing drain on it, and most London wells were then deepened, new wells being almost universally carried into the Chalk."—Whitaker, ' Guide to the Geology of London,' p. 20.

[†] " It was, probably, on the shores of the dry land of this period (the Thanet Sands), that the innumerable flint pebbles so perfectly rounded—a process indicating a vast lapse of time—which we find in higher portions of the Lower Tertiary strata, as at Blackheath and Addington, were formed; these accumulations of shore-pebbles having been spread out over the Thanet Sands at that next succeeding Lower Tertiary period. After the period of the Thanet Sands a further subsidence of the northern part of the southern continental area took place, and the sea then spread itself over the greater part of the Isle of Wight and Paris Tertiary districts, leaving some of the higher lands as islands. One of these islands occupied probably the area now forming the Weald of Kent and Surrey, then not denuded of all its chalk dome. It was during this second period that the strata of the Woolwich and Reading series were formed."—Prestwich, ' The Ground Beneath Us,' p. 73 ; see also ' Quart. Journ. Geol. Soc.,' vol. x. p. 135.

M. Elie de Beaumont, also, suggests that probably, at the Lower Tertiary period, an island extended somewhere in the present position of the Wealden and part of the north of France, and a smaller one of the elevated land, the *Pays de Bray.* See his memoir " Sur l'Etendue du Système Tertiaire inférieur," in the ' Mém. Soc. Géol. de France,' ser. 1, vol. i. pp. 111, 112, and pl. 7, fig. 5.

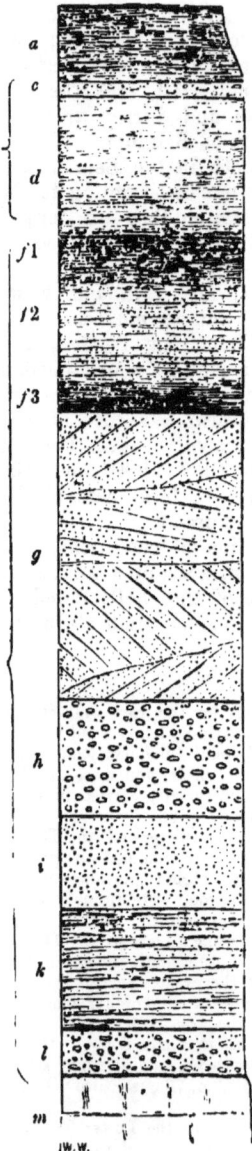

Fig. 1.—*General Section at Bushey Kiln, near Watford.**

(Scale, 8 feet to an inch.)

Drifted clay, in parts sandy, with flint-pebbles, thickness variable.

FEET.

London Clay.
(a) Brown Clay.

Basement Bed.
(c) Pebble-bed; some of the pebbles large ... ½ (or more)

(d) Brown sandy clay; "large oyster-shells at the bottom" (R. Trench)... about 6

Reading Beds, 35 or 36 feet.

(f 1) Green clay, with "race" (irregular calcareous concretions) passing into the bed below.
(f 2) Greenish and brown clayey sand . . . . . .
(f 3) Clay.
At the eastern part of the yard these three beds are so full of race that they become a marl . . . . .
} over 7

(g) Light-coloured false-bedded sand . . . . about 12
The beds below this were not to be seen, but Mr. Trench was told that they were as follows:—
(h) Pebble-bed . . . . about 5
(i) Sand 4
(k) Loam 5
(l) Flints in sand 2

Chalk (m).

* Whitaker, Mem. Geol. Surv. vol. iv. p. 222, fig. 55.

FIG. 2.—*General Section at Watford Heath Kiln.*[*]

(Scale, 8 feet to an inch.)

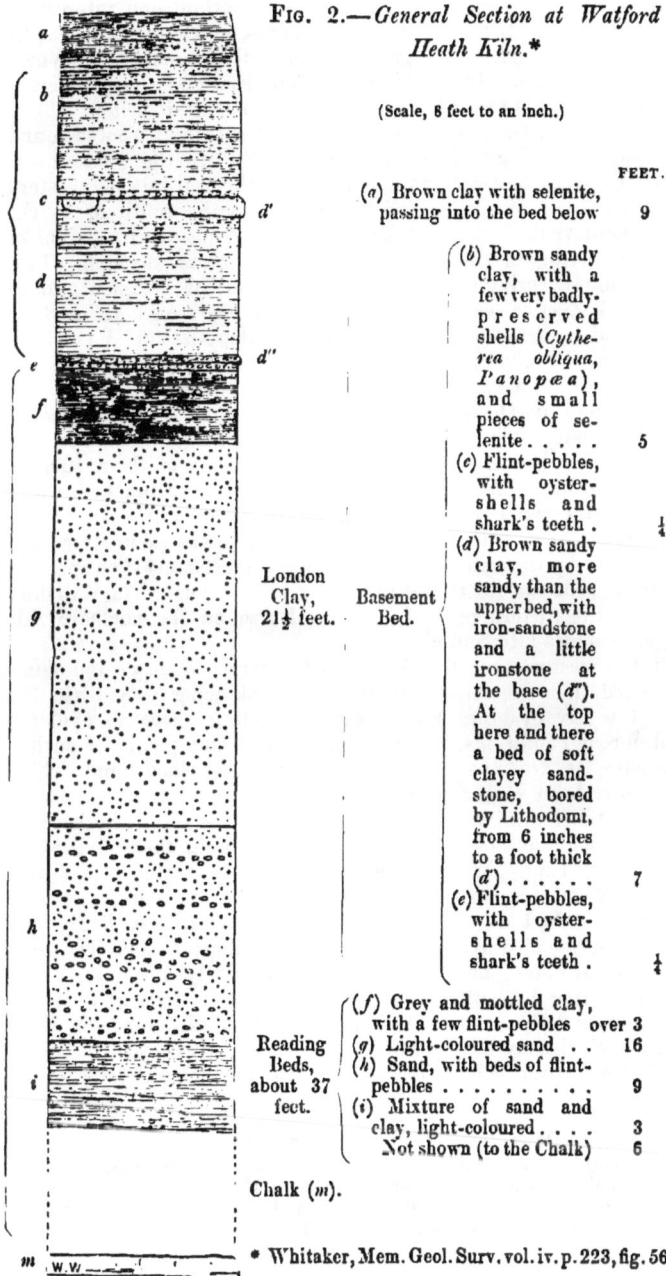

FEET.

(*a*) Brown clay with selenite, passing into the bed below   9

(*b*) Brown sandy clay, with a few very badly-preserved shells (*Cytherea obliqua, Panopæa*), and small pieces of selenite   5

(*c*) Flint-pebbles, with oyster-shells and shark's teeth .   ¼

London Clay, 21½ feet.   Basement Bed.

(*d*) Brown sandy clay, more sandy than the upper bed, with iron-sandstone and a little ironstone at the base (*d''*). At the top here and there a bed of soft clayey sandstone, bored by Lithodomi, from 6 inches to a foot thick (*d'*)   7

(*e*) Flint-pebbles, with oyster-shells and shark's teeth .   ¼

(*f*) Grey and mottled clay, with a few flint-pebbles over 3

Reading Beds, about 37 feet.

(*g*) Light-coloured sand . .   16

(*h*) Sand, with beds of flint-pebbles   9

(*i*) Mixture of sand and clay, light-coloured   3

Not shown (to the Chalk)   6

Chalk (*m*).

* Whitaker, Mem. Geol. Surv. vol. iv. p. 223, fig. 56.

Overlying the Thanet Beds occurs an important and interesting group, showing still more marked changes in the physical conditions of the period. This group is generally known as the WOOL-WICH AND READING BEDS, which were deposited under very different conditions from those of the pre-existing marine beds below. They present two distinct local facies; hence the term "Woolwich and Reading Series," given by Prof. Prestwich. In the western and northern area they are more marine, in the central and eastern more fluviatile and estuarine.* It was to the south or to the south-west that there must have existed a considerable extent of land consisting of the Chalk and Wealden rocks, through which rivers flowed, bringing down a vast amount of sediment, to be deposited over a considerable portion of the southern part of the London area, as marked by the deposits at Woolwich, Lewisham, Peckham, and in other districts. These indicate old river-courses flowing into an estuary, from what is known of the shells found in them. These shells, such as *Unio*, *Paludina*, *Neritina*, only exist in rivers, or some at least, at the mouths of rivers, where brackish water prevails; for many of them, such as *Cyrena*, *Melania*, *Melanopsis*, *Ostrea*, *Cerithium*, are brackish-water forms. But what is understood in relation to this and other localities is, that a far larger area of country was then submerged or covered by deposits than at the preceding Thanet Sand period : for these beds can be traced from beyond Hungerford in Wiltshire towards the eastern part of Kent, and also on the northern side of the Thames into Suffolk.

In the western area they consist of a series of clays and muds deposited in a comparatively deep sea, showing very little life except a few oysters; but towards Reading there is evidence of different conditions. Here occur plants, and plants of such a character as are known only to grow upon land, and which must have been carried on to the old sea bed. Further eastward are seen the formations indicating the great series of fresh-water and brackish deposits, evidence of rivers draining themselves from a southern land. When, however, we trace them over a still more eastern area, we find them becoming more marine in their character. Just as we should expect to find in any large tidal river a series of fluviatile, estuarine, and marine deposits, sometimes intercalated, or with the mollusca partly intermixed ; so the respective deposits of the Woolwich beds, as seen at Dulwich, Charlton, and Upnor, seem to indicate a slight difference in their faunas, which may have resulted from their having been accumulated at a greater or less distance from the ancient estuary.†

* Prestwich, Quart. Journ. Geol. Soc., vol. x. p. 78.

† At Peckham and Dulwich *Paludina* and *Unio* are abundant, with some plants and also mammals, as *Coryphodon*, etc. At Upnor *Cytherea* and *Pectunculus* are common, associated with *Cyrena ;* at Charlton the chief brackish or marine form is *Ostrea*, mixed with *Cyrena* and *Melania*.

It is these beds on the northern parts of the Thames that are more interesting in relation to the geology of Watford; for they are the first of the Tertiary series here overlying the Chalk. If you examine the sections at the Bushey Kiln, at the Watford Heath Kiln, at Chorley Wood and Woodcock Hill in the neighbourhood of Rickmansworth, at Hatfield Park, and near Hertford (Figs. 1, 2, 3, 4), you will find that there are certain strata immediately overlying the Chalk, which are referred to the Woolwich and Reading series. They are almost unfossiliferous, or indicate that they were not deposited under fresh-water conditions, for the remains found in them are only a few *Ostreæ*. Hence, therefore, you will see the necessity of carefully working out the characters and contents of deposits in order to learn the conditions under which they were formed.* It is not improbable that while to the southern side of the Thames, rivers existed, as before mentioned, on the northern side there was more or less open sea in which marine sand or mud accumulated. But these beds have equivalents in the western area of the London Basin, and also in the Hampshire Basin, where the red clays which lie against the Chalk in Alum and White Cliff Bays are the representatives of the beds in the neighbourhood of Watford. In the Paris or Belgian area at this period marine conditions partly prevailed, but around Epernay are found similar fresh-water strata to those in the neighbourhood of Woolwich. Hence you see a great physical change must have taken place in the geography of the period during the deposition of the Woolwich series.†

Perhaps it might be interesting to notice that if we compare the fertility of the Chalk hills of Hertfordshire with that of the Downs south of the Thames, it will be found that a great part of the fertility of the Chalk district is due to the spreading over it of more or less of these Woolwich clays or sands, and hence, therefore, the difference in the wooded and agricultural character of the

* "In Surrey, west of Croydon, and along the north-western outcrop in Buckinghamshire and Hertfordshire, the other or Reading type occurs exclusively. It is unfossiliferous (?), and characterized by the presence of soapy mottled plastic clay, of various and often rich colours, some shade of red generally showing; but sand is mostly present also, and sometimes with pebbles; at the northern margin of the district, between Aldenham and Shenley, there is a regular pebble-bed, hardened into stone of just the same kind as the blocks of the well-known 'Hertfordshire pudding-stone,' which are found so commonly over the Chalk-tract beyond, and were indeed most likely derived from this bed." —Whitaker, 'Guide to the Geology of London,' p. 31.

† "The reasons for believing that the temperature of the sea at the 'Thanet sands' period was lower than that which prevailed during the period of the London Clay, apply in some measure probably less forcibly to this intermediate epoch of the Woolwich and Reading series. The general character both of the fauna and flora shows a preponderance of forms such as, on the whole, we might expect to meet with at present in more moderate climates than the one in which the more tropical-seeming vegetation and animals of the London Clay could have flourished."—Prestwich, 'Quart. Journ. Geol. Soc.' vol. x. p. 136. See also Dr. Hooker's Note on the Fossil Plants from Reading (vol. x. p. 163), in which he states that they "represent a vegetation differing in no important respect from that at present inhabiting the north temperate zone."

FIG. 3.—*General Section of the Tertiary Beds at Hatfield Park Kiln.**

(Scale, 8 feet to an inch.)

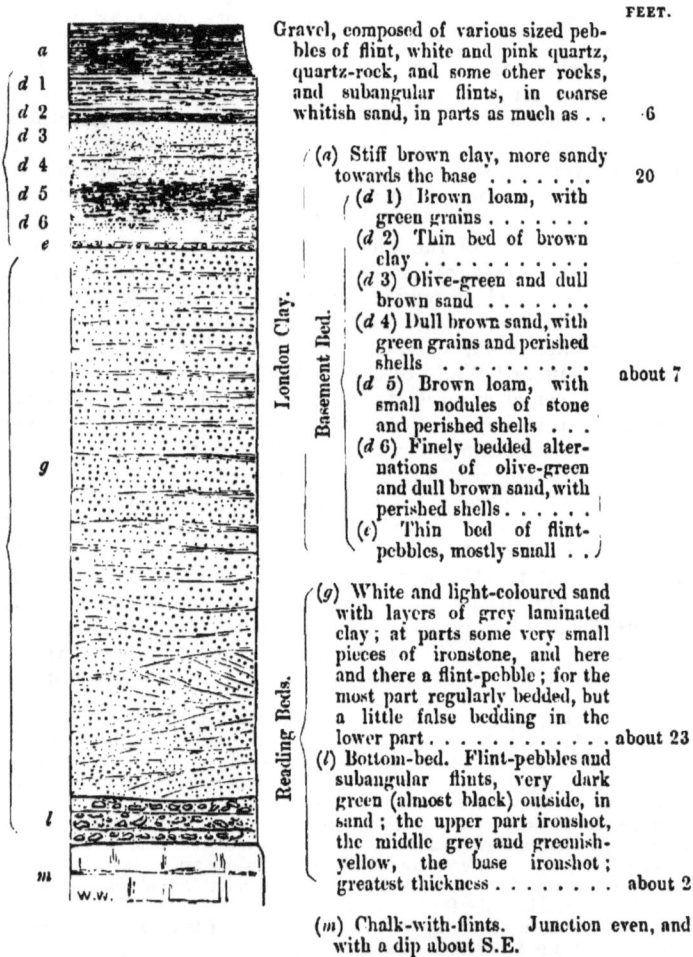

FEET.

Gravel, composed of various sized pebbles of flint, white and pink quartz, quartz-rock, and some other rocks, and subangular flints, in coarse whitish sand, in parts as much as . .   ·6

(a) Stiff brown clay, more sandy towards the base   20

(d 1) Brown loam, with green grains . . . .

(d 2) Thin bed of brown clay . . . .

(d 3) Olive-green and dull brown sand . . . .

(d 4) Dull brown sand, with green grains and perished shells . . . .   about 7

(d 5) Brown loam, with small nodules of stone and perished shells . . .

(d 6) Finely bedded alternations of olive-green and dull brown sand, with perished shells . . . . . .

(e) Thin bed of flint-pebbles, mostly small . . .

(g) White and light-coloured sand with layers of grey laminated clay ; at parts some very small pieces of ironstone, and here and there a flint-pebble ; for the most part regularly bedded, but a little false bedding in the lower part . . . . about 23

(l) Bottom-bed. Flint-pebbles and subangular flints, very dark green (almost black) outside, in sand ; the upper part ironshot, the middle grey and greenish-yellow, the base ironshot ; greatest thickness . . . .   about 2

(m) Chalk-with-flints. Junction even, and with a dip about S.E.

* " At Hatfield Park Kiln, at the eastern edge of the park, the pits give a very good section from the high-level gravel down to the Chalk. On the eastern side of the road, the higher pit shows the former over London Clay, and the lower, London Clay and its basement-bed over the Reading Beds; whilst on the other side the higher pit also shows London Clay with a little gravel, and the lower one all the beds from the basement-bed to the Chalk."—Whitaker, ' Mem. Geol. Surv.' vol. iv. p. 226, fig. 57. See also Prestwich, ' Quart. Journ. Geol. Soc.' vol. vi. p. 270.

Fig. 4.—*General Section at Mr. Line's Brickyard,
near Hertford.**

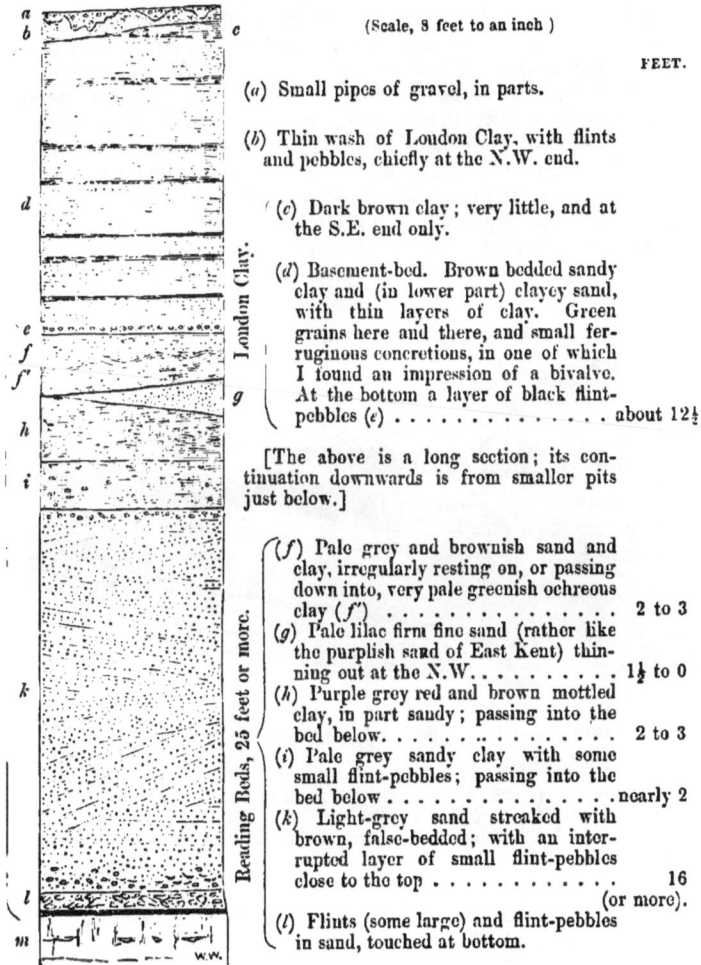

(Scale, 8 feet to an inch.)

FEET.

(*a*) Small pipes of gravel, in parts.

(*b*) Thin wash of London Clay, with flints
and pebbles, chiefly at the N.W. end.

(*c*) Dark brown clay; very little, and at
the S.E. end only.

(*d*) Basement-bed. Brown bedded sandy
clay and (in lower part) clayey sand,
with thin layers of clay. Green
grains here and there, and small ferruginous concretions, in one of which
I found an impression of a bivalve.
At the bottom a layer of black flint-
pebbles (*e*) . . . . about 12½

[The above is a long section; its continuation downwards is from smaller pits
just below.]

(*f*) Pale grey and brownish sand and
clay, irregularly resting on, or passing
down into, very pale greenish ochreous
clay (*f'*) . . . . 2 to 3

(*g*) Pale lilac firm fine sand (rather like
the purplish sand of East Kent) thinning out at the N.W. . . . . 1½ to 0

(*h*) Purple grey red and brown mottled
clay, in part sandy; passing into the
bed below. . . . . 2 to 3

(*i*) Pale grey sandy clay with some
small flint-pebbles; passing into the
bed below . . . . nearly 2

(*k*) Light-grey sand streaked with
brown, false-bedded; with an inter-
rupted layer of small flint-pebbles
close to the top 16
(or more).

(*l*) Flints (some large) and flint-pebbles
in sand, touched at bottom.

Left margin labels: London Clay. | Reading Beds, 25 feet or more.

---

* " For some way east of Hatfield Kiln sections of any sort are rare. . . . .
However, there is a clear spot at the kiln half a mile south-west of Rush Green
near Hertford. In an old overgrown pit close to and east of the house there is
London Clay. The present pits (1869) are north-west of the house, and give the
only good section in the neighbourhood."—Whitaker, ' Mem. Geol. Surv.' vol.
iv. p. 227, fig. 58.

northern Chalk lands compared with the open downs of uncovered
Chalk on the southern side of the Thames.*

Overlying the Woolwich beds in some parts of the London
Basin, but apparently not found in this district, are pebble beds
and sands, of variable thickness. These have been termed by Mr.
Whitaker the OLDHAVEN AND BLACKHEATH BEDS; their molluscan
fauna is both estuarine and marine, and is somewhat related to
the beds below and the London Clay above, of which latter formation these beds have been considered the base. These perfectly
rounded pebbles, like those of the Woolwich beds below, are so
well marked that they can be readily detected amongst the mass of
superficial gravels of later age spread over the district. Their
nature and form indicate that they were derived from the Chalk,
and rolled upon some shore for ages, having been subsequently
spread over a larger area (far perhaps from their parent source)
by the changes to which the sea or estuarine bed was subjected.

FIG. 5.—*General Section on Railway, Bushey Cutting.*

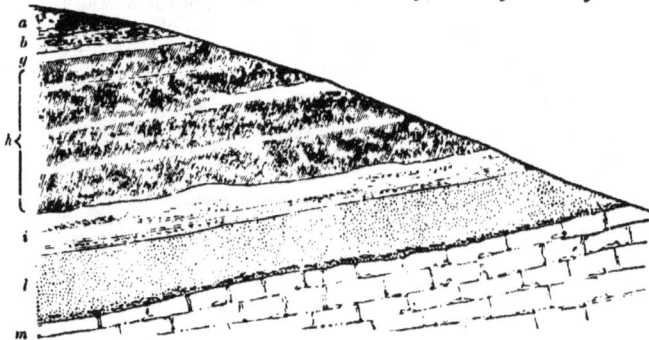

(*a*) London Clay
(*b*) Basement-bed of the London Clay, with numerous fossils . . . . . .   5 ?

		FEET.
	(*g*) Sands	3 ?
	(*h*) Mottled clays with a few beds of sand	35
Reading Beds.	(*i*) Sand nearly white, with a few layers and patches of flint-pebbles	10
	(*l*) Shingle bed of flint-pebbles in ochreous sand . . .	15

(*m*) Chalk.

After the deposition of these estuarine beds, the geology of the
London area shows that another physical change took place, probably of still greater interest. The Woolwich Beds indicate moderately temperate conditions; but the overlying stratum—that which
is known as the LONDON CLAY—presents a very different character:
firstly, with regard to its mode of accumulation; and secondly, as

---

* "The chalk hills which bound the Tertiary area on the north, unlike the
chalk of Salisbury Plain, present but a small extent of open downs, and are
well wooded on their summits. This arises in part from a covering of clay

to the nature of its fossil contents. The lowest beds of this clay are those which are exposed in the neighbourhood of Watford.

Referring to the sections south of the Bushey Station (Fig. 5), the brick-kilns at Watford Heath and Bushey, and near Hertford, at Woodcock Hill, and at Hatfield Park kiln, we shall find, overlying the Woolwich beds, layers of pebbles, sands, and loam, with some marine remains, forming the base of the London Clay proper. It is these which Mr. Prestwich calls the "Basement Bed." See Figs. 1, 2, 3, 4.

There are traces of the London Clay in Hertfordshire, but it is of no great thickness—in the northern district it is almost wanting,*—but it attains the thickness of four or five hundred feet in some parts of the London Basin, and consists of a brownish or bluish clay, quietly but successively deposited in a comparatively deep sea, and that sea to some extent open to the north. The fossil forms are of a tropical character; yet there are indications also of a moderately temperate condition, and this thick deposit of the London Clay, forming one of the chief features of the London Basin, shows us therefore that it was accumulated in a tolerably deep sea, with adjacent land, as is evident from the plant and mammalian remains found in it.

This Clay is not restricted to the present London Basin area. It occurs in the Hampshire Basin; but, singularly enough, the sea does not appear to have covered any considerable portion of the Paris Basin. There are traces of it in the neighbourhood of Dieppe and Dunkirk, but considerably more is spread over a portion of Belgium, where it is known as the *Système Yprésien*. Possibly, says Mr. Prestwich, the London Clay may have been formed during a period unrepresented, or only very partially represented, in the French series.

When we consider the nature of the Fauna and Flora—the animal and vegetable life which existed at the time—we shall find a very instructive lesson. There are, so far as at present known, between four and five hundred species of animal remains. These belong to nearly all the divisions of the animal kingdom,—the largest number being the Mollusca, of which there are between 200 and 250 species. But all the other departments are

drift and in part from thin cappings of the lower Tertiary beds, the latter being especially frequent to the north and north-west of Reading, and again around Beaconsfield, Penn, and Amersham. They are also found to some extent near St. Albans, Welwyn, and to the north of Hertford, and between Ware and Bishop's Stortford."—Prestwich, ' Quart. Journ. Geol. Soc.,' vol. x. p. 19.—" In the north-western corner of our district, in Bucks and Herts, there is absolutely no downland, and the greater part of the tract consists of ploughed land diversified by woods and parks."—Whitaker, ' Guide to the Geology of London,' p. 21.

* "The *London Clay* forms the greater part of the London Tertiary district, stretching eastward from the neighbourhood of Hungerford to that of Canterbury on the south, and to that of Bishop's Stortford on the north, and having a breadth therefore of twenty miles and more at London: on the west, however, where the succeeding series is in force and the dip high, and as the formation gets thinner, the outcrop is comparatively narrow, less than a mile wide sometimes."—Whitaker, ' Mem. Geol. Survey,' vol. iv. 1872, p. 9.

represented. Amongst the Vertebrata we have each class represented—Fishes, Reptiles, Birds, and Mammals. Amongst the most numerous are some very curious forms of fish. The fish of the London Clay period indicate to us a great Natural History fact —that whereas, of the fish in the Chalk period most of the forms are now extinct, or belong to the shark and ray tribe, and there were only a very few species related to the present most abundant fish-life forms, in the London Clay there were not only sharks and rays, as shown by their well-preserved teeth and palates, but a great number of forms allied to those which constitute the larger portion of the existing fish fauna, the Cycloid and Ctenoid, or Teleostean fishes. This therefore shows that, in one group at least of fishes,—the Teleostei, there has been a gradual increase from the Chalk period to the present time ; and the phœnogamous plants exhibit a similar increase.

Besides the fish, there are numerous forms of reptile life— the Crocodiles, and also the Ophidia (snakes), which here appear for the first time ; for no traces of this order have been noticed before. In the London Clay also is found another interesting order—the Chelonia or group of turtles. No less than nine different species of turtle occur, whereas at the present time in all the seas of the globe there are only five known living species, and they are widely distributed. These indicate warm conditions ; and with them are found river turtles and tortoises. Many species of Crustacea, *Xanthopsis, Hoploparia*, etc., some Echinodermata, numerous Foraminifera, and Entomostraca, also occur. Of the more remarkable Mollusca is the *Nautilus*, with eight or ten fossil species, although there are only two living ones ; and there are also numerous species of *Voluta, Fusus, Cypræa, Pleurotoma*, which afford another indication of comparatively tropical conditions.

But besides the crocodiles and turtles as evidence of rivers and shores, we find imbedded in the clay of Sheppey and other districts remains of certain Mammalia of curious forms (*Hyracotherium, Pliolophus*)—not of existing genera, but related to existing genera—which must have lived on the land of that period ; and still more interesting, in the neighbourhood of Sheppey and elsewhere are found abundant traces of vegetation of large growth and of different characters : fruits and seeds, which by a careful comparison of existing forms indicate the very singular flora which grew upon the high and low lands of the London Clay period, and some curious forms of Coniferæ which yielded the Highgate resin or fossil amber, and of Proteaceæ, a family almost only represented at the present day in the arid forests of Australia.

Fruits related to the Acacia, Gourd, Melon, and Custard-apple families are associated with a large number of so-called "fossil figs" (*Nipadites*), which bear a close resemblance to the remarkable genus *Nipa*, growing so abundantly in the Molucca Islands and the region of the Ganges, and which frequently come down the river in such numbers as almost to stop the navigation.

Hence it will be seen that a careful study and comparison of present forms with those of past times, yields us evidence that the London Clay was deposited under tropical conditions, or in a climate very different from that at present prevailing in the same area.

The London Clay, as I pointed out to you, is but little spread over the area of Hertfordshire.* What remains of the Tertiary series is that which belonged to the Woolwich beds and the basement bed of the London Clay, with only a small portion of the Clay itself.

One interesting point which some of the members of the Society may have noticed is that in some parts of Hertfordshire, as near Radlett, there occur masses of rounded pebbles frequently cemented together into hard stone. These plum-pudding stones, as they are called, are merely the consolidated pebble-beds of the Woolwich series. These pebbles were not only rolled upon some shore where they were deposited, but were subsequently cemented by infiltration of siliceous matter, so as to form a solid rock. These old conglomerate masses were formerly made into querns or hand-mills for grinding corn, having been so used because, probably, the softer parts between the pebbles more readily give way than the harder, hence forming a continued roughened surface.

Besides the characteristics which I alluded to in the London Clay, there is another interesting point bearing upon the life of the period. Many of you may probably have observed in your visits to some of our sea-shores, pieces of wood, or sometimes pieces at the bottom of old piles, bored by a kind of shipworm called the *Teredo*. Other specimens, which are not at all uncommon in the London Clay, tell a somewhat similar story. The wood which, from its structure, is known to be coniferous, grew upon land, and was subsequently drifted into the sea; during the drifting it became the home of the *Teredina*, and ultimately becoming water-logged, sank to the bottom. This and other facts noticed, therefore show that the London Clay was formed not only in a deep sea and gradually accumulated, but that there was contemporaneous land on which vegetation grew and animals lived whose remains were washed down by the streams and imbedded in the accumulating mud.

This Clay period at last terminated, and the other Eocene deposits newer than the London Clay are not represented in Hertfordshire.

The next formed beds were sands (the Lower Bagshot), and are still found capping as outliers the London Clay of Harrow and Hampstead Hills, and are remnants of similar strata which

---

* "Along the northern boundary the escarpment (of the London Clay) is again conspicuous for the most part, as on the south of Windsor, and along the valley of the Colne: Stanmore Heath, indeed, with its capping of pebble-gravel, being the highest ground in Middlesex."—Whitaker, 'Geology of London,' p. 42.

constitute the fine and extensive heaths of Pirbright, Frimley, and Bagshot; these may formerly have extended over the area of Hertfordshire, but have been subsequently washed away by the denuding agencies to which the county has been subjected.

Between the London Clay period and the next overlying formations in this district, there is a great hiatus—a great geological break—during which extensive and different accumulations of strata took place (*i.e.* the Middle and Upper Eocene, Miocene, and Pliocene), not only in England, but also on the Continent, such as those which now constitute a considerable portion of the rocks forming some of the higher parts of the Pyrenees, Alps, and Himalaya; for those mountains, high as they are, have been considerably elevated since the London Clay period. Most of the chief cities of Europe are built either upon the Eocene or Miocene strata.

In this neighbourhood the next series of strata are those which I alluded to in the former part of the lecture as belonging to the Pleistocene period, and the agencies concerned in their formation have partly tended to modify the features of the district.   In descending order they have been divided as follows:—*

	Alluvium (recent river deposits).
Old River Drift, Post-glacial...	{ Brick-earth (loam). { Gravel and sand.
	Plateau gravel (of doubtful age).
Surface deposits on the Chalk-tract..............................	{ Brick-earth (and pebbly loam). { Clay with flints (of doubtful age).
Glacial Drift	{ Boulder-clay. { Loam, gravel, and sand.
? Pre-glacial	Pebble gravel.

Those members of the Society who have attended the field meetings which have been held in the neighbourhood of Watford, have been shown that there are certain accumulations of gravel and clay spread over the district, which do not present any regular stratified appearance.   These are referred to what geologists call the Glacial Period, and they are of different kinds and ages.

Firstly, there are the gravels which are found at Stanmore Heath. If we examine a section from the neighbourhood of Bushey Grove to Stanmore, we observe a little escarpment of the Chalk, covered, as we ascend, by the Woolwich beds, and these again by the London Clay, until we reach the gravel of Stanmore Heath, as well shown in Mr. Whitaker's diagram (fig. 6).   These gravels are the first of the series referable to this period.   They are apparently due to the spreading by the water at the first commencement of, or previously to, the Glacial Period.   By Mr. Whitaker they

---

* Whitaker, Geology of London, p. 3.

Fig. 6.—*Section from a Point about a quarter of a mile S.W. of Bushey Grove to Stanmore Heath.**

N.W.   BUSHEY   Stanmore Heath.   S.E

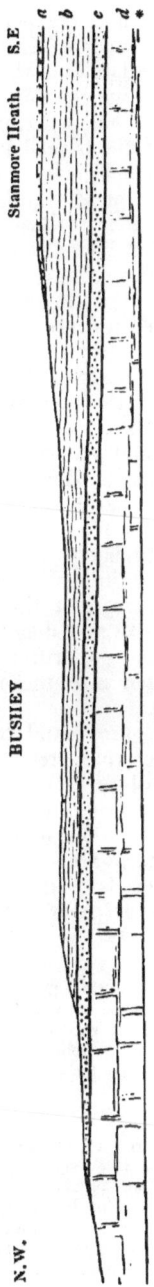

Horizontal scale, 3 inches to a mile; vertical scale, twice as large (880 feet to an inch).

* Sea-level (approximate).   *a.* Pebble-gravel.   *b.* London Clay.   *c.* Reading Beds.   *d.* Chalk.

The coming on of the London Clay over the Reading Beds has been made too abrupt, and the ground at and to the left of Bushey has been drawn rather too high, so that the slope on the right is hardly exaggerated.

* Whitaker, Mem. Geol. Surv. vol. iv. p. 374, fig. 88.

** The figures 1, 2, 3, 4, and 6, from Mr. Whitaker's 'Memoir,' are inserted by permission of Mr. H. W. Bristow, Director of the Geological Survey of England, and figure 5, from Mr. Prestwich's paper in 'Quart. Journ. Geol. Soc.' vol. x. p. 91, by permission of the Council of the Geological Society.

are supposed to be pre-glacial, and are known as the pebble-gravel in this district, and similar gravels are found at Hemel Hempstead and other places.* Secondly, of later date than these pebble-gravels are still more instructive beds, and which afford far better indications of great physical and climatic changes. Hertfordshire presents us with some marked features of the Glacial Period ; for in certain districts occurs a deposit of sand and gravel, with foreign rocks not belonging to the present County of Hertford, as in the gravel-pits west of Watford, the chalk-pit near to Bushey Station, and the pit on the hill east of the railway, at Radlett near Watford.

Overlying that again, as at Bricket Wood, is a more or less thick accumulation of clay, known as Boulder-clay.† The lower sands are of middle glacial age ; where they are wanting, the Boulder-clay rests directly on the older Tertiary beds. This clay presents some remarkable features, and the study of its origin may assist in explaining the causes by which the present contour of the country has been partly produced. Some of you have probably read of the "Great Ice Period," and geologists refer this superficial covering spread over some portion of Hertfordshire, and other parts of England, to that earlier period of the earth's history when higher mountains existed in Wales and Scotland, down which large glaciers moved, and probably extended as a great ice-sheet, like that of Greenland, over the lower land to the border of the old icy sea. From the margin of this old shore, masses of ice loaded with their *débris* of earth and stones protruded into the sea, and becoming detached as icebergs, drifted away, and when melted deposited their earthy burden over the old sea-bed in the more temperate region to the south.

For in the north-east of Hertfordshire are found boulders of limestone, which cannot have come nearer than from the Derbyshire hills, and also other rocks from still further north. It is evident, therefore, that these superficial coverings indicate a very different period from that of the London Clay,—one of intense cold, when there existed to the north large glaciers and snowy mountains, from which were derived the materials of the wide-spread deposits and far-brought boulders found over parts of the present area of Hertfordshire.‡

* "On the whole, it seems safer to conclude that this gravel is the oldest Drift of the district, and is a bed of somewhat local occurrence. The chief localities are Stanmore Heath, from Shenley south-eastward, west and north of Barnet, and at Totteridge, in Middlesex ; at Highbeach, Jack's Hill, and Gayne's Park, east of Epping, in Essex ; and at Shooter's Hill, in Kent."— Whitaker, 'Geology of London,' p. 51.

† Prestwich, The Geologist, vol. i. p. 241.

‡ "The chief tracts of Boulder-clay in our area are on the north-east of Watford, our most westerly patch ; at Finchley, its most southerly point, where it ends off at the northern slope of the ridge that bounds the valley of the Thames ; and in Essex on the north and north-west of Brentwood, whence it spreads over a very large district, beyond our bounds."—Whitaker, l.c. p. 54. —" From an examination of the sections that have been exposed during the last seven years, in making the double line of the London and North-Western

It will be observed, from the few brief observations I have made, that the formations in Hertfordshire are of different kinds, and belong to different periods. If the beds remained as originally formed, and horizontal, the same stratum probably would only have been exposed over the area; but you must remember this fact as taught by geology—that the physical features of the district are due to two primary causes: firstly, to the disturbance which the strata of the neighbourhood have undergone, by which undulations of the surface were occasioned, and hence brought up this or that rock to the surface; and secondly, to the great planing agency, acting differently on the hard and soft materials, partly due to the effects of the great Glacial Period, but probably more largely to the action of rain and rivers, ice and snow, modifying those undulations produced by primary disturbance, and thus presenting us with the varied physical features which contribute so much not only to the picturesque beauty of this neighbourhood, but to that of all districts where glacial effects and other meteoric actions have operated.

Although the geology of the vicinity of Watford shows only the remnants of strata which in other districts are much thicker and occupy far larger areas, still it affords evidence of considerable change of land and sea. of the life of the period, and of climatal conditions; and the more we study the Natural History of these formations, and of the others which constitute the crust of the globe, the more we shall find indubitable evidence of the harmony and unity of design in a Creative intelligence, which, as at the present, so in all past time, has adapted the animal and vegetable life to the existing inorganic conditions.

Whilst the broader characters of a district (geologically speaking) are known, it should not be forgotten that local and working Natural History Societies have their duties and utility. If previous workers have sketched out the larger natural features, still there remain many minute points for investigation by the local naturalist; and therefore it will be well for us to remember, that by detailed work in the field—by carefully examining the pebbles, rocks, and fossils, which apparently seem to teach us little unless we read them rightly—we may all perhaps add something additional to the facts which previous geologists have taught us, as well as to our knowledge of the great physical changes the earth has undergone.

Railway, between Hertfordshire and Lancashire, I have been led to believe that the sands and overlying Boulder-clays are of the same age in the one County as in the other; but whether this be so or not, it is certain that these deposits represent *the close of the Glacial* submergence, and that this submergence of the land lessened in extent southwards, so that the whole of the country south of the Thames was a long island, as suggested by Mr. Godwin-Austen."—C. E. De Rance, On the Relative Age of some Valleys in the North and South of England, ' Proc. Geol. Assoc.,' vol. iv. p. 242.

108

13.—Miscellaneous Notes and Observations.

ENTOMOLOGY.

[Read 14th October, 1875.]

Appearance of Sphinx Convolvuli.—The Meteorological Society having requested that occasional appearances in considerable numbers, of insects usually scarce, should be noted with a view to the elucidation of "seasonal phenomena," it is proper to record the capture during the past few weeks of several specimens of *Sphinx Convolvuli* (the convolvulus hawk-moth), an insect not usually by any means common.

I have heard of seven specimens having been taken in Watford, and of an eighth having been seen since, which has as yet escaped capture. Of the seven which have been taken, two or three were found at rest in early morning upon door-knockers. One, a very fine male, so taken by Mr. Hodgson, one of our letter-carriers, has been very kindly presented to me by the captor. Mr. Hodgson took two others, one of which is in his own collection, and the other in that of Mr. Jonathan Chater, who has two more captured this year. One, which flew into a florist's shop, is in Dr. Brett's possession; and Mr. Clarence Fry has captured one flying over some petunias in his garden, and has seen another, but at present has failed to take it. Mr. Lawford has taken three at Hitchin hovering over flowers at dusk, and Mr. Fry has had two sent to him from Norfolk.

Probably the next issue of the Entomological Journals will contain records of captures of this insect in many other parts of the country, as it is one of those that is usually scarce, but in some years appears in abundance over a large district. These occasional appearances are at present quite unaccounted for, and I am inclined to doubt whether any connexion will be discovered between them and seasonal phenomena.—*Arthur Cottam, Watford.*

BOTANY.

[Read 11th November, 1875.]

Botany of West Suffolk.—I find the Botany of West Suffolk very different from that of Middlesex. I have not yet met with anything that is specially rare. I have, however, in a small area, marked down upwards of 500 plants—among them several of considerable interest, as *Holtonia palustris, Hydrocharis Morsus-ranæ, Parnassia palustris, Antirrhinum Orontium, Sisymbrium Sophia, Iberis amara, Thlaspi arvense, Turritis glabra, Scleranthus perennis, Nepeta Cataria,* and *Rumex pulcher.*—[*Rev.*] *W. M. Hind, Honington Rectory, Bury St. Edmunds.*

14.—On the supposed Chalybeate Spring at Watford, and on other Medicinal Waters in Herts.

By R. A. PRYOR, B.A., F.L.S.

[Read 13th January, 1876.]

At page 63 of the second part of our 'Transactions' there is an inquiry as to a mineral spring, which, on the authority of the 'National Gazetteer of Great Britain and Ireland,' is supposed to have existed at Watford. I cannot help suspecting some error, probably from careless copying, on the part of the topographer quoted.

Sir Henry Chauncy, in the 'Historical Antiquities of Hertfordshire' (p. 6,—1700), in his account of the "Waters in this county that are physical," mentions a spring at Watton that was "discovered about the year 1682, and by some experiments found of very good use. It is of the nature with the waters of *Tunbridge*, but some think stronger; it yields a very black tincture with galls, and will, if close stopped, do so after it hath been four days from the spring; it is very useful to create an appetite," with other beneficial effects, into the exact details of which it is not now necessary to enter. The account in the 'Gazetteer' is so evidently taken from the passage just given, that there can be little doubt that the confusion has arisen from the similarity of name of the two places.

The Watton chalybeate does not appear to have attracted much public attention, and I am not aware that its properties have been subjected to any further analysis. There were, however, other waters in the county of a medicinal character, one at least of which enjoyed for some time a considerable notoriety. Three such are noticed by Chauncy.* The most celebrated was that "in the Common, near Barnet." Of this the first mention is, I believe, to be found in Fuller's 'Worthies of England,' published posthumously in 1662. It had about that time "lately been discovered in a *Common*, as generally *sanative springs* are found in such places, as if Nature therein intimated her intention, designing them for publique profit, not private employment ; it is conceived to run through veins of *alome* by the taste thereof. It coagulateth milk, and the end thereof is an excellent plaister for any green wounds, besides several other operations. But," he goes on to observe, "as *Alexander* was wont to applaud *Achilles*, not as the most valiant, but the most fortunate of men, having *Homer* to trumpet forth his actions; so are these waters much advantaged with the vicinitie of *London*, whose citizens proclaim the praise thereof. And indeed, *London* in this kind is stately attended, having three *Medicinal Waters* (Tunbridge, Epshom, Barnet) within one dayes journey thereof. The catalogue of the cures done by this *spring*," he continues, " amounting to a great number, insomuch that there

* Hist. Antiq. Herts.

is hope, in process of time, *the water rising here* will repay the *blood shed* hard by, and save as many lives as were lost in the fatal battel at *Barnet* betwixt the two houses of *Yorke* and *Lancaster*,"* an anticipation that was hardly, I fear, destined to be fully realised.

Four years afterwards it was again noticed by Merret in his 'Pinax,' where, however, he wrongly places the " fontes purgantes ad Barnet" " in Middlesexia." †

In such repute was it now held, that in 1677 Mr. Alderman Owen left the sum of £1 per annum to keep the well in repair " as long as it should be of service to the parish." ‡ The same benefactor added £8 per annum to the endowment of Queen Elizabeth's Free School at Barnet, to be paid by the Fishmongers' Company.§ It is possible that the Company were trustees of the other bequest also, and that their records may be able to furnish additional particulars. I have been able to glean nothing as to the subsequent history of the trust.

At no great distance, but of secondary importance, were the wells " in the common at *Northal*," now Northaw. These are alluded to by Doody, the botanist and correspondent of Ray, in his notes in the appendix to the second edition of the 'Synopsis,' where he speaks of " Belbar" as " *haud procul ab aquis medicatis* Northallensibus." ‖

Another spring in the same parish is, I believe, mentioned only by Chauncy; it was at the place called Cuffely, now Coffleys.¶

In each case, according to the last-named writer, " The Mineral that they are impregnated with is supposed to be Allom, but most certainly a mixt fixt Salt, of which 'tis hard to determine," ** an explanation that does not throw very much light on the matter. He goes on, however, to describe their medicinal virtues at considerable length, and there can be no doubt that the Barnet waters at all events were at one time extensively in use.

To much the same effect is the account given a few years later by Salmon in his ' History of Hertfordshire ' (in 1728). " There are," he tells us, " Mineral Waters of the *Epsom* kind at *Northall* and *Barnet*, of the *Tunbridge* Sort at *Welwyn* and *Watton*.†† They are known by their Effects, but 'tis hard to say with what impregnated." ‡‡

The Welwyn chalybeate is noticed also by Gough in his additions to Camden's 'Britannia' (vol. i. p. 343) in 1789, where he

* Fuller, Worthies, p. 18.   † Merret, Pinax Rer. Nat. Brit. p. 220.—1666.
‡ Lysons, Envir. Lond. vol. iv. p. 8.   § Salmon, Hist. Herts, p. 56.
‖ Ray, Syn. ed. 2, p. 334.—1696.
¶ In the neighbourhood of North Mims and Hatfield, there are many springs " of a sulphureous or ferruginous nature."—Encycl. Brit. ed. 7, vol. xi. p. 284.
** Chauncy, l c.
†† " In a Miller's Garden of this (Watton) Parish, just by the Beane, is a Well of the *Tunbridge* Kind, which hath a higher *Chalybeate* Taste than that of Welwyn."—Salmon, l.c. p. 219.
‡‡ Salmon, l.c. p. 1.

localises it "at the corner of the rector's garden." I am not aware of any other particulars as to its history.*

Coming down to more recent times, we find Clutterbuck also in his 'History' making mention of mineral springs " in the parishes of Chipping Barnet, Northaw, and Watton," † adding further that "the waters of the two first were analysed some years since [*i.e.* previous to 1815] by Dr. Rutty of Dublin. A gallon of the Barnet water, according to his analysis, yielded, upon evaporation, 323 grains of sediment, consisting of 297 grains of saline, and 26 of earthy matter, mostly calcareous. The same quantity of Northaw water yielded 250 grains of sediment, consisting of 225 grains of saline, and 25 earthy matter, mostly calcareous." ‡

A still later, but perhaps not altogether trustworthy, authority goes into more detail as to the Barnet water, which is said to contain "a considerable portion of calcareous glauber, with a small portion of sea-salt," § a description that would perhaps hardly satisfy the requirements of a modern analyst.

Besides the above, there were also, according to Chauncy, "petrifying Springs in the grounds of *Broadfield*, and in the Parish of *Clothall*." ‖ These, however, can hardly be reckoned among medicinal waters. I do not find mention of them in any other writer.

So much I have been able to gather as to the past history of the mineral springs in this county; their present condition I must leave to the investigation of others. All alike have now dropped out of general notice, but of several the local tradition must yet survive; and analyses of their properties might not unusefully be undertaken by those who have the requisite facilities.

---

* There was also "a chalybeat water" at Hitchin, " in the Sun inn yard."—Gough, l.c. p. 342.
† Clutterbuck, Hist. Herts, vol. i. p. 3.—1815.
‡ G. Monro, Mineral Waters, vol. i. p. 148.
§ Lewis, Topog. Dict. vol. i. p. 86.—1831.   ‖ Chauncy, l.c.

15.—THE RAINFALL IN 1875.

[Summary of Quarterly Reports read 10th June and 11th Nov. 1875, and 13th Jan. 1876]

THE following table shows the monthly fall of rain, in 1875, as recorded at Watford House by Dr. Brett, at Harwood's Farm by Mr. Swanston, at Cassiobury House by the Earl of Essex,* at Oaklands, Hempstead Road, by Mr. Edward Harrison, and at Nash Mills, Hemel Hempstead, by the President, Mr. John Evans, F.R.S. The localities are grouped, firstly, under the river-basins, in accordance with the botanical districts into which Mr. R. A. Pryor has divided the county ;† and secondly, according to their distance from Watford and their proximity to each other,—an arrangement the advantage of which will be more apparent if reports are received from more distant parts of the county. The reports for the first quarter of the year, previously published in the 'Transactions,'‡ are incorporated, and the mean monthly fall at Nash Mills in the decade 1860—69, computed as before, is given in the last column.

RIVER DISTRICTS.		LOWER COLNE.			BULBORNE.
LOCALITIES.	Watford House.	Har- wood's Farm.	Cassio- bury.	Oak- lands.	Nash Mills, Hemel Hemp- stead.
OBSERVERS.	DR. BRETT.	MR. SWANS- TON.	LORD ESSEX.	MR. E. HARRI- SON.	MR. JOHN EVANS.
Height of Rain Gauge { Above Ground. } { Above Sea-level. }	1 ft. 3 in. 250 ft.		1ft. 3 in. 258 ft.	5 ft. 6in. 273 ft.	2ft. 9 in. 237 ft.	Mean Fall 1860-69.
January	3·68	3·90	[3·91]	3·92	3·13	2·88
February	0·62	0·56	[0·84]	1·13	1·03	1·58
March	1·05	1·19	[1·02]	0·85	0·68	2·03
April	1·62	1·45	[1·46]	1·47	1·48	1·45
May	2·03	2·17	2·17	2·05	2·11	2·27
June	2·89	2·13	3·00	3·09	2·35	2·48
July	6 48	6·08	6·43	5·63	5·58	1·85
August	1·22	1·78	1·56	1·34	1·25	2·59
September	2·25	1·58	2·49	2·10	2·23	2·61
October	3·80	3·80	4·39	4·18	4·92	2·35
November	3·28	3·40	3·86	3·89	3·66	2·08
December	1·16	1·03	0·75	0·88	0·93	2·22
Totals .	30·08	29·07	31·88	30·53	29·35	26·39

*Absence from home having prevented the Earl of Essex furnishing returns for the first four months in the year, the means of the amounts recorded at Harwood's Farm and Oaklands for these months are inserted in brackets.

† Transactions, vol. i. p. 67. See also plate 1.   ‡ *ib.* p. 63.

16.—ANNIVERSARY ADDRESS.

By the PRESIDENT, JOHN EVANS, F.R.S., F.S.A., F.G.S., etc.

[Delivered at the Annual Meeting, 10th February, 1876.]

LADIES AND GENTLEMEN,—

It now becomes my duty, as President of this Society, to offer you a few remarks by way of address, and I must express my regret that, owing to other occupations, I have really not had time to prepare anything that will be worthy of your acceptance. I must therefore beg of you to excuse me if in the remarks I address to you I seem to repeat observations I have already made at the opening meeting of this Society.

Before proceeding further, I must congratulate the Society upon its successful entry into life and into business. We number something like 150 members, and our finances are in a satisfactory condition. It is true that our income is not much in excess of our expenditure, but still you must bear in mind that in the first year of the existence of any society there are a certain number of expenses which are not likely to be repeated at subsequent periods, and I therefore think the position so far as regards the pecuniary condition of our Society is good. We have held nine evening meetings since our commencement, and have also attempted to hold a fair number of field meetings, which, owing to the unfortunate weather that prevailed upon the days selected, we were not in all cases able to carry out.

The papers on various subjects which have been read during the past year have already been enumerated in the Report of the Council. We have had, in the first place, geological papers from Mr. Lobley, Professor Morris, and Mr. Whitaker. That from Mr. Lobley was an interesting account of the "Cretaceous Rocks of England," in which we are here more especially interested; and that of Professor Morris was on the "Geology of the London Basin," also one of our neighbours. Mr. Whitaker's paper was "A List of Works on the Geology of Hertfordshire," and therefore of great value to those who are likely to investigate what has been written on the subject. In Botany, we have had some valuable papers from Mr. Cottam, on the "Flora of the Watford District;" and from Mr. R. A. Pryor, "Notes on a proposed re-issue of the Flora of Hertfordshire," and also on the "Botanical Work of the past Season."

Mr. Littleboy, also, has given us a very interesting paper, " A Few
Words about our Local Ferns," and we have further recorded in the
pages of our ' Transactions' the discovery of two or three plants
which are new to Hertfordshire — *Myosotis sylvatica*, *Poterium
muricatum*, and *Impatiens fulva*. In Meteorology and Botany combined, showing the relationship of one to the other, we have had
papers,—from Dr. Hind, " Notes on the Plants on which the Meteorological Society invites Observation as to their Time of Flowering ; " and from Mr. Hopkinson, "On the Observation of Periodical
Natural Phenomena." Mr. Cottam has also given us some " Notes
on the Observation of Insects in Connexion with Investigations on
Seasonal Phenomena." With regard to Meteorology, we have had
meteorological observations taken at Cassiobury by the Earl of
Essex, and I believe we shall also have a report from Dr. Brett at
Watford House. We have also had reports of the rainfall from
several observers, and Mr. Heather has just given us a paper " On the
Construction, Adjustment, and Use of Meteorological Instruments."
In Natural History generally we have had a paper from Mr.
Harting on the study of Natural History, relating more particularly to the observation of the migration and habits of birds ; and
in Entomology two notices from Mr. J. H. James, on the "Destruction of an Oak-tree by the Larvæ of the Goat Moth," and
on " The Death's Head Moth at Watford ; " while Mr. Cottam has
given us a notice relative to the appearance of *Sphinx Convolvuli*.
We have also had, from various authors, several minor notices on
Botany, etc., and at our evening meetings some very interesting
microscopical exhibitions.

We may therefore look back with satisfaction on the work of
the past year, and I think, judging from what has already been
communicated here, we may fairly hope for the future that those
gentlemen who have so readily given us so much will give us
more ; and others will no doubt follow the good example set them,
especially when they come to consider how much lies within our
reach, and comes within our area of observation.

Up to the present time our papers seem to have been mainly
devoted to geology, botany, and meteorology; but our area is sufficiently wide to embrace the whole field of Natural History. We
have only at present extended our investigations to two or three
departments, while the whole of that vast area of Natural History
is open before us; and it has occurred to me that on the present
occasion it might be well if I were to call attention to a few of the

subjects which strike me as being such as would interest the members of the Society, and which lie within easy reach of nearly all of us, especially of those, of course, who have paid any particular attention to the departments of Natural History under which each subject lies.

In Geology we have had, as I said before, Mr. Lobley's paper on the Chalk, and Professor Morris's paper on the London Basin. Mr. Lobley, in his very interesting paper, gave us some account of the method in which the Chalk had probably been deposited, and you will find in the illustrations of his paper some of those minute organisms which have been washed out of the Chalk placed side by side and compared with other organisms of a similar character which have been dredged up from the deep sea in the course of the expedition of the *Challenger*. That expedition of the *Challenger* will, I think, throw a very material amount of light upon the origin, not only of the Chalk, but of various other rocks; for it is found in the course of their soundings that they have brought up, at the very least, four different kinds of sea-bottom. In shallow water they brought up something, which to all appearance was sand of a greenish colour, but which, after close examination under the microscope, proved to be casts of small animals of the *Foraminifera* class, which had been converted into a mixture of flint, clay, and iron, which has this greenish appearance. Chemically it is spoken of as glauconite, or silicate of iron and alumina. This foraminiferal sand is characteristic of some of the beds at the base of the Chalk, what we call the Greensand consisting to some extent of similar fossilized organisms converted in the same manner. There is a point which, I think, might very well be investigated by members of this Society, by examination under the microscope, as to whether in the Leighton sands, which are frequently brought into this neighbourhood for building purposes, they could not find some of those organisms which have been converted into this peculiar greensand or glauconite. But at greater depths the soundings have brought up a white ooze, consisting mainly of the same shells, but mixed also with the spikes of very minute organisms which seem to live on the surface of the sea,— little animals like sea-urchins, with spines all over them; the spines of which fall to the bottom of the sea, and fill up the spaces left by the larger, but still very minute organisms. Similar remains are to be found in the Chalk, and there again is a subject that some of our microscopists might take in hand. But going to

a greater depth, some of those organisms from the bottom of the
sea, which, when taken from a depth of about two thousand
fathoms, appear to be white and moderately firm, assume a rotten
appearance, and become grey; and at still greater depths they
gradually turn into a red clay. The curious feature is this—that
it would appear as if this red clay consisted mainly of the remains
of organic life.

Whether there is in the shells of these minute organisms a
sufficient portion of aluminous matter to constitute this red
clay, when all the chalk is dissolved away, is somewhat
disputed between Professor Wyville Thomson and Dr. Carpenter.
Professor Wyville Thomson is of opinion that two per cent. of
the otherwise calcareous shells is insoluble, while Dr. Carpenter
thinks that the appearance is not due to the presence of clay itself,
but rather to the disintegration of the greensand, which itself is
due to the decomposition of the fleshy matter, the sarcode of the
animals. It has long been known that over various portions of
the Chalk area and various limestone districts we have red clays,
and in all probability these red clays are in a similar manner due
to the solution of the lime—the chalky matter—from the original
chalk or limestone, leaving this insoluble portion on the top of the
rock. In the same way, it is supposed that at the bottom of the
sea there is a current of cold water, not improbably the result of
ice melting at the poles, containing a sufficient quantity of carbonic acid to dissolve away the lime and leave the insoluble
portions at the bottom. No doubt these discoveries would tend to
throw some light on the conditions under which our Chalk has
been deposited. But what I would call attention to is the desira-
bility of making some experiments with our chalk, in order to
ascertain by actual investigation what portion remains insoluble
when exposed for a length of time to water charged with carbonic
acid. I think we have some chemists among our body, and that
there would be no difficulty in carrying out experiments which will
be not only of local but general interest.

Another question to which the attention of the members of the
Society might well be directed is that of the origin of flint. In
certain portions of the sea at the present time there are a vast
number of those minute organisms, the diatoms, which have the
power of secreting a flinty instead of a calcareous shell from the
water of the sea, which contains not only lime, but a certain
amount of flint in solution. Sponges have the same peculiarity of

constructing their skeletons of flint, and the spicules in the interior of white flint are very beautiful objects under the microscope. They also testify to the probability of a great portion of the flint in chalk having been originally organic. I think some investigations might be carried on to ascertain how far any of these diatoms may be traced in our flint, and also to ascertain how far the dissolution and formation of flint may be going on at the present day ; for water has the power of dissolving a very minute amount of flint, and under certain circumstances of parting with that flint. If, for instance, water, with a certain amount of flint in solution, gets into the interior of a flint, there seems a difficulty in its getting out with the flint in solution, and therefore it deposits it in minute layers in the interior. I have no doubt you have noticed in the interior of hollow flints those beautiful pieces of chalcedony like bunches of grapes, and if you examine them under the microscope, you will find that they have been deposited in layers by the infiltration of water containing flint in solution. In some cases, instead of the flint being deposited in thin films, it has been deposited in crystals, and there is a curious change observable occasionally, in which the flint, having been deposited in crystals, after a certain length of time seems to change its character, and is deposited in films over the original crystals, and on breaking the chalcedony the crystals are seen like radii through the circular protuberances.

There are various pieces of geological work which may be done in the neighbourhood. There is one interesting deposit in the Chalk to which Mr. Whitaker has given the name of the "chalk rock." It comes about the middle of the Chalk, midway between the Upper and Lower Chalk, and consists of a very hard rocky stone, which may be seen on the railway in the neighbourhood of Berkhampstead projecting from the sides of the cutting in large blocks, and it is often met with in sinking wells a little to the north of Watford. The shells of the organisms in it are distinct from those in the chalk above and below it ; so that it seems to have been deposited under somewhat different conditions. It would be interesting to you to find how far the chalk rock extends, at what depth it is, and to examine the organisms to be found in it. The best locality is the pit on Rough-down in the neighbourhood of Boxmoor Station, where I have found the greater number of the shells characteristic of this chalk rock.

Another geological subject which lies before us is to form some

idea as to the distribution of the drift or gravels of the neighbourhood; for we have here two different kinds, if not more, of this
series of drifted rocks. We have what is known as the Glacial
Drift, and we have along our valleys the River Drift; the Glacial
Drift being probably due to the last submergence of the country
below the sea, and the River Drift to the excavation of the valleys
by the rivers themselves or by rivers running in much the same
course. All those members of the Society who have paid any
attention to geology are perfectly aware that at the time the
glacial drift was deposited, there is every probability that the
climate was much colder than it is at present, and that those clays
in which we find small fragments of chalk, and foreign pebbles,
were either brought by icebergs or formed by the action of a large
coating of ice on the surface of the country. It is an open question,
whether to a certain extent the valleys in the Chalk have not been
excavated by large local glaciers; whether we have had here at
some time or other a thick coating of ice, which, working towards
the sea, ploughed out a portion of our valleys; but whether this
is the case or not, we have evidence, in the gravels, of rocks having
been brought here from a very considerable distance. I think it
would be worth the attention of any of us to form a collection of
the different pebbles found in the Watford gravels, with the view
of ascertaining the general proportion of each, and then of tracing
the countries from which they came; for many of the stones must
have been brought, probably by the action of floating icebergs,
fifty, a hundred, and in some cases some hundreds of miles.

In the valley gravels you find some of the remains of the older
gravels mixed with the flints washed out of the chalk by the rivers.
It is therefore rather difficult to distinguish between those gravels
which are of marine origin and those of fresh-water origin. But
still, if you find in the gravels the remains of the animals which
must have lived on land, the probability is that those gravels were
deposited by the action of streams running through the land, and
not by the sea. In some cases the remains of the large mammoth—
the large hairy elephant—have been found in these valleys. On one
occasion the tooth of an elephant was found at Bricket Wood; and
in the valley of the Gade, at Two Waters, an elephant's tooth was
dug up in the gravel, in the excavation for the Canal. In the
valley of the Gade I have myself found one or two instruments
of flint, which bear testimony to the fact of man living in this
country at the same time as the animals of what is known as the
Quaternary fauna.

The Brick Earths of the neighbourhood would also repay investigation. In some of these there are laminated beds of clay between which impressions of leaves may be found; they are extremely rare however, and it is difficult to say whether those beds containing leaves belong to Tertiary times, or to a period when the brick earth itself was deposited.

There is only one other geological point upon which I will address you; and I hope you will excuse me for dwelling more on geology than other parts of Natural History, as I feel myself more at home in that domain than in some of the others. There is a geological deposit essentially known as belonging to Hertfordshire —the Hertfordshire plum-pudding stone. At the present time there are not more than one or two places known where it can be met with in the actual position in which it has been formed. There is one place near Radlett where you will find the Woolwich and Reading beds (which are below the London Clay) cemented together with flinty cement into a band of pudding stone. This is in its original position, with the upper portion worn away as if by the action of ice or some strong abrading material over it. It would be interesting to see if we could find upon any rock of that character in position, those striations or ice-markings which are so characteristic of local glaciers.

With regard to Botany, I must at the outset say that I know very little about it. But there are several points which it appears to me may be very well investigated by those better acquainted with the subject than myself; and one of these is the connexion of the geology of the country with the plants found on its surface. Mr. Pryor has made some suggestions with regard to dividing the county into certain districts, more especially according to the river-basins; but I think it also desirable for botanists to notice, not only the nature of the sub-soil as shown on the geological map, but the drift, or surface soil that comes above it. There is no doubt that there is a very intimate connexion between the Botany of a district and its geological formation; in fact, geologists not unfrequently are led to discover outliers of clay from the woods growing upon them. In olden times the London Clay was not so easily drained as at present, and in consequence portions of it existing in Chalk areas, being too heavy for cultivation, were left as sites for woods. It is generally the case that wherever there is a Tertiary outlier, there is a wood upon it; and thus the outlines of the country are such as in many cases to suggest to geologists the spots where Tertiary outliers may be looked for.

The ferns of our county, which everybody admires so much, have already been brought under our notice by Mr. Littleboy, and I imagine there will not be many additions to the list with which he has furnished us ; but I think the mosses of the district have not been touched upon, and that they would be an exceedingly interesting subject of study to anybody who will take it up. The fungi, also, appear to me to be very worthy of observation, and I hope we may have some communications on the subject of these lower plants in the course of our next session. But even without going into the fields to botanize, there are other subjects which you may observe at home; and I think anybody who has read those interesting books of Darwin's, on climbing plants, for instance, must feel how many objects of interest there are for those who only have a few flower-pots or the smallest portion of garden ground. It is interesting to observe the almost instinctive properties of certain plants. Whether in twisting round so as to obtain a support on which to rest, or in turning to the light, they seem in some instances to approximate to the instinct of animals. The carnivorous plants, as to whose flesh-eating habits Darwin has also written, might possibly be experimented upon ; and I am sure the members of this Society will be extremely indebted to any one who will bring before them the results of their experiments, illustrated by the plants themselves.

As to Zoology, we have had no papers on the higher animals. There are in this district a fair number of wild Mammalia still in existence—the badger, the hedgehog, the mole, and various other animals, as to whose habits observations may be directed, which would be of interest to the Society.

We have also not heard much of Ornithology, though we have had one paper on the seasonal migration of birds ; but any one who has read Gilbert White's 'Natural History of Selborne' must have seen how extremely interesting are observations in connexion with the habits of birds. Whether it is with regard to the question of the food on which they live ; whether it is the connexion which exists between the birds, the insects, and the fruit of a district; or whether it is with regard to their habits of migration, they are among the most interesting subjects of observation which the naturalist can have. If, in addition, some meteorological observations, as to the season, the temperature, and other probable causes which bring the birds amongst us, are made, some special interest will be given to the subject.

We have done nothing either with the reptiles, the fishes, or the land and fresh-water shells of the county. All of them are fitting subjects for investigation, and I hope we shall find among us some who will take these questions up. Fresh-water shells are, I think, as abundant in this county as in any other part of England, and their collection and classification would be an interesting employment, especially for our younger members, during the ensuing summer.

Nor have we done much in the matter of Entomology, though Mr. Cottam has contributed one paper with regard to the observation of insects, and another on the appearance of the convolvulus hawk-moth in our neighbourhood. There is a very popular though scientific book, a translation from the French, by Professor Duncan, on the 'Transformations of Insects.' If it is not in the library, I would recommend any one interested to procure the book, and he will find in it a vast number of subjects, which may induce him to bring observations before us of interest to the Society. Even the common cabbage butterfly, if traced up from its birth, will fill a long chapter in the history of insects —its struggles to escape from some of its clothing, the manner in which it ties itself up, and other matters, are as interesting as the events in many a novel.

With regard to the habits of bees, wasps, and ants, anybody who has noticed those very remarkable papers by my friend Sir John Lubbock, will see a field of observation open for all of us. The way in which ants have actually contrived to have, one may say, domestic cattle among them—the way in which they employ other insects for certain purposes, leads one to regard them as possessing a greater amount of intelligence than we are naturally inclined to assign to them. Probably the habits of bees and wasps are rather indicative of acquired instinct than of reason, but they are such as to repay the amplest amount of attention that can be directed to them.

With regard to Meteorology, we have already in the district several rain-gauges kept, and I am glad to hear that one or two other observations are likely to be taken within the county. I hope we shall have the stations extended at which proper meteorological observations will be taken, and the results communicated to us.

In addition to the ordinary rain-gauge, the firm of which I am a member has been in the habit for a considerable number of years

of keeping gauges which ascertain not only the amount of rain
which falls from the heavens, but the rain which finds its way
through a certain amount of soil. These observations have been
extended over a period of upwards of thirty years, and I am sorry
to say that but few other observations of the kind have been made.
I should be glad if some member of the Society, taking up meteorology, would also have a certain number of gauges of this kind, and
carry on observations simultaneously with ourselves, so that we
may have some means of comparing our results with those of
others, and be able to place a greater amount of reliance upon
them. The instrument is of the simplest kind. In consists of a
cast-iron cylinder turned to a knife edge at the top, and with a
pipe from the bottom leading to a gauge like an ordinary rain-
gauge. The cylinder is sunk so that its top edge is nearly level
with the ground, and it is filled with soil, the surface of which is
sown with grass, so that it does not appear in any way different
from the field or piece of ground in which it is buried. The
results of the measurement of the amount of rain which percolates
through the soil in the gauge are very different from what might
have been supposed. I will not go deeply into the subject, but it
appears, generally speaking, that of the whole amount of rain
which falls from April to October, in the ordinary soil of this
district, hardly a drop finds its way to a depth of three feet from
the surface. A greater amount finds its way through the Chalk in
summer, though often not one inch, although seventeen or eighteen
inches of rain may fall. In the winter months, when the growth
of vegetation is not going on to the same extent, and there is less
evaporation, a greater amount finds its way down, and percolates
to the springs which feed our rivers ; but still, in different years it
varies from two or three inches to as much as fourteen or fifteen
inches. It is a question which throws a very considerable amount
of light on the nature of the streams which flow through the
country, and indirectly upon the general water supply. If any one
is inclined to take up the subject, I shall be only too happy to put
him in the way of carrying out his experiments.

With regard to microscopic investigations, a considerable number
of our members have taken up that branch of study, and anything
more interesting than the revelations of the microscope it is
certainly impossible to imagine. We find organisms so minute
that we can hardly conceive the possibility of their existence.
We are able to trace the conditions under which life is carried on,

and almost to see the process of digestion going on. We find, even in the smallest things, the most wonderful perfection. It calls to my mind a passage of one of the oldest writers on Natural History, Pliny, who says that "the nature of things is never more complete than in the smallest"—"*Cum natura rerum nusquam magis quam in minimis tota sit.*"

> "Nature hath made no thing so base but can
> Read some instruction to the wisest man."

And it is, I think, by means of the microscope that we can form the best idea of the marvellous power of the Creator.

I have now just touched upon some of those subjects which fall within our domain.

Our field meetings unfortunately were not so successful last year as could have been wished, but I hope may during the ensuing season be more prosperous. It seems to me that in planning these expeditions it is desirable not to make them cover too large an extent of country ; it is much better to make our excursions short, and to explore the country we intend to examine, well, rather than find ourselves compelled to hurry and neglect some interesting point to catch a train or to return home by daylight. In planning our excursions no doubt it is very desirable, as far as possible, to make the objects varied, so that on one occasion the botanist may find something more especially to interest him, on another the entomologist, and on another the geologist—but it is impossible to take an excursion of the kind without finding some objects for all.

We have around us in this county, and in the neighbouring counties, a sufficient field for us to be able to make interesting excursions during a long series of years. We are well placed, with regard to railway communication, for exploring what lies more immediately in our own neighbourhood, or for varying expeditions in the neighbourhood with those to a greater distance. We may, I think, occasionally venture to explore some new districts where we shall find a new soil, new plants, new animals, and new insects. It will be a matter for our excellent Secretary to consider. I am sure, if the Society has in any way been successful, it is in great measure to the efforts of our Secretary it is due. The pains which he has taken in organizing our excursions have been enormous, and I can only regret that on one or two occasions, owing to unfavourable weather, they have been in vain.

I have now given you at greater length than I intended, but I hope at no greater length than has been sufficient to interest you, some slight account of what I consider the general objects of our Society, and what remains for us to do.   We have the whole domain of Natural History before us, and in tracing the marvellous inter-connexion of the whole of the phenomena of animated nature, I think we shall feel how wonderful are those links which seem to exist between every variety of living beings.   Whether we regard each form of being as the result of special creation, or whether we take the more modern view of development—the theory of their springing from second causes—the whole seems to form one chain :

> .   .   .   .   .   .   " Each moss,
> Each shell, each crawling insect, holds a rank
> Important in the plan of Him who framed
> This scale of beings : holds a rank which lost
> Would break the chain and leave behind a gap
> Which Nature's self would rue."

The whole fabric testifies indeed to the infinite power of the one First Cause, and we shall, as Milton says, "in contemplation of created things, by steps ascend to God."

17.—THE GEOLOGY AND WATER SUPPLY OF THE NEIGHBOURHOOD
OF WATFORD.

By the Rev. JAMES C. CLUTTERBUCK, M.A.

Communicated by A. T. BRETT, M.D., Vice-President.

[Read 11th May, 1876.]

THE Geology and Water Supply of any district are so inseparably
connected, that it needs no excuse for considering them together.

It is proposed in the following paper to consider the one with
special reference to and as depending entirely on the other. In
attempting to describe the geology of the immediate neighbourhood of Watford, it will not be necessary to enter into minute
details, but to take a general view of the subject. First as to the
extent of the area which may be considered the immediate neighbourhood of Watford. Taking the Parish Church as a well-defined
centre, a circle with a radius of five miles will include examples of
the characteristic features of the geology of the greater part of
Hertfordshire, which may be described as forming a portion of the
northern limb of the Chalk basin of London. The river Colne in
its course from north-east to south-west divides the district into
two nearly equal parts; that to the north-west to be accounted as
Chalk, that to the south and south-west presenting a band or belt of
the Chalk bounded on the north by the river Colne and on the south
by the Tertiary beds which overlie the Chalk; this band varying
from a mile to two miles and a half in width. The physical
features of the district are to a certain extent indexes of its
geological conditions. The centre of the northern portion of the
district is intersected from north to south by the river Gade, the
north-western limb by the river Chess,—two rivers characteristic of
their origin from the Chalk, which run in deep valleys, by which
the otherwise slightly undulating surface of the district is furrowed.

The Chalk, whether to the north or south of the river Colne,
presents little if any exposed surface, being covered by beds of
flint-gravel, sand, or loam, varying in thickness; with the exception of certain isolated and outlying patches of Tertiary clay and
sand, in situ, which again are frequently covered with beds or
traces of the higher level gravel.

To the south the Chalk, except the belt or band before mentioned, is covered by the Tertiary strata. These rise in ill-defined
escarpments at their junction with the Chalk. The highest levels
are at Bushey Heath and Stanmore Common, being capped by
traces of the Bagshot sands and gravel in beds of considerable
extent. Such is a somewhat rough description of the leading
geological features of the immediate neighbourhood of Watford.

The cuttings of the London and North Western Railway furnish
well-defined sections of the strata more or less exposed to view.
Beginning with that at the southern end of the tunnel, the Chalk
is exposed with very remarkable undulations of surface; the
cavities (sometimes called pipes) being filled with sand or gravel.

It may be remarked that on the immediate surface of the Chalk there is usually a thin band of dark red clay, called by Dr. Buckland a "pargetting," said often to contain traces of manganese.

Passing over the valley of the Colne by the lofty viaduct, the Chalk and Tertiary beds may be seen in a chalk pit to the east of the line, and on the entrance of the cutting on the London side of the Bushey Station. The first partly exposed bed consists of sand sometimes intermixed with rolled pebbles, sometimes coloured, sometimes of a singular purity and brightness, known as silver sand, and quarried for household, trade, or horticultural purposes. Above the sand beds are the clays formerly bearing the term "plastic," as indicating their nature. They are of various and beautiful colours and consistency. A good exposed section may be seen in Mr. Blackwell's brick field. Immediately resting on the clay in the cutting is a bed of black silt in which sharks' teeth are found. This is capped by an outcropping bed of the London Clay, which here completes the series, the whole dipping towards and passing under London and finding its outcrop in the bed of the Thames above Woolwich, which gives a name to some of these Tertiary beds. The silt bed seems to crop out in the river about the spot where the tunnel was made, and it is believed that much of the difficulty encountered in its construction was due to the fact that this bed being of the nature of quick or running sand, the water of the river thereby found a too ready access to the works, hence their consequent serious hindrance. This is confirmed by the fact that a recent subway has been constructed near the Tower of London with little difficulty, where the stiff London Clay was pierced, and the ingress of water thereby prevented.

It is now to be considered how the geological condition of the district will account for the presence or absence of water. To begin with the upper beds—those found on the higher levels. It may be sufficient to speak of these as beds of sand and gravel resting on clay. It may be remarked that such spots were fixed on of old for habitation; a rule which will extend to cities and towns as well as country villages. The site of ancient London is nearly if not entirely co-extensive with beds of gravel resting on the London clay. Hampstead, Highgate, Harrow, Hendon, and other towns were placed where there is a certain amount of water, though the increase of population has required additional quantities to be obtained often at great trouble and expense. The water in such places is easily reached by sinking shallow wells into the gravel or sand, the water being upheld by the clay beneath. Where there is only a thin bed of gravel or sand, ponds are sunk, which, if they receive the drainage of a considerable area, will sometimes furnish a supply through the year. These sources of water when they show themselves above ground are usually called land springs; they will run till the bed of water in the sand or gravel is exhausted or reduced to so low a level that the pressure of the water is not sufficient to force it to the surface. The deeper or more abundant sources of water are usually called main springs.

There is a considerable amount of water in the gravel or sand in the district known as Bushey Heath, or Stanmore Common ; hence of late years the population there has increased, and seems to have outrun the natural water supply. The site of the village of Abbot's Langley, with its hamlet Bedmont, presents a different feature. The Chalk here rises to a considerable elevation—about 450 feet above the level of the sea. It is capped by an outlying bed of the "plastic clay," *in situ*. which may be seen cropping out on the roadside bank between Trolly Bottom and the village. This is covered by a bed of gravel in which the water accumulates. If, in sinking a well, of which there are many, as well as open ponds, the clay is pierced till reaching the chalk beneath, the water will disappear. At Bedmont, on one occasion at least, in order to clean out a large pond fed by the natural supply from the gravel, the head or stank of the pond being cut for that purpose, the water which immediately found its way into the Chalk sensibly augmented the supply of water in the wells near at hand, though at least 170 feet below.

To return to the district east and south-east of the Colne. Where the London Clay is not covered by beds of sand or gravel, the water is thrown from the surface sometimes augmented in its passage to the river by artificial agricultural drainage; these waters flow in open water courses, which here and there furrow the escarpment which overhangs the Colne. When it arrives at the junction of the clay with the sand outcropping beneath it, the water wholly or in part sinks into the earth through natural apertures usually called swallow-holes, descends into the subjacent chalk, and is added to the water in that so-called water-bearing stratum by which the river is augmented and maintained. As the water which finds its way into the chalk by these swallow-holes is derived from the surface drainage of the Tertiary clays, and as their surface must not only be saturated but flooded before the water will be discharged from the surface, the supply from this source must necessarily be irregular and periodical. In some years there are no such floods ; in others, such as 1875–6, the quantity of water must in many cases be more than the swallow-holes can take in. Among the most remarkable are those found in the carrier which conveys the water from the Elstree reservoir to the river, which must be plugged when the water is discharged, to prevent the waste of a greater part if not the entire volume. At another, near Letchmore Heath, in the parish of Aldenham, where a large body of water sinks in a deep depression or pit into the earth, at the junction of the sand of the Tertiary beds and the Chalk, this sand may be seen cropping out close at hand. It has been supposed that there is some connexion between this irruption of water and the well-known copious issue of water at Otterspool. There are stories of ducks having found their way thither by some subterranean passage ; and measurements of the level at which the water stands in the wells thereabout and in the direction of the pool, show an irregularity not easily accounted for but by

the existence of some fault or fissure in that direction. After
heavy rain the pool becomes slightly turbid, and in a dry season it
has been known to cease flowing over the dam by which it is confined and over which the water usually falls. There are other
swallow-holes to the north and south of Bushey Grove, in the
direction of Hillfield Lodge, and Cold Harbour; in the latter the
overflowing water might be seen this year running to waste in
augmentation of the floods in the rivers across the park. Again
there is a remarkable instance in a meadow through which the
footpath runs from Crook Log to Bushey Church, the orifice sometimes being insufficient to take in all the water flowing down the
watercourse. When the water thus finds its way through the
sand, or in some cases direct into the chalk, it here as elsewhere
causes a rise in the water in the chalk sometimes of 20 feet at a
distance of say half a mile from the river or outfall. By the slow
discharge of these waters that of the river is augmented, though
from the uncertainty due to the confined area of the chalk which
can receive the rainfall south of the river, the perennial flow
cannot be great. The amount to be calculated on as delivered from
this source might be to a certain extent estimated by the measurement of any wells in a line between the swallow-holes and river;
the wells near the river will not only rise with the irruption of the
water at the swallow-holes; but whether they be shallow or deep
shafts sunk into the chalk, or deep borings, they will, if near the
river, rise and fall as the river may be flooded, or in dry seasons be
reduced in volume or level.

It is well known that the Chalk and Tertiary strata, such as
they are seen in the district under consideration, dip towards
London, that their outcrop is in the bed of the Thames above
Woolwich, and that the height to which water will rise between
Watford and the Thames mean tide level would be described by a
line drawn from a point about 20 feet above the River Colne to
mean tide level in the Thames, or an inclination of about 13 feet
per mile, and that within a certain range near London the deep
wells are reduced 60 feet at the point of greatest depression, by
the aggregate pumping from the wells sunk into the sand of the
Tertiary beds and the Chalk beneath, and that when there is a rise
in the wells which receive the drainage of the Tertiary clay
through swallow-holes, the deep wells in London are also found
to rise. The depression of the water-level under London 60 feet
below Trinity high-water mark among other things shows clearly
the fallacy of the assertion that the water in the Chalk might be
arrested in its passage to the sea by deep wells sunk near Watford,
whereas under London the drainage is absolutely reversed.

Now to turn to the district north of the Colne. The Chalk
district within the limits assigned by this paper forms but a small
part of an extensive area which reaches from the Colne to the
range of the Chiltern Hills. Though only a part of this area, the
water falling on its surface and given out in rivers is regulated by
the same laws and presents the same natural phenomena as the

wider and entire district. The Chalk is often spoken of as a water-bearing stratum. That it is the great source of water to the Thames and its tributaries is beyond all doubt, and this, because it receives the rainfall on an extended surface, and a certain portion of that rainfall sinking into the earth forms an extensive reservoir, whence the Thames and most of its tributaries derive their waters. That the subterranean water in the Chalk stratum is due to the rainfall on its surface needs no argument. It has been calculated that after the summer months, when generally there is no percolation of water to the subterranean reservoir, it requires at least three inches of continuous rainfall to replace the evaporation from the soil. When the soil is saturated, a considerable per-centage sinks into the earth and an accumulation of water takes place; and as the water moves, by natural gravitation, towards its vent or outfall—the rivers which run in the lowest valleys—in its passage thither it encounters a resistance which so retards its progress that it assumes an inclined surface, which is the balance between this resistance in the medium in which the water flows, and the hydrostatic force by which its progress towards its vent is quickened. This inclination of surface varies with the presence or absence of cracks, fissures, and orifices, through which alone the water in the Chalk can flow. The distance from the outfall regulates the amount of storage in this subterranean reservoir in the Chalk. The whole average inclination of the surface of the water, from the Chiltern Hills to the Colne, is 13 feet in the mile. Besides this, which may be called the longitudinal, there is a lateral adjustment of inclination of surface rising from the river on either side to the centre between two rivers, flowing in parallel lines towards the south. Thus the river Gade, at or about Cassio Bridge, and the River Colne, at some points between Watford Mill and the site of the old Bushey Mill, will be found on a level. Draw a line connecting these two points, and take the four cross-roads as a centre between them, and it will be found that the water there is never less than 10 feet above the rivers, and that this height decreases progressively towards the rivers, and, moreover, that in very wet seasons there will be an additional rise of about 10 feet at the top of Watford, varying with the amount of rainfall percolating to the water-level in the Chalk. Take a third line following the course of the High Street of Watford, and this will be found to agree with the other lines. At one time the Chalk under Watford was perforated with wells; they are now mostly, if not all, filled up, but the measurements of the varying level of the waters have been retained, as well as those from the top of Watford to Cassio Bridge. The way in which the water-level in the Chalk maintains its regularity, and its ratio of rise and fall, may be deemed an interesting phenomenon of natural geological hydraulics.

It is by the replenishment and exhaustion of the rain-water sinking into the Chalk that the rivers are fed and maintain their volume, the water in wells following the same natural law. There are several methods by which attempts have been made to measure the amount of the storage and discharge of the water in the Chalk. Any mere average of rainfall is no certain guide; it depends more on the conditions under which the rain falls, than on the amount falling. The heaviest summer rain will scarcely replace that evaporated from the surface, whereas a moderate rainfall in the winter, when the soil is wet, will descend to augment the stock of water in the Chalk. This is clearly shown by the records of a rain gauge bearing the name of the great Dalton, kept for more than a generation by the late Mr. John Dickinson, and now by Mr. John Evans, which registers the rainfall percolating three feet of earth, and thereby indicates the amount which sinks to the level of the subterranean Chalk water. Some have contented themselves with the measurement of wells, a somewhat troublesome process, but where a conveniently situated line of wells can be found, being well worth the while of those who take an interest in such matters. The writer of this paper has always—in these days when the water-supply question increases in interest and importance—protested against abstracting large quantities of water from the Chalk as the great water-bearing stratum, and he ventures to quote what he said in evidence when examined before the Royal Commission, and which was quoted with approval by the Ministers of the Crown in both Houses of Parliament :—" Take the water as it flows above ground, but do not tamper with it below."

It may be asked what effects will be produced by pumping water at the Colne Valley Water Works. I have heard Mr. Bateman distinctly disclaim any particular knowledge of water supply in the Chalk districts, when examined before the Committee of the House of Lords ; and in a discussion on a paper by the late Mr. F. Braithwaite, on the rise and fall of the Wandle, he said that he was but slightly acquainted with the question of water supply in the Chalk districts. I venture to claim some knowledge on the subject, especially in the immediate vicinity of the spot where the Water Works are placed. I have a record of the rise and fall of the wells near at hand for the years 1841-2, the winter of the former being a very wet season with a rainfall of 12·68 inches in the months of September, October, and November, with a percolation in Dalton's gauge of 10·86 in those months, therefore specially favourable to observation on the alternations of the Chalk water-level, and the effects of the irruption of water by swallow-holes, and the coincident rise and fall of the river and wells. I am informed that the well is made water-tight to the depth, I think, of 60 feet, with a view of excluding the water of the river. It will be found that the water in the well rises and falls with the water in the river. Therefore this so-called precaution is quite unnecessary. The well would of course be " steined " till it reached the solid Chalk, but beyond this any money so expended would be simple waste. Proof of this may be found in the record of an experiment made by the Grand Junction Canal Company, when the late Mr. John Dickinson opposed the sinking a well at the head of the Bulborne.

An experimental well was steined and puddled by the workmen of the Canal Company, pumps were worked before and after this process, and in both cases the effects of draining the stream were the same. And so it would be at the new Water Works. I am informed that in sinking the Water Works well the water came in greater volume from the side away from the river. This is easily explained by the fact that the water in the Chalk to the east received through the swallow-holes in one of the wettest seasons on record stood at an inclination rising from the river of from 40 to 50 feet in the mile, hence the greater pressure and consequent more rapid flow into the well. When the exhaustion of water by pumping is daily carried on, the water in the Chalk to the east will, naturally in dry seasons, and artificially by pumping, be gradually reduced, the pressure from that quarter will be lessened, the level of water in the well will be lowered, and the abstraction of water from the river increased in proportion to the amount of water pumped. If that quantity amounts to, say, 2,000,000 gallons per day, the power of the mills below will be sensibly diminished. The natural effect of the rise and fall of the surface of the water in the river will be like that of tidal wells on the sea-coast, where the Chalk waters outfall into the sea, the alternation of level of water in the wells within a certain range being regulated by the height of the tide. At Liverpool, under the direction of the late Mr. Robert Stephenson, an experiment was made to test the possibility of supplying the town with water from the Red Sandstone formation on which the town stands. Large quantities were obtained from several wells. At length, when the level of the wells was reduced, the tidal waters found their way into the wells. Read river for tidal waters and the same will take place at Bushey meadows. I have lately heard of the abandonment of wells as a source of supply to an important and thickly inhabited district from the fouling of the wells from proximity to a tidal river. If the proposal to extend the supply from the well now in question should be carried out, at certain seasons a great portion of the water must of necessity be drawn from the river, and in flood time, such as has been of late, there will be the danger of the water in the well becoming turbid and thus furnishing unmistakable evidence of the source whence it is derived.

18.—Meteorological Observations taken at Cassiobury House from May to December, 1875.

By the Right Honourable the Earl of Essex.

[Read 13th January, 1876.]

Abstract.*

May.—The mean pressure of the atmosphere was 30·06 ins.; the highest reading, 30·45 ins. on the 11th; the lowest, 29·34 on the 6th; range, 1·11 in.

The mean temperature of the air was 55°·6; the highest, 78° on the 15th; the lowest, 36° on the 31st; range, 42°: the mean high day temperature, 66°·7; the mean low night temperature, 44°·5; mean daily range, 22°·2. The highest temperature in the sun was 105° on the 15th.

The direction of the wind was N.W. on 7 days, N.E. on 4, E. on 2, S.E. on 1, S.W. on 13, and W. on 4. Westerly winds (N.W. to S.W.) mostly prevailed for the first half of the month, and north-easterly only on the last few days.

Rain fell on 6 days, the total amount being 2·17 ins., and the greatest fall in one day 0·87 in. on the 6th.

A "heavy blight" was noticed at 2 p.m. on the 27th.

June.—The mean pressure of the atmosphere was 29·90 ins.; the highest reading, 30·30 ins. on the 24th; the lowest, 29·55 ins. on the 15th; range, 0·75 in.

The mean temperature of the air was 59°·6; the highest, 80° on the 4th;† the lowest, 41° on the 1st; range, 39°: the mean high day temperature, 69°·5; the mean low night temperature, 49°·9; mean daily range, 19°·6. The highest temperature in the sun was 103° on the 3rd.

The direction of the wind was N.E. on 6 days, E. on 1, S.E. on 2, S. on 3, S.W. on 14, and W. on 4. Easterly winds prevailed for the first few days, and then south-westerly to the 17th, and again towards the end of the month.

Rain fell on 16 days, from the 8th to the 20th inclusive, and on the last 3 days; the total amount being 3·00 ins., and the greatest fall in one day 0·50 in. on the 9th.

There was a slight thunderstorm at 2 p.m. on the 9th.

July.—The mean pressure of the atmosphere was 30·05 ins.; the highest reading, 30·40 ins. on the 6th and 28th; the lowest, 29·60 ins. on the 11th; range, 0·80 in.

---

* In preparing this summary of the Earl's daily observations no corrections have been applied to any of the readings; but as the barometer reads about 0·28 in. too high, and the height above the sea is 258 feet, the figures given represent approximately the sea-level pressure. The mean temperatures are deduced from the daily readings of the maximum and minimum thermometers. The observations were taken at 9 a.m.—Ed.

† The only day in the year on which the shade temperature is recorded as having reached 80°.

The mean temperature of the air was 57°·4; the highest, 73° on the 29th; the lowest, 40° on the 13th; range, 33°: the mean high day temperature, 64°·8; the mean low night temperature, 50°·0; mean daily range, 14°·8. The highest temperature in the sun was 95° on the 29th.

The direction of the wind was N.W. on 2 days, N.E. on 9, E. on 4, S. on 5, S.W. on 6, and W. on 5. North-easterly winds prevailed most at the beginning of the month, and westerly or south-westerly towards the end.

Rain fell on 18 days, on every day from the 14th to the 23rd inclusive; the total amount being 6·43 ins., and the greatest fall in one day 1·16 in. on the 14th. (On the 21st 1·06 in. fell.)

Thunder was heard at 3 p.m. on the 3rd, and hail fell at 6 p.m. on the 25th.

AUGUST.—The mean pressure of the atmosphere was 30·11 ins.; the highest reading, 30·40 ins. on the 21st; the lowest, 29·88 ins. on the 13th; range, 0·52 in.

The mean temperature of the air was 61°·4; the highest, 79° on the 18th; the lowest, 40° on the 30th; range, 39°: the mean high day temperature, 70°·0; the mean low night temperature, 52°·8; mean daily range, 17°·2. The highest temperature in the sun was 98° on the 23rd.

The direction of the wind was N.W. on 6 days, N. on 3, N.E. on 7, S.E. on 1, S. on 6, and S.W. on 8. North-easterly winds prevailed at the beginning of the month (to the 7th), then south-westerly, and north-westerly for the last few days.

Rain fell on 11 days, the total amount being 1·56 in., and the greatest fall in one day 0·70 in. on the 3rd.

This day (the 3rd) was "thundery," and heavy rain fell at 4 p.m. Thunder was also heard at 2 p.m. on the 7th.

SEPTEMBER.—The mean pressure of the atmosphere was 30·12 ins.; the highest reading, 30·40 ins. on the 6th and 12th; the lowest, 29·80 ins. on the 22nd and 28th; range, 0·60 in.

The mean temperature of the air was 59°·3; the highest, 80° on the 19th; the lowest, 42° on the 29th; range, 38°: the mean high day temperature, 69°·1; the mean low night temperature, 49°·5; mean daily range, 19°·6. The highest temperature in the sun was 96° on the 28th.

The direction of the wind was N.W. on 4 days, N.E. on 2, E. on 9, S.E. on 3, S.W. on 8, and W. on 4. Westerly winds mostly prevailed at the beginning of the month, easterly in the middle, and westerly again towards the end.

Rain fell on 13 days, on every day from the 19th to the 28th inclusive; the total amount being 2·49 ins., and the greatest fall in one day 0·75 in. on the 21st.

OCTOBER.—The mean pressure of the atmosphere was 29·84; the highest reading, 30·40 ins. on the 7th; the lowest, 29·30 ins. on the 13th; range, 1·10 in.

The mean temperature of the air was 45°·3; the highest, 65° on the 4th ; the lowest, 26° on the 25th ; range, 39˙: the mean high day temperature, 52˙·4 ; the mean low night temperature, 38°·2 ; mean daily range, 14°·2. The highest temperature in the sun was 71° on the 8th.

The direction of the wind was N.W. on 4 days, N.E. on 3, E. on 5, S.E. on 6, S. on 3, S.W. on 6, and W. on 4. Westerly winds prevailed for the first half of the month, and easterly for the last half.

Rain fell on 15 days, the total amount being 4·39 ins., and the greatest fall in one day 0·68 in. on the 20th.

The temperature sank to below freezing-point on 5 nights : 5 days were foggy.

NOVEMBER.—The mean pressure of the atmosphere was 29·85 ins. ; the highest reading, 30·20 ins. on the 15th and 23rd ; the lowest, 29·15 on the 11th and 14th ; range, 1·05 in.

The mean temperature of the air was 37°·4 ; the highest, 55˙ on the 4th and 18th ; the lowest, 17° on the 26th ; range, 38° : the mean high day temperature, 43˙·1 ; the mean low night temperature, 31°·7 ; mean daily range, 11°·4. The highest temperature in the sun was 64° on the 18th.

The direction of the wind was N.W. on 5 days, N. on 3, N.E. on 7, E. on 2, S.E. on 3, S. on 1, S.W. on 5, and W. on 4. Southerly (S.E. and S.W.) winds prevailed for the first few days, then westerly, and north-easterly towards the end of the month.

Rain fell on 14 days, the total amount being 3·86 ins., and the greatest fall in one day 0·70 in. on the 10th. Snow fell on the 26th and 27th. The amount is not included, as melted snow, in the rainfall recorded.

The temperature sank to below freezing-point on 19 nights, and to below 20° on the 26th and 27th. Fog prevailed on 4 days.

DECEMBER.—The mean pressure of the atmosphere was 30·12 ins. ; the highest reading, 30·50 ins. on the 28th ; the lowest, 29·70 ins. on the 20th and 28th ; range, 0·80 in.

The mean temperature of the air was 33°·9 ; the highest, 51° on the 22nd ; the lowest, 10° on the 4th ; range, 41° : the mean high day temperature, 38°·6 ; the mean low night temperature, 29°·3 ; mean daily range, 9°·3. The highest temperature in the sun was 52° on the 22nd.

The direction of the wind was N.W. on 3 days, N. on 4, N.E. on 3, E. on 4, S. on 4, S.W. on 8, and W. on 5. Easterly winds prevailed for the first week, northerly for the second, and south-westerly to the end of the month.

Rain fell on 5 days, the total amount being 0·75 in., and the greatest fall in one day, 0·33 in. on the 10th. Snow fell on the 2nd, 3rd, 4th, 6th, and 8th. The amount, as in November, is not included in the rainfall recorded.

The temperature sank to below freezing-point on 19 nights, and to below 20° on the 4th, 6th, and 14th. Fog prevailed on 5 days.

135

19.—MISCELLANEOUS NOTES AND OBSERVATIONS.

[Read 8th June, 1876.]

GEOLOGY.

Section of the Strata passed through in boring at the Colne Valley Waterworks —From the level of the engine-house floor * a well of 10 feet diameter is sunk to a depth of 95 feet in chalk and flints. To a depth of 140 feet below this there is a bore of 11 inches diameter, which passes through the following strata:—chalk and flints, 87 feet,—hard rock chalk, 12 feet,—soft chalk, 3 feet,—hard rock chalk, 16 feet,—soft chalk, 1 foot 6 inches,—hard grey rock chalk, 20 feet 6 inches,—Total depth 235 feet.—*William Verini, Bushey Heath.*

BOTANY.

The Ermine Street traced by its Vegetation.—Some years ago, while driving between Hertford and Ware, I noticed that the buttercups and other meadow flowers grew in such a manner as to make a distinct broad band across the meads near the New River Head. About that time I happened to ride along that portion of the old Roman road, the Ermine Street—or, as the authors of the 'Flora Hertfordiensis' call it, Herman Street—and I was struck with the fact that the road was much of the same width as the band of buttercups. On examining the Ordnance Map, I find that the floral band and Roman road are in exactly a straight line, and further, that this straight line produced joins the present north road beyond Buntingford, and coincides with it as far as, if not farther than Royston.† I mentioned this to a very intelligent man, and he told me that in a certain field north of the River Lee, now used as a nursery garden, the corn used to change colour in a similar band; and I find this field is also in the direct straight line. I have some hopes of finding some further links between Ware and Buntingford, but hitherto I have not been able to spare the time required for such a purpose. Since the year I first noticed the band of flowers I have again seen it, but with nothing like the same sharpness of outline.—*Richard B. Croft, Great Cozens, Ware.*

ENTOMOLOGY.

Note on the Larvæ of the Goat Moth.—In the spring of 1875 I sent a short account of the finding of a number of larvæ of the goat moth (*Cossus ligniperda*) in the trunk of an oak tree then

* The engine-house floor is 203 feet above mean sea-level.—ED.

† According to Chauncy ('Hist. Antiq. Herts,'—1700) the Ermine Street passed " thro' Hertford, on the south side of Ware Park, to Wadesmill, and so forward to Royston," coinciding, as shown on his map, with the present north road from Wadesmill to Royston.—ED.

recently felled on this place.* Of these, the majority survived
their imprisonment in a tin box but a few weeks; several, however, took freely to the oak splinters provided as food, and buried
themselves in the wood, where, although too deep to be seen, I
believe them to be now alive. One, of large size, about the end of
September spun for himself a cocoon in the angle of the bottom
of the box, under about two inches of dry earth, and was then
supposed to have passed into the pupa state. A few days ago this
same caterpillar emerged from his cocoon in his original form, but
much increased in size, and is now as vigorous as ever. He must
have been wholly without food for upwards of six months. As is
well known, the larva of this moth retains its form for three years,
and its ordinary habitat, deep in the trunk of a tree, is consistent
with hybernation; but I do not remember any entomological
authority for asserting that it can exist for long periods without
food, so that the case above stated may be of some value and
interest. Perhaps some member of the Society will inform us
what is known touching the condition in winter of these insects in
a natural state.—*J. Henry James, Kingswood, Watford.*

ORNITHOLOGY.

Notes on the Cuckoo.—On the 26th, 28th, and 30th of May,
1876, a female cuckoo came hovering about a stable wall covered
with ivy a few yards from, and opposite, Wiggenhall House, Watford; apparently she was endeavouring to find food or a nest. She
remained from one to two hours each time. She did not make any
cry. In 1875 a cuckoo was hatched in a pied wagtail's nest built
in a corn rick, and another in ivy covering a wall. One was found
on the ground dead, perhaps starved. Mr. J. King has had it
stuffed. In 1874 a cuckoo was hatched in a swallow's nest in a
potting shed near the house at Wiggenhall. I saw it quite filling
the nest, which appeared to be much too small for it. Two facts
seemed to me unusual—first, that the cuckoo should lay an egg in
a nest under cover so near the house; secondly, that she should
lay in a swallow's nest. No mention is made by Yarrell in his
'History of British Birds' (2nd ed. vol. ii. p. 191) of the nest of
this bird as one of those in which the cuckoo lays.—*Alfred T.
Brett, M.D., Watford House.*

---

* *Vide* 'Transactions,' vol. i. pt. 2, p. 64.

20.—The Hertfordshire Bourne.

By the President, John Evans, F.R.S., V.P.S.A., F.G.S., etc.

[Read 8th June, 1876.]

The paper which I have been requested to read this evening is, I am sorry to say, unwritten, for I have not had time to reduce it to writing. It is on the Hertfordshire Bourne—one of those intermittent rivers which are not unfrequent under certain conditions.

What is the meaning of the term "bourne"? It is identical, I think, with the German "brunnen" and the Scotch "burn," a brook. We find it also used as indicating a boundary, for brooks very frequently form boundaries, especially between different counties; and in this instance, during a considerable part of its course, the Bourne forms the boundary between Hertfordshire and Buckinghamshire. It is not "the bourne" mentioned by Shakespeare, from which "no traveller returns;" for I am happy to say that I visited its source this morning and I am here this evening.

I may, first of all, mention the spot where it flows into the Bulbourne, a better-known Hertfordshire river. It is at a small hamlet called Bourne End, which lies about two miles to the south-east of Berkhampstead, and year after year the travellers along the high road from Watford to Tring may pass over the spot where its course traverses the road, without having the slightest idea that a moderately-sized brook occasionally flows there, and that, according to tradition, a man was once drowned at the end of the usually dry culvert which passes under the road. For this Bourne only flows occasionally, at intervals in general of from three to seven years. On the present occasion it is flowing with moderate force. I did not gauge it; but it is a sufficient stream to fill a culvert, which is something like a foot in diameter, through which it runs with moderate velocity. At the present time the stream rises about three miles up the valley, in the direction of Chesham. I found its source about 70 yards north-east of the road going to Harratt's End, and it has been flowing since about the end of April. The last time I visited it, which was the last time it flowed, was in the year 1873. At that time it rose at a spot nearly half a mile further to the south-west, and was flowing in considerably greater volume. Its source was midway between White Hill and Ashley Green. That was in the month of February, so that on that occasion the stream commenced flowing at a much earlier period than it did this year. It has also flowed at different times during various previous years, but unfortunately I find that I have no note of all the years in which it flowed. In those days there was no Hertfordshire Naturalists' Society to take notice of such phenomena. But I have a note of my visit in March, 1853—twenty-three years ago. At that time the Bourne rose rather higher up the valley than it does in the present year. Looking at the records of the rainfall and the percolation, I think that the stream must have flowed in the year 1860, and probably in 1866. This is the more probable, as I find that the Bourne near Croydon, in the Caterham Valley, flowed in 1841, 1852, 1866, and 1873, in which latter year it began to flow about the middle of January.

There are, you will observe, other Bournes in England which are perhaps better known than this in Hertfordshire. They flow generally in the same years as this, and the question arises, What is the theory and meaning of these intermittent rivers, which seem to flow in such a capricious manner—in some years flowing in considerable force, and in other years being invisible? In order to understand the origin and theory of these bournes, you must consider what is the origin and nature of all the streams which run through a porous rock like the Chalk.

Mr. Clutterbuck, in his lecture last month, gave you some account of the generally accepted theory with regard to such rivers. Taking, for instance, a valley with Chalk hills on each side, and a river flowing down the valley, you will find that the water which percolates through the Chalk goes down until it arrives at a plane of permanent saturation. That plane of permanent saturation is not level, but is inclined towards those places where the water finds its way to the surface in the form of springs. It varies at different times in the year, sometimes being inclined at an angle of 20 feet and sometimes of 25 feet to the mile, and at others being on a slope represented by not more than 12 feet to the mile. The rain which falls during the winter months finds its way through the Chalk, and raises the level of the subterranean reservoir on account of the water coming in from above faster than it can find its way out to the rivers; and although no rain may find its way to the reservoir during the summer months, yet the water already there is delivered out by springs, and the level gradually falls, and you can tell by the variation in the wells what the fall is. In a well at Studham, some miles from any stream, I have found the level of the water in two successive years vary as much as 70 feet.

If we take the inclination of the rivers flowing past Watford and St. Albans, we find that they have an inclination of about 12 feet 6 inches to the mile in the lower portion of their course, and 18 feet 6 inches in the upper portion. That shows what is the amount of impediment to water passing through the Chalk in a lateral direction. For, assuming that water could find its way through the Chalk at a less inclination than 12 feet 6 inches to the mile, these rivers would cease to flow, or at all events you would never see the streams upon the surface. The whole of the Chalk being porous and pervious, unless there were a sufficiently saturated bed beneath the river to hold the water up at an inclination at least equal to that of the river, it would die in its bed and disappear. The inclination of subterranean water passing through Chalk must therefore be at least 12 feet 6 inches or thereabouts to the mile in this district. If, starting from the level of an existing spring, you carried an artificial valley through a Chalk district at an inclination of 10 feet to the mile, it would be less than that at which the water finds its way underground, and there would be a constant stream of water through it, as it would afford the readiest means of delivery from the underground reservoir. But take a natural valley, with an inclination of 16 or 17 feet to the mile. Under ordinary circumstances water finding its way at an inclination of 12 feet 6 inches to the mile would not show upon the surface. Suppose, however, that in a very wet winter the water in the subterranean reservoir was raised so as to be at an inclination of 25 feet to the mile, it would at once appear on the surface, at the bottom of such a valley, because it would find its way more readily over the surface than underground.

Thus with regard to the valley of the Bourne. In certain years the subterranean water is raised in the body of the hills, and this valley, cut at right angles or nearly so to the main stream, intersects the general surface of the plane of saturation, and the water appears on the surface. It, of course, is not the case that the slope of any valley is absolutely in one uniform line; generally speaking there are some small undulations. In looking at the Bourne, I found this theory of intermittent streams being due to the intersection of the plane of saturation very prettily illustrated, because in one place I found the Bourne running, and when I arrived at a certain spot it had disappeared; further on it ran again, and again disappeared. The plane of saturation was more even than the surface, and where there was an elevation of the surface the water found its way underground instead of running over it. At one spot, where there was a depression, there was water five or six inches deep, all over the road, and I found that while the water was visible near Harratt's End Lane, it disappeared further down the valley. Past Bottom Farm the water ran in considerable volume, but before it arrived about half-way to Bourne End, it disappeared altogether, and though a pond which was dry last year had six feet of water in it, the stream did not run out of it, but re-commenced running a few yards below it.

I must now refer to the observations made as to the rainfall during the years which have been marked by the flowing of the Bourne. I mentioned that in March, 1853, it was flowing. I find that during the six winter months of 1852 and 1853 there had been through our gauges for ascertaining the amount of percolation, 10·74 ins. of rain. The stream was running in March, and in March, 1853, the percolation through the soil had ceased. But during that winter a much larger quantity of water than usual found its way into the Chalk, for the average winter percolation is not more than five or six inches. Taking another of these years; the Bourne was flowing on February 16th, 1873. The amount of rain which during the six winter months found its way to the subterranean reservoir was 11·25 inches. This year the Bourne did not commence flowing until April, and judging from our gauges, which at any rate give an approximate measure, its appearance is due to a less amount of infiltration of water than

usual. There had only been, during the six months ending the
31st March, about six inches, and in April another half-inch of
rain, which passed down through three feet of soil.   That is rather
a small amount of rain to enable the Bourne to flow; but when we
look at the amount of rᵃinfall there has been for some years, I
think the reservoir has not been at so low a level when the
infiltration commenced, as on some other occasions, and although
generally speaking the flow of the Bourne is connected with the
amount of infiltration of water during the six months or so
preceding, yet we must take into account the state of the springs
and subterranean reservoir during the previous years.

I will not go into the question of the infiltration into the
subterranean reservoir, as I hope to lay some observations on this
subject before the Society in a printed form, having embodied them
in a communication to the Society of Civil Engineers.*

NOTE.—January 31st, 1877.   The Bourne is again running,
having commenced to flow on the evening of the 6th, or the
morning of the 7th.   I was at Bourne End on the afternoon of
the 6th, and the bed of the stream, where it passes under the road,
was free from water.   On the 7th, Mr. Littleboy visited the spot,
and found the stream running.   I have since seen the Bourne
flowing in considerable volume, and have ascertained that the
position of its present source is as nearly as possible the same as
it was in February, 1873.   The Bourne in the Caterham Valley,
near Croydon, is also flowing in a powerful stream.—J. E.

* Proc. Inst. C.E. vol. xlv. Feb. 29, 1876.

21.—The Hertfordshire Ordnance Bench Marks, from the 'Abstracts of Levelling' of the Ordnance Survey.

Communicated by John Hopkinson, Hon. Sec.

[Read 9th November, 1876.]

The work from which the following levels are taken [*] gives the height, above the Datum Level for Great Britain—the level of mean tide at Liverpool—of every bench mark in sixty-three separate lines of levelling, with branches to trigonometrical stations situated near the different lines. "The levels established on these lines, and marked ⋀ upon permanent objects on the ground, furnish definite points all over the kingdom from which the lines of levels for the contours and the detail plans of every part of the country are carried, and thus all the levels on the Ordnance plans refer to one common datum level." [†]

Two of these lines of levelling run through Hertfordshire. One is that from Birmingham to London. It is in an almost direct line from north-west to south-east, following the coach road through the towns of Coventry, Dunchurch, Towcester, Dunstable, St. Albans, and Barnet. It was commenced on the 19th of January, 1848, and completed on the 7th of April in the same year. The other is that from London to Dunstable. This takes a much more circuitous route, being first carried in a northerly direction along the road through the towns of Tottenham, Cheshunt, and Hoddesdon, to Ware, thence turning west through Hertford, north-west through Stevenage to Hitchin, south-west to Luton, and again north-west to Dunstable, where it joins the former line. It was commenced on the 11th of July, 1848, and completed on the 26th of July, 1851.

The height above the datum level, as already defined, is given in feet, and carried to three places of decimals, or to the thousandth part of a foot.

There are two kinds of bench marks. The "Mark," which consists of a vertical broad arrow cut into some permanent object, and a horizontal line above it, the centre of which indicates the exact level; and the "Bolt," a first-class "Mark," which is distinguished by a piece of copper bolt driven into the object, which in this case is usually the stone wall of a church tower, a public building such as a town-hall, or a bridge.

Besides these levels, others are given by the Ordnance Survey in the "Parish Maps" on the scale of $\frac{1}{2500}$, or 25·344 inches to the mile, but the maps of only a few parishes in the county are as yet published. The parish of Watford has recently been completed.

---

[*] 'Abstracts of the Principal Lines of Spirit Levelling in England and Wales.' By Colonel Sir Henry James, R.E., F.R.S., etc., Director of the Ordnance Survey. 1861.

[†] *l.c.* p. v.

I.—BIRMINGHAM TO LONDON.

The line of levelling from Birmingham to London enters Hertfordshire from Bedfordshire at about a mile from Dunstable, and leaves it for Middlesex at about the same distance beyond Barnet. Between South Mimms and Barnet the line is in Middlesex, and to preserve the continuity of the levelling I have included this portion.

DUNSTABLE TO ST. ALBANS.

	Altitudes in Feet.
Mark on corner of Mr. Osborne's house, boot and shoe maker, Dunstable; 3·59 ft. above centre of road *	483·458
Mark on the 32nd milestone from London and 12th from St. Albans	538·590
Mark on south-west corner of house, nearly opposite Dunstable Toll-house; 4·29 ft above centre of road . .	558·334
Mark on brick over pipe at east side of road; 0·70 ft. below centre of road	552·535
Mark on the 31st milestone from London and 11th from St. Albans; 2·64 ft. above centre of road	527·250
Mark on north-east corner of house, at west side of road; 2·83 ft. above centre of road	500·994
Mark on the 30th milestone from London and 3rd from Dunstable; 4·83 ft. above centre of road	478·152
Mark on north-west corner of house, opposite the Pack Horse Inn; 3·02 ft. above centre of road	448·997
Mark on south-west corner of Mr. Stanley's house, at east side of road; 2·01ft. above centre of road	439·971
Mark on top of the 29th milestone from London; 1·57 ft above centre of road	434·006
Mark on north-west corner of Thomas Powel's public-house, at north end of Market-street Village; 1·97 ft. above centre of road	443·182
Mark on south-west corner of Mr. Dell's house, at north side of Market-street Village; 1·82 ft. above surface	422·076
Mark on corner of house, nearly opposite Pickford-lane, Market-street Village; 1·26ft. above centre of road . .	406·851
Mark on top of the 28th milestone from London and 5th from Dunstable; 2·35 ft. above centre of road	407·192
Mark on brick over pipe at east side of road, 3 chains south of cross roads; 0·87 ft. above centre of road	383·914
Mark on south corner of Friars Wash public-house; 0·26 ft. below centre of road	359·389
Mark on north-east corner of small house at Friars Wash Toll-house; 1·28 ft above centre of road	354·941
Mark on the 26th milestone from London and 6th from St. Albans; 1·50 ft. above centre of road	373·957
Mark on brick over pipe at iron grating, east side of road, opposite gravel pit; 0·23 ft. below centre of road. .	413·871

* In Bedfordshire.

Mark on east battlement of small bridge at east side of road; 1·98 ft. above centre of road .. ..   410·821

Mark on the 25th milestone from London and 5th from St. Albans; 2·35 ft. above centre of road   .. .. ..   406·240

Mark on south-west corner of Mr. Farr's house, at east side of Redbourn Village; 1·50 ft. above centre of road..   351·547

Mark on corner of the George and Dragon Inn, Redbourn Village; 2·47 ft. above centre of road .. .. ..   323·064

Mark on south-east corner of James Foster's house, at north-east end of Redbourn Village; 1·47 ft. above centre of road   .. ..   309·409

Mark on the 24th milestone from London and 4th from St. Albans; 1·77 ft. above centre of road   .. ..   314·445

Mark on wall at east side of road, 173 links north of mill; 1·76 ft. above centre of road .. ..   303·594

Mark on east end of pipe at junction of roads; 0·67 ft. below centre of road .. ..   307·728

Mark on the 23rd milestone from London and 3rd from St. Albans; 1·77 ft. above centre of road .. .. ..   304·343

Mark on north-east end of pipe crossing under road; 1·39 ft. below centre of road .. ..   291·144

Mark on the 22nd milestone from London and 2nd from St. Albans; 1·12 ft. above centre of road   .. .. ..   287·646

Mark on east face of west battlement of bridge over stream; 1·97 ft. below top of battlement   .. .. ..   280·375

Mark on flag over pipe crossing under footpath, at west side of road; 0 52 ft. below centre of road .. .. ..   292·212

Mark on south end of pipe at entrance to house west side of road; 0·56 ft. below centre of road .. .. ..   304·900

Mark on the 21st milestone from London and 1st from St. Albans; 0·64 ft. above centre of road .. .. ..   295·859

Mark on south-east corner of storehouse at brewery, west side of road; 2·42 ft. above centre of road .. ..   296·665

Mark on corner of the Queen Victoria Inn, Spencer-street, St. Albans; 2·84 ft. above centre of road .. ..   351·714

BRANCH LEVELLING, ST. ALBANS.

Town Hall, St. Albans. Bolt in north corner; 1·57 ft. above surface .. .. : .. .. ..   379·957

St. Peter's Church, St. Albans. Bolt in north side; 2·76 ft. above surface   .. ..   402·509

ST. ALBANS TO CHIPPING BARNET.

Mark on south-west corner of the Red Lion Inn, at junction of streets, St. Albans; 1·65 ft. above centre of road   .. ..   363·860

Mark on Mr. Cooper's house, coach builder, St. Albans; 2·37 ft. above centre of road   .. ..   354·652

Mark on south-east corner of Mr. Hopkins' house, at west side of road, St. Albans; 0·72 ft. above surface ..   300·941

Mark on the 20th milestone from London and 1st from
St. Albans; 1·16 ft. above centre of road.. .. .. .. 289·453

Mark on north-east corner of the Mile House public-
house, at west side of road; 1·78 ft. above centre of road 295·052

Mark on the 19th milestone from London and 2nd
from St. Albans; 0·79 ft. above centre of road .. .. 285·661

Mark on brick at end of pipe, west side of road; 1·41 ft.
below centre of road .. .. 261·334

Mark on the 18th milestone from London and 3rd from
St. Albans; 0·83 ft. above centre of road.. .. .. .. 235·943

Mark on south-east corner of house at junction of road,
north end of London Colney; 2·79 ft. above centre of road 244·801

Mark on north face of south battlement of London
Colney Bridge; 2·44 ft. below top of battlement .. .. 227·418

Mark on south-east corner of house at west side of road,
London Colney; 2·98 ft. above centre of road .. .. 231·494

Mark on top of the 17th milestone from London and
6th from Chipping Barnet; 1·79 ft. above centre of road 238·758

Mark on south end of pipe at east side of road; 0·10 ft.
below centre of road .. .. 258·724

Mark on end of pipe at east side of road; 0·16 ft. below
centre of road .. .. 299·196

Mark on top of the 16th milestone from London and
5th from Chipping Barnet; 3·31 ft. above centre of road 402·440

Mark on end of pipe at gate, east side of road; 0·33 ft.
above centre of road .. .. 349·127

Mark on the 15th milestone from London; 0·30 ft.
above centre of road * .. .. 290·302

Bolt in south-west buttress of South Mimms Church
tower; 1·62 ft. above sill of door, and 0·86 ft. above mark * 319·705

Mark on the 14th milestone from London; 1·64 ft.
above surface * .. .. 314·391

Mark on top of west battlement of bridge; 2·70 ft.
above centre of road, and 5·10 ft. above surface of key-
stone * .. .. 292·979

Mark on top of west battlement of bridge over stream;
3·02 ft. above centre of road * .. .. 293·388

Mark on north-east corner of the Green Dragon Inn;
2·57 ft. above centre of road * .. .. 312·638

Mark on the 12th milestone from London and 1st from
Chipping Barnet; 1·73 ft. above centre of road * .. .. 353·367

Mark on end of pipe at west side of road; 0·67 ft.
below centre of road * .. .. 392·889

Mark on north-east corner of house, nearly opposite
Christ Church, Chipping Barnet; 1·41 ft. above surface * 427·613

Mark on south corner of Mr. Jacob's house, surgeon,
at junction of roads, Chipping Barnet; 2·35 ft. above
centre of road * .. .. 431·296

* In Middlesex.

Bolt in south side of door, at west end of Chipping
Barnet Church; 1·56 ft. above sill of door in tower   ..   429·751

BRANCH LEVELLING, LONDON COLNEY.

London Colney Chapel of Ease. Bolt in upper step of
door; 0·13 ft. below top of upper step .. ..   223·914

BRANCH LEVELLING, BARNET.

Christ Christ, Chipping Barnet. Bolt in east jamb of
small door; 1·99 ft. above surface * .. ..   427·008

CHIPPING BARNET TO LONDON.

Mark on south-west corner of Mr. Bower's house,
wine-merchant, Chipping Barnet; 3·24 ft. above centre
of road .. ..   396·619
Mark on south-east corner of coach-house, at west side
of road; 2·50 ft. above centre of road .. ..   301·898
Mark on the 10th milestone from London; 2·19 ft.
above centre of road .. ..   293·560
Mark on plinth of gate pier at junction of road to East
Barnet; 0·70 ft. above centre of road .. ..   303·358
Mark on step at entrance to house, west side of road;
1·56 ft. above centre of road .. ..   312·456

II.—LONDON TO DUNSTABLE.

The line of levelling from London to Dunstable enters Hertfordshire from Middlesex at Waltham Cross, and leaves it for
Bedfordshire at about two miles from Luton.

TOTTENHAM TO BROXBOURNE.

Mark on south-east angle of the White Hart Inn;
1·49 ft. above surface .. ..   72·481
Bolt in pillar of Chapel of Ease, Waltham Cross;
2·39 ft. above surface .. ..   75·806
Mark on front of Trinity Cottage, Crossbrook-street;
2·62 ft. above surface .. ..   76·682
Mark on brick column at entrance to Mr. Stobart's
house, Turner's Hill; 1·68 ft. above surface .. .. ..   81·084
Mark on north-east angle of Police Station-house,
Cheshunt; 2·46 ft. above surface .. ..   84·060
Mark on base of railing in front of Cuba Cottage,
Turner's-hill; 0·52 ft. above surface .. ..   85·263
Mark on angle of Mrs. Shepherd's house, at junction
of Church-lane, Cheshunt; 1·75 ft. above surface .. ..   90·432
Mark on Messrs. Paul and Sons' seed shop, Cheshunt-
street; 2·10 ft. above surface .. ..   91·404
Mark on Mrs. King's house, near junction of Brook-
lane, Cheshunt-street; 2·59 ft. above surface.. .. ..   82·151

* In Middlesex.

Mark on brick culvert at east side of road; 1·52 ft.
below surface .. ..   77·950
Mark on south-west angle of the Old Bull's Head beer-
shop, Turnford; 2 05 ft. above surface .. ..   82·797
Mark on base of railing in front of Mr. Codson's house,
Wormley; 1·76 ft above surface .. ..   103·128
Mark on front of the Globe Inn, Wormley; 2·20 ft.
above surface .. ..   105·504
Mark on base of railing in front of Mr. Martin's house,
Broxbourne; 1·93 ft. above surface.. .. ..   102·726
Mark on base of railing of Mr. Pemer's house, Brox-
bourne; 0·54 ft. above surface.. .. ..   119 625

BROXBOURNE TO HODDESDON.

Mark on corner of the Bull Inn, Broxbourne; 1·99 ft.
above surface .. ..   121·841
Mark on south-east angle of Cheshunt Toll-house;
1·37 ft. above surface .. ..   133·024
Mark on east battlement of Spital Bridge; 3·03 ft. above
surface .. ..   114·326
Mark on angle of brick wall, at junction of road to
Hoddesdon Railway Station; 1·63 ft. above surface ..   140·145
Mark on base of railing in front of Mr. Howley's
house, High-street; 1·41 ft. above surface .. .. ..   148·797
Mark on sill of window of the Police Station-house,
Hoddesdon; 3·45 ft. above surface .. ..   149·153
Mark on east battlement of bridge, near Girls' School-
house, Hoddesdon; 1·35 ft. above surface .. .. ..   121·112

BRANCH LEVELLING TO BROXBOURNE CHURCH.

Broxbourne Church. Bolt in jamb of door in west
face of tower; 3 62 ft. above surface .. ..   113·840

HODDESDON TO WARE.

Mark on the Duke William public-house, at junction
of Duke-street; 1·77 ft. above surface .. ..   127·257
Mark on brick culvert at east side of road; 0·79 ft.
below surface .. ..   128·206
Mark on water-trough at west side of road; 1·19 ft.
above surface .. ..   150·866
Mark on culvert at east side of road; 1·07 ft. above
surface .. ..   143·045
Mark on gatepost at junction of footpath, east side of
road; 1·28 ft. above surface .. ..   181·478
Mark on bow window of the Waggon and Horses Inn,
Pepper-hill; 1·88 ft. above surface .. ..   196·994
Mark on gatepost in front of Amwell Bury Lodge;
1·66 ft. above surface.. .. ..   166·117
Mark on wooden post in front of Amwell-hill Engine-
house; 2·00 ft. above surface .. ..   140·315

Mark on gatepost at west side of road, opposite road
to Amwell; 2·05 ft. above surface .. ..   112·089
Mark on bow window of the Red House Inn, one mile
from Ware; 1·52 ft. above surface .. ..   113·207
Mark on wooden post at north side of metal bridge, at
junction of new and old roads, south end of Ware; 1·85 ft.
above surface .. ..   114·562
Mark on angle of Mr. Lyon's house, Amwell End,
Ware, at junction of road to Hertford Heath; 1·60 ft.
above surface .. ..   113·221

BRANCH LEVELLING TO AMWELL CHURCH.

Mark on brick column, at entrance to Mrs. Crowder's
house, and junction of road to Ware; 1·87 ft. above surface   202·017
Mark on Mrs. Crowder's garden wall, at junction of
Church-passage, Amwell-lane; 1·40 ft. above surface ..   159·549
Amwell Church. Bolt in north-west angle of tower;
2·82 ft. above surface.. .. ..   148·319

BRANCH LEVELLING TO WARE CHURCH.

Bolt in front of Mr. Haggar's house, Amwell-lane;
1·74 ft. above surface.. .. ..   111·240
Bolt in west pier of Ware Bridge, over the River Lea;
1 57 ft. above surface.. .. ..   118·339
Bolt in front of the Star Inn, Water-street, Ware;
2·01 ft. above surface.. .. ..   113·357
Bolt in front of house in Water-street; opposite Red-
lane; 1·85 ft. above surface .. ..   114·717
Mark on front of house in High-street, opposite Church-
lane; 1·65 ft. above surface .. ..   116·141
Bolt in north-west abutment of Ware Church tower;
1·62 ft. above surface .. ..   119·285

WARE TO HERTFORD.

Mark on base of railing at junction of Amwell End
and Hertford-road, south end of Ware; 0·44 ft. above
surface .. ..   113·430
Mark on post of gate at south side of Hertford-road;
1·83 ft. above surface.. .. ..   116·520
Mark on the 21st milestone from London; 2·00 ft.
above surface .. ..   129·245
Mark on west gable of cottage, at south side of road;
0·71 ft. above surface.. .. ..   160·835
Mark on corner of the Halfway House, at south side
of road; 0·70 ft. above surface.. .. ..   154·726
Mark on brick culvert at junction of roads, near Hertford Union Workhouse; 2·10 ft. below surface .. ..   131·275
Mark on corner pier of wall of Hertford Gaol; 0·80 ft.
above surface .. ..   134·446

Mark on pier of gate to the Blue Coat School, Fore-street, Hertford; 0·77 ft. above surface .. ..   136·427
Mark on front of Hertford Town Hall; 1·17 ft. above surface .. ..   133·014
Mark on north-west corner of St. Andrew's Church tower, Hertford; 2·60 ft. above surface .. ..   137·529

HERTFORD TO STEVENAGE.

Mark on brick pier of wall nearly opposite the Infirmary; 1·35 ft. above surface.. .. ..   132·078
Mark on parish boundary stone, marked S. L. A. B., at west side of road; 1·12 ft. above surface .. .. ..   158·110
Mark on the 23rd milestone from London; 2·24 ft. above surface .. ..   142·959
Mark on north-east corner of cottage, at south end of Waterford Village, west side of road; 0·77 ft. above surface   172·249
Mark on front of the Old Windmill public-house; 1·48 ft. above surface.. .. ..   148·174
Mark on the 24th milestone from London; 0·92 ft. above surface .. ..   179·747
Mark on corner of cottage at south-west side of road, Stapleford; 1·11ft. above surface .. ..   159·937
Mark on south-east corner of the Woodhall Arms public-house; 0·85 ft. above surface .. ..   162·891
Mark on pier of gate at east side of road, near Woodhall Park Lodge; 1·35 ft. above surface .. ..   211·540
Mark on brick wall at north-east side of road; 0·80 ft. above surface .. ..   196·076
Bolt in corner of cottage, at south end of Watton Village, north-east side of road; 1·19 ft. above surface..   190·346
Mark on corner of The Jolly Thatcher public-house; 1·06 ft. above surface .. ..   197·803
Mark on corner of cottage, opposite junction of road to Walkern; 1·78 ft. above surface .. ..   210·648
Mark on the 27th milestone from London; 1·25 ft. above surface .. ..   204·355
Mark on corner of barn at Oaks Cross Farm; 2·92 ft. above surface .. ..   217·859
Mark on front of the Three Horse Shoes public-house; 0·62 ft. above surface .. ..   218·632
Mark on front of The Chequers public-house, Bragbury End; 1·30 ft. above surface .. ..   228·961
Mark on the 29th milestone from London; 1·24 ft. above surface .. ..   276·664
Mark on south-east corner of cottage, 59 links off south side of road; 1·19 ft. above surface .. .. ..   254·021
Mark on pier of gate at north-east side of road; 1·50 ft. above surface .. ..   251·786
Mark on corner of the Roebuck Inn, Broadwater Village; 2·02 ft. above surface .. ..   263·992

Mark on culvert at north-east side of road; 0·15 ft. above centre of road .. ..   261·987
Mark on culvert at south-west side of road; 0·60 ft. above surface .. ..   279·448
Mark on pier of gate at Six Hills, west side of road; 1·43 ft. above surface.. .. ..   299·158
Mark on pier of gate in front of cottages, at east side of road; 1·39 ft. above surface.. .. ..   297·865
Mark on Gothic cottage at junction of roads, Stevenage; 1·71 ft. above surface .. ..   298·797
Bolt in north-east corner of the White Lion Inn, Stevenage; 1·76 ft. above surface .. ..   306·288

STEVENAGE TO HITCHIN.

Mark on corner of smithy at west side of road; 1·67 ft. above surface .. ..   311·497
Mark on front of Corey's Mill public-house, east side of road; 2·14 ft. above surface.. .. ..   300·475
Mark on culvert at south-west side of road; 0·59 ft. below centre of road .. ..   285·320
Mark on culvert at junction of roads, south-west side of road; 1·10 ft. below centre of road .. .. ..   265·266
Bolt in north-east corner of railway viaduct, at Little Wymondley; 1·29 ft. above surface.. .. ..   253·701
Mark on corner of Little Wymondley farm-house; 1·09 ft. above surface.. .. ..   248·648
Mark on culvert at junction of roads, north side of road; 2·00 ft. below centre of road .. ..   240·811
Mark on corner of cottage in Ashbrook Village, at north side of road; 1·30 ft. above surface .. .. ..   242·160
Mark on corner of brick culvert over stream, at junction of roads; 1·18 ft. below centre of road .. ..   216·313
Mark on pier of gate at north side of road and summit of Wymondley Hill; 1·04 ft. above surface .. .. ..   252·575
Mark on south-east side of small bridge over Hitchin township boundary stream; 2·12 ft. below centre of road   214·860
Mark on west corner of cottage, at end of The Folly and junction of roads, south end of Hitchin; 1·40 ft. above surface .. ..   233·298

BRANCH LEVELLING TO HITCHIN CHURCH.

Mark on corner of cottage, at junction of Hitchin Boundary-road with Hertford-road; 0·77 ft. above surface   243·859
Mark on south-west corner of the Orange Tree public-house, The Folly; 1·19 ft. above surface .. .. ..   246·333
Mark on north-east corner of house, in Hitchin Newtown, Hitchin-hill; 0·97 ft. above surface .. .. ..   274·068
Mark on obelisk finger post, at junction of London-road and Hertford-road; 0·70 ft. above surface .. .. ..   287·600

Mark on gullet at junction of Gosmore-road with London-road; 0 18 ft. above surface of road .. .. .. 249·585
Mark on corner of wall opposite the Falcon Inn, Hitchin-hill; 1·26 ft. above surface .. .. 233·964
Mark on angle of house opposite Bull's Corner, at junction of Bridge-street and Dead-street; 1·02 ft. above surface .. .. 217·892
Bolt in west side of bridge over the River Hiz, New Bridge-street; 1·05 ft. above surface .. .. 212·374
Mark on south-west corner of the Sun Inn, Sun-street; 2·38 ft. above surface.. .. .. 213·098
Mark on corner of house, at opening between buildings, Market-square; 1·27 ft. above surface .. .. .. 218·703
Bolt in south-west corner of Hitchin Church tower; 0·83 ft. above surface .. .. 216·374

HITCHIN TO LUTON.

Bolt in end of granary at junction of roads, New England Farm; 1·25 ft. above surface .. .. 263·813
Mark on front of New England House; 1·19 ft. above surface .. .. 273·862
Bolt in south-east corner of New England Cottage, at junction of roads; 2·56 ft. above surface .. .. .. 269·178
Mark on pier of gate at junction of footpath, through Priory Park; 1·28 ft. above surface.. .. .. 279·128
Mark on pier of stile at junction of roads; 1·49 ft. above surface .. .. 283·191
Mark on pier of gate at cross roads, Wellhead-hill; 0·88 ft. above surface .. .. 298·939
Mark on east end of cottage at junction of footpath, west side of road, Wellhead; 3·32 ft. above surface .. 250·462
Mark on wooden post at angle of fence near river, south-east side of road; 0·96 ft. above surface .. .. 238·186
Mark on gatepost at junction of roads, south-east side of road; 1·24 ft. above surface.. .. .. 254·573
Mark on wooden posts at junction of roads, south-east side of road; 1·45 ft. above surface .. .. 273·265
Mark on pier of gate at junction of footpath, south-east side of road; 0·99 ft. above surface.. .. .. .. 302·783
Mark on gatepost at junction of hedge, north-west side of road; 0·92 ft. above surface.. .. .. .. 341·705
Mark on stone of culvert over boundary stream of Hitchin and Great Offley townships.. .. .. 298·455
Mark on post of gate at south side of road; 1·57 ft. above surface .. .. 337·618
Mark on post of gate at south-east side of road; 2·24 ft. above surface .. .. 322·940
Mark on post of paling at junction of footpath through Offley Park; 1·21 ft. above surface .. .. 386·475

Bolt in corner of house, at junction of road to Great
Offley Church; 1·48 ft. above surface .. ..   524·247
Mark on corner of The Windmill public-house; 1·81ft.
above surface .. ..   491·194
Mark on pier of gate at south-east side of road; 1·79 ft.
above surface .. ..   439·878
Mark on barn opposite junction of road to Lilley;
2·01 ft. above surface .. ..   428·935
Mark on pier of gate at entrance to Putteridge Bury
Park; 0·94 ft. above surface .. ..   486·596
Mark on post of gate at north-west side of road;
2·19 ft. above surface * .. ..   546·020

BRANCH LEVELLING.

Great Offley Church. Bolt in west end of tower;
1·06 ft. above surface.. .. ..   524·671
Lilley Church. Bolt in south jamb of vestry door;
1·37 ft. above surface.. .. ..   440·316

* The continuation of this line of levelling, to Luton, and thence to Dunstable,
is in Bedfordshire.

22.—THE POLARISATION OF LIGHT.

By JAMES U. HARFORD.

[Abstract of Lecture delivered 12th October, 1876.]

PLATE II.

THE subject of Polarisation of Light forms part of the general one of Physical Optics. In attempting its special consideration, therefore, it is difficult, if not impossible, to avoid reference to the more extended and complete range of study with which it is connected. An endeavour will, however, be made to confine the attention as closely as possible to the proper and peculiar phenomena of polarisation, and general references will be made only where they may be found absolutely indispensable.

Light must be understood, without further definition, to mean that combination or mutual relation that is known and acknowledged to exist between the "luminous" or "light-giving" body, and the "sensation" of light for which provision is made in the animal organisation. The external cause on the one hand and the animal sensation on the other—light and vision—must both be taken into account as completing our notion and idea of light. Physical cause and human perception are, therefore, the simplest data on which ground can be broken on this occasion.

The first thing to be done now is to make a simple and clear distinction or contrast between what we understand as *ordinary* light and *polarised* light respectively. To all ordinary view the two are alike, and it is only when some test or method of examination and analysis is applied that the difference is discovered. Ordinary light has been described, with fair propriety, as "all sided," polarised light as "one sided." Let this be explained. Ordinary light (Fig. 1) may be viewed in all directions—may be transmitted through all transparent media in all directions of position of the latter—may be reflected from all surfaces at whatever the angle of position of the reflecting surface, without any apparent hindrance or alteration in its properties. Polarised light, on the contrary, will *not* bear reflexion at a certain angle of the reflecting surface, and will *not* bear transmission through a transparent medium in certain positions of the two relatively. These positions, on the one hand of complete transmission or reflexion, and on the other of total obstruction of transmission or reflexion, are found to be at right angles with each other (Fig. 2). At intermediate positions or relations the transmission or reflexion are proportionately partial.

Thus polarised light possesses relations to two lines of direction at right angles to each other; and from this circumstance, in analogy with the poles of the earth or sphere, light in the condition termed "polarised" owes in part its distinctive appellation. The term "in part" is used, because, when we come to consider some of the phenomena in connexion with crystallisation, there seems a further reason for the appropriateness of the term.

We will now proceed to exemplify and explain in a more precise and practical way these general remarks. 1st. To investigate the effect of reflexion. A beam of ordinary light let fall on a reflecting surface, not metallic—say glass—at an angle of 56½° of incidence, or making an angle with the glass of 33½°, is partly reflected and partly transmitted (Fig. 3), as, in fact, would be the case at any other angle of reflexion. But at this particular angle the light that is reflected becomes completely polarised. I say "completely" because at any other angle only partial polarisation takes place; and the angle of 56½° is therefore called the polarising angle for glass,* other reflecting bodies having each a particular angle of maximum polarisation. Now this light so reflected is capable of being reflected again from a second reflecting plate at any angle of position, so that the reflexion takes place in the same plane, but will not bear reflexion in a plane deviating from the plane of incidence and first reflexion, and its inability of reflexion increases up to the angle of 90 degrees, a right angle with the first plane, at which angle no light is reflected by the second reflector. The light reflected by the first plate at the given angle is therefore said to be polarised in the plane of reflexion. Now what becomes of the portion of light that passes through the first glass plate? By testing it in a similar way by a second reflector, it is found to be capable of second reflexion just in the directions in which it refused to pass by reflexion from the first reflecting surface, and incapable of reflexion in the original plane of incidence. Thus, then, the light that passes through the first plate is said to be polarised by refraction. It is necessary to state here that refraction through a single plate is insufficient to polarise the whole of the transmitted light; but by the use of several plates superposed, called "a bundle," the effect is proportionately increased until nearly entire polarisation ensues. We have now to notice a further and most interesting form of polarisation attendant on what is known as double refraction. The most remarkable substance exemplifying this property is Iceland spar. A beam of light in passing through this mineral in any direction (except one, hereafter to be considered) is divided into two (Fig. 4). An object, therefore, seen through a plate of this crystal, appears doubled. A small hole in a card, or a black spot on paper, will appear doubled; and what concerns our subject is this—that the two beams into which the original one is divided are polarised at right angles to each other. What glass plates and bundles have effected by reflexion and transmission respectively, is in the case of Iceland spar effected by transmission solely, through the separation of the beam of light into two.

This subject of double refraction opens up a wide field of research in connexion with Mineralogy and Crystallography, and also has to do with a great class of most interesting and beautiful

* The polarising angle varies, however, according to the index of refraction of the glass. Deschanel, in his 'Elementary Treatise on Natural Philosophy' (edition by Prof. Everett, page 1034), states that the polarising angle for crown-glass varies from 56° 51' to 57° 23', and for flint-glass from 57° 36' to 58° 40'.—Ed.

phenomena in connexion with polarised light. First as regards
crystals. It is not to be concluded that Iceland spar is the only
substance possessing the property of double refraction. All crys-
talline forms, for the purpose of the present inquiry, may be
classified under three, or even two divisions. 1st, the cubic series,
including all forms that are based on or derived from the funda-
mental form of the cube. 2nd, the prismatic, which may be taken
to include the 3rd, the oblique. Now it is to be particularly noted
that the property of double refraction is possessed by the latter
only of these classes of forms, the cubic series of forms having no
such property. Then further note—first, that, in the cubic forms,
the axes of form, *i.e.* those lines which directly intersect the
crystal, are equal; second, that experiment has shown that these
forms, when capable of expansion, are expansible or elastic equally
in all directions of their axes. On the contrary, the axes of the
oblique and prismatic forms are unequal, and experiment has
shown that their expansibility or elasticity is also unequal in
different directions. It is fairly inferred from these considerations,
that in the structure (or architecture, as it has been called) of
crystals, the molecules of which they are built up have arranged
themselves in accordance with the properties above stated—viz.
that in the cubic crystals the density of the molecular arrangement
is equal in all directions; or, in other words, that the attractive
force that holds them together is equal in all directions; or again,
that the tension is similarly equal in all directions. Now in the
case of the oblique and prismatic forms all the foregoing conditions
are different. They are found by experiment to be unequally
elastic and expansible. The density, attractive force, and tension,
therefore, in the arrangement of the molecules, are held to be
unequal in different directions. There is, in evident connexion
with these respective properties of crystals, the fact that a ray of
light suffers no separation in passing through a cubic form, but is
divided into two in passing through an oblique or prismatic form.

The various substances or preparations used as illustrating under
the microscope some of the phenomena of polarisation may be
noticed here, as possessing the characteristics of unequal tension,
such as animal and vegetable tissue, bone, horn, fibres of silk,
wool and hair, seeds and seed vessels, and artificially prepared
bodies such as gum, jellies, resins, etc. Of the same character
may be instanced the optical property in respect to polarisation
exhibited by unannealed glass. A moulded form of glass is greatly
heated and then allowed to cool rapidly. The effect is to contract
the outer surface in the act of cooling, in excess as compared with
the interior. Thus the molecular condition, or in other terms, the
tension, of the whole mass, is unequal.

The consideration of the possible law which governs the arrangement of the molecules of matter when they pass from the fluid to
the solid state in the act of crystallising, furnishes the additional
support to the use of the term "polar" as applied to light. It is
clear that the particles of matter arrange or build themselves up in

a crystal under a definite system, and it is not venturing far into
the domain of speculation to imagine that the law is that of attrac-
tion and repulsion; or, in other words, polarity of some kind, as
exemplified in the ordinary magnetic property. Thus, if the architecture of crystals is assumed to be governed by a species of
polarity, certain phenomena of light which are intimately connected
with crystallography may not inappropriately borrow or adopt the
same term.

Before leaving this part of the subject some further peculiar
properties of the doubly refracted beam must be noticed. 1st.
When the beam passes directly along the axis of the crystal, *i.e.*,
the line connecting the obtuse angles of the rhomb, it is not
divided. This again seems to denote the symmetry of arrangement
and equal and uniform density in the molecular arrangement along
that line. 2nd. In every other direction (increasing to a maximum
at what may be termed the equator of the crystal) a separation
of the rays takes place. One of these, called the ordinary ray,
is refracted in accordance with the law established by Snell,
viz., that refraction takes place in the plane of incidence of the
light, and that the sine of the angle of refraction bears a constant
relation to the sine of the angle of incidence. A reference to Fig. 5
will make this matter more intelligible. The refraction of the
other ray, called the extraordinary ray, does not obey this law. It
is *not* refracted constantly in the plane of incidence, and its index
of refraction is *not* constant. The index for the ordinary ray is
1·654; that for the extraordinary ray is 1·483 to 1·654. The
refractive power of the crystal is therefore greatest in the direction
traversed by the ordinary ray, again proving that the molecular
arrangement is more dense in that direction than it is in the other.
The greater refraction of the ordinary ray is at once observed by
placing a crystal of the spar over a piece of paper on which a black
spot or other mark is made. One spot of the two, resulting from
double refraction, which seems to be raised to a higher level than
the other, is the ordinary ray.

This difference between the refractive powers of the crystal in
relation to the ordinary and extraordinary rays is applied very
ingeniously in the construction of the optical instrument so well
known as Nicol's prism. By reference to Fig. 6, it is seen that an
elongated prism of Iceland spar is cut diagonally in its length
through the two obtuse angles, and the two parts are then re-united
with Canada balsam. The refractive power of this stands between
those of the ordinary and the extraordinary ray. A ray of ordinary
light, therefore, impinging on the first surface of the prism is as
usual split into two in traversing the first portion of the crystal.
The extraordinary ray, passing from a medium of less density into
the Canada balsam, which exceeds it in refractive power, is bent in
the usual way inwards, then issues from the balsam into the spar,
and pursues its course through the second half of the prism and
finally issues in the polarised state. The ordinary ray is altogether
reflected out of the prism, because it passes from the greater re-

fractive power of the spar upon the lower power of the balsam at so slight an angle that it is, in accordance with a well-known law, which time will not allow of explaining here, incapable of penetrating it, and is wholly reflected. Thus, for optical purposes, and the microscope especially, a provision is secured for obtaining a pure beam of polarised light, *i.e.* the beam that issues from the crystal.

In reference to the doubly refracting power of the oblique and prismatic class of crystals, it is further to be observed that in the great majority of cases the separation of the two rays (ordinary and extraordinary) is so slight as to be altogether imperceptible to common observation. It is detected and proved, however, by other means, chiefly by the remarkable effects of colour, which will be treated of in a subsequent part of this lecture.

There is one other mode in which light may become polarised, and that is by what is called *absorption.* Take a thin slice of the mineral tourmaline, cut in a direction parallel to the axis, and it is found that the light passing through this plate is polarised, and its property can be proved in the usual modes. Take a second similar cutting, and it is observed that when both plates are placed over each other in the same direction as their position in the natural crystal—or one of them in the position vertical to it—the light passes through both with no alteration beyond what is due to the diminution of light owing to the increased thickness. Place, however, the two plates across each other at a relative position rectangular to the former, and the light is wholly stopped. In this instance it is to be remarked that the tourmaline belongs to the class of prismatic forms; that in this case double refraction occurs in all directions except along the axis; and that double refraction ought to occur, therefore, in the passage of light through the plates just referred to. It does so, but one of the rays is obstructed, suppressed, or absorbed in its passage; and one only, and that polarised, emerges.

All the foregoing considerations seem to point towards the first step of the theory which is adopted in explanation. Without attempting a lengthened dissertation, it may briefly be stated thus : light consists of, is caused by, or accompanied by, whichever term may be most appropriate or intelligible, vibrations—oscillations—movements to and fro—of particles of a highly elastic fluid medium called the " luminiferous ether." These vibrations take place in directions transverse to the line of direction of the propagation of the light. The law under which these vibrations combine to produce what are termed waves or undulations will be considered later. In ordinary light these vibrations occur in all directions round the line of progression of light In polarised light, on the contrary, they are assorted into definite directions, and in the case of a ray divided into two, either by ordinary or double refraction, the arrangement of the vibrations is such that the planes of these vibrations are at right angles to each other. A little thought will suffice to make this theory apply to the several cases of polarisation already noticed.

An exceedingly interesting department of the subject must now be taken into consideration, that is, coloured polarisation. The beautiful phenomena, usually displayed by means of the microscope with a polariscope attached, are amongst the most interesting as well as the most gorgeous revelations of natural science. It will now be our object to illustrate and explain the principles on which they depend The subject of colour in general would alone furnish matter for long and interesting research, but on this occasion we are restricted to so much of the subject as is concerned with polarisation only. All colour is caused by light, and thus so many things are common to the whole subject that we must be allowed some extent of comprehension and collateral remark in treating even a subdivision. The colours exhibited by objects examined by the aid of polarised light are caused by what is called theoretically, "interference," i.e., interference of waves of light. Thus a theory of waves is involved, or the so-called undulatory theory. Now whatever may be the exact character or form of the so-called waves of light, there is clearly, from the result of observation and experiment, a close, exact analogy with the theory and action of waves in general. If nothing else is proved, this characteristic at least is undoubted, viz. a regular recurrence of intervals, or periodicity, in the action of light; and it may also be affirmed that this periodicity is capable of being made the basis of exact calculation on the mechanical principles which govern the theory of wave action generally.

The principal points may be here enumerated, and the undulatory theory of light will be found in accordance, if not in actual form, at least, in strict analogy. 1st. Wave motion commences at a central point of disturbance, and is propagated in all directions around, by regular equal-timed waves. Fig. 7 will explain this principle, both in reference to water and air, the latter producing sound. 2nd. The wave is formed by the vibrating movement of particles of the medium to and fro,—in water, transverse to the line of propagation of the wave,—in air, longitudinally; each half wave being contrary to the adjoining half in respect to the state or *phase* of its vibrations. 3rd. The wave, or rather the wave form, travels, and not the particles of the medium, which merely oscillate to and fro; the front of the wave being formed of particles in the upward phase, the back of the wave of particles in the downward phase. 4th. When two waves encounter each other, the result for water or other liquid is an increase of height or intensity of form at those points of intersection where summit and summit or hollow and hollow coincide, and a calm or mutual extinction where summit and hollow intersect. At all intermediate points the interference is proportionate to the relative distances from the points of complete intersection. (Figs. 8, 9, 10, 11.) In air the effect is analogous, taking condensation and rarefaction as analogous to summit and hollow, and intensity and calm as analogous to sound and silence. In all these particulars the undulatory theory of light is in strict analogy. 1st. The equal and equal-

timed intervals. This may be demonstrated by reference to the
colours of Newton's rings, the successive intervals of thickness
producing a repetition of the same order of colours being in direct
arithmetical progression—1, 2, 3, 4, etc; also by the effect of the
passage of light through a narrow slit. This is easily demonstrated practically, but can hardly be well explained without a
diagram. In looking through a narrow slit the figure of the
opening will be seen covered with narrow dark lines, due to the
interference of waves of light passing through, or what is called
diffracted, from the boundary edges of the slit. 2nd. The theory
of the vibrating movement of particles of luminiferous ether transverse to the line of propagation has already been referred to. It
is probable and natural that a longitudinal alternate compression
and dilation should take place in the ether analogous to the action
of air in sound. Each half-wave is contrary in phase to the adjoining half, consequently under such circumstances the interference of
waves of light results in darkness. This may be illustrated by
means of a diffraction slit, or Frauenhofer's gratings, and also by
the dark intervals between the successive Newton's rings, which
are explained by Fig. 12. 3rd. It is as difficult to conceive of the
possibility of the emission of particles from a luminous body at
the speed of 190,000 miles per second as it is of the emission of
particles of matter from a sounding body to the ear. The wave
theory seems simpler and more satisfactory, to say nothing of other
reasons. The *wave* theory of light addresses itself to our knowledge, the *emission* theory to our ignorance. 4th. The interference
of waves of light at the half-wave interval results in the extinction
of light; but at intermediate points the extinction is partial in
proportion to the amount of interference, and fringes of colour
result. These seem due to the effect on the eye of the residue of
the vibrations and their continuous impression on the sensation of
sight. This is somewhat analogous to the beats of sound which
are heard when two musical notes of discordant pitch are sounded
together. The coincidences produce an augmented sound, and
when following slowly may be counted, but if in rapid succession
produce a sustained effect on the ear.

On the principle of interference may be explained most of the
phenomena of colour in ordinary light as well as those observed in
polarised light. In all cases one ray of light is found or made to
run concurrently with another in such a manner that the phases of
the vibrations shall in some part counteract or neutralise one
another, and the resulting vibrations produce the effect of colour
as being part only of the combined effect of the total vibrations
constituting the wave. For instance, in the case of thin films part
of the light is reflected at the first surface, another part enters the
film and is reflected from the second interior surface, and emerges
in close proximity with the first reflected beam (Fig. 13). If the
difference owing to the internal refraction and reflexion amounts to
a complete and exact wave, the two waves of reflexion will concur
in their respective phases,—no interference will take place, and the

light remains unchanged, *i.e.* white. If the difference amounts to more or less than an entire wave, the two reflected waves are in a condition of interference, part of the vibrations is suppressed or neutralised by the mutual opposition, and a residue only is observed, and this residue is coloured. The tint of colour will be according to the amount of interference, or, *pari passu*, the thickness of the film. In the case of the double refraction it will be remembered that the refracted beams pass through strata of unequal densities, and therefore unequal refractive power. One, therefore—*i.e.* the ordinary ray—suffers more obstruction than the other, or, to use the recognized word, is "retarded," and this retardation serves the same office as reflexion and refraction in the former instance, when by means of a proper contrivance two beams in the same *plane* of polarisation, but in different *phases* as to vibration, are made concurrent. Reference to Fig. 14 will help to make this apparent. Let *a* represent a beam of polarised light. This passing through a thin slice of selenite *b* cut parallel to the axis of the crystal is separated into *two* rays *c* and *c'*. This separation, however, is so small as to be invisible. The light may simply be said to be dislocated, or the separation started. This light is then analysed by passing through a crystal of Iceland spar *d* which has the power of completely separating the rays, and *each* ray *c* and *c'* is divided into *two*, making *four* in all—*e e'* derived from one ray, say the ordinary ray, and *f f'* from the other, the extraordinary ray. In each case the separation is accompanied by polarisation in opposite planes. This separation into *four* is invisible. The visible result is that *two* rays *g* and *g'* are seen, each being compounded of two rays respectively in the same plane, but in a state of interference. For note that *g* is formed by concurrence of *e* and *f*, and *g'* by concurrence of *e'* and *f'*. Now *e* and *f* come from different sources—*e* from the ordinary ray, and *f* from the extraordinary ray, and are consequently in different phases of vibration. The same may be stated in reference to *e'* and *f'*. The colours in the result are *complementary*, *i.e.* by their union *white* light is made complete, one colour being the *complement* to the other in this respect.

This paper being intended simply as an abstract of a lecture on the subject, in the course of which specimens, apparatus, and diagrams were freely used, it is obvious that to render the paper as complete and effective as the lecture it would expand into a treatise and prove unnecessarily voluminous. One other topic only, concerned with the subject, will be alluded to.. The consideration has hitherto been devoted to what is termed *plane* polarisation, meaning that the polarisation that takes place has reference to two planes at right angles to each other. The term *rectangular* polarisation is sometimes more correctly applied. There are, however, phenomena of polarisation that belong not to two rectangular planes only, but are exhibited at all planes in succession around the central point. The phenomena of colour in this case, instead of taking place in reference to two opposite planes alternately, are also shown all round.   This kind of polarisation is termed *circular*, and the crystal quartz exhibits the property in a remarkable way. Of the same character is also what is termed *elliptical* polarisation. The subject altogether is too extensive for hasty treatment, but the object of the lecture has been to bring under notice its most prominent features, and it is hoped that the effort will not have proved unavailing.

EXPLANATION OF PLATE II.

Fig.   1. Section of beam of ordinary light.

Fig.   2. Sections of beams (*a b*) of polarised light.

Fig.   3. Polarisation by reflexion and refraction : *a*, ray of ordinary light; *b*, portion of ray polarised by reflexion from surface of glass plate ; *c*, portion of ray polarised by refraction through it.

Fig.   4. Polarisation by double refraction: *a*, ray of ordinary light; *b*, ordinary ray, and *e*, extraordinary ray, polarised in planes at right angles to each other by transmission through prism of Iceland spar (*d d*).

Fig.   5. Snell's Law of Sines : as the sine, *a b*, of the angle of incidence (in air) is to the sine, *a' b'*, of the angle of refraction (in water), so is 1⅓ to 1.

Fig.   6. Nicol's Prism: *a*, ray of ordinary light; *b*, ordinary ray reflected from Canada balsam and thrown out of the prism ; *c*, extraordinary ray transmitted through it; *d*, Iceland spar ; *e*, Canada balsam.

Fig.   7. Propagation of waves : the lines denote summits.

Fig.   8. Wave motion: the arrows show the direction of the particles of the wave and their upward and downward movement.

Fig.   9. Two waves coinciding.

Fig. 10. Two waves totally interfering.

Fig. 11. Two waves partially interfering.

Fig. 12. Newton's Rings (curve of upper glass plate exaggerated): Nos. 1, 2, 3, 4, 5, 6, and 7 denote repetitions of the same colour ; i, ii, iii, iv, etc., equal intervals of the passage of light.

Fig. 13. Films (thickness exaggerated): *a*, reflected from upper surface; *a'*, reflected from lower surface ; *b*, refracted direct; *b'*, refracted by reflexion from upper surface.

Fig. 14. Production of colour by polarised light : *a*, polarised beam ; *b*, selenite film ; *c c'*, beams separated but not visibly: *d*, Iceland spar ; *e e'*, and *f f'*, the two foregoing beams each doubly refracted; *g g'*, two colours complementary.

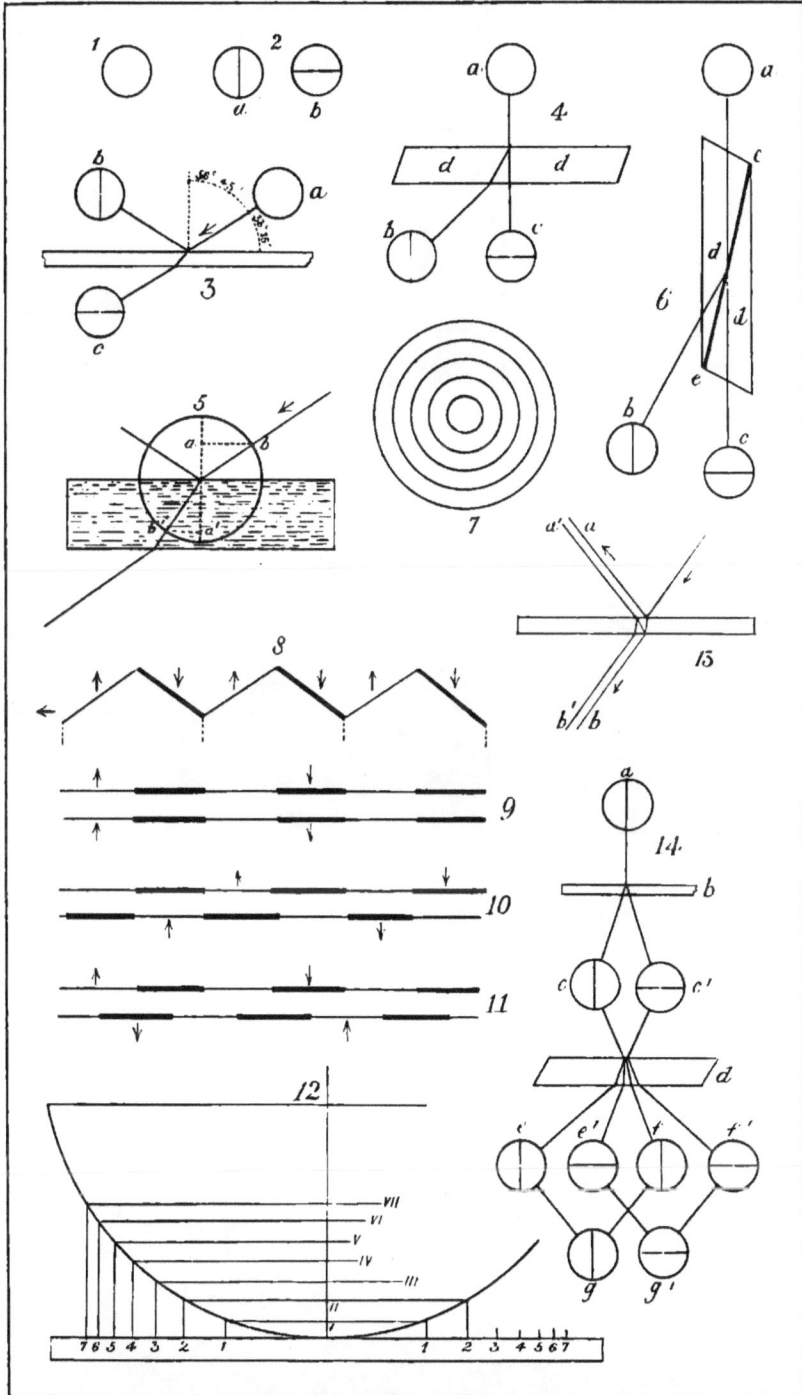

POLARISATION OF LIGHT.

Fiddle & Buchman, Lith.

23.—THE EOCENES OF ENGLAND AND THEIR EXTENSION IN HERTFORDSHIRE.

By J. LOGAN LOBLEY, F.G.S., F.R.G.S.

[A Lecture delivered 11th December, 1876.]

WHEN I previously had the honour of addressing the members of the Watford Natural History Society, a brief description of the Cretaceous group of British rocks was attempted. This series of strata includes the Chalk—that great limestone formation which forms as it were the foundation-stone of Hertfordshire. Above the Chalk lie superimposed a series of beds, some of which only, however, are to be found in this county, which have been deposited since the Cretaceous epoch; and it is the lower portion of this series, that lying immediately on the Chalk, to which I wish to ask your attention this evening.

As you are aware, the entire series of sedimentary rocks is divided into three great divisions:—the Primary or Palæozoic, the Secondary or Mesozoic, and the Tertiary or Cainozoic. The Chalk is the highest of the British Secondary rocks. The beds, therefore, lying upon the Chalk in regular sequence, form the lowermost division of the Tertiary. To this division the name Eocene· has been given, the precise meaning of which name may be briefly explained. From investigations made by M. Deshayes upwards of forty years ago, it appeared possible to Sir Charles Lyell to name the three divisions of the Tertiary deposits in accordance with the proportion of recent species found among the fossil shells of each. To the lower beds, in which a small proportion of recent shells were found, the name *Eocene*, from *eos*, dawn, and *cainos*, recent, was accordingly given. The middle beds, in which less than half of the fossil shells were recent, were named Miocene, from *meion*, less; and the upper beds, containing an assemblage of shells of which considerably more than half were recent species, were called the Pliocene, from *pleion*, more.

The Eocene, or the dawn of the recent, is, therefore, the division which includes the beds formed during that period of the earth's history when the fauna of the present day began to make its appearance, and though our higher forms of life were then unrepresented, yet many genera and a few species of our existing Mollusca were at that period inhabitants of the waters, if not of the lands of the globe.

The Eocene beds of England are found occupying two areas distinctly separated by a large and elevated district. One of these areas is triangular in shape, and stretches from Hungerford in Berkshire to the German Ocean, along the course of the Thames, but chiefly on its northern side; and to this extension of Lower Tertiary beds the name London Basin has been given. The second area, including as it does a large portion of the county of Hants and the northern part of the Isle of Wight, is known by the name of the Hampshire Basin. No beds of Eocene age occur in Great Britain outside these areas. The physical features of the Eocene districts of England are not striking, the elevations being inconsiderable, and the valleys broad; but a luxuriant growth of timber trees of large size gives a rich appearance to a great portion of each area, while utterly barren wastes occupy a by no means inconsiderable portion of the London Basin.

But though the single name Eocene has been given to the whole of the lower division of the Tertiaries, this group of strata is by no means uniform either lithologically or palæontologically. On the contrary, it consists of siliceous, calcareous, and argillaceous beds, some marine, some estuarine, and some freshwater, with, as a consequence, markedly distinct assemblages of fossils. There are therefore abundant grounds for distinguishing the various beds by different names, and thus it is that the term the *Eocenes* of England is used.

The following are the various divisions of the Eocene group of British strata (in descending order) :—

Bembridge Series.
Osborne or St. Helen's Beds. } UPPER EOCENE.
Headon Series.

Upper Bagshot Beds.
Bracklesham and Barton Beds. } MIDDLE EOCENE.
Lower Bagshot Beds.

London Clay and Bognor Rock.
Oldhaven Beds.
Woolwich and Reading Series. } LOWER EOCENE.
Thanet Sands.

THE LOWER EOCENES.

THE THANET SANDS.—Above the Chalk in the London Basin we find a series of beds chiefly of sand extending from the east of Thanet to a little west of London, lying chiefly south of the Thames. To these beds the name Thanet Sands has been given. Resting immediately upon the Chalk, the surface of which is irregularly eroded, lies a bed of large flints, unworn, but all covered with a green coating which has been ascertained to be silicate of iron. These flints are obviously Chalk flints, and since they are unworn, it is concluded that they, being siliceous and therefore insoluble bodies, have been left by the removal of a bed of Chalk, not by running water, but by its solution by carbonated water which has percolated through overlying beds, and that the flints are a measure of the amount of chalk so removed. The bed of green-coated flints, or Bull Head bed, with argillaceous matter, forms the base or lowest bed of the Thanet Sands, which are divisible in the typical locality of Pegwell Bay into five distinct beds. They are described in detail by Mr. Whitaker in his paper "On the Lower London Tertiaries of Kent," in the 'Quarterly Journal of the Geological Society,' vol. xxii. p. 414, and the result of his observations may be summarized by a table thus:—

e 30 feet.	Fine sharp sand. (Silicified fossils.)	Reculvers and Pegwell Bay.
d 93 feet in Belgium.	Sandy marl. (Fossils: *Cyprina Morrisii*, *Pholadomya cuneata*, etc.)	Near Canterbury.
c 60 feet.	Fine soft pale buff sand. (No fossils, except cast of *Pholadomya*.)	Begins east of Canterbury; dies out west of London.
b	Brown clay and loam.	East of Faversham, Pegwell Bay (local).
a 2 to 5 feet.	Clayey bed with green-coated flints.	Persistent everywhere.

As we travel westward from the neighbourhood of Ramsgate, the formation becomes less diversified, and between the Medway and London only two of the five divisions are found ; these are *a* and *c*, the latter of which has increased to a very considerable thickness, 60 feet in some places, and forms the typical Thanet Sand. Very good sections of the bed may be seen at Charlton, near Woolwich, and lower down the river at Erith, where the sand has been excavated for a long period of time to serve as ballast for Tyne-returning colliers, and afterwards to do duty for casting purposes at the great iron works of the north of England. Its fitness for casting operations is due to its soft loamy character, which is so marked that it is called by the men who work it not sand but loam. Thick as is this bed, and extensively as it has been worked for many years, only a doubtful cast of a *Pholadomya* has been found in it. The bed *d*, however, at several places—Pegwell Bay, near Herne Bay, etc.—is very fossiliferous, one species especially being most abundant; this is the *Cyprina Morrisii*, which is found in a beautiful state of preservation. Other species in the Thanet Sands are *Astarte tenera*, *Corbula regulbiensis*, and *Pholadomya Konincki*.

Though the Thanet Sands of England have a very limited extension, and are not found at all in the Hampshire Basin, they are not confined to this country, but are met with in Belgium on the east, and in France on the south of the Channel, where they are called *Sables de Bracheaux*. From the character of the fauna it has been inferred that the Thanet Sands sea was a comparatively cold one, considerably colder than the sea which succeeded it.

Climatal conditions in various parts of the world at the present time show that places in the same latitude may have very different temperatures. The British Islands enjoy a much milder climate than the lands on the west of the Atlantic equally distant from the pole. This is doubtless caused to a great extent by the configuration of the land on the globe, the central part of the American continent deflecting the great equatorial current, and causing a great flow of warm water from the tropics to the north-western coasts of Europe, and which great body of warm water warms and renders humid the winds which blow over it during so many days in the year from the south-west. This will indicate how we may account for the various climatal conditions of the Eocene Epoch, though the hypothesis of an alteration of the inclination of the earth's axis has been called in to explain the great changes of temperature which have occurred during the later geological periods. If then we suppose the small and shallow Thanet Sands sea to have been closed to the south and open to the north, open to the influx of the cold polar waters, we shall have conditions that will suffice to give a sea of such a temperature as to be favourable to the life and development of the genera represented in these beds.

The Woolwich and Reading Series.—A series of deposits of great interest overlies and overlaps the Thanet Sands, for the Woolwich and Reading Series has a much greater extension in England than the underlying formation, which terminates westward between London and Windsor, and is little seen north of the Thames. Nor are the Woolwich beds confined to the London Basin, for in the Isle of Wight they are seen resting against the upheaved Chalk. The fauna and the flora of these beds clearly indicate that the deposition took place during a period in which several alterations in the relative level of land and water took place, —alterations which at one time gave a river, at another an estuary, and at another an open sea over the same area; for freshwater, estuarine, and marine shells alternate in the various beds composing the Woolwich and Reading Series.

In the extreme west—the Isle of Wight—the Woolwich Beds, consisting of clays of mottled colours, and called from their consistence the "Plastic Clay," are quite devoid of fossils. In the neighbourhood of Reading argillaceous beds prevail, with oysters in abundance, while in the eastern part of the London Basin the beds vary greatly in character, and yield many species of Mollusca, including some river shells, and, in addition, an assemblage of plant-remains, which also tell us of the proximity of land. Perhaps the most marked feature of the Woolwich and Reading Series is the occurrence of beds almost entirely composed of shells. These beds contain, in some instances, shells of *Cyrena* mingled with those of oysters, but in others the cyrenas are free from intermingled oysters, and in others again the oysters are free from cyrenas. The thickness of the formation in the London Basin is about eighty feet, and in the Isle of Wight, where the beds are nearly vertical, it is 160 feet thick.

Among the fossils the following are the best-known :—Mollusca : *Melania inquinata, Paludina lenta, Cerithium funatum, Cyrena cuneiformis, C. deperdita, Ostrea Bellovacina, O. tenera.* Plants : *Dryandroides Prestwichii, Ficus Forbesi, Laurus Hookeri.*

The Oldhaven Beds.—The shell beds and clays of the Woolwich Series give place in Kent to pebble-beds of great thickness, which have been named the Oldhaven Beds, though at Oldhaven Gap the beds of this horizon are rather clayey than stony. Bounding the south side of the Thames Valley extends a series of flat-topped hills, with deeply-cut indentations which being usually richly wooded add greatly to the beauty of the district. The high-level flats are formed of the Oldhaven pebble-beds, and the pretty dells are due to the erosion of the easily disintegrated beds by the water which is stopped in its downward course by the argillaceous beds below, and which has found an outlet at various points along the escarpment.

Nowhere perhaps are these remarkable beds of pebbles better seen than at Blackheath, one of the plateaux formed by them. The pebbles are found to be completely rounded or oval, without the admixture of any angular or even subangular ones. Moreover they are all of one material. They are all flint pebbles of a blue-black colour. We have no difficulty in concluding, therefore, that the Oldhaven pebble-beds are derived from the waste of a Chalk district, and the belief is entertained that they have formed originally a great shingle bank well out at sea, and were not shingle *beaches* at the foot of a chalk cliff, for in that case subangular flints would have been plentifully intermingled with those which had been longer exposed to the rolling action of the sea waves, and which consequently were more completely rounded.

THE LONDON CLAY.—To give anything like a description of the succeeding formation, the great argillaceous deposit known as the London Clay, with its interesting fauna and flora, much more time than is at our disposal this evening would be required. So much was, however, said on this member of the Eocenes by Professor Morris in his learned lecture last year to the members of this Society, and printed in the 'Transactions,' that it will be unnecessary for me to do more than remind you of the salient facts recorded by investigators of the London Clay. In the London Tertiary Basin the London Clay occupies a very extensive area, stretching from near Hungerford in the west to the coast of Essex in the east, and forming the greater part of the counties of Middlesex and Essex, while in the Hampshire Basin the London Clay is seen resting against the Plastic Clay of the Isle of Wight. At some depth below the surface this deposit is a blue clay of uniform consistency; but where exposure has taken place the colour is brown, consequent upon the more complete oxidation of the iron contained in the clay, and crystals of selenite are abundant, while the clay itself is less compact and uniform in character.

The fauna as well as the flora of the London Clay indicate warmer conditions than prevailed during the Thanet Sands or the subsequent Woolwich Series period, and indeed to some geologists give conclusive evidence of a warm or even a hot climate. Certain it is that the inhabitants of tropical seas at the present time, such as turtles, nautili, volutes, and the plants growing on the banks of tropical rivers, such as palms, had representatives in the London

Clay epoch. In Sheppey the remains of more species of turtles than are now known to exist have been found. Nautili and volutes and allied genera are abundant in the London area; while the fossil fruits of the palm (*Nipadites*) are extremely common in the Sheppey district.

Well-sinkings in the London district give a maximum thickness of 400 feet to the London Clay. This is much diminished in the lower parts of the Thames Valley, which has been cut out of this formation by the river. Thus, near the river we find the clay about 200 feet thick, while at Hampstead it is about 400 feet. The upper beds are sandy in character, and contain a small *Pectunculus* (*P. decussatus*) in abundance, with nautili of several species.

It is an interesting question, Whence came this large accumulation of argillaceous matter? Since each of the sedimentary rocks is made up of the waste of those deposits which have formed the land of the period of its deposition, we must look to older rocks than the London Clay to find the source of the material of which it is composed. The decomposition of one of the hardest rocks—granite—affords a pure clay, and doubtless a large portion of the London Clay was derived from the waste of the granitic rocks to the west, though much may have come from Gault and Oxford Clay areas.

The London Clay is not made up entirely of argillaceous matter, for we find in it concretionary masses of carbonate of lime, with an abundance of crystals of selenite and nodules of iron pyrites. The first and last of these mineral concretions are so abundant that in Sheppey the disintegration of the sea-cliffs yields them freely enough for their collection to form a considerable industry. The concretions of carbonate of lime (known as *septaria*) are ground for cement, and the iron pyrites is used for the manufacture of sulphuric acid. Of the age of the London Clay also, at Bognor in Sussex, silicceo-calcareous masses form what is called the Bognor Rock, which is so hard as to well withstand the waves of that exposed coast.

Though the fossils are of many species and very numerous, they are not scattered uniformly through the formation, but are in colonies as it were. Thus we have Chelonia and plant-remains abundant in Sheppey, nautili and volutes common at Highgate in the upper beds, *Ditrupa* in masses in a band in the Isle of Wight, fish and other vertebrate remains in the lower basement beds. The following are a few of the characteristic fossils of the London Clay :—Vertebrata : *Hyracotherium leporinum, Chelone breviceps, Palæophis Toliapicus, Lamna elegans.* Invertebrata : *Nautilus imperialis, Aturia ziczac, Voluta nodosa, Aporrhais Sowerbyi, Rostellaria rimosa, Pholadomya margaritacea, Pectunculus decussatus, Vermicularia bognoriensis, Ditrupa plana, Ophiura Wetherelli.* Plants : *Nipadites ellipticus, Pterophiloides Richardsoni.*

THE MIDDLE EOCENES.

The Middle Eocenes of England have a total thickness equal to that of the Lower, and consist of the Lower Bagshot Sands, the Bracklesham and Barton Beds, and the Upper Bagshot Sands.

THE LOWER BAGSHOT SANDS, which repose on the London Clay, are, in the London Basin, sterile siliceous sands and gravels, devoid of fossils, forming extensive heaths and wastes in the south-west of the district, and constituting the well-known Hampstead Heath on the north of the Thames. In addition to this, outliers of the Lower Bagshots occur at corresponding elevations at Highgate, Harrow, and High Beach in Epping Forest. In the Isle of Wight they are represented by the coloured sands of Alum Bay, which have interbedded bands of white pipe-clay, containing dicotyledonous leaves in abundance; and these plant-remains are also found in beds of the same age at Bournemouth.

THE UPPER BAGSHOT BEDS are similarly devoid of fossils, and, equally with the Lower, consist of sterile sands. They form wide-spreading heaths near Sandhurst.

But while we look in vain for the remains of animal existence in these great siliceous beds, the BRACKLESHAM AND BARTON argillaceous beds of the same age are filled with fossils, warning us that absence of organic remains in any group of strata must not be considered evidence of paucity of life at the period of deposition, but rather that the conditions at a particular locality were not favourable to animal life, and that in other areas, where conditions were more favourable, life at the time was doubtless in undiminished abundance.

The following fossils indicate the prevailing character of the Middle Eocene fauna:—*Palæophis typhæus, Ototus obliquus, Voluta athleta, Mitra scalera, Typhis pungens, Crassatella sulcata, Cardita planicosta, Nummulites lævigatus.*

It may be noted here that the great limestone of the Paris Basin, the Nummulitic Limestone of Egypt which yielded the blocks for the Great Pyramid, and which extends eastwards to India and even to China, is of Middle Eocene age. A very extensive sea, therefore, spread its waters over the present great continental area of the Old World at this epoch. The nummulites which characterize the Middle Eocene are of the same class—the Foraminifera—to which belong the myriads of minute organisms which almost entirely make up that other oceanic deposit, the Chalk.

At this period of the earth's history some of the greatest ranges of mountains must have had no existence, since nummulites of this age are found in the Pyrenees, 6,000 feet above the level of the sea, and in the Himalayas as much as 16,000 feet, while both the Himalayas and the Alps are partly composed of rocks of a still later age. The Middle Eocenes of England by their horizontality indicate clearly that this area has not partaken of the great seismic movements which have elevated the great ranges of mountains just named. Nevertheless, at Alum Bay we have the Chalk vertical, with the Eocenes, Lower and Middle, resting against it and giving proof of considerable local disturbance since the Eocene epoch. The lithological character of the mass of the Bagshot Beds, and the flora of the argillaceous bands, alike show that the Middle Eocenes of England were shallow-water deposits, probably littoral deposits of the wide-spreading sea wherein the great limestone was being formed.

THE UPPER EOCENES.

To the marine Middle Eocenes succeed a series of strata, partly marine and partly freshwater, and called from this the Fluvio-marine Beds. These are quite local, being confined in their extension to the Isle of Wight, if we except a fragment at Brockenhurst in the New Forest.

The lowest group is named the HEADON SERIES, from Headon Hill, near Alum Bay; but these beds are also well seen in Whitecliff Bay, at the east end of the Isle of Wight. They consist of sands, marls, and bands of limestone of, as their fossils indicate, fresh-water, estuarine, and marine origin. The lowermost of the three divisions into which the Headon Series has been divided is a fresh-water and brackish-water deposit. The Middle Headon is marine and brackish-water; and the Upper is like the Lower, fresh and brackish-water. The three divisions are all highly fossiliferous, and the fossils are in a beautiful state of preservation. Amongst the fresh-water species the *Planorbis euomphalus* and *Limnæa longiseata* are perhaps the most abundant. *Cytherea incrassata* distinctly characterizes the marine beds, and in the brackish-water deposits *Ostrea flabellula* and *Potamides cinctus* are abundant.

THE OSBORNE or ST. HELEN'S SERIES, seen at St. Helen's and along the shore in front of Osborne House, succeed. These beds are largely composed of green clays, with bands of red and green mottled clays. Bands of limestone, sandstone, and sands are interbedded with the clays. The Osborne Series is evidently a fresh-water deposit, abounding, as it does, with such shells as *Limnæa, Melanopsis, Paludina,* and *Planorbis.*

THE BEMBRIDGE SERIES, considered either palæontologically or economically, is more important than either the Headon or the Osborne Series. It forms the greater portion of the Tertiary area of the Isle of Wight, and affords the chief building stone of the island, while the organic remains include, besides sixty species of Mollusca, the bones of the earliest large Mammalia yet found. The lower division is the well-known Bembridge Limestone, which has for ages been quarried at Binstead, near Ryde; and the upper consists of marls and clays. Although the limestone is certainly fresh-water, the Bembridge beds yield, some at least, estuarine or brackish-water genera, as *Ostrea, Mytilus,* and *Cytherea.* Of the fresh-water species *Planorbis discus* and *Lymnæa longiseata* are the most abundant, and *Bulimus ellipticus, Cyrena obovata, C. tenuistriata,* and *Cerithium mutabile,* are common. It was in the Binstead quarries that the mammalian remains were discovered. These, on examination, were found to correspond with the bones obtained by Cuvier from the gypseous beds of Montmartre at Paris, which were determined by that great naturalist to be the remains of tapir-like animals, having a short proboscis, but with teeth resembling those of the Rhinoceros. The following species have been determined :—*Anoplotherium commune, A. secundarium, Chæropotamus Cuvieri, Dichobune Cervineum, Palæotherium crassum, P. magnum, P. medium, P. minus.*

THE EOCENES OF HERTFORDSHIRE.

The extension of the Eocenes in this county will be at once learnt from an inspection of the Geological Survey map of the district, which, not showing the superficial Post-Pliocene deposits, indicates conspicuously the entire extent of the Lower Tertiaries. Disregarding the Post-Pliocene superficial deposits, the County of Hertford is occupied chiefly by the Chalk, and it is only in the southern part of the county that this formation is overlain by Tertiary beds. These are a portion of the northern margin of the London Tertiary Basin, the boundary of which in Hertfordshire extends from near Rickmansworth in the west, by Bushey, Shenley, and Hatfield, to the neighbourhood of Bishop's Stortford in the east, thus forming a line trending in a north-easterly direction, and giving the Eocenes to the south and south-east parts of the county. Beyond, however, the line I have described, there are in several places to the north patches of Tertiary deposits lying on the Chalk quite detached from each other and from the main mass. These occur at the following places: Micklefield Hall, Micklefield Green, Sarratt, Abbot's Langley, Bedmont, Bennet's End, Leverstock Green, and at the St. Peter's side of St. Albans. These outliers clearly prove the former extension of the Eocenes to a considerable distance beyond the present boundary, since they are undoubtedly fragments of once continuous beds, which have more or less escaped denudation. To the south of the boundary-line the Tertiaries are continuous, with the exception of a small area near Northaw, where an inlier of Chalk is uncovered by Tertiary beds. Roughly parallel with the edge or escarpment of the Tertiaries, and at a short distance from it, the river Colne runs from Colney-street to Rickmansworth.

In Hertfordshire we have only the Woolwich Beds and the London Clay—the Thanet Sands, the Middle, and the Upper Eocenes, being absent. The lowest formation, therefore—the Thanet Sands—so conspicuous in Kent, must not be looked for here, and although immediately outside the boundary of the county, at Harrow, a patch of the Bagshot Sands occurs on the summit of the hill, these and all the succeeding Eocenes are absent within the boundary.

The Woolwich and Reading Beds are exposed, as might be expected, along the edge of the Tertiary area, where they are seen at many points covering over the Chalk. At Watford Heath, at Bushey, in the neighbourhood of Hertford, and on the eastern edge of Hatfield Park, good sections are exposed, and at these places the variable character of the Woolwich Beds, even within short distances, may be observed. One section shows clays, another sands, and another mingled clays and sands, indicating the changing conditions of deposition which marked the Woolwich and Reading period. In this county the Woolwich Beds are not of that fossiliferous character which distinguishes them in the Kentish area; but still a diligent search may be rewarded by the discovery of a few species. Most of the sections show at their summits a portion of the Basement Bed of the London Clay, with its characteristic scattered small blue-black pebbles, but without those thick beds of pebbles—the Oldhaven Beds—seen at Blackheath and other parts of Kent, and which in that county underlie the London Clay.

Occupying the whole of the Tertiary area, excepting the fringe, and two small areas near Northaw, where streams have cut through to the Woolwich Beds, the London Clay forms the base on which rest all the superficial Post-Pliocene or Drift deposits of this part of the county. The thickness of the clay varies considerably, as may be seen from the well-sections in the county, given by Mr. Whitaker in his 'Geology of the London Basin,' which work should be consulted by all who desire to have a good knowledge of the geology of this district.

As only the basement and lower beds of the London Clay are present, the London Clay fossils of Hertfordshire do not adequately represent the fauna of the formation, and we consequently look in vain for the chelonian remains, the great nautili, and the abundant gasteropods and lamellibranchs of other areas. It must not be supposed, however, that the organic remains found in the Eocenes of Hertfordshire are devoid of interest. This is far from being the case. Teeth of fishes of the genus *Lamna* are common, and Mr. Whitaker mentions the following species of Mollusca as occurring at Bushey :—

Aporrhais Sowerbyi, Mant.	*Cytherea ovalis*, Sby.
Cardium nitens, Sby.	*Nucula*, sp.
„ *Plumsteadiense*, Sby.	*Panopæa intermedia*, Sby.
Cytherea obliqua, Desh.	

Besides these, a member of our Society, Mr. W. T. Stone, some years since was fortunate enough to secure for science a fossil determined by Prof. Owen to be a portion of a bone of a monkey (*Hyracotherium leporinum*). The palæontology of the Eocenes of Hertfordshire is therefore worthy of the attention of our geological members, who I hope may be able to add largely in future years to our knowledge of the fossils of these beds, and I trust, from what has been said of Hertfordshire, members generally may be encouraged to devote some time to the study in the field of the very interesting science of Geology.

APPENDIX.

WELL-SECTIONS IN HERTFORDSHIRE.

(Abstracts of Sections in Whitaker's 'Geology of the London Basin,' part 1, pp. 447-456.)

AMWELL END.
Rough Gravel .... 36 feet.
  Chalk.

BARNET, EAST. Lion's Down.
London Clay .... 113½ „
Woolwich Beds................... 48½ „
  Chalk.

BARNET, NEW. Railway Station.
London Clay .... 115 „
Woolwich Beds................... 44 „
  Chalk.

BARNET, NEW. Trial-boring near Railway Station.
London Clay .... 111½ feet.
Woolwich Beds................... 58 „
  Chalk.

———— The Absorbing Well.
London Clay .... 73 „
Woolwich Beds................... 68 „

BAYFORD.
To Chalk .... 150 „

BISHOP'S STORTFORD. Chantrey Road.
Brick-earth	30	feet.
Sand	18	,,
Chalk.		

——— Dunmow Road.
Brown Loam	3	,,
Gravel and Sand	40	,,
Mottled Loam	4	,,

——— Dunmow Road.
Boulder Clay	45	,,
Sand and Gravel	15	,,
Sand	12	,,

——— Hadham Road.
London Clay	27	,,
Woolwich Beds	20	,,
Chalk.		

——— Hadham Road.
Brick-earth and Sand	28	,,
Chalk.		

——— New Road.
Drift	10	,,
London Clay ?	30	,,
Woolwich Beds	16	,,
Chalk.		

——— Training College.
Drift	65	,,
Woolwich Beds	25	,,
Chalk.		

——— Waterworks.
Boulder Clay	17	,,
London Clay	54	,,
Woolwich Beds	45½	,,
Chalk.		

BROXBOURNE.
To Chalk	84	,,

BUSHEY. L. & N. W. Railway.
Surface earth	3	,,
Clay with large stones	10	,,
Chalk.		

——— Oak Lodge.
London Clay	110	,,
Woolwich Beds	35	,,
Chalk.		

CHESHUNT.
Gravel	8½	,,
London Clay	40	,,
Woolwich Beds	60½	,,
Chalk.		

——— Beaumont Green.
Mould	1	,,
Drift	16	,,
London Clay }	108	,,
Woolwich Beds }		
Soft White Sand	1½	,,

——— Upper Park Farm.
Gravel	5	,,
London Clay	59	,,
Woolwich Beds	57½	,,
Chalk.		

CHESHUNT. Engine House.
Surface Earth	1½	feet.
Gravel	8	,,
London Clay	47	,,
Woolwich Beds	51	,,
Chalk.		

CHORLEY WOOD. Parsonage.
Clay	60	,,
Flints	2	,,
Chalk.		

ELSTREE.
London Clay	183	,,
Woolwich Beds	19	,,
Chalk.		

HADHAM. Berry Green.
Boulder Clay	20	,,
Yellow Sand	15	,,
Brown Clay	25	,,
Chalk.		

HAREFIELD PARK.
Gravel	5	,,
Woolwich Beds	17	,,

HERTFORD. Haileybury College.
To Chalk	150	,,

HITCHIN. Brewery.
Made Ground	3	,,
Drift	77	,,
Chalk.		

HODDESDON. Brewery.
Gravel	20	,,
London Clay }	70	,,
Woolwich Beds }		
Chalk.		

——— New River Company.
Soil	1	,,
Valley Drift	23½	,,
Chalk.		

WALTHAM CROSS.
Mould	2	,,
Valley Drift	14	,,
London Clay	40	,,
Woolwich Beds	51	,,

WATFORD. L. & N. W. Railway.
Surface-earth	2	,,
Clay	8	,,
Gravel	2	,,
Chalk.		

WORMLEY. Nunsbury.
Made Ground & Gravel	6	,,
London Clay	27	,,
Woolwich Beds	47½	,,

——— West End.
Surface-earth	1	,,
Loam	9	,,
London Clay	22	,,
Woolwich Beds	40	,,
Chalk.		

WORMLEY END.
To Chalk	100	,,

24.—MISCELLANEOUS NOTES AND OBSERVATIONS.

[Read 9th November, 1876.]

GEOLOGY.

Boulders in the Neighbourhood of Buntingford, Herts.—I have recently found, in the parish of Westmill, near Buntingford, several boulders from one to two feet in diameter, and more or less sub-angular or rounded in shape, which appear to be undoubtedly Mountain Limestone, and which in all probability have been transported by ice from the hills of Derbyshire, as this district is the nearest, and at the same time the most elevated, in which the Mountain Limestone is found on this side of the eastern watershed of England. Several of these blocks I noticed in draining a stiffish soil, about two feet below the surface, and some twenty feet probably above the surface of the Chalk, and at a height of about fifty feet above the River Rib. They do not show any groovings or striations. Smaller pieces of the same rock are not uncommon in these parts, and I have found one small mass which appears to consist of Millstone-grit, also a well-known Derbyshire rock.

Large boulder stones in this neighbourhood are not of common occurrence. The largest I have noticed consist of the well-known Hertfordshire "plum-pudding stone." There is one at Standon which is over five feet in length, and from one to two feet in width. Boulders of the older Palæozoic rocks I have not yet noticed, but small boulders of more recent rocks, frequently consisting of a fine-grained compact sandstone, distinctly glaciated and striated, and generally sub-angular in character, are not of unfrequent occurrence.

The country about here is all Chalk, more or less covered with stiffish soil, clay, and flint-gravel. The valleys trend from north to south. The gravel beds apparently do not contain either implements of any kind, or any fragments of rocks transported from a distance.—*R. P. Greg, Coles Park, Buntingford.*

MALACOLOGY.

Supposed Recent Extinction of Cyclostoma elegans in North Herts.—In this, the northern part of the county, *Cyclostoma elegans* seems to be extinct, and I am anxious to know whether it is found in other parts of the county. The shells are here, however, very numerous in the sub-soil and chalk rubble forming the superficial part of Tumuli and other scattered remnants of the old surface of the land as it existed anterior to the present state of cultivation. They are rarely found with the operculum, but this does occasionally remain in the mouth of the shell. I presume therefore that as far as this locality is concerned *Cyclostoma elegans* may be regarded as the latest fossil form, having but recently become extinct. In Dr. S. P. Woodward's 'Manual of the Mollusca,' *C. elegans* is figured from Charlton, Kent, and its habitat is given as "calcareous soils." As it is the only British species there can be no doubt, I suppose, on the question of identity.

The points which seem to me likely to be of interest, if they have not already been settled, are :—1. What is the area in England at present inhabited by *C. elegans*? 2. What is the area in which its remains are found in a fossil or sub-fossil state? 3. When did it become extinct in the localities in which its shell only is found? 4. What is the cause of its extinction, and what natural changes can be inferred from its extinction? It is obvious, I think, that the fact of its disappearance cannot be ascribed to cultivation of the land, for although it would doubtless become extinct over the greater part of the country, there are yet large areas of Chalk downs on which it would still thrive. Climate may perhaps have slightly changed, and have brought with its change necessary changes in life, both animal and vegetable.

I enclose a few specimens of the shell of *Cyclostoma elegans* from Highly Hill Tumulus, near Ashwell, Herts.—*H. George Fordham, Odsey, Royston*.

BOTANY.

Is the Anacharis Alsinastrum dying out in the River Colne at Watford?—I do not know the exact date in which this plant, which used to be called the "new American water-weed," first made its appearance at Watford. I remember it being regarded as a troublesome intruder about twenty-five years ago. It increased so rapidly as to threaten to fill up the smaller streams. Mr. King, of Wiggen Hall, tells me that it used to be so plentiful as to appear on the surface of the water in the river, and in two of his fish ponds, and that it had to be removed three or four times a year. The last few years he says that it has become much less common, and seems to be dying out. It is still plentiful at the Fountain Pond in the High Street, Watford.

If it is really dying out, it is an interesting fact, and it might be owing to the female plant only being found in this country. It is not propagated by seed, and therefore it might only survive the life of the original plant from which it has been derived. Many kinds of fruit trees are dying out in this way, and I believe the explanation is that they only live as long as the original tree. Perhaps some enthusiastic botanist will introduce the male *Anacharis Alsinastrum*. We have only lately had the male spotted laurel in England, although we have had the female for many years.

One singular fact with regard to the *Anacharis* is that it has not appeared in Mr. King's largest pond. He has three ponds for the breeding of fish. They all communicate with the Colne and with each other, but the water plant has never appeared in the first and largest pond.—*A. T. Brett, M.D., Watford House.*

Plants New to the Neighbourhood of Watford.—During the past month I have had one or two opportunities of paying a flying visit to the south and south-west of the county, and have been rewarded by the discovery of new stations for several of our rarer plants.

Some of these are in the neighbourhood of Watford. Such are:—
Ulex nanus, Rowley Green; *Myriophyllum alterniflorum*, Chorley
Wood Common; *Filago minima*, Rickmansworth; *Jasione montana*,
Rickmansworth; *Gentiana germanica*, Sarratt; *Scutellaria minor*,
Rowley Green; and *Rumex palustris*, near High Canons. This
last has been gathered but once before in the county, at Totteridge,
where it has probably been extinct for the last thirty years.—*R.*
A. Pryor, Hatfield.

Recent Blossoming of Spring Flowers.—I do not know whether
any of the members of our Society have noticed the unusual
number of spring flowers that have been in blossom for the last
few weeks (during the month of October and the first week in
November); and that, not in the way of a solitary instance, but
repeatedly and in widely separated localities. Such are:—*Caltha*
palustris, *Stellaria Holostea*, *Fragaria vesca*, *Potentilla Fragarias-*
trum, *Chærophyllum silvestre*, and other of our commoner species.
Spiræa Ulmaria, *Chærophyllum temulum*, and many others, which
belong strictly to the summer season, have also bloomed for a
second time, and such cases are deserving of some attention, as the
growths, which are thus produced out of due time, are apt not
unfrequently to vary conspicuously from those of the normal
period.—*R. A. Pryor.*

ENTOMOLOGY.

Capture of Chærocampa Nerii at Hemel Hempstead.—I have
great pleasure in formally recording the capture of a grand addition
to our Hertfordshire fauna. A fine specimen of the oleander hawk-
moth, *Chærocampa Nerii*, was taken at Hemel Hempstead, on the
13th of October, by a working man who brought it to Dr. Pitts, of
the West Herts Infirmary, Hemel Hempstead, in whose possession
it now is. Most of us saw the insect at the recent conversazione
at the Public Library. It was exhibited by Dr. Pitts, who saw it
alive and set it out. The specimen is a male, and with the exception of a bit which has been nipped out of one of its wings, is
in fair condition.

Chærocampa Nerii is tolerably common in Southern Italy, and
probably wherever the oleander, upon which plant the larvæ of *C.*
Nerii feed, is indigenous. There are, however, only two instances
of its capture in this country on record. One specimen was taken
"at light" at Brighton, on August 16th, 1857. It flew in at an
open window near the old church. This was confirmed by a Mr.
Tidy whom I know, and also by a Mr. Thorncroft, who recorded
the "Illustrious Stranger" in the 'Entomologists' Weekly Intelli-
gencer' of Aug. 29th, 1857. The other also was taken at Brighton,
by a school-boy, and its capture was recorded in a local paper.—
Clarence E. Fry, The Little Elms, Watford.

175

25.—Notes and Queries on the River Colne, Watford.

By Alfred T. Brett, M.D.

[Read 11th January, 1877.]

Chauncy says: "The *Colne*, which springs forth near *Tittenhanger*, thence passeth the Road at *Colny-street*, and running above two Miles in length, meets the *Verlume* near *Park-street*, but tho' the *Verlume* is much the greater Stream, yet the *Colne* usurps the Glory of her own Name, and floweth thence to *Watford*, (a large Market Town)."* And if Chauncy had lived now, I think he would have added, "where there is a good Public Library and a flourishing Natural History Society and Hertfordshire Field Club." Two thoughts suggest themselves to me in the above passage. Firstly: What is the meaning of the word Colne? Secondly: Why should the Ver, being the larger stream, lose her name, and the smaller stream Colne give the name to the river? Firstly: What does the word Colne mean? As my friend, the Rev. N. Price, very early in life distinguished himself as a philologist, I asked him, and he kindly wrote me this letter:—

"Not having a satisfactory account to give of the word Colne as a river name, I have put the question to others, and here is the result. 1. Mr. Furnivall says, ' Unless Colne is *colonia*, as in Lincoln, Colchester, I don't know what it is. The rivers Colne are all over the country.' 2. A friend of Mr. Furnivall's thinks it is a word of Celtic origin, meaning water or some attribute of water. 3. Dr. Gee quotes from Newcome's History of St. Albans. Newcome says *colonia* in Colchester, Colne, is a latinized form of the British word *cóllen*, which signifies hazels. I only give you a summary. I retain the opinion that it is a word like many other names of natural features, surviving from a præ-Celtic language spoken in this country, which word meant water or some attribute of water. The root might possibly be found in the Euskarian or Basque language. What in my opinion makes Newcome's derivation doubtful is that there are so many rivers Colne, a fact which seems almost to prove that the word means water. It is remarkable that all the derivations given may be reconciled, if you put it in this way: Colne is from *colonia*, which, however, is a word used by the Celts, but simulating a Latin origin, and meaning hazels (or water)."

It thus seems probable that the Hertfordshire men during the Stone Age called our river the Colne; and what were the manners and customs of that remarkable race no one in Europe is so well able to tell us as our learned President. Secondly: Why called Colne rather than Ver? Mr. Waghorne (who has lived at the junction of the river Colne and the Ver at the Nether Wyld nearly all his life) tells me that some forty years ago a scheme was proposed to form a lake or reservoir from the water of the Ver in order to supply London with water, and that the engineers were much struck with the relative size of the two rivers, the Ver having much more water and also being a trout stream, which the Colne is not till it joins the Ver. I have not given much thought to the names of rivers, yet it seems to me to be most natural that the larger stream should retain the name; or if the two streams should be nearly equal, that some name should be found combining the two.

* Hist. Antiq. Herts., p. 2.

For instance, another Hertfordshire stream, the Thame, rises at Tring, and after a time, according to Chauncy, "congratulates the *Isis;* but both emulating each other for the Name, and neither yielding, they are complicated by that of *Thamisis*" or Thames—a river more famous, perhaps, than any in the world. It may be that the relative size of the two streams has changed during the last 1500 years or so. I may remark that the two rivers meet, not at Park-street, but at the common meadows between Munden and the Nether Wyld.

Is the river Colne at Watford improving or not as a stream for fish? Before we discuss this question I should like to call your attention to a peculiarity of the river in the low meadows from Bushey Mill to the town. In many places the river is much above the level of the meadows, and the banks of the river require constant attention in order to prevent the water overflowing. Mr. Robert Clutterbuck, to whom the meadows on this side until recently belonged, says in a letter to me:—

" Has it ever struck you that the bed of the Colne from Otterspool to Watford must clearly be an artificial one ? In many places if the banks are not drawn up, the water runs on the meadows. I have never met with or heard of any evidence of this alteration of the level to serve, no doubt, the mills ; nor have I ever heard of any in Herts."

It is a very general opinion that there are not so many fish in the river at Watford as there used to be. I have heard the late Mr. W. Capel (who was a good sportsman and a keen and accurate observer of nature, and on whose sporting adventures a book full of interest might be written) say that formerly he could always have a brace of trout brought him if he wished it, but now he seldom saw a trout. Mr. E. Mead, who owns the Watford Flour Mill, says: "We think the river is better for roach and dace, not so good for trout or for minnows." Mr. Jonathan King says: "We have no fish in the river now; very few minnows or gudgeons, and no trout." I presume he refers to the Colne at Wiggenhall ; where, in 1856, he caught with the net 54lbs. of trout in one day. And another friend tells me that twenty-five years ago he used to take out of the Colne about 150lbs. of trout in a year.

I should think that minnows were more plentiful formerly than they are now. Mr. W. Johnson, a good fisherman, tells me that it was the custom formerly to hold a minnow-feast each year at the Leathersellers' Arms, Watford. The way the fish were caught was somewhat singular. A miller's sack used to be placed in the shallow part of the stream, and the fish would go into the sack, and a peck might be caught at one time. I doubt if we could catch as many now. I have often seen men catch minnows at Cashio Bridge which they say are for the animals at the Zoological Gardens. I have not seen them come to the Colne. The Colne used to have a good reputation for trout. Boccius says, in 1848:— "The river which I have restored for many miles is the Colne."*

* Fish in Rivers and Streams, p. 5.

I presume our Colne. I should think that the river Gade at Cassiobury also had a good reputation as a fishing stream, for.I read in 'The Ingoldsby Legends,' in the Irishman's Account of the Coronation :—

> "All in the gallery you might persave ;
> But Lord Brougham was missing and gone a fishing,
> Ounly the crass Lord Essex would not give him lave."

I need not say the late Lord Essex is meant.

The facts that I have now mentioned would lead us to infer that the Colne is not so full of fish as it used to be. I will now mention some facts on the other side. A pike was lately caught in the water at Aldenham Abbey weighing 14½lbs. Mr. Durham has had it stuffed, and he has kindly lent it for the Society to see. A friend of mine told me he lately saw in the Ver, within a hundred yards, three trout, twenty inches long. Mr. Arthur H. Hibbert, of Munden, says in a letter to me :—

> "In 1873, with one rod, eight trout averaging over 2½lbs. were caught in six days; in 1874, in five days, six averaging 2½lbs. were caught; in 1875, in eight days, ten averaging 2lbs. ; and in 1876, in seven days, seventeen averaging just over 2½lbs. ; so last year was the best. In the above I have counted every fish that was caught, but you can hardly judge from the statements I give as to the quantity of trout in the river, as it is only fished for eight days at the most. One trout caught last year, weighing 2¾lbs., had seventy odd large minnows in him. The largest trout was 3½lbs., and this is the largest caught since 1873."

I wrote also to my friend Mr. Henry Howard, formerly of Watford, now of St. Albans, for facts regarding his fishing. He says with regard to the different fish and rivers :—

> "I can only send you a list of the fish that I myself have captured, with the date, weight, and place where caught. All the fish from Boxmoor were from the small river Bulbourne, which flows into the Gade at Two Waters. Some years ago, Mr. J. King caught (netting) one trout, I believe over 8lbs., between the Rookery and Hamper Mill. Of the Ver I now know nothing, but on the 8th July, 1858, I killed one trout, at Bowbridge, of 3lbs., and since then, about four years since, I have landed three fish in one day averaging 3½lbs., from the Ver, for Major Gape."

With regard to eels, I should say they are not less plentiful. Mr. Mead says the largest quantity caught on any one day was three hundredweight. Three hundred and thirty-six pounds weight of fish is a good haul.

The practical point that we have to discuss is this : If the fish are decreasing, why are they, and are the causes remediable ?

Lord Essex tells me that in the year 1876 there has been a disease in the trout in the Gade, at Cassiobury. The symptoms are the following :—A film forms over the eyes, the body turns black and emaciated, the head seems enlarged in consequence, and a mildew or fungus seems to spread over the body ; many fish die and sink to the bottom of the water. I do not know the cause of this. Could caustic lime have got into the water ? For I read that "alkali is death to every species of fish."* It is singular that the same disease, or a similar one, attacked the gold fish that Lord Essex had in the large aquarium in the conser-

---

* Boccius, *l. c.*, p. 28.

vatory, and the water used there was not taken from the river
Gade.. Mr. Forsdyke, sen., has seen the same disease in fish many
years ago. Now a few words for the cure. Mr. Frank Buckland's
cure is, rub salt on the back of the fish, but, as in putting salt on
the tail of the bird, you must first catch him. Mr. J. King once
tried the salt cure, and the men put so much salt on that the skin
of the fish came off and the fish died. Keepers tell me that a little
salt will do good to fish which have mildew or mould on them. I
think that disease in the fish kept in aquariums is caused by neg-
lecting to have water-weeds in the water, or not enough. You
may have too many fish in an aquarium, but it is almost impossible
to have too much of water-weeds. The weeds give both food and
air to the fish. I am told that after a thunderstorm and sudden
heavy rain, quantities of dead fish may sometimes be seen floating
down the Colne at Hamper Mill. I cannot think it is the sewage
that kills the fish, because formerly all the sewage of Watford
went into the stream and now very little goes in, and very soon
no sewage will pollute the stream, because the Board of Health
intend to put into force the Rivers' Pollution Act of last year.

One cause of the decrease of trout may be that there is so much
mud in the river. When I bathe in the Colne I find the bathing
place itself is pretty free from mud, but if I swim up the stream a
little way and then put my feet to the ground I sink into mud
above my knees. Now trout hate mud; they like a gravelly bottom.
Some trout died at Rickmansworth, and as they were thought to
be poisoned, they were sent to Mr. Frank Buckland, who found
that they died suffocated by mud and weeds. The late Sir
James Willes, when he first went to live at Otterspool, found the
bed of the river very full of mud. It had no trout. He had
taken out some hundreds of loads of dirt and broken crockery,
ginger-beer and soda-water bottles, champagne bottles, etc.
The presence of these was explained by the fact that Otterspool was formerly a fashionable hotel and much frequented by
Londoners. Well, the river having been cleaned, the trout returned, and after a time the Judge had several tame trout which
he used to feed, and on no account would he allow them to be
caught. Some were the Geneva trout. The late Mr. Joseph Hill
used to have some tame trout in the stream which flows past his
garden, at Frogmore. Mr. Hill used to think that the Colne trout
and the Gade trout were of different kinds. Mr. J. King has had
taken out of the river some 4000 loads of mud, and there is
plenty left.

26.—FISH-HATCHING AND FISH-CULTURE IN HERTFORDSHIRE.

By ALFRED T. BRETT, M.D.

With NOTES ON PISCICULTURE, by PETER HOOD, M.D.

[Read 11th January, 1877.]

THE science and art of Pisciculture is so interesting and so important that I have ventured to bring it before the notice of our Society.

The interest of the subject is evident whether we regard it as naturalists, as physiologists, or as political economists. It affords great pleasure to the student of nature to observe the instincts and habits of fish during the breeding season; how the fish when she wishes to lay her eggs first proceeds to make the nest for them, "salmon and trout making use of stones for this purpose; other fish, especially sea-fish, making use of vegetable material, either, as in the case of the stickle-back, building a true nest, or else depositing the eggs upon the fronds and leaves of plants."

To the physiologist the study of the young fish is full of interest. Mr. Frank Buckland says :—" Get out the microscope and place a young new-born salmon under a low power, and you shall see one of the most beautiful sights ever beheld by human eye. You shall see the tiny heart, which is situate just underneath the lower jaw, going pit-a-pat, pit-a-pat; you shall see the blood at one instant in one cavity of the heart (where it appears like a red speck), at the next instant it is in the other side of the heart; and so it goes on, day and night, never ceasing, never tired—a great forcing pump, propelling the blood to all parts of the body. . . . Again, down the centre of the transparent body of the fish can be seen, with the unassisted eye, two tiny streaks. The microscope shows that these also are blood-vessels, and that the blood in one is running towards the heart, and in the other towards the tail. A more complete and beautiful demonstration of the circulation of the blood never was yet placed under a microscope."*

I will not detain you with other examples of the facts to be learnt from the study of new-born fish. To watch the gradual development of that mysterious something we call life excites in us wonder and great interest.

For the political economist fish-culture is of great national importance. For if, as it has been well said, he deserves well of his country who makes two blades of grass grow where one grew before, I think he deserves great praise who makes ten fish swim where one swam before. Here then, as Lord Essex once said, "is a mine of wealth under water. as much as under ground;" and if for a moment you look at a map of the globe, you will see that about three-fourths of the whole earth is covered by water. But

* Fish-Hatching, pp. 131, 133.

while we devote (and properly devote) much study to agriculture, we neglect aquaculture—cultivation of the water.

My intention this evening is not to speak of pisciculture in general, but to record what has been done in this useful work in our own county; for as we are a Hertfordshire Field Club, I think it desirable that our members should observe and record all the facts that they can connected with Natural History, and although the facts may not be of very general interest, yet they have an interest peculiar to them as belonging to our own county.

As far as I know, fish-breeding has only been carried out in Hertfordshire in three rivers—the Colne, the Gade, and the Chess; and chiefly by three members of our Society—Dr. Hood, of Upton House, Mr. Jonathan King, of Wiggen Hall, and the Earl of Essex. I mention them in the order in which they began their experiments. Fish-breeding has also been carried out by the late Mr. C. Longman and by the late Mrs. Hibbert, of Munden ; and Colonel Goodlake, of the Fisheries, at Denham, is very successful in breeding fish.

I asked Dr. Hood (to whom I look up as to a second Isaac Walton in all matters piscatorial) to give me the results of his experience, and he kindly sent me a paper, which I will ask our Secretary to read.*

To Mr. Jonathan King I am indebted for much valuable information, not only in pisciculture, but in other departments of Natural History, for at eighty-four he has as much enthusiasm in watching (as far as he can) the habits of birds, beasts, and fishes, as any boy. It is of great advantage to us to retain in old age, as he does, a cheerful and youthful mind.

Mr. King was first induced to hatch fish through the advice of Mr. Frank Buckland. He had a house built on purpose to breed fish. It is a thatched wood house, 10ft. by 15ft. The apparatus he uses is the same as that used by Mr. Ponder, of Hampton, and fully described in Mr. Buckland's book on 'Fish Hatching,' which I should recommend our members to read. He has kindly lent me the apparatus which I here show you.

Filtered Colne water was used; the eggs were looked at daily, and the dead ones removed. The fish-hatching was carried on for ten years, from 1864 to 1874. In each year about 5000 fish were hatched. The kinds of fish bred were salmon, sea-trout, Neuchatel (or Geneva) trout, trout from the Colne and the Gade, and trout from Loch Farraline in Inverness-shire.

There is about half an acre of water communicating with the river, and with a current of water flowing slowly through it. The water is divided into three ponds—upper, middle, and lower. When the young fish grow to the size of an inch long, they are placed in one of these ponds, and kept for some time till they are large enough to be removed into the river.

I have had an enlarged drawing made of the salmon ova and

* See page 185.

newly-hatched fish. You observe that fish obey the universal law of *omne vivum ex ovo.*

The eggs are known to be alive when the eyes of the fish become visible like two small jet-black specks, and this is the sign that they will bear transport. They should not be removed till then. When the eggs are dead, they become of a dull opaque white. The best way to pack the eggs is in wet moss—a few eggs, and then a layer of moss, and so on. The eggs do *not* grow, *i.e.* they do not increase in diameter; but the fish inside them most certainly increase in bulk, till at last the egg-shell suddenly bursts and out comes the young fish. Mr. Buckland says, " I have never yet seen a more beautiful sight than the gradual development of the young Salmon and Trout. We begin with a globule of albumen (or white of egg); we see within it a faint line, and two black spots; day by day these become larger till the young fish is born. Time goes on; the umbilical vesicle is absorbed, the colour appears on the scales, the long single crests which one observes at birth as running down the upper and lower parts of the body, resolve themselves, as it were by magic, into the various fins distinctive of the adult creature, and we have a perfect fish before us. Nature, ever wonderful in her works, surpasses herself in the beauty and minuteness of finish of these little fish."* The time occupied in the hatching varies according to the temperature—the colder the water, the stronger the fish, and the longer the process. The young fish do not require feeding until the umbilical vesicle is absorbed, which happens in about six weeks. After that they may be fed with raw beef grated very fine, and not too much at a time, so as to decompose and injure the water.

Mr. King has kindly furnished me with some of his notes.

" February 12th, 1864.—I received from Neuchatel, Switzerland, 1500 eggs of trout. They left Switzerland February 8th, at 8 p.m., packed in a box with wet moss; arrived at Wiggenhall February 12th, at 9.30 p.m., and commenced hatching on the 15th. March 9th, all out.

" January 16th, 1865.—I had from the Gade 1200 eggs of trout. Commenced hatching April 12th.

" March 21st, 1865.—I received from Worcester 200 salmon eggs (108 were bad on their arrival). Commenced hatching April 10th; all out on the 11th.

" January 30th, 1867.—I had 1000 trout eggs from Loch Farraline, Scotland; they were one day in coming. Commenced hatching February 12th; all out on the 25th."

With regard to the trout in Loch Farraline I should like to mention a fact which seems to me singular, and I do not know if it is common to other lakes. When I was at Farraline we caught about forty trout in one afternoon, and the flesh of the trout was in some pink, in some yellow, and in some white, in the same part of the water; and they were all of the same size, not quite a pound in weight, and in equal condition. I do not know if they were of different species, or whether the colour varied according to the food. We thought the pink of the best flavour, then the yellow, then the white. It is also singular that the char (which I believe

* Fish-Hatching, p. 105.

was introduced by those ardent pisciculturists the Romans) will be found in some lakes and not in others, although the lakes may communicate.

I will now allude to the third of our members who has bred fish in Hertfordshire—the Earl of Essex.

Trout-hatching was carried on for two or three years. They were Gade trout, and when they were hatched they were put into the river Gade. Lord Essex tells me that he will breed fish again, and that he intends to get some trout ova from France in order to change the breed of the fish. He says that in France pisciculture is followed with such care and success that the rivers and streams are full of fish.

Our President, Mr. Evans, to whom I applied for information, has kindly told me by letter that some years ago the late Mr. Charles Longman tried the experiment of fish-hatching with trout at Nash Mills, but not with much success. There were, however, a fair number of young fish hatched, so far as he remembers, but the difficulty was that the stream, having the canal incorporated with it, is not well adapted for trout. With a pure trout stream he thinks that artificial fish-breeding might be carried on with advantage.

The late Mrs. Hibbert, of Munden, carried on fish-hatching for five years, under the direction of her game-keeper, Haylock. Fish were bred every year from 1869 to 1873. Mr. Arthur Henry Hibbert, of Munden, one of our members, to whom I applied for information, says, "I am very glad to hear that interest is taken in fish-breeding in Hertfordshire, as some day I hope to follow in my grandmother's footsteps, and preserve for the Colne." Mr. Frank Buckland instructed Haylock, and superintended the putting up of the breeding boxes. Mr. Hibbert kindly directed Haylock to give me any information in his power. He says that from a 4lb. fish he has got 3000 eggs. This corresponds with Mr. Buckland's observation, who says, from each 1lb. weight of fish you may get 1000 eggs. Haylock used to catch the fish on the 3rd of January, and 3000 to 4000 were bred each year. He did not use pump water, but Colne water filtered through charcoal and gravel and white sand. Four troughs were used and a large cistern at the end. The troughs were three feet long and three inches deep. After the fish were hatched they were placed in a ditch communicating with the river Colne. He thinks it would improve the river as a trout stream if it were dragged twice a year, and the chub and the pike taken out.

Colonel Goodlake, of the Denham Fishery, Uxbridge, says in a letter to me, dated January 7th, 1877 :—

"I have only got some 80,000 trout in my boxes at present, instead of 260,000, which I could have easily procured had this deluge not been against me. A curious circumstance has occurred in my Fishery. About October I placed some 200 Fontinalis (that is, *Salmo Fontinalis*, American brook trout) of about 1lb. weight in one of my grated streams for spawning purposes, taken from about 4000 at haphazard. About December I only saw two fish at work on the gravel, so I caught a few to see why they were so late; finding these were all males, I kept on catching them, and I found in the end that I had only three females among 200 fish. I need not say this has been a good lesson to me, as next year I shall be more careful in the selection of sexes. I have now given the Fontinalis a good trial. I think they are easier to rear the first year, and grow quicker than the common trout; but they are much more voracious, and a much bolder fish. After the first year, given the same food as common trout, and under the same conditions, they do not grow so fast, and decidedly grow to head, but with a double allowance of food they will about hold their own. I have had a Committee of Taste, and it was decided that they were inferior in flavour to the common trout. This, taken together with my humble opinion that they are more voracious and destructive to the fry of other fish than common trout, causes me unwillingly not to be so sweet upon them as I was. The only advantage that I see in their cultivation is the pleasure it gives in catching with the fly a different variety, and I fancy that when they arrive at 4 or 5lbs. in weight they would take a fly freer than the common trout of the same size. I have kept them together with common trout (of 1lb. weight) in a glass aquarium, and I found that if I gave the Fontinalis only as much as they could eat they never allowed their commoner brethren a share, and would starve them in time. Also that they were great bullies, biting them severely. I must apologize for writing so fully on a subject that doubtless you are well acquainted with, but, as I dare say you know, our hobby is apt to run away with us."

I do not know if the grayling has ever been introduced into the rivers of Herts. In Walton's 'Angler' I read : "The grayling .... lives in such rivers as the Trout does, and is usually taken with the same baits as the Trout is and after the same manner; ... he is of a fine shape, his flesh is white, his teeth, those little ones that he has, are in his throat." Mr. James Hopkinson thinks grayling would do well in the Ver and the Gade ; and he says that they afford good sport, and are in season when the trout are not. He has noticed that the rivers in the neighbourhood of Abbeys in the North of England always have grayling in them, which he supposes have been introduced by the monks. I wonder that the Hertfordshire monks at St. Albans did not introduce the grayling into the Ver and Colne. It is not too late now to remedy the omission, and I should be glad to see grayling introduced into our rivers. I see that in 1863 the Thames Angling Preservation Society were about to introduce grayling into the Thames. Mr. Buckland says that grayling are much more delicate than trout ova, and seem to die at the least provocation. They are beautifully transparent, and when viewed in the sun, of a lovely opalescent hue. The body of the fish is perfectly visible in nine days, and the fish will actually hatch out of the egg in fourteen days.

I have not yet alluded to the fecundity of fish. · It seems that a 20lb. codfish may have more eggs in her than there are people in London, namely 4,870,000. The ova of fish need be very abundant, because they have so many enemies, as the larvæ of the May-fly and the larvæ of the dragon-fly, and birds, as dabchicks, swans, ducks, etc.

Perhaps it would not be scientifically correct to include under the term pisciculture the cultivation of the molluscs, such as the oyster, the mussel, and the snail; and the crustacea, as the lobster, the crayfish, the shrimp, the prawn, etc.; yet it is a subject so nearly connected with it that I may be excused if I make a passing allusion to it. The only two of the animals just mentioned that it would be possible for us to cultivate here are the crayfish and the snail. The crayfish is plentiful in the Colne, and I wonder that it is not caught for food. I have seen it at the *table d'hôte* at Nancy, in France, and it makes a very pretty, if not a very satisfying dish. No doubt it might be cultivated in our streams in Hertfordshire to any extent. Pope says, " Let me to crack live crayfish recommend." With regard to the snail I am told that it is an esteemed article of food on the Continent among what are called the Latin nations. I suppose nothing but ignorant prejudice prevents the natives of Hertfordshire cultivating and eating snails. I expect snail-culture was followed by the Romans when they lived in our county, which they did for three or four centuries.

In the North of France and in Switzerland the apple snail, *Helix pomatia*, is a much-prized mollusc as an article of diet. I should think, with a little care, favoured by our humid climate, we might soon get a good quantity of edible snails. I have had an instance of the fondness of the Romans for molluscs brought before my notice by the Rev. James Clutterbuck. There was found in a field in Oxfordshire a silver Roman spoon. I send round a drawing of it, and also three silver Roman spoons brought by the President from his Museum. You see that one end is shaped like our spoons to eat eggs with; the other end is pointed to hook out the snails and molluscs with, in the same manner that we now use a pin to pick out the winkles which, I suppose, are sea snails. The name of spoon, *Cochleare*, was derived from its shelling properties, as may be seen from an epigram of Martial :

> " *Sum cochleis habilis, sed nec minus utilis ovis,*
> *Namquid scis potius cur cochleare vocer.*"

which may be freely translated,

> " I am clever at winkles, and for eggs not less fit,
> Then why I'm called cochleare question your wit."

I have now, in a fragmentary manner, endeavoured to direct your attention to fish-culture, and although I may not have added to your knowledge, yet if I have excited interest enough to cause some of you to study the subject, I shall consider the time not ill spent.

We should make use of our natural advantages, for our county, as Chauncy says, " is pleasantly water'd with many small Brooks and Rivers, which .... produce Variety of Fish, as Eels, Millersthumbs, Cray-fish, Trouts, Gudgeons, Breame, Carps, Tench, Pearch, Roach, and the River *Lea*, some Salmons ; .... and if these Fish had free Passage by the Mills, ... they would greatly encrease in that River, and be of great benefit, as well to the City of *London* as the Country ; for some Water-men have observed, that they delight in this Stream and play much about those Sluices near *Waltham.*"*

* Hist. Antiq. Herts., p. 2.

I will now conclude in the words of Boccius, who studied this subject fifty years ago:—" All the fresh waters of these United Kingdoms, it is not too much to say, are grossly neglected, and the rivers especially are imperfectly understood."* In this age of knowledge it is greatly to be regretted that water should not be cultivated as much as land, and more especially when it is a matter of fact that water is far more capable of producing abundance of food than any element in the great laboratory of nature. Why then should such a source of plenty be neglected?

APPENDIX.

NOTES ON PISCICULTURE IN HERTFORDSHIRE.

By PETER HOOD, M.D.

Mr. Boccius was the first person who, thirty-five years ago, wrote a treatise on Pisciculture.† To the Chinese, however, belongs the credit of having first of all practised the artificial hatching of fish. They placed the ovum of a fish in an egg-shell half-full of water, and watched the progress of hatching with as much interest as we would the growth of a rare plant. The spawn of the fish they watched were those belonging to the Cypridæ, or carp tribe, fish that inhabit still waters. If they had tried the same experiment on trout ova—had they possessed any—they would have failed to accomplish their design, as the spawn of the Salmonidæ, like the fish themselves, require running water to hatch them, as those fish do to exist in.

Twenty years ago I engaged the services of Mr. Ramsbotham, of Clitheroe, who had taken up the practice of Pisciculture. He operated on a large quantity of ova taken from trout belonging to the River Colne, at Rickmansworth, but the result was not attended with success, owing to the fact not being then recognised, that for the perfect hatching of trout ova, *clear* water was an indispensable requisite. If I had paid attention to the dictum of Lord Ebury's ancient keeper, Green, that "the Colne was a bad breeding river, but an excellent feeding one," I might have taken it as a warning of non-success, for, when the ova failed to hatch, the reason was patent enough,—they were all covered with alluvial deposit, which abounds in this river in the winter-time, and the ova were, so to speak, suffocated.

The next experiment I tried was on the river Chess, whose water runs clear winter and summer—at least it did so then, before it was polluted by the existing paper mill. The late Mr. Marston, who then rented Rickmansworth Park, kindly gave me permission. I tapped the bank of the river with a 2in. pipe, the

* Fish in Rivers and Streams, p. 36.
† Gottlieb Boccius was the author of *two* works on Pisciculture, the first of which, entitled ' A Treatise on the Management of Fresh-water Fish,' was published in 1841, and gave the result of many years' observations; the second, ' A Treatise on the Management of Fish in Rivers and Streams,' was published in 1848.—ED.

water from which flowed into a large tub. From this tub another
pipe carried the water into a series of long boxes, covered at the
bottom with fine gravel, on which the ova were deposited. By
this simple contrivance the ova were hatched in thousands, but
what ultimately became of them we never learned. The boxes
were far away from the keeper's house, and they never had that
attention paid to them which is so essential to command success.
Mr. Frank Buckland suggested to me that it was most probably
the result of a raid by a "fresh-water mouse." As I have never
seen that animal, I can say no more about it. That this simple
method of breeding fish has succeeded in other hands I am
well aware, in Hampshire, Surrey, and other counties, where
thousands of young trout are reared, and command a high price;
but it cannot compare with such a perfect apparatus as that
belonging to my friend, Mr. Jonathan King, and also that employed by Messrs. Ponder and Buckland, at Hampton, consisting
of a series of slate troughs, one below another, like the shelves of
a greenhouse, the water flowing from one into the other. The
great advantage of this construction is that any unfertilised ova
can be at once detected and removed from the others, which if
they were allowed to remain would injure those near them.

I need scarcely refer to the numerous salmon river proprietors in
Scotland and elsewhere, who have most extensive breeding apparatus, which pay well, for it is estimated that not more than
one in a thousand of the eggs laid naturally by a salmon ever
reaches the adult stage of a fish, from the number of enemies
and other causes that are adverse to them.

To refer to what I have previously mentioned, as to the Colne
being a good "feeding" river, I will state a fact that can only be
paralleled by the rapid growth of a salmon when it returns from
the sea after its first visit there. Some years ago Mr. Jonathan
King gave me some Geneva lake trout, the size of small minnows,
the ova of which he had procured from Switzerland. I placed
these little fish in the Colne. At the end of two years I killed, one
afternoon, five of these fish, which weighed 15lbs.—their average
weight thus being 3lbs. each.

27.—ANNIVERSARY ADDRESS.

By the PRESIDENT, JOHN EVANS, F.R.S., V.P.S.A., F.G.S., etc.

[Delivered at the Annual Meeting, 8th February, 1877.]

LADIES AND GENTLEMEN,—

I am now, as President, called upon to deliver an Anniversary Address, though I regret that I am not able to present to you much that will be worthy of attention, as I have not had time to prepare anything in a written form. Before proceeding to treat of any particular subject, I think I may fairly congratulate the Society, as the Council has already done, on the progress it has made during the first two years of its existence. It is indeed now fully established, and has been and is doing good work. When we look back at the Proceedings of the past year, we see that we have had a series of papers communicated to us of greater or less importance on those different Natural History subjects to which we ought to devote our principal attention. We have had interesting papers on Phenological Phenomena, and on the Botany of the Ermine Street, by Lieutenant Croft; another paper from the northern part of the county, by Mr. Fordham, on the supposed extinction of *Cyclostoma elegans*, the most beautiful of the British land-shells, and comparatively abundant in this part of the county. We have had papers on *Anacharis alsinastrum* in the Colne; on Fish-culture in Hertfordshire, the River Colne, the Cuckoo, and other minor subjects, from Dr. Brett. We have also had some Entomological notices, on the Larvæ of the Goat-Moth, from Mr. J. H. James, and on the Oleander Hawk-Moth, a very rare moth in this country, from Mr. Fry. Mr. Pryor, who is distinguished as a botanist, not only here but elsewhere, has communicated to us a list of plants found in new situations in the neighbourhood of Watford, and has also called attention to the late blossoming of certain spring flowers which bloomed in October and November, as well as early in the spring. But, perhaps, we may especially congratulate ourselves on one of our members—a lady member, Miss Willshin—having discovered the *Campanula latifolia* in the neighbourhood of St. Albans, and also a new variety of a thistle and a heath. With regard to another subject—Meteorology—we have had the records of several observers communicated to us; and from the Report of the Council, it appears that we are likely to have

a succession of Meteorological Observations kept in this county.
Geology has had—partly, I imagine, owing to the geological pro-
clivities of your Secretary, and possibly of your President—a very
fair amount of attention shown it during the past year. We
have had an admirable lecture on "The Eocenes of England and
their Extension in Hertfordshire," by Mr. Lobley; we have had
a notice of the "Hertfordshire Ordnance Bench Marks," by Mr.
John Hopkinson; an account of some "Boulders near Buntingford,"
by Mr. R. P. Greg; and, what is of more immediate interest to
the inhabitants of this part of the county, a paper on "The Geology
and Water Supply of the Neighbourhood of Watford," by the Rev.
James C. Clutterbuck. I have also communicated a short paper on
"The Hertfordshire Bourne," and "Notes on Earth Pyramids in
the Neighbourhood of Botzen in the Tyrol." In addition to all
this, you have had two excellent lectures "On the Polarisation of
Light," from Mr. Harford; notes on "Microscopical Mounting,"
by Mr. Cottam; and hints for a new field naturalist's microscope, by Lieutenant Croft. I think that this list shows that we
have been extending our operations over a very considerable field,
and I hope with satisfactory results.

In the Address which I had the honour of delivering last year, I
pointed out the various branches of inquiry which seemed to me to
come within the field of such a society as this; and it appears to
me that I did enough on that occasion in the way of indicating
the methods which might be adopted, and the subjects which required investigation; for we shall all agree that there is still a
great deal to be done by the Society before all the fields then
pointed out may be considered to have been fully explored. I
therefore thought that on this occasion it was not worth while to
give an address in any way similar in character to that which I gave
last year. It next occurred to me whether it would be possible
to give some account of the advances made last year in Natural
History generally; but although we have had an Arctic Expedition,
and other Expeditions undertaken with the view of bringing within
our knowledge a greater amount of the Natural History of various
parts of the world than has been before obtained, yet, to make an
address adapted for a society of this kind would have required
considerable more time, and perhaps ability, than I was able to
bestow upon it. I then considered whether it was possible that
any of the recent works on Natural History that have issued from
the press would afford me material on which to speak to you. It
crossed my mind whether the works of Mr. Darwin on Climbing
Plants, and on Cross-fertilisation, or any other of his admirable

books, would afford me foundation for an address; but I thought that, after all, it was preferable for those who take an interest in Science to read the works themselves, to hearing a garbled report of them second-hand. I therefore felt that I must take up some other subject; but before I proceed, I may just mention one point to which I alluded in my last address, that was curiously illustrated in our Church decorations of last Christmas.

Every one must have noticed the remarkable absence of holly berries in this district, and the same scarcity was felt over a considerable portion of England. The question arose, "How is it that holly berries are so scarce?" It was attributed by some persons to the early frosts; but I for one expressed an opinion that it was due to a want of certain insects in the spring; and I am glad to perceive that in a letter addressed by Mr. Darwin to the 'Gardener's Chronicle,' he bears out entirely that view. He points out that the holly is what is known as a diœcious tree—that is, there are separate male and female plants,—and it is requisite that the pollen from the one shall be brought to the other before the flowers are fertilised to produce seed. This is done generally by means of bees, as he has ascertained by actual experiment some years ago. It appears, therefore, that the absence of holly berries arose from the deficiency of bees. Mr. Darwin also observed, in looking over the clover fields which were in flower in his neighbourhood, that there was there also comparatively a small number of humble-bees; and it crossed his mind whether—in consequence of this—there might not prove to be some failure in clover seed, as clover is mainly fertilised by means of humble-bees. Curiously enough, he subsequently received a letter telling him that there *was* a deficiency in clover seed, and farmers could not understand why the seed had not set. I do not know whether the clover seed was affected to any great extent in this neighbourhood; but there is no doubt this is one of those cases in which "great effects from little causes spring," and that the presence or absence of a few insects affects the prosperity of farmers and others engaged in agricultural pursuits. As Fuller observes of our Hertfordshire Pope, Adrian the Fourth, who was choked by a fly—"Anything next nothing, be it but advantageously planted, is big enough to batter a man's life down to the ground." No doubt the absence of his seed-crop is not equal to the battering down of a farmer's life, but still it may materially affect him.

But to return from this digression. I was saying that I found a difficulty in deciding what would be best adapted to speak upon this evening. I thought probably that you would have had during this year almost enough of purely geological subjects. It then struck me that possibly something in connexion with Archæology might be of interest to you; but then I considered that this Society is a Field Club of Naturalists, and does not include any branches of Archæology within its province. In many counties, however, Field Clubs and Naturalists' Societies study Archæology. I think that even we have ventured into churches, and found that they added interest to what was an interesting excursion in connexion with Natural History. Archæology, after all, appears to me but a branch of the natural history of man, which of course comes within the range of our inquiry; and when we get beyond the domain of written records, and attempt to study primeval man, his antiquity and early history,—when, indeed, we have to trust to monuments alone,—the study of Archæology must, to a certain extent, follow the methods of Natural History, and may be regarded as a branch of it. Your Secretary, moreover, suggested to me that I might say this evening something with regard to that border province between Geology and Archæology in which we find the earliest traces of man on the globe. Acting on his advice, I have brought here a few implements found under peculiar geological conditions, about which I shall have to speak to you; and I propose giving you some account of the discoveries made in the province known as Archæo-geology, and offering you some few remarks with regard to the antiquity of man in this and other countries, and the geological formations in which the discoveries of the last twenty years have been made.

All of you are aware that the history of man has been divided into different Periods—that is to say, that of late years it has been the habit to speak of an Iron Period, a Bronze Period, and a Stone Period, and, possibly, of subdivisions of these periods. The use of this general classification is, I think, evident; because, though strictly speaking during the Iron Period bronze and stone were not excluded, and though during the Bronze Period stone was not absolutely disused, yet there is a great distinction between the people who were in so low a stage of civilization that they used stone instruments only, and those who were acquainted with the use of metal. We live in the Iron Age or Steel Age; but some 2000 years ago, say 300 or 400 years B.C., the knowledge of iron was extremely limited in this country; and instead of iron the ordinary tools and weapons were made of brass, or strictly speaking bronze, that is to say, formed of a mixture of copper and tin, and not of copper and zinc. Not only do we find, in examining the relics which have come down to us, an evident development from the forms in one metal to those in another; but in history there are traces of the use of bronze before that of iron. In the time when the Homeric poems were written, iron was extremely rare, and the weapons were of copper or bronze ; and it will be very interesting, when we see the results of Dr. Schliemann's explorations at Mycenæ, to observe how far the weapons and other ornaments which have been found there correspond with what may be supposed to have been the arms and ornaments in use when the scenes of the Homeric poems were laid. It is a remarkable fact that in these tombs of Agamemnon, or other royal personages at Mycenæ, no traces of iron have been found, but the swords and other weapons are of bronze. There are also found ornaments of gold, and pottery, some of very fine manufacture, and some stones or gems which have been admirably worked—showing that the absence of the knowledge of iron is not incompatible with a certain high degree of civilization. As further evidence of the succession of iron to bronze, we find traces of the use of bronze surviving in religious rites, where the earlier form of sacrificial instruments was preserved after iron had come into use for other purposes, and for some religious rites stone instruments have also prevailed even into the Iron Period. We know, also, that during the Bronze Period in this country, while bronze was in use for knives and other articles, arrow-heads were still made of flint, probably because they were liable to be lost, and flint was cheaper than metal. We find, too, that stone battle-axes were in use after the period when bronze was introduced for the formation of daggers. In a similar manner we find bronze overlapping beyond the introduction of iron ; so that generally we have the three divisions shading off one into the other, as I have elsewhere remarked, like the principal colours of the rainbow.

It must never be forgotten that these so-called ages are simply indicative of different stages of civilization, and are not of any chronological value. It does not by any means follow that when the inhabitants of this country were in their Stone Age, the inhabitants of Greece were also in it at the same time. In all probability, while the inhabitants of the south of Europe were using bronze and even iron, the inhabitants of the north still used stone for their cutting tools and other weapons. At the present time we find many savages who—although we are thoroughly in our Iron Age, in almost too full development—are still in their Stone Period ; and I have brought some specimens to show the kind of tools in use among savages of the present day, by way of illustration of those of ancient date which we find in this country. Here, for instance, is a stone axe from Polynesia, bound to its haft by a piece of cord,

showing a very simple form of mounting an axe. Here is another
from New Caledonia, showing how far the development of art had
gone while stone was still in use. The blade is inserted into a
wooden socket, bound round in the most artistic way to prevent it
from splitting, and attached to a stout handle in a very ingenious
manner.

In tracing back our antiquities in this country, we also come to
a period when nothing but stone was in use for cutting purposes.
We find, for instance, hatchets made of stone carefully ground to
an edge, and shaped in a similar manner to those in use in New
Guinea and various islands of the Pacific. These belong to the
Polished Stone Period, or Neolithic Period—the period which pre-
ceded the use of bronze. Now we know that at the time of Julius
Cæsar, iron was already beginning to be known in Britain, and
bronze was dying or had died out of use. The use of bronze in
this country probably extended over about a thousand years, which
would give a date of 1000 or 1200 B.C. for the more recent of the
ordinary stone instruments. How much further back their use
might be carried it is impossible to say; but however far back,
we find they belong to what must be regarded as a comparatively
recent period, when compared with the period in which certain
other implements were made. The later or Polished Stone Period
received the name Neolithic (New Stone) or Surface Period, from
these things being found on the surface; and the other the Palæolithic (Old Stone) or Drift Period, inasmuch as the implements were
found, as a rule, not on the surface, but in deposits of a late
geological age, and associated with animals in many cases not
living in the districts at the present time, but which are either
extinct or have migrated from the places where they originally
lived. It is with regard to this Palæolithic Age that I am going
to say a few words this evening.

The Palæolithic instruments may be roughly divided into two
classes—those found in caves, and those found in the gravels.
There is some difficulty in ascertaining the relative chronology of
these two classes of deposits; but in all probability many of the
caves belong to a more recent period than the older of the gravels.
But with regard to the question of chronology I shall have more
to say when I get further into the subject.

The fact of the association of man with the extinct animals
in cavern deposits is by no means a new one. It has been treated
of by Tournal, Christol, Schmerling, and others in France and
Belgium; and about fifty years ago Mr. MacEnery also observed
it in Kent's Cavern, in Devonshire, though induced to suppress

his discoveries to a certain extent by the late Dr. Buckland. But in late years a vast number of these caves have been explored, and they throw a great amount of light on the character of the inhabitants of Europe at the period when they were occupied. We find that in the south of France men were in the habit of living, not so much in actual caves, as in shelters below rocks—that they fed on reindeer, which have now disappeared from that part of the globe, on horses to a certain extent, and oxen and deer, whose bones we find broken up; and mixed with these bones, the instruments of which they made use. They seem to have been, like the Esquimaux, devotedly attached to marrow, for almost every bone is smashed. In the hammers with which they smashed the bones, the flint tools with which they fashioned their harpoons and other instruments made from the horns of the reindeer, the stones, heated probably for boiling water, we find the whole history of their method of life. I have brought here a few arrow-heads, lance-heads, and deer-horn harpoons, round-ended instruments known as scrapers, and one or two other objects. With regard to the scrapers, it is curious that in the present century the Esquimaux were using similar instruments as planes for working wood, and sometimes as scrapers for the inner side of skins. But not only have we the instruments with which the Cave-dwellers prepared their leather, but the needles with which they sewed the skins together. You will see that the needles are not quite so fine as our own, but still very fine when you consider that they were made by means of flint tools only. The late Dr. Falconer tried to make some bone needles like them without the present modern appliances, using only flint tools, and he succeeded perfectly. In one corner of the case before you, you will see a piece of hæmatite, or iron ore, of a reddish colour, which has been scraped. There is very little doubt that at that time the savages were given to ornament and colour very much in the same manner as at the present day, and the red stone was used to produce paint. They may even have put on war paint when going into battle. The caves seem to vary considerably in age; but any dissertation on their chronology would be out of place here. I will, therefore, not trouble you beyond saying that in all probability there were four successive ages of caves, and the tools found in the earliest of these approximate most nearly in form to those found in the river gravels. By way of illustrating the great distinction in time there must have been between the period of the cavern people, when reindeer formed the staple article of food, and the more recent Neolithic Period, I may mention that in the neighbourhood of the Swiss Lakes, where so many articles

of the Neolithic Stone Period have been found, there is a cave at
Mont Salève, near Geneva, where reindeer remains occur with
instruments like these ; while in the lake dwellings of the Polished
Stone Period, reindeer are entirely absent. Of our English caverns,
the principal is Kent's Cavern, near Torquay, undergoing exploration by a Committee of the British Association, of which Mr.
Pengelly and Mr. Vivian are the most active members. In that
cave a number of remains of extinct animals have been found,
associated in a few cases with instruments like those from the
French caves, including barbed harpoons of reindeer horn. In a
lower deposit, beneath large masses of stalagmite, there have been
found a certain number of stone instruments of the same character
as those which have been found in the river gravels. Much the
same class of remains, that is to say, bones of extinct animals side
by side with implements fashioned by the hand of man, were found
in a cave near Wookey Hole, explored by Mr. Boyd Dawkins some
years ago.

  I think that I have now said enough to you with regard to the
cave instruments to show that the fauna with which they are
associated is distinct in its character from that which belonged to
the ordinary Stone Period. I now turn to those found in old river
drift—that is to say, in gravels which appear to have been deposited in old river-beds by water flowing at a higher elevation
than that at which the rivers now flow. It is only of late
years that much attention has been called to these deposits. M.
Boucher de Perthes, in 1846, was the first who published any
account of the instruments found in the gravels of the River
Somme, and he was followed up by Dr. Rigollot at Amiens. In
1858 Dr. Falconer visited M. de Perthes' collection, and mentioned
the subject to Mr. Prestwich. In April, 1859, Mr. Prestwich and
I visited the spot, and satisfied ourselves as to the authenticity of
M. Boucher de Perthes' discoveries.

  The discoveries have since been multiplied to a very great extent,
and now there is hardly an important river-valley in France in
which such implements have not been discovered. Researches
which have extended over the greater part of southern England
have also been well rewarded. With regard to the beds of Amiens,
I may give you some short account of them as typical examples of
the nature of the beds in which these instruments occur. At the
surface you have a varying depth of from nine to ten feet of brick
earth, gravelly at its base, containing but few fossils; but from time
to time there are found imbedded in this brick earth implements
of flint, which, though whitened by age, have not undergone any

process of rolling, but retain their edges as sharp as on the day they were made. Below there is a silt, in which is found a considerable number of species of river-shells and some land-shells; and below that again (the thickness of the silt being six or seven feet, and there being often seams of gravel intermixed in it), is found a bed of coarse, and in some cases finer gravel, five or six feet thick, in which implements more commonly occur, as forming constituent parts of the gravel itself. The late Mr. Flower, of Croydon, dug out, from a depth of twenty feet, a well-formed instrument, which he bequeathed to my collection, and I have myself extracted some from about the same depth at Amiens, which were pointed out to me *in situ* by the workmen.

After the discoveries at Amiens and Abbeville became known, Mr. Prestwich and I thought that in all probability there were places in this country where such instruments ought to be discovered, and we visited many places which, from analogy, appeared likely to produce such implements, amongst which were Bedford and Salisbury; but our search was unsuccessful. Attention, however, having been directed to the subject, and the gravel-pits carefully searched by geologists living on the spots, flint implements were eventually found associated with the same mammalian fauna as that of the valley of the Somme, and with fresh-water shells nearly similar to those at Amiens. In the valley of the Lark, in the valley of the Little Ouse and Waveney, in the valley of the Thames at Acton and Ealing, and in several other river-valleys, they have also now been discovered.

Further down the valley of the Thames, at Reculvers, in the neighbourhood of Herne Bay; in the south of England, at Southampton, and other places along the south coast, these things have also been found. Perhaps one of the most curious of these discoveries is that at Southampton, and along the southern shores of the counties of Dorset and Hampshire. There you have a cliff now close to the sea, which is capped with gravel at something like 90 feet above high-water mark, and in this gravel these implements have been discovered.

It is not a little remarkable that, in addition to their occurring, as I have pointed out, in France and England, and also in Spain and other parts of Europe (but not generally throughout Europe), they are found in the East Indies in beds of laterite of great antiquity.

Having now mentioned some of the places where these implements have been found, and having alluded to the circumstances under which they have been discovered, it will be well to say a

little with regard to the character of the implements.   First of all,
the simplest form is a mere flint " flake," as it is termed—a piece
dislodged from the flint by a single blow, with a sharp edge on
each side, being a tool valuable for various purposes.   As an
instance of the modern use of these flakes, I may tell you that at
the time of the Spanish conquest of Mexico, the natives shaved
themselves with flakes of obsidian.   So readily were they made
that it was easier to make a new one than to sharpen and go on
shaving with the old one.   Knives constructed in that very simple
manner have been in use all over the world among savage tribes.
Among other places I may mention Queensland, Australia, where
knives are usually made of basalt, the handle being of kangaroo
skin, attached by gum to the butt end, thus forming a knife that
is very serviceable, although of the rudest possible construction.
As an instance of the effect of the contact with civilization on the
construction of these instruments, I may say that, having a friend
in Queensland, I requested him to procure me one of these knives,
and he sent me one.   It is made of a beautiful transparent
material, with the handle tied on and coated with gum; but I
find, on examining it, that, instead of its being kangaroo skin, it
is a piece of coarse Manchester cotton.   Though the gum is there,
the string which holds it on is probably of European manufacture,
and the blade is merely the fragment of a gin-bottle.   No doubt it
is a better purpose to which to apply gin-bottles than those to
which they are generally applied; but it is a very curious result
of the approach of civilization to a barbarous people, who made
use of the material brought to them in converting it to what we
may call a non-natural purpose.   On the coast of America old
porter-bottles have been used as a material for arrow-heads.

To return to the various forms of instruments found in the river-
gravels.   There are various pointed tools adapted to be held in the
hand.   Some are oval-shaped with a sharp edge all round; others
nearly round, and in other cases they are almond-shaped.   These
are, generally speaking, the forms in which they occur.   As to the
purposes to which they are applied, it is almost impossible to
determine, though in all probability the bulk of them were used
for much the same purposes as we use the knife and axe.   It has
been suggested that some were used for cutting holes in the ice for
fishing, or grubbing holes in the earth for roots, and for killing
animals, and it is impossible to say what they have not been used
for.   All I have to say is that I agree with Professor Ramsay that
they are instruments as distinctly worked by the hand of man, as a
Sheffield whittle is at the present day.

The earliest discovery of the instruments of which any record has been kept, took place in 1699 or 1700, in Gray's Inn Lane, in London, when an implement was found associated with the remains of an elephant. At that time there were no questions raised as to the antiquity of man, and no doubts were thrown on the discovery, the instrument being supposed to have been used by a Briton to kill an elephant which had been imported by Cæsar. Subsequently, at the end of the last century, Mr. Frere communicated a notice to the Society of Antiquaries, giving an account of the discovery of a number of these tools at Hoxne, in Suffolk, and stating that they were found in a brick-pit with the remains of large animals, and under such circumstances as to make it appear that they belonged to what he called "another world." I myself have carried out some explorations in that pit, and here is the butt end of one of these instruments, which I saw thrown out from a depth of eight feet of undisturbed gravel. That gives you an idea of the great amount of accumulation found in some cases over these instruments. In other cases they are found upon the surface. Here is one I found on the surface between Abbot's Langley and Bedmond. Here is another from Nash Mills. I found it within a quarter of a mile of my own house on some gravel that was being used for repairing the towing path, which I think had been dredged from the bottom of the valley.

The levels at which these implements occur are usually far beyond the reach of existing floods. In the case of Highbury, near London, one was found nearly 100 feet above the Thames; and at Ealing they occur something like 90 feet above the river; but it is impossible to suppose that at any period the floods of the Thames in its valley, as at present existing, reached to such a height; and even if they did, that they could have deposited the veins of gravel in which the implements occur, and, in addition to these, the beds of sand and brick-earth above them.

Then the question arises, in what manner can we satisfactorily account for the deposits in which the implements are found? As I said before, they appear to be drift deposited by the action of rivers, following much the same courses as the rivers of the present day, but flowing at a different level, and it is from the conditions under which they are deposited, and the associated fauna, that we make some inferences as to their antiquity. I have already said that with them have been found the remains of the mammoth, and in addition there is the rhinoceros, the cave-lion, the hippopotamus, and other animals no longer living in this country, and which had become extinct or had migrated by the time the beds were deposited which now form the bottom of our valleys. Such a change in the fauna must be significant of a great lapse of time.

And there is another feature in the case. In nearly all instances there is a great similarity in the deposits in which the implements occur, and in the localities in which they are found. The beds cannot be due to any great cataclysm or wave traversing the country, because the materials of which the gravels are formed are confined to the valleys through which the rivers now pass. For instance, if there were such beds in the valley of the Colne, you would only in these gravels get pebbles derived from the Chalk or Tertiary beds above, including, however, the Glacial beds, in which the older rocks occur. In France, in the gravels of rivers which have passed through granitic districts, there are found granitic pebbles; whereas where the rivers do not traverse granitic districts, no such pebbles are to be seen. Other and conclusive evidence of the gravels having been deposited by the action of rivers is afforded by the presence of fresh-water shells. We are therefore driven to the conclusion that they were deposited by rivers flowing from much the same watersheds as at present, but at a very different elevation. One theory was that the valleys had already been excavated in pre-glacial times and subsequently re-excavated. But in this there is a difficulty, because it is very doubtful whether in certain soils it was not easier for the rivers to cut out new valleys than for them to excavate the beds which had been deposited in glacial times. I think, therefore, that this was not the case, but that the valleys, even when in existence in a shallower form in pre-glacial times, have been cut much deeper in post-glacial times by the rivers which have flowed through them. We can hardly form an estimate of what the old rivers were like when they received a much greater amount of rainfall than at present, and were left in a state of nature. Indeed, if the rainfall were increased to a not immoderate extent, all the conditions of the case would be altered, especially in Chalk districts, in which these implements have been mainly found. If, for instance, instead of the level of saturation being 70 or 80 feet below the surface, as in this district, the rainfall saturated the Chalk to the top,—which would not require a very excessive amount,—the rain falling on the saturated surface would act in the same manner as if falling in a clay country, and there would be enormous floods in districts where they are now unknown. I think this is one of the reasons which conduced to the formation of valleys of such depths by streams which at present appear so inadequate to the work which we have every reason to believe they performed.

A river, assuming that it were liable to floods of this kind, would constantly scour out its bed,—deepen it by transporting the materials to the sea, or by removing them and depositing them in fresh places. In that manner small portions of the original bed of the river which had escaped the action of succeeding floods would be left as land-marks at the side of the valleys at a far higher level than the beds now being formed at the bottom of the valley—in fact, the old river-bed would be cut through and small portions left as memorials of its existence at high levels. That such is the case with the gravel-beds now 90 or 100 feet above the streams is also borne out by the fact that above the gravels we find the fine silt or brick-earth already mentioned. Gravel can only be carried by water flowing with considerable velocity. Where the velocity is not so great, it is deposited; where water flows slowly, sand falls to the bottom; and where it is nearly stagnant, turbid water will deposit mud. All these deposits might be formed at the same time, the gravel along the bed of the main stream, and silt and mud at spots only accessible by flood-waters. At the period when the rivers ran at a high level, the bottoms of the valleys were probably much wider than at present, and you may readily conceive how from any meandering of the streams from one side of the valley to the other, parts of the old bed were left at some distance from the main stream, which were liable to receive a coating of sand, and subsequently, as the river got further away, were merely exposed to the almost stagnant waters of floods, and received a coating of brick-earth.

And not only have we the evidence of this great deepening of the valleys, which must have required an enormous amount of time; but we have that curious feature, to which I have already alluded, of gravels of fresh-water formation capping the cliffs on the south coast of England. At Bournemouth the cliffs are about ninety feet high, with this gravel above, and, judging from analogy, we cannot but regard it as having been formed in the bed of a river. But the southern side of the valley through which that river flowed has now entirely disappeared, and in order to reconstruct the country through which it flowed, you must regard the great range of Chalk hills which passes through the Isle of Wight as being continuous to Ballard Down, near Corfe Castle, and fill up the great bay between Studland and the Isle of Wight with one hundred square miles of high ground sloping to the north.

That this was in all probability the early condition of that part of England, and that the capping of the cliffs at Bournemouth is merely the bed of an ancient river, is shown by

the fact that between the Isle of Wight and the mainland
there exists a channel, the Solent Sea, which seems to be only a
portion of the old river that flowed by Bournemouth, widened out.
You can easily imagine that when once the sea had made a breach
in the land so as to intersect the course of that old river, it would
in process of time widen it out. Looking at the fact that all along
the shores of Southampton Water we find gravel with these implements, showing that a great branch river flowed southwards into
the Solent, and that along the northern sides of the Solent Sea we
have gravels capping the cliffs at Barton, also with implements,
and that on the opposite side of the Solent these implements have
likewise been found, near the Foreland in the Isle of Wight ; I
think there is good evidence for regarding that Solent Sea, which is
now a great highway for the British Navy, as having been only a
portion of a river, at a time when this part of the world was already
occupied by man. It is not a little remarkable that at Southampton
Common, where we get these gravels, they occur at 150 or 160
feet above high-water mark. Here is an implement said to have
been found at 180 feet, but certainly at above 140 feet. Its edges
are not sharp, but are waterworn, showing that it has been subject
to the abrading action of water.

But I am afraid I have detained you full long upon this
interesting subject. You may ask, probably, what antiquity
is to be assigned to these objects, and I frankly say I cannot
tell you. You must imagine to yourselves the amount of time
required for a river having a watershed or basin of the same area
as the existing River Thames to excavate the valley in which
London now stands, some three miles in width and 80 feet in
depth, and add to the period which would be necessary for this to
be effected, the whole of the Stone, Bronze, and Iron Periods which
are embraced in ordinary history. You must for yourselves reconstruct the map of England, and connect the Isle of Wight with
the mainland ; and picture to yourselves the amount of time
requisite to wash away the whole of the southern part of the valley
of the River Solent and widen out the course of the stream where
is now the Solent Sea. If you are mentally able to conceive the
amount of time which would be necessary for producing such effects,
I think that you will agree with me that the antiquity of man is
something which requires strong powers of the imagination to
realize.

28.—THE FERTILISATION OF PLANTS.

By the Rev. GEORGE HENSLOW, M.A., F.L.S., F.G.S.,
Lecturer on Botany at St. Bartholomew's Hospital.

[A Lecture delivered 8th March, 1877.]

I PURPOSE giving you this evening a short account of a new work by Mr. Darwin. As you are all doubtless aware, whatever he undertakes he does thoroughly, and his book on "The Cross- and Self-Fertilisation of Plants," which came out last January, contains observations upon experiments he has been making for several years past. It is a book that takes, I had almost said months, certainly weeks, to digest thoroughly; and although no one can gainsay the majority of his conclusions, there is one point from which, I think, he has drawn a wrong inference; and I shall comment upon it. I mean "Self-Fertilisation." My first idea was to make that the subject of this lecture, but I shall take the whole question, and then put before you wherein I think lies his mistake, and I shall be very glad if any one will criticise my views.

It is just two hundred years ago since Sir Thomas Millington detected the use of the pollen for the fertilisation of the stigma. As soon as that necessity was recognised, the idea very soon followed that flowers were adapted to secure their own seeds by the pollen falling on the stigma of the same flower. I think it was Linnæus to whom is attributed the statement that both pendulous and erect flowers have the stigmas *below* the anthers, so that the pollen may fall from the latter upon them. Further observations would have shown that this is not universally true. Take, for instance, the common crocus. In the purple variety the stigma is erect and forms a brush, but the stamens are below it. The tops of the anthers only reach a height below the point where the stigmas branch, so that this is a case in which the rule fails. It was soon found that in many instances it would not apply, and it was also noticed that all flowers had not both stamens and pistils in the same flower, *e.g.* cucumbers and melons; and similarly with regard to several trees, such as the willow; so that it was clear there must be some other law than that the pollen should fall on the stigma of the same flower. Hence "intercrossing" was suspected, and Sprengel, a German, in 1790, wrote a very interesting book, in which he noticed a great many plants, the pollen of which it is necessary for insects to carry from one flower to another. We have, however, to thank Mr. Darwin for elucidating the fact, and establishing, on a thoroughly scientific basis, the necessity for insects to visit conspicuous flowers and carry the pollen from one to another. He was the first English botanist who established that fact, although he has had a great number of followers since; and anybody who searches regularly into flowers is pretty sure to find some new contrivance. I will mention one of a few recorded by myself, viz. that of the crocus. As soon as the bees come out in spring, you can easily see how they succeed in intercrossing this plant. The perianth of the crocus is contracted at the base, so that if the bee alights on the inner surface of it, she cannot get down to the bottom where the honey lies, and so she alights on the brush-like stigma, and goes head downwards, grasping the whole column of stamens with her legs; consequently the anthers dust the bee on the under-side with pollen. It should be noticed that the anthers do not burst inwards, as is ordinarily the case in flowers, but outwards, so that the bee smears herself over with pollen; she then flies to another flower, alights on the brush-like stigmas, and these of course sweep off the pollen which the bee has brought. That is just an instance of the intercrossing of flowers. Mr. Darwin's work on the 'Fertilisation of Orchids' is a most interesting book, and deals with one particular family; but intercrossing occurs in nearly all orders of the Vegetable Kingdom.

Having thus detected that the pollen was necessary to fertilise the pistil, intercrossing was looked upon to some extent as a necessity. It was a sort of general surmise that plants produced by the resulting seeds were benefited if the pollen had come from any other flower than its own; but the *exact value* was never known; and it is remarkable that Dean Herbert, in his work on the *Amaryllideæ* (1836) says: "I am inclined to think I have derived advantage from impregnating the flowers from which I wish to obtain seeds, from individuals of another variety or another flower rather than its own, and especially of any grown in different soil or aspect." That is a remarkable sentence, and we have been forty years without having this fact established, so that the great value of Mr. Darwin's new book lies in the fact that it gives us the exact value of these three kinds of crossing.

Let us, then, start from this point, and we will take four kinds of combination. The first is when the pollen of flowers falls on their own stigmas: that is self-fertilisation. The second kind of union is that of crossing different flowers, but on the same plant. The third is the intercrossing plants of the same stock, grown in the same garden, and sprung from the same ancestor, and consequently all of close kinship. Lastly, there is the crossing plants from distinct stocks; one, say, growing in Mr. Darwin's garden, and the other brought from Colchester or elsewhere, and of course grown under different circumstances.

Mr. Darwin went through an elaborate series of experiments on fifty-four species of thirty distinct natural orders, and I will give you the main results. The first case upon which he experimented he carried out more fully than all the others. He cultivated the so-called "Convolvulus major" (*Ipomæa purpurea*) for ten years, year by year, and his method was to fertilise the flowers artificially with their own pollen, and collect the seeds from those flowers: he called them "self-fertilised seeds." On the other hand, he fertilised the flowers of plants with the pollen of other flowers growing in his garden, and called the result "intercrossed seeds." Then he allowed both kinds to germinate, and as soon as he got pairs of exactly the same height, he planted them on opposite sides of a pot, the mould and moisture, etc., being the same, and the plants subject to exactly the same conditions. Then he allowed these pairs to grow up, and when they were fully grown he measured their heights in inches, always calculating the "intercrossed" as 100 for convenience, and the resulting ratios were recorded for ten years. He grew five or six pots every year, and in each pot five or six pairs of plants, thus raising an immense number of plants altogether. He added up the heights, and then divided by the number of plants, so as to get the average. In the first year's growth the heights were as 100 to 76 ; 100 representing the "intercrossed" and 76 representing the self-fertilised. It went down to 68 the third year; and in every year the self-fertilised fell short of 100. The interpretation of this, therefore, was that intercrossing did a great deal of good, as shown by the "inter-crossed plants" being higher than the "self-fertilised." Grouping the years in threes, another result comes out. Thus the averages of the first three years give the ratio of 100 to 74. The averages of the fourth, fifth, and sixth years give the ratio of 100 to 78, *i.e.* they are nearer equality; and the average of the next three years gives the ratio of 100 to 88, *i.e.* still nearer equality. *Hence the ratio is becoming approximately equal to unity as the generations go on.* It shows however that the intercrossing was beneficial for the first few years, but as it proceeded the benefit apparently began to die out, and the plants became approximated to the self-fertilised. You get the very same result when you take the ratios of fertility, as represented by the average number of seeds developed in the capsule. Mr. Darwin has not tabulated this, but I have calculated it from his book. There are two generations in the proportion of 100 to 93 ; the next two generations are as 100 to 94 ; one generation, the fifth, gives a ratio of 100 to 107, while the eighth gives a ratio, by calculation, of 100 to 114! Hence there is a gradual approximation to unity, or 100 to 100, as years go on, in two respects. Intercrossing appears to be beneficial at first ; but after-wards the benefit dies out, and then the plants show no improvement upon the self-fertilised. On the contrary, self-fertilisation proves to be more beneficial than intercrossing.

This is also shown in another way. When Mr. Darwin first cultivated the plants, there was an immense variety in the colours; but subsequently they got less variable, the intercrossed gradually assumed one and the same colour, though never absolute uniformity ; whereas the self-fertilised became absolutely uniform in colour. This brings out an important horticultural fact. If a gardener wishes to keep any particular strain, he must be very particular not to cross it by another strain, but propagate it either by slips, bulbs, etc., or *self-fertilise it*, for such fixes the colour.

We will now consider the crossing of flowers on the same plant. Unfortunately Mr. Darwin has not gone into this so fully, and one cannot therefore draw very safe deductions from his experiments ;

but the conclusion, as far as it goes, appears to be this. He tried first of all the *Ipomæa purpurea*, and found the relative heights of plants grown from seed of the intercrossed flowers on the same plant, to the self-fertilised, were as 100 to 105. That showed it was better for a flower to be self-fertilised than to be crossed with another flower on the same plant. He cut down both the self-fertilised and crossed plants, *i.e.* those which had been the result of a seed of flowers fertilised respectively as stated, and the ratio of their weights was as 100 to 124, so that in height and weight it showed that the self-fertilisation was better than the crossing. This was a different result from what was anticipated. Botanists had been inclined to take it for granted that it was always beneficial to cross flowers even on the same plant, as Dean Herbert had surmised. Mr. Darwin only tried five plants. Of *Mimulus luteus* the height was as 100 to 101, and the weight 100 to 103, the benefit being on the side of the self-fertilised. *Digitalis purpurea* gave ratios 100 to 94 in height, the weight 100 to 78, showing no slight benefit in crossing the flowers. In another part of his book Mr. Darwin alludes to what some other botanists had found, viz. that no difference occurred with *Reseda*, *Dianthus*, or *Abutilon*; but a slight beneficial effect appeared in thus crossing *Eschscholtzia*, *Oncidium* and *Corydalis cava*. A curious fact is noticeable here. All the plants which derived a benefit were naturally more or less *self-sterile* plants, as stated in his list of self-sterile plants, *i.e.* which cannot naturally set seed of themselves. Therefore I think we may at least suspect, if not generalise, that the benefit derived from crossing flowers on the same plant may prove to be more or less limited to those naturally self-sterile.

Next, we must consider the effects of introducing a new stock. He did this with some half-dozen plants, and then the benefit was something very great indeed. He has given a table (C) in the book, and by tabulating the mean results of it, and taking 100 as the standard for the new stock, we arrive at the following conclusions:

Mean of heights of crossed to intercrossed = 100 : 85.
„   „   „   self-fertilised = 100 : 75.
„   fertility   „   intercrossed = 100 : 40.
„   „   „   self-fertilised = 100 : 25.
„   weight   „   intercrossed = 100 : 116.
„   „   „   self-fertilised = 100 : 53.

" Crossed " signifies crossed with a new stock; " intercrossed " signifies crossed with the same stock.

You see that in this table nearly all these numbers are considerably less than 100, showing as a rule that the benefit derived from crossing with a new stock, whether in height, weight, or fertility (estimated by the number of seeds), is immense. But it is not absolute—there are exceptions, and the number 116 stands out as an exception. That, however, is the mean of only three plants, too few from which to generalise.

I will enumerate some of the benefits which Mr. Darwin observed;

although you cannot generalise from these effects, yet they occurred in individual cases, where the crossed plants showed some special or particular advantage in other respects than height, weight, and fertility; for example, on one occasion he planted the self-fertilised some hours, or even a day or two before the others, and then the crossed overtook them and beat them in the race. Then he found they were better able to resist unfavourable conditions of various kinds : such as a sudden removal from the greenhouse to the open ground, which checked the self-fertilised, whereas the others were able to stand it. But this was only in particular instances. They also better withstood cold and intemperate weather, and a severe frost on one occasion. The period of flowering of the intercrossed was earlier than that of the self-fertilised, sometimes days, or even, as in the case of *Cyclamen*, three weeks. To sum up the results, we find that the experiments establish these main facts. By introducing a new stock, the cross benefits the plants in every way, they grow higher, their leaves are larger and greener, and they become altogether finer and more bushy plants, and produce a greater profusion of flowers, while the flowers are subject to greater variations of colour. Secondly, by intercrossing two plants of the same stock, you get a certain amount of benefit, but in a lesser degree ; but if one continues to cultivate the same stock year after year, the benefit derived at first gradually disappears, the plants finally become as if they fertilised themselves, and the flowers retain the same uniform colour.

Then we come to the process of self-fertilisation. We have considered the three kinds : a distinct cross, *i.e.* with different stock ; crossing the same stock ; and crossing flowers on the same plant ; but self-fertilisation is the subject on which I join issue with Mr. Darwin. Throughout the book he uses the phrases "evil effects of," and "injurious effects of," in regard to self-fertilisation. Of course he has proved the benefits of crossing ; but to say that the opposite process is "injurious" is, I think, misleading. For when you read of "injurious effects" you infer some unhealthiness or infertility. Cases amongst cultivated plants may occur where something like "injurious effects" may be recognised, but apart from individual and exceptional cases, to lay it down as a broad general rule is, I think, erroneous. Mr. Darwin heads a section on p. 303 as follows :—"On the preservation of the good effects from a cross and the evil effects from self-fertilisation." But out of the seventy-four cases he has cultivated, he has only got three plants to bring forward. The first one, *Nemophila insignis*, must be struck out altogether, because he says : "This experiment was quite worthless." That reduces us to two cases only. One is the common pansy, and the way in which he wished to show the benefit was by taking two plants cultivated for one generation ; the one crossed, the other self-fertilised, and the ratio of the two was as 100 to 42, showing a very great benefit to the intercrossed. He now crossed the seedlings of *both* of these two ; and he thought the one doubly-crossed would show the transmitted benefit and be

thus superior to the (now crossed) self-fertilised. It did, as the
ratio, 100 to 82, indicates. This is nearer to unity than before,
but it only shows that the self-fertilised plant was now benefited
by its being crossed, while the (twice) intercrossed retained some
benefit, but did not acquire any proportionally increased advantage. The next was the sweet pea. In the first generations,
the intercrossed to the self-fertilised was 100 to 80, the next
year 100 to 88. Then he allowed *both* to be *self-fertilised*, and
the ratio was 100 to 90, or nearly 90. Then, he says, some were
cultivated in very unfavourable situations, and showed in an "unmistakable manner" the superior constitutional vigour in those
which had been intercrossed. He put some in a pot containing a
large *Brugmansia*, and in poor soil, and the ratio was 100 to 88,
exactly that of the previous year. Again, when planted on poor soil
in the shrubbery, others reached 100 to 98, or practically showing
no difference between the intercrossed and self-fertilised, *i.e.* the
benefit of intercrossing was *not* transmitted. So from these two
cases I do not see that he is justified in attributing "evil effects
to self-fertilisation." He established the fact that the benefits of
the cross may be handed down, but the "evil effects" of self-
fertilisation are not proved. The self-fertilised were just as healthy.
He remarks that both produced a profusion of pods, and, in fact,
under the shrubbery they were practically equal in height.

He adds a remarkable instance, where he says the effect of the
cross was carried on for a long period. A variety of the common
pea was raised by Mr. Knight by crossing distinct varieties, and it
retained its characters by self-fertilisation alone *for upwards of
sixty years.* If it was not superseded for sixty years as a market-
able product, the words "evil effects" are surely misleading. The
crossing has to thank the self-fertilising power of the pea for
keeping it up so long !

Now I will give you what seem to me the grounds for believing
in the benefits of self-fertilisation. You may think it strange after
what I have been saying, but in many cases I think it is true, and
Mr. Darwin himself admits it. Although he talks about the "evil
effects," yet he admits that in some cases self-fertilisation must be
beneficial. This was the case when the results were compared
with those of crossing flowers on the same plant. The self-fertilised
plants of *Ipomœa* were higher than the intercrossed. He says :
"This is a remarkable fact, which seems to show that self-fertilisation is more advantageous, *unless* the crossing brings some decided
and appreciable advantage." This is the clue to the whole thing.
Crossing is only a means to an end, and that end is the introduction
of new constitutional elements. Hence by means of intercrossing,
different plants, which are living under slightly different circumstances, have new elements of constitution introduced into each other;
and from this arises the benefit. The mere act of crossing does no
good. It is similar or analogous to ourselves going to a different
part of the country for change of air. An invalid likes change and
new scenery, for they invigorate the constitution. So as long as a

plant goes on fertilising itself, it cannot introduce new constitutional elements; but carry it into a new country, and you may see a surprising difference. The water-cress, which is self-fertilising, now growing in New Zealand, retains the same form that it has here, but it grows twelve feet long, and nearly an inch thick, and has increased so that the Government expends large sums every year in keeping the rivers clear of it. It is not only far superior to, but is completely driving out the native water-plants.

I will now enumerate several facts which will, I think, make out the case of self-fertilisation. 1. The majority of flowering plants are self-fertile. Mr. Darwin's book brought that out more than I suspected to be the case. The general idea was that conspicuous flowers are adapted solely for intercrossing. That is not quite true; though a large number of conspicuous flowers are strongly "proterandrous," that is, mature their stamens before their stigmas, and so cannot be self-fertilised ; as the common clove pink ; but the *Ipomœa purpurea*, which is a very conspicuous flower, though freely crossed by bees, yet will fertilise itself if we keep the bees away. 2. Very few plants are known to be physiologically self-sterile. It is a remarkable fact that some plants are in this condition ; but put the pollen on another flower, and it is effective. 3. Many are morphologically self-sterile. That means, the pollen cannot reach the stigma of the same flower unless artificially put there, but it is then effective. 4. Self-sterile plants may become self-fertile by many causes. Some of these causes want a little more establishing, it is true; but they have at least been noticed in certain cases. For instance, the withering of the corolla. Mr. Darwin mentions the case of the pansy. I have noticed the same thing in plants in the autumn, when it is getting too cold for the corolla to expand. You may find the corolla withered and pressed down upon the stamens and pistil, which then seeds abundantly. Such a case I have observed in *Tradescantia*. 5. Loss of colour. That means loss of energy ; because it is known that if you keep balsams without ammonia in the soil, they will be white, but with ammonia they become pink again. The conclusion I draw is that from whatever cause the energy in a plant is destroyed, its loss may be indicated by a white or pale-coloured corolla. Loss of energy appears to be favourable for self-fertilisation ; but the converse is not necessarily true. In Mr. Darwin's book there are about half a dozen instances where he mentions that pale flowers and white flowers are more self-fertile than others. 6. The absence of insects. It appears that some flowers which are habitually crossed in their own country by insects, on transportation to another country, where there are none of those insects, may become self-fertilising. Three common examples are the sweet pea, the garden pea, and the dwarf kidney-bean. The pea is really adapted for insect agency, but it is self-fertilising in this country, apparently because we have not the proper insect to fertilise it. If plants therefore do not receive visits from the right insects, the probability is that they will generally die out, and we have reason to suppose that many have died out on that account; but the pea and others may be regarded as exceptions which have become self-fertilising instead. 7. Highly self-fertile forms may arise under cultivation. In cultivating the *Ipomœa purpurea* for three years, not one single plant of the self-fertilised appeared taller than the crossed; in every individual case the intercrossed was taller than the self-fertilised; but in the third generation one plant grew to a greater height, and Mr. Darwin says he was so much surprised that he saved the seed to see what would happen. However, it only beat its competitor by ·6 p.c., that is, the ratio of the intercrossed to the self-fertilised was 100 to 100·6; which is practically one of equality. He called that plant " Hero," and saved the seed, to see whether the seedlings would show any tendency to be taller than the intercrossed. The descendants did exert a power of growth quite equal to the ordinary intercrossed, and became more fertile than is usually the case, for they had a higher average of seeds per capsule than in any other cases. No benefit followed from intercrossing, and not even any benefit from crossing with new stock! So that this was a very remarkable individual, for its descendants had great self-fertilising powers and always beat their competitors. When one studies the details of the experiments with the different species, there is scarcely a single table where there are not three or more self-fertilised seedlings which beat their competitors. So that Hero was not by any means an exceptional case of a self-fertilised plant growing taller and being more vigorous than the others. Indeed it seems to have been a very common thing indeed. Hero was the first, and therefore Mr. Darwin studied that individual. 8. Special adaptations occur for self-fertilisation. We have had so much literature on the subject of intercrossing published of late years, that the peculiarities of self-fertilisation have been rather neglected. Take, for instance, the two common mallows, *Malva rotundifolia* and *sylvestris*; the latter is a conspicuous large flowering species, and is " proterandrous," *i.e.* the stamens all shed their pollen long before the styles and stigma rise up and are ready to receive it; so that it cannot possibly be self-fertilising. *Malva rotundifolia*, on the other hand, is self-fertile: the styles rise up and are mature at the same time as the stamens. They curl backwards, inserting the stigmas amongst the anthers, and thus secure the pollen on their own stigmas, and the plant is self-fertilised. The pansy (*Viola tricolor*) does not usually set seed of itself, but requires to be intercrossed. It is a self-sterile plant. Hermann Müller, who has especially studied these conditions, found some very small and inconspicuous varieties, in which the stigma was turned towards the stamens, and received the pollen directly from them. It will be found to be a general rule that small inconspicuous forms are self-fertilising, while larger and brightly-coloured flowers require insects. Inconspicuous flowers are therefore probably always self-fertile, without, however, precluding the possibility of their being crossed. I have examined a very large number of our common weeds, and I found the pollen grains always penetrating the stigma. Many of them fertilise themselves in the bud without opening at all. The common chickweed and the *Spergula arvensis* in the winter never open; but the anthers will be found clustering round the stigmas, and the flower seeding itself rapidly in that state. They fertilise themselves with great ease and great rapidity. It is astonishing how soon the seeds ripen and escape. 9. "Cleistogamous" flowers. Certain plants, besides bearing conspicuous flowers, as the common violet, have inconspicuous, almost microscopic flowers as well, which never open. Now the ordinary violet-blossoms rarely set any seed; but if you turn up the leaves in the summer, you will find a great number of minute buds, not much bigger than a large pin's head, but they often have no petals, and the stamens are reduced to two or three, and the anthers are pressed down on the stigma, and the result is that these minute flowers are self-fertilising and set seed in profusion. *Oxalis*, or the wood sorrel, is another instance; as is one of the balsams; and *Lamium amplexicaule* also has cleistogamous flowers. 10. The relative fertility may equal or surpass that of crossed plants. Very often the number of seeds per capsule did not differ much between the intercrossed and the self-fertilised in Mr. Darwin's experiments; but the intercrossed being more vigorous produced more flowers, so that the absolute fertility was very greatly in favour of the intercrossed, but the number of seeds per capsule did not materially differ. Then, again, the fertility does not decrease. If there were injurious effects in self-fertilisation, one would think that the fertility would decrease in successive generations, but it does not; and in some cases plants usually requiring to be intercrossed became very self-fertile, by the anthers maturing with the stigma instead of before them, and Mr. Darwin found the fertility then increased in successive generations. This was the case with the clove pink. 11. When the plants were grown in competition on opposite sides of the pot, so long as they were seedlings, there was no difference; but as soon as they began to increase in size, competition set in. It was with that object he put them in the same pot, to resemble the "struggle" which occurs in nature. But it is generally plants of different orders that compete together in nature, and not plants of the same kind; and two plants of totally different orders will grow together where plants of the same kind will not, for they do not require exactly the same food; but two of the same kind want the same things, and so compete for the same elements. Therefore it is not quite the same condition as happens in nature. When, however, the seedlings were planted in the open ground, there was often very little difference between them, and when transferred from the pots to the open ground, although still in favour of the intercrossed, it was much less so. There are only two alternatives to explain this; either the intercrossed *lost* vigour from being moved, or else the self-fertilised *gained* vigour faster than the intercrossed, and so became nearly equal to them. In Mr. Darwin's book on the "Variation of

Animals and Plants under Domestication," he says that it is
necessary to put them under competition, otherwise little or no
difference may be seen in the results, showing, therefore, that,
apart from the competition, there is not so much benefit to the
intercrossed over the self-fertilised as might be expected. 12.
Naturalised abroad, self-fertilised plants often gain great vigour,
and are the fittest to survive in the struggle for life.   I have
noted down all the British plants from a number of different
lists of floras of foreign countries, to see what was the distribution
of our own wild flowers over the world; and what at once struck
me as peculiar was that they are, for the most part, the inconspicuous and self-fertilising flowers.   Thus *Cardamine hirsuta* is a
good example.   You probably know *C. pratensis*, the "cuckoo
flower" of our meadows.   While this is solely European, *C. hirsuta*
is found in many countries scattered over the world.   *Stellaria
media*, the chickweed, is found in a great many places, but *Stellaria
Holostea*, the common stitchwort, which is large flowered and requires insects, is nowhere to be found out of Europe.   No other
species of *Malva* except *M. rotundifolia* is widely dispersed : with
the sole exception of *M. sylvestris*, which is in Japan.   There is no
reason why the conspicuous-flowered plants should not have become
dispersed as well as the others.   Again, *Solanum nigrum*, the little
white flowering night-shade, is found dispersed, while *Solanum
Dulcamara* is nowhere seen but here.   *Polygonum aviculare*, which
bears little inconspicuous green flowers, and is self-fertilising, is found
in Australia and elsewhere; but the large purple one, *P. Bistorta*, is
only met with here.   Moreover the former, a small weed in this
country, in New Zealand is completely ousting the native flowers.
It is described as being four feet long, and with roots of several feet
in length.   Now if such is the case, what are we to infer?   That
there is no appreciable reason why the conspicuous and insect-
requiring plants should not travel about as much as the inconspicuous ones ; but that if they did, and have disappeared, it is
because no insects visited them.   Inasmuch as insects, as a rule,
keep to particular flowers, and the native insects in foreign countries
would continue to visit their own flowers, and would not take the
trouble to go to the newly-imported individuals, I infer that,
whenever conspicuous forms requiring insect agency have migrated,
they have generally perished—in other words, that the self-fertilising are the fittest to survive in the struggle for life.

—

29.—Instructions for taking Meteorological Observations.

By WILLIAM MARRIOTT, F.M.S.,
Assistant Secretary of the Meteorological Society.

Communicated by J. HOPKINSON, Hon. Sec.

[Read 12th April, 1877.]

As this Society will naturally take an interest in the science of Meteorology, and as some of its members may make, or intend making, observations with the view of determining the climate, etc., of Hertfordshire, I have much pleasure in acceding to the request of your Secretary to give a few instructions upon the best method of taking meteorological observations.

Meteorological observations to be of any scientific value must be made on a uniform plan at all stations, otherwise the results will not be comparable. The Meteorological Society is very stringent in this matter of uniformity, and only accepts those observers who will comply with its requirements, and whose stations and instruments are found to be satisfactory on inspection.

Instruments.—The necessary instruments are:—Standard Barometer; Dry-bulb Thermometer; Wet-bulb Thermometer; Maximum Thermometer; Minimum Thermometer; Rain-gauge; and Stevenson's Thermometer Stand. It is also desirable to have a Black-bulb Maximum Thermometer in vacuo; a Minimum Thermometer for terrestrial radiation; and an Anemometer.

All the instruments should be verified at the Kew Observatory, so that the corrections for index error may be ascertained.

Barometer.—The Barometer may be either a Fortin or a Kew Standard. It should be mounted in a room which is only subject to very slight changes of temperature, must hang vertically, and be in a good light.

When the mercury in the tube falls, that in the cistern rises in a corresponding proportion, and *vice versâ*, and unless this variation be taken into account, the readings will not be correct. In the Fortin barometer this difficulty is overcome by having an adjustable cistern, so that the mercury can always be maintained at a constant level by being brought into contact with a fixed ivory point. In the Kew barometer the cistern is closed, but the error arising from the change of level in the cistern (technically termed "the error of capacity") is overcome by contracting the divisions on the scale, so that the inches are somewhat less than true inches. The height of the mercury is determined by bringing the bottom of the vernier to form a tangent to the top of the column, and then reading off the divisions on the scale and vernier.

All barometers have a thermometer attached to them, with the bulb inserted in the brass case, so as to be between it and the glass tube; this is supposed to show the same temperature as the mercury in the barometer. By its means we are able to determine the proper correction to be applied to the reading of the barometer to reduce it to a fixed temperature, viz. the freezing-point, 32°. The mode of taking the observation is this:—First note the reading of the attached thermometer to the nearest degree; then (if the barometer is a Fortin) adjust the mercury in the cistern by turning the screw at the bottom so that the ivory point is *just* brought into contact with the surface of the mercury, but does not depress it; the ivory point and its reflected image in the mercury should appear to touch each other and form a double cone. The next thing is to adjust the vernier so that the lower edge shall form a tangent to the convex surface of the mercury—in fact, the front and back edges of the vernier and the top of the mercury must be in the same straight line. The scale on the tube is divided to inches, tenths, and half-tenths, or five-hundredths of an inch, and the vernier is made equal to 24 divisions of the scale, and is divided into 25 equal parts. Each division of the vernier is therefore smaller than each division of the scale, by the 25th part of ·05; which is ·002 inch. First read off the division on the scale at, or below which the lower edge of the vernier stands. Suppose it is between 29·70 inches and 29·75 inches; we should call this 29·70 inches. Next look along the vernier until one of its lines is found to agree with a line on the scale. Suppose this is at the second division above the figure 2. As each of the figures marked on the vernier count as hundredths, and each intermediate division as two thousandths, our reading of the vernier will be ·024 inch. The reading of the barometer is therefore 29·70 + ·024 = 29·724 inches.

Having obtained the actual reading of the barometer, it now requires corrections for (1) index error, (2) temperature, and (3) height above sea-level.

1. The correction for index error is ascertained by comparing the barometer with a standard instrument, such as that at the Kew Observatory; the correction is always given on the certificate of comparison.

2. As the mercury in the barometer expands by heat, the height of the column is affected by temperature; it is therefore necessary to reduce the readings to a uniform temperature: 32° is the point now adopted. Tables of corrections have been prepared for this purpose, and will be found in most treatises on Meteorology.

3. In comparing barometric observations made at different places, account must be taken of their respective heights above sea-level; for, the higher the station is, the lower will the reading of the barometer be. The height of the cistern of the barometer above sea-level must therefore be accurately ascertained, which can be done by levelling, etc., from the nearest bench-mark. The proper corrections for altitude can then be calculated from the tables given in most treatises.

A form of table has been devised for combining all the above corrections, and is the means of saving many troublesome calculations, besides greatly reducing the liability to error. (See 'Quarterly Journal of the Meteorological Society,' vol. iii., p. 1.)

Thermometers.—The Maximum Thermometer may be on either Negretti and Zambra's or Phillips' principle. Negretti's registers in the following manner :—The tube is bent and contracted near the bulb in such a way that it allows the mercury to pass in expanding, but on contraction the column of mercury in the tube is broken off, and the extremity shows the highest temperature that has been attained. It is set by simply holding the instrument bulb downwards and shaking it. It is to be mounted horizontally. In Phillips' thermometer the index is formed by a small portion of the mercurial column, separated from the main thread by a minute air-bubble, and is pushed on before the column when it expands, but does not return with it when it contracts. It therefore rests at the extreme position to which it has advanced, and the end furthest from the bulb registers the highest temperature which has been attained. As the air-bubble is liable to be displaced, and the instrument to be put out of order, Negretti's thermometer is the more trustworthy of the two.

The Minimum Thermometer generally used is that known as Rutherford's. The fluid used is spirit, and in it there is immersed a steel index. When the temperature falls, the spirit draws the index along with it, but on rising again, the spirit passes by the index, leaving it at the lowest point to which it has been drawn, thus registering the minimum temperature. The instrument is set by raising the bulb and allowing the index to flow to the end of the column of spirit. The thermometer should be mounted very nearly horizontally, the bulb being a trifle lower than the other end.

The Dry- and Wet-bulb Thermometers should be of precisely the same make, have small bulbs, and be about four inches apart. The wet-bulb should be covered with a single piece of very fine muslin, in the form of a jacket to fit the bulb if it is cylindrical, and should project a little below it. A conducting thread of six or eight strands of darning cotton should be tied round the neck of the bulb over the muslin, the other end passing into a water receptacle through a small orifice at the top, placed about three inches from the bulb. Clean rain-water alone should be employed. The muslin and conducting thread must be washed in boiling water prior to use, and must be changed at least once a month, and oftener if there is any appearance of dirt or deposit. In damp and foggy weather the thermometers should be carefully wiped about five minutes before the observation. When the temperature is below the freezing-point, the wet-bulb requires careful management. Instead of a film of water round the bulb, there must be a coating of ice, which can be obtained by applying, with a camel's hair brush, water taken from under ice. This must be done half an hour or so before the time of observation. It is best to remove the muslin entirely, as a lower and more correct reading will be obtained if the coating of ice is on the naked bulb; for this purpose thermometers with roughened or ground bulbs should be used, as the ice will form more readily on them than on smooth bulbs. As soon as the temperature rises above the freezing-point, the bulb and conducting thread should be washed with warm water, so that every particle of ice may be melted off, otherwise the thermometer will give too low a reading.

The thermometers must be mounted in a Stevenson's screen, which has double louvres all round, allowing a free current of air to pass through, and preventing the sun shining on the thermometers. The screen should be placed over grass in a freely exposed situation; it is desirable that it should never be in the shade, and it must not be placed within ten feet of any wall. It must be mounted on four posts, so that the bulbs of the dry- and wet-thermometers shall be four feet above the ground; and the door should open to the north. The thermometers should be placed as near the centre of the stand as possible. A convenient arrangement is to mount the maximum and minimum on two small uprights in front of the dry and wet, in such a way that the scales of the latter can be seen between the two former.

The observations are made as follows :—Having let down the door of the screen, the dry- and wet-bulb thermometers are to be read first, so that they may not be affected by the nearness of the observer. The minimum thermometer is to be read next by noting the position of the end of the index farthest from the bulb. (The end of the column of spirit shows the temperature at the time of observation.) The maximum thermometer is read last by noting the degree at which the end of the column of mercury is lying. When this has been done, the instruments should be looked at again to see that no mistake has been made in reading them; the maximum and minimum should then be set in the manner already explained, and the door closed.

Spirit thermometers are liable to a serious fault, viz. the evaporation of the spirit from the column, and its condensation at the top of the tube. We sometimes see in the newspapers accounts of extremely low temperatures having been registered at certain places, but they are very often traceable to this fault, for the thermometers may have as much as 5° or 10° of spirit lodged at the top of the tube. As it is not always possible to see the spirit at the top, it is very desirable to occasionally place all the thermometers in a basin of water and compare them together, for we can then see if the thermometers are working properly or have gone wrong.

The instrument used for measuring solar radiation is what is called the "Black-bulb Thermometer in vacuo." It consists of a sensitive maximum thermometer, which has its bulb and one inch of the stem coated with dull lamp-black; this thermometer is inclosed in a glass jacket, from which the air is completely exhausted. It should be mounted on a post four feet above the ground, with the bulb directed to the S.E. The difference between the maximum in the sun and in the shade is the amount of solar radiation.

For determining the intensity of terrestrial radiation a sensitive spirit minimum thermometer must be used, and placed upon short grass.

Rain-gauge.—The Rain-gauge should be made of copper, and have a funnel of five or eight inches diameter. It is very desirable that it have also a deep rim. It should be set in an open and well-exposed situation, entirely free from trees, walls, and buildings. It must be firmly fixed so that it cannot be blown over; the top of the funnel should be one foot above the ground and must be quite level. The measurement of the rain simply consists in pouring out the contents of the bottle or can into the glass measure, which must be held quite vertically, and reading off the division to which the water rises. The amount should always be written down before the water is thrown away. The gauge must be emptied every morning at 9 a.m., and the rain-fall entered to the *previous* day. If it is known that no rain has fallen, the gauge should, nevertheless, be examined, and a line or dash inserted in the register. It is desirable that very heavy falls of rain should be measured on their termination, and the particulars entered in the remarks; but if this be done, the water should be returned to the gauge, so that the next ordinary registration may not be interfered with. When snow falls, that which is collected in the funnel is to be melted and measured as rain. It is also desirable to measure with a rule the depth of snow in a place where it has not drifted, and enter it in the remarks.

Wind.—The direction and force of the wind may be ascertained by estimation, or from a vane and anemometer, where such are available. It is absolutely necessary to first obtain and mark a fixed point of the compass—N. is the best; this may be done by observing Polaris, the North Star, on a clear night, or noting the shadow of a building, etc., when the sun is *due* S. about noon. The direction of the wind is that point of the compass *from* which it is blowing. Care must be taken that the direction is that of the general current of air passing over the place, and that it is not locally affected. The wind is influenced by so many local causes, that anemometers, unless they are very well exposed, can hardly ever record its *true* direction and force. The direction can be obtained by observing the drift of smoke from tall chimneys or low clouds. The force is generally obtained by estimation, the scale employed being the following :—

0	= Calm	= 3 miles per hour.		7 = Moderate gale = 40 miles per hour.			
1	= Light air	= 8	,, ,,	8 = Fresh	,,	= 48	,, ,,
2	= Light breeze	= 13	,, ,,	9 = Strong	,,	= 56	,, ,,
3	= Gentle ,,	= 18	,, ,,	10 = Whole	,,	= 65	,, ,,
4	= Moderate ,,	= 23	,, ,,	11 = Storm		= 75	,, ,,
5	= Fresh ,,	= 28	,, ,,	12 = Hurricane		= 90	,, ,,
6	= Strong ,,	= 34	,, ,,				

If a Robinson's cup anemometer be used, it must be mounted on a pole in a freely-exposed situation, so as to be quite uninfluenced by buildings, trees, etc.

Clouds.—The proportion of sky covered with cloud must be observed. This is done by estimation, the scale adopted being 0 to 10,—0 representing a cloudless sky, and 10 a completely covered or overcast sky. It is also desirable to note the kind of cloud prevalent at the time, and the direction from which it is coming.

The different modifications and forms of cloud are Cirrus, Cirro-cumulus, Cirro-stratus, Cumulus, Cumulo-stratus, Stratus, and Nimbus.

The Cirrus cloud consists of parallel wavy or diverging fibres which may increase in any or in all directions. It is that very high cloud which looks like hair or feathers, and is formed of ice crystals. The Cirro-cumulus is composed of small, well-defined, roundish masses lying near each other, and quite separated by intervals of sky. This cloud forms what is generally known as a "mackerel sky." The Cirro-stratus consists of horizontal or slightly inclined masses thinned towards a part of the circumference, bent downwards or undulated, and either separate or in groups. It is in this cloud that halos and coronæ are formed. The Cumulus is of a convex or well-rounded shape, and is generally a cloud of the day. The Cumulo-stratus is formed by the Cirro-stratus blending with the Cumulus, either among its piled-up heaps, or spreading underneath its base as a horizontal layer of vapour. The Stratus is a widely extended continuous sheet of cloud, increasing from below upwards. It is the lowest kind of cloud, its lower surface commonly resting on the earth. The Nimbus is the well-known *rain-cloud*, consisting of a cloud, or system of clouds, from which rain is falling.

In addition to the foregoing observations, it is very desirable to note the state of the weather and any phenomena that may have occurred since the last observation, such as thunder-storms, halos, etc. These may be entered in the register in an abbreviated form by the letters of Beaufort's notation, which is as follows:—

b = blue sky.	*p* = passing temporary showers.
c = cloudy, but detached clouds.	*q* = squally.
d = drizzling rain.	*r* = rain.
f = foggy.	*s* = snow.
g = dark, gloomy weather.	*t* = thunder.
h = hail.	*u* = "ugly," threatening appearance
l = lightning.	of the weather.
m = misty, hazy atmosphere.	*v* = visibility of distant objects.
o = overcast, the whole sky being covered with an impervious cloud.	*w* = wet, dew.

The hours of observation are 9 a.m. and 9 p.m., and must be punctually attended to. The maximum and minimum thermometers are to be read and set at 9 p.m., and the readings entered to the same day.

Omissions must be carefully avoided, otherwise the register will be incomplete, and true means cannot be obtained; it is, therefore, necessary to have a deputy to take the observations in the absence of the regular observer.

30.—Meteorological Observations taken at Holly Bank, Watford, during the year ending 28th February, 1877.

By John Hopkinson, F.L.S., F.M.S., etc., Hon. Sec.

[Read 12th April, 1877.]

The meteorological observations, some of the results of which I propose to give in this communication, were in part commenced in January, 1876; but, as it was not until the end of February that the barometer and thermometers were obtained, to complete a year the first two months of 1877 are included.

Though it is to be regretted that the results of observations in the entire year 1876 cannot be given, there is one advantage in the arrangement adopted—by commencing in March we can divide the year into its four seasons.

The result we wish more particularly to arrive at being a knowledge of the climate of the neighbourhood of Watford, obtained by data which will enable us to compare its climate with that of other places where similar observations are carried on, by dividing the year into the four seasons—Spring, Summer, Autumn, and Winter—and taking the means for each season, a more satisfactory comparison may be made than by taking only the means for the year, and a more comprehensive and less tedious one than by comparing with each other the monthly means.

This being the first report, it will be necessary to give certain particulars as to the locality, the instruments used, their position, and the time and method of observation.

The locality is perhaps as suitable a one as could be chosen in the immediate neighbourhood of Watford. The position as related to the surrounding country is high, the ground falling slightly in every direction, either immediately or at the distance of a few hundred yards; and, with the exception of a belt of trees forming the eastern margin of Cassiobury Park, which perhaps gives some slight protection against westerly winds, there is nothing to interfere with a free current of air in every direction.

The longitude is 0° 24′ 10″ W. (of Greenwich), and the latitude 51° 40′ 5″ N. The town of Watford is about a mile to the south-east. The ground-level is about 268 feet above Ordnance Datum (mean sea-level), 30 feet higher than the centre of the town of Watford, and 10 feet higher than the ground on which the trees on the west, already mentioned, are situated.

The instruments used are by Mr. J. J. Hicks, of Hatton Garden, London, and they have been verified at the Kew Observatory.

The barometer (No. 473) is a standard on Fortin's principle. The tube is half an inch in internal diameter, and the correction required, according to the Kew certificate, is +0·004 inch, of which +0·003 is due to capillarity, the error of construction or "index error" being therefore only 0·001 inch. The cistern of the instrument is about 272 feet above Ordnance Datum. The readings are first entered without any correction, but the monthly means and other readings here given are corrected for index error and capillarity, reduced to 32° in accordance with the readings of the attached thermometer (No. 39031), and to sea-level, taking into account the temperature of the external air.

The thermometers consist of a Negretti maximum, a Rutherford minimum, and a dry- and wet-bulb, or hygrometer. They are placed in a Stevenson screen, over grass, and at a considerable distance from any wall or building. Their bulbs are about four feet above the ground. Their readings are corrected for index errors only. The dry- and wet-bulb thermometers are practically correct, their maximum error, 0°·1, being too slight to necessitate a correction being made. The maximum requires a slight correction when at or above 62°, and the minimum when as low as 12°. The following are the precise corrections:—

MINIMUM. (No. 39076.)	MAXIMUM. (No. 39077.)	DRY-BULB. (No. 39078.)	WET-BULB. (No. 39079.)
At 12°..........+0°·3	At 32°.......... 0°·0	At 32°.......... 0°·0	At 32°.......... 0°·0
22°..........+0 ·1	42°..........+0 ·1	42°.......... 0 ·0	42°.......... 0 ·0
32°.......... 0 ·0	52°.......... 0 ·0	52°.......... 0 ·0	52°.......... 0 ·0
42°.......... 0 ·0	62°..........+0 ·2	62°.......... 0 ·0	62°..........—0 ·1
52°.......... 0 ·0	72°..........+0 ·2	72°..........+0 ·1	72°.......... 0 ·0
62°.......... 0 ·0	82°..........+0 ·2	82°.......... 0 ·0	82°.......... 0 ·0
72°..........—0 ·1	92°..........+0 ·2	92°..........—0 ·1	92°..........—0 ·1

The rain gauge used during the year 1876 is a "Howard," by R. and J. Beck. From the commencement of the year 1877 a "Snowdon" gauge, by J. J. Hicks, has been used for the daily observations, and the Howard has been read weekly and at the end of each month, as a check upon the daily readings of the Snowdon gauge. Both gauges are five inches in diameter. The Howard has not been verified, the Snowdon (No. 103) has, and is correct throughout the scale. They are placed about two feet from each other, with their rims one foot above the ground. Their exposure is very open, no trees or buildings being near.

The rain gauges are read at 9 a.m., and the amounts entered to the previous day (or week); the maximum and minimum thermometers are read at 9 p.m., and entered to the same day; and the other instruments are read at both 9 a.m. and 9 p.m., when the direction and force of the wind (estimated), and the amount of cloud, or proportion of sky covered by cloud, are also entered.

The accompanying table gives the monthly means of these observations, and of other results deduced from them. The direction of the wind is given entirely from the morning observations, as I have frequently been uncertain as to its direction at night. For the first three months also the dry- and wet-bulb thermometers were not read at 9 p.m., nor were the amount of

RESULTS OF METEOROLOGICAL OBSERVATIONS TAKEN AT HOLLY BANK, WATFORD.

Months.	Mean Pressure.	Air Temperature.								Tension of Vapour.	Relative Humidity.
		Mean.	Means of		Mean Daily Range.	Absolute Min. and Max.					
			Min.	Max.		Min.	Day.	Max.	Day.		
	ins.	°	°	°	°	°		°		ins.	%
March, 1876	29·589	42·0	33·4	47·4	14·0	23·1	21st	58·9	30th	·225	85
April	29·881	47·6	39·0	54·8	15·8	28·6	13th	68·6	8th	·254	77
May	30·156	50·2	38·6	56·8	18·2	30·0	4th	66·4	29th	·245	68
June	30·005	58·6	48·0	66·8	18·8	37·7	11th	80·8	21st	·348	71
July	30·077	63·2	50·7	74·7	24·0	49·4	11th	88·2	15th	·412	71
August	29·949	63·5	48·7	72·1	23·4	41·6	24th	89·0	13th	·409	70
September	29·802	55·4	48·8	62·2	13·4	41·3	13th	69·0	22nd	·365	82
October	29·958	51·4	47·0	57·5	10·5	30·5	25th	67·2	6th	·330	87
November	29·895	42·3	37·7	48·0	10·3	23·4	11th	58·8	16th	·244	90
December	29·512	42·5	39·9	46·2	6·3	28·0	22nd	55·4	2nd	·247	91
January, 1877	29·837	40·9	37·6	48·0	10·4	26·6	21st	55·5	19th	·215	84
February	29·948	42·1	39·0	47·7	8·7	24·7	28th	55·7	7th	·242	89
Year	29·884	50·0	42·4	56·9	14·5					·295	80

Months.	Amount of Cloud 0–10.	Force of Wind 0–12.	Rainfall.			No. of days of		Wind—No. of observations of.								
			Total.	Max.	Day.	Rain.	Snow.	N.	N.E.	E.	S.E.	S.	S.W.	W.	N.W.	Calm.
March, 1876	6·8		2·84	·64	12th	13	6	1	3	3	1	4	4	10	5	0
April	6·0		2·55	·77	10th	12	5	1	5	3	2	3	6	6	4	0
May	6·0	2·9	0·65	·30	22nd	8	0	5	8	7	2	0	2	1	3	3
June	6·1	3·1	1·44	·50	15th	13	0	5	6	1	3	0	8	3	3	1
July	7·4	2·7	1·22	·48	31st	8	0	2	2	0	0	3	6	5	8	5
August	3·9	1·6	1·91	·42	4th	13	0	1	4	1	9	5	6	2
September	6·1	2·5	4·82	1·13	5th	26	0	5	2	0	5	2	2	7	5	2
October	6·4	1·8	1·68	·46	10th	16	0	2	6	1	5	3	9	0	1	4
November	7·0	1·7	3·59	·58	11th	17	1	5	2	3	5	2	3	3	4	3
December	8·3	2·1	5·67	·66	23rd	22	3	3	0	4	3	8	5	2	1	5
January, 1877	6·6	2·0	4·93	·70	3rd	27	0	1	1	2	6	12	3	3	3
February	6·5	2·2	1·92	·35	14th	17	3	4	1	0	0	1	7	9	5	1
Year	6·4		33·22			192	18	33	39	24	32	33	73	54	48	29

To face p. 218.

cloud and force of the wind observed at that hour; and in some of the other months there are several days on which no evening observations were made, but the omissions are not so numerous as to sensibly affect the monthly means. The mean temperature is deduced from the observations of the dry-bulb thermometer at 9 a.m. and 9 p.m., and it will be seen to differ very slightly from the mean of the maximum and minimum. The dew point having been obtained from the readings of the dry- and wet-bulb by means of Mr. Marriott's 'Table for faciliating the Determination of the Dew-point' (1874), Mr. Glaisher's 'Hygrometrical Tables' (6th edition, 1876) were used in the calculation of the tension (or elastic force) of vapour, and the relative humidity.

Grouping into seasons some of the most important results here expressed, we have the following table, which admits of ready comparison with observations taken at other places.

WATFORD.

Seasons 1876-77.	Mean Pressure.	Mean Temperature.	Mean Daily Range.	Tension of Vapour.	Relative Humidity.	Rainfall.
	ins.	°	°	ins.	%	ins.
Spring..........	29·875	46·6	16·0	·241	77	6·04
Summer	30·010	61·8	22·1	·390	71	4·57
Autumn	29·885	49·7	11·4	·313	86	10·09
Winter	29·766	41·8	8·5	·235	88	12·52
Year	29·884	50·0	14·5	·295	80	33·22

I will take for example the observations made at the Royal Observatory at Greenwich, as given in Mr. Glaisher's "Remarks on the Weather," in the Quarterly Reports of the Registrar-General. The values given for the mean pressure of the atmosphere are corrected for elevation above the sea (160 feet), Mr. Glaisher's monthly means not being reduced to sea-level. No other correction has been applied.

GREENWICH.

Seasons 1876-77.	Mean Pressure.	Mean Temperature.	Mean Daily Range.	Tension of Vapour.	Relative Humidity.	Rainfall.
	ins.	°	°	ins.	%	ins.
Spring..........	29·853	45·9	18·2	·236	77	4·70
Summer	30·000	62·7	23·6	·403	73	3·80
Autumn·.....	29·869	50·9	13·5	·316	84	7·30
Winter	29·754	43·4	9·9	·245	85	11·90
Year	29·869	50·7	16·3	·300	80	27·70

The most noticeable features in the year (March 1876 to February 1877) were the great barometric depressions in March and December, the excessive heat in July and August, and the heavy rainfall in September, December, and January. With the exception of the rainfall, these and other phenomena of which mention should be made are not shown in the table. In the following notes on the months these exceptional occurrences are specially alluded to, and an endeavour is made to give an account of the principal changes in the weather, which—read in conjunction with the table, to which they are merely supplementary—may serve in some measure as a substitute for the daily register. All the values given are fully corrected.

MARCH.—During the first week the weather was mild, the mean temperature being about 45°; the wind was W. to S.W., and rain fell every day but the 3rd. On the 9th a fall of temperature occurred, with a strong easterly wind and slight snowstorm. Atmospheric pressure, which during the first week had been between 29½ and 30 inches, decreased on the 8th from 29·726 inches at 9 a.m. to 28·958 at 9 p.m., continuing to decrease until at 9 p.m. on the 9th it was 28·686. The barometer had risen slightly the next morning, and continued to rise until at 9 p.m. on the 11th it stood at 29·231, the wind being N.W. A remarkably sudden fall then occurred, and between noon and 1 p.m. on the 12th, during a violent gale and snowstorm, the barometer reached its lowest point, after which it rose even more rapidly than it had fallen. The readings taken on the 12th were :—

At 9·0 a.m.	28·667 ins.	Wind		S.E.
„ 0·30 p.m.	28·464 „		„	N E.
„ 3·0 p.m.	28·763 „		„	E.
„ 6·0 p.m.	29·119 „		„	N.W.
„ 9·0 p m.	29·252 „		„	W.

The temperature at 9 a.m. was 34°. The minimum the previous night was 31°. The snowstorm commenced at 8·30 a.m. and continued till about 3 p.m. The wind continued W. to N. to the 21st, with occasional slight falls of snow, and it then changed to S., was easterly for the next six days, and southerly to the end of the month. During this time the temperature was very variable, but there was a sudden rise from 36° at 9 a.m. on the 27th to 48° on the 28th, and the weather continued warm to the 10th of April. A lunar halo* was seen on the evening of the 11th.

APRIL.—Pressure was very variable, mostly higher the first half of the month than the last half. The barometer was below 29 ins. on the 19th only, and never reached 30½ ins. The mean temperature for the first nine days was 51°·6. On the 10th there was a heavy fall of snow and a cold period set in, lasting until the 18th, with snow almost daily,—the mean for this period being 42°·6. On the 13th there was a terrific gale and snowstorm, very similar to that on the 12th of March, but not accompanied by any

---

* This is a ring of (usually) white light at a distance from the moon, and must not be confounded with the corona, a ring of prismatic colours bordering the moon.

great barometric depression. The storm commenced at about noon and reached its height in the evening. The day will be remembered as that of one of the evening meetings of our Society, access to which the storm rendered almost impossible. In the neighbourhood of Hitchin the snowstorm was more violent than at Watford, the drift there being in some places six feet deep, and vehicles had to be left on the roads completely buried in the snow. The next morning it measured a foot deep where it had not drifted. For the first half of the month the wind was very variable, but most often westerly to the 14th, when it changed to N.E. On the 18th it changed to S.W., the prevailing direction to the end of the month, and on this day the temperature again rose to nearly 49°, the mean of the remaining days in the month. No rain fell until the 9th, but rain or snow almost daily from then.

MAY.—Atmospheric pressure was above 30 ins. every day except from the 22nd to the 27th, and then it was only slightly less. The mean temperature to the 19th was about the same as the mean of the previous month, the slight increase of 2°·6 shown in the table being due to the warmer weather which set in on the 20th. The minimum in both April and May was below 32° on five days. Until the 20th the wind was mostly easterly, but after then westerly (or S. to N.W.). All the rain in the month fell on the six days when the barometer was below 30 inches, excepting ·02 in. on the 2nd, and the same amount on the 15th. This was the driest month in the year, both in respect to the rainfall and the humidity of the air, as may be seen by the table.

JUNE.—Atmospheric pressure was remarkably uniform, the maximum range being only half an inch, from 29·724 at 9 a.m. on the 9th to 30·196 at 9 p.m. on the 27th. No considerable rise in the temperature occurred until the 12th, which was 10° warmer, at 9 a.m., than the previous day. The warmest days were the 20th and 21st—the temperature being respectively, at 9 a.m., 73 and 73°·4. The maximum was above 80° on the 21st only. The wind was N.W. to S.W. to the 9th, when it changed to N.E., which direction it maintained for three days, after which it became N., and then for the latter half of the month mostly easterly but very variable. Rain was pretty evenly distributed over the month, but none fell the last six days.

JULY.—For the first twelve days the mean temperature was 63°·3, the maximum during this period being 75°. On the 13th the maximum had reached 82°, on the 14th 87°·2, and on the 15th 88°·2, this being the hottest day. The temperature then gradually became lower, and towards the end of the month was lower than at the beginning. The maximum was above 80° on nine days. The prevailing direction of the wind was westerly (S.W. to N.W.). Scarcely any rain fell until the end of the month, but the last two days were very wet, ·30 in. falling on the 30th and ·48 on the 31st. There was a severe thunderstorm on the 23rd. Owing to my absence from home the latter part of the month, the barometric and some other observations are incomplete.

AUGUST.—The temperature increased gradually and almost uniformly to about the middle of the month, decreasing similarly to the end, when it was slightly lower than at the beginning. The maximum was above 80° on seven days, and was highest on the 13th, when it reached 89°, the hottest day in the year and for several years past. On that day, at 3 p.m., there was a difference of more than 20° between the dry- and the wet-bulb, which stood respectively at 88°·4 and 68°·1, showing an extreme dryness of the air. The excessively hot period extended from the 9th to the 17th, when the readings of the dry- and wet-bulb at 9 a.m., and maximum and minimum thermometers, were as follows:—

	DRY.	WET.	MAX.	MIN.
August 9	72°·0	65°·3	82°·5	52°·9
„ 10	64 ·1	57 ·7	78 ·2	54 ·9
„ 11	63 ·2	57 ·4	76 ·0	44 ·7
„ 12	69 ·0	61 ·4	81 ·6	51 ·2
„ 13	78 ·4	66 ·6	89 ·0	59 ·6
„ 14	74 ·5	66 ·7	86 ·8	55 ·5
„ 15	74 ·9	63 ·3	85 ·9	59 ·9
„ 16	74 ·3	68 ·0	81 ·7	61 ·3
„ 17	64 ·5	59 ·7	85 ·8	55 ·6

At the close of this hot period there were several thunderstorms. Thunder was heard on the 15th at about 6 p.m., and on the evening of the following day, when lightning was also seen, but no rain fell. On the 18th there was a violent thunderstorm from 4 to 6 a.m., with rain, which continued to fall for some time after. On the following day there was another thunderstorm from noon to 2 p.m., with heavy rain. Half an inch of rain fell in the two days. A considerable amount fell on the 2nd and 4th, but none from then to the 18th. The wind was westerly until the hot period, then mostly S.E. to N.E., and westerly (S.W. to N.W.) again from the 21st to the end of the month. Pressure varied very slightly until the 30th, when the mercury fell (at 9 a.m.) to 29·176 ins., a little lower next morning, and rose again before night. Both these were wet days.

SEPTEMBER. — The considerable decrease in *mean* temperature from last month was mostly due to a few cold days about the middle of the month (11th, 12th, and 13th especially) reducing the mean, and the few hot days in August raising the mean of that month, the *average* temperature of the two months being about the same. The wind was S.W. by W. to N. until the 20th, when it changed to S.E., the prevailing direction to the end of the month. Rain fell every day but the 12th, 19th, 20th, and 21st. From the 1st to the 7th inclusive 3·10 ins. fell, and the maximum fall of the year (1·13 in. on the 5th) fell in a few hours during the night. Excepting on the 19th, 20th, and 21st, three of the four days on which no rain fell, pressure was invariably below 30 inches. The mean of the six observations on these days was 30·312 ins. Thunder was heard on the night of the 17th.

OCTOBER.—For the first three weeks the temperature was about the same as in September,—the cold weather, which commenced on the 21st, being the entire cause of the slight reduction of 3° in the mean temperature of the whole month. The minimum was below 32° on the 25th only. Pressure was almost invariably below 30 inches until the 20th—the warm period. During the succeeding cold period it was above 30 ins. without a single exception. The rainfall was almost entirely confined to the first 16 days, for 12 of which the wind was S. or S.W. The prevailing direction during the dry period which followed was N.E. A remarkable phenomenon was observed on the 6th. At about 10·45 a.m. a dense black cloud suddenly formed and it became as dark as in the worst London fogs. In a few minutes rain began to fall and it was quite light. At about 11 a.m. the rain ceased, the cloud again formed, and it became nearly as dark as before, when rain again fell and dispersed the cloud. The difference between the dry- and the wet-bulb thermometer at the time was less than half a degree, showing an excessive moisture of the air. There was a thunderstorm at 8 p.m. on the 5th. On several mornings there was a dense mist on the ground, clearing off before 9 a.m.

NOVEMBER.—Atmospheric pressure was high, above 30 inches, at the beginning of the month, decreasing to 29·171 ins. at 9 p.m. on the 12th, increasing again to the 22nd (30·294 at 9 a.m.), and then again decreasing. The cold weather which commenced on the 21st of October continued throughout the month, the only warm period being from the 14th to the 19th. The mean of these six days was 50°·3, being 8° above the mean of the entire month. The minimum was below 32° on six days, all between the 1st and 13th, and on the 11th was lower than on any other day in the three winter months—December, 1876, and January and February, 1877. The wind was mostly northerly to the 10th, variable (easterly prevailing) from the 11th to the 26th, and S.W. the last four days. The rainfall was pretty equally distributed over the month. There was a slight fall of snow on the 8th.

DECEMBER.—A remarkable depression of the barometer occurred on the 4th, exceeding that of the 12th of March, but it was not (at Watford) accompanied like it by any great atmospheric disturbance. Pressure was generally slight, but very variable, as the following daily readings of the barometer at 9 a.m. will show. The mean will be found to be 29·490 ins., differing very slightly from the mean of the 9 a.m and 9 p.m. readings together, as given in the table (opposite p. 218).

	ins.		ins.		ins.		ins.
1 ...	29·439	9 ...	30·126	17 ...	29·531	25 ...	29·758
2 ...	·280	10 ...	·204	18 ...	·325	26 ...	30·194
3 ...	·093	11 ...	·142	19 ...	·164	27 ...	29·786
4 ...	28·395	12 ...	29·743	20 ...	28·776	28 ...	·691
5 ...	·927	13 ...	·731	21 ...	·793	29 ...	·812
6 .	29·041	14 ...	·934	22 ...	29·141	30 ...	·543
7 ...	·179	15 ...	·936	23 ...	·377	31 ...	·275
8 ...	·526	16 ...	·820	24 ...	·493		

It will be seen that there are two principal minima, first that of the 4th, and secondly that of the 20th, on which day at 9 p.m. the barometer had fallen to 28·670 ins. The month was unusually warm, the mean temperature being higher than in November. The minimum was below 32° on six days, five of which were between the 23rd and 27th inclusive. The wind was chiefly southerly, verging mostly to W. at the beginning and end of the month, and to E. from the 14th to the 20th. The only days free from rain or snow were the 8th, 9th, 10th, 14th, 21st, and 22nd, the days of snow being the 23rd, 25th, and 26th.

JANUARY.—Until the 10th the temperature was about the same as the mean of December, and from the 10th to the 15th it was lower, higher again from the 16th to the 20th, suddenly lower on the 21st, and about the mean of the entire month to the end. The minimum was below 32° on five days. The wind was south-westerly almost throughout the month, inclining rather to S. until the 24th, from which date it was more westerly, sometimes N.W. Pressure varied considerably. The lowest reading of the barometer was 28·673 ins. at 9 a.m. on the 2nd, and the highest 30·663 at 9 a.m. on the 21st, the range being therefore about two inches. Rain fell every day but the 12th, 20th, 21st, and 22nd, the three consecutive days without rain coinciding with the high barometer. A lunar halo was observed on the evening of the 24th.

FEBRUARY.—The temperature remained about the same as during the last week of January. It was rather higher from the 7th to the 15th (the mean during this period being 46°) and much lower towards the end of the month. The mean of the last three days was 31°·8. The minimum was below 32° on three days. It was lowest the last day of the month, which also, if we exclude November as an autumnal month, was the coldest day of the winter of 1876–77. Pressure was much more equable than during the two previous months. The lowest reading of the barometer was 29·172 ins. at 9 a.m. on the 20th and the highest 30·366 at 9 p.m. on the 4th. The prevailing direction of the wind was westerly, inclining to S.W. to the 19th, and to N. or N.W. afterwards. The fall of rain was pretty evenly distributed over the month. Snow fell on the 20th, 25th, and 26th.

31.—REPORT ON THE RAINFALL IN HERTFORDSHIRE IN 1876.

By JOHN HOPKINSON, F.L.S., F.M.S., Hon. Sec.

[Read 12th April, 1877.]

IN Part 4 of our 'Transactions' (p. 112) will be found a summary of reports of the rainfall in 1875, which had been communicated quarterly at our meetings. These quarterly reports were compiled from the returns of five observers, and if it had not been thought desirable to solicit the co-operation of a greater number of observers in the county, there would have been little difficulty in continuing the system of quarterly reports.

Feeling, however, that it would be desirable to obtain as many records of the rainfall as possible, I obtained the permission of our Hon. Member, Mr. G. J. Symons, to publish in our 'Transactions' returns from the observers the results of whose observations are published by him in his 'British Rainfall'; the quarterly reports were discontinued; and I wrote to all his observers in the county, whom I here desire to thank for their ready response to my request for their returns of the rainfall.

The returns which have been received comprise the records of 23 rain gauges, as given in the following table :—

STATION.	OBSERVER.	Diameter of Gauge.	Height of Gauge above Ground	Height of Gauge above Sea-level.
		ins.	ft. ins.	ft.
Watford—Bushey Station	Robert Savill	5	0 8	220
„ Watford House	Alfred T. Brett, M.D.	8	1 3	240
„ Holly Bank	John Hopkinson	5	1 0	270
„ Oaklands	Edward Harrison	5	5 6	273
„ Cassiobury	Lord Essex	5	1 3	258
„ Harwood's Farm	W. Swanston	5	1 3	
Rickmansworth—Moor Park.	Lord Ebury	5	2 0	340
St. Albans—Gorhambury	J. Thompson	6	2 9	
Harpenden—Rothamsted	Lawes and Gilbert	5	2 0	420
„ „ (2nd gauge)	„ „	*	0 9	420
Dunstable—Kensworth	Miss Grace Jones	5	1 0	902
Hemel Hempsted—Nash Mills	John Evans, F.R.S.	12	3 9	237
Berkhampstead—High St.	William Squire	8	1 6	370
„ Ashlyns	William Longman	5	1 0	550
Tring—Cowroast	Hubert Thomas, C.E.	10	4 2	345
Hoddesdon—Feildes Weir	Beardmore and Barnes	20	3 0	82
Hertford—Bayfordbury	W. Clinton Baker	8	0 4	250
Welwyn	Rev. C. L. Wingfield	5	0 4	
Ware—Much Hadham	Rev. H. S. Mott	5	1 0	222
Stevenage	Rev. J. B. Seager	8	2 0	319
Buntingford—Aspenden	Rev. A. P. Sanderson.	5	1 1	329
Hitchin	William Lucas	9	1 6	238
Royston	Hale Wortham	8	0 6	269

* This gauge has a receiving area of $\frac{1}{1000}$ of an acre.

The localities are here arranged in the same order as before, *i.e.* grouped according to Mr. Pryor's botanical divisions* and their distance from Watford. Four out of his five divisions are represented,—the one from which we have no return being the Brent, a fragment (about four square miles) of Hertfordshire which may fairly be said to be situated in Middlesex, as it is almost entirely surrounded by that county. Of the sixteen minor districts we have returns from twelve. Those for which we require observers are the Upper Colne, the Chess, the Brent, and the Stort; all but the Upper Colne being outlying districts of very small extent.

The accompanying table (p. 227) gives the monthly and annual rainfall † at each station. It is seen by this table to have been very unevenly distributed over the year; and by breaking the year into three periods of four months each the inequality is rendered even more apparent. From January to April (inclusive) 9·73 inches fell; from May to August 5·45, or a little more than half the previous quantity; and from September to December 15·59, nearly three times the fall of the four summer months.

The next table gives the mean rainfall for each of the larger divisions or main river-basins, and also for each of the smaller districts or lesser river-basins and their sub-divisions. With the exception of the districts of the Lower Colne, the Ver, and the Bulborne, all of which are comprised in the Colne division, in which we are here more immediately interested, each of the districts is dependent upon a single observer, whose return we are therefore obliged to consider as representing the mean fall in the district.

Colne...32·28	Lower Colne...	29·61	Lea......29·08	Lower Lea...	26·60
	Ver	33·00		Upper Lea...	30·50
	Bulborne	34·23		Mimram......	30·27
Thame 34·09	Thame	34·09		Ash............	28·85
Ouse ...28·52	Ivel	30·26		Beane.........	28·93
	Cam	26·78		Rib............	29·36

Of the 22 observers 18 have taken their observations daily throughout the year, and they give the number of days in each month on which ·01 inch or more fell. The mean of these for the different months is as follows :—

Jan. ..... 9·7	April ...... 15·0	July ...... 7·8	Oct. ...... 12·0
Feb. ...... 19·2	May ...... 7·8	Aug....... 12·5	Nov....... 17·7
March ... 18·1	June ...... 10·2	Sept....... 20·2	Dec....... 22·7

giving a mean for the year of 172·9, or (say) 173 days. The least number of days of rain were at Ashlyns, Berkhampstead (142), Buntingford (143), and Rickmansworth (144); the greatest, at Holly Bank, Watford (195), Hitchin (199), and Harpenden (204). The numbers nearest the mean were at Royston (165), and at Hertford (178).

These 18 returns also give the greatest amount of rain which fell

* 'Transactions,' Vol. I. p. 67, and map, Plate I.
† The amounts entered as rain here and throughout this report include melted snow.

HERTFORDSHIRE RAINFALL IN 1876.

(All values in inches.)

District	Sub-district	Station	Jan.	Feb.	Mar.	Apl.	May.	June.	July.	Aug.	Sept.	Oct.	Nov.	Dec.	Total.
COLNE	Lower Colne	Watford—Bushey Station	·90	2·03	3·40	2·28	·55	1·54	·79	2·38	5·04	1·62	3·30	5·71	29·54
		„ Watford House	1·24	2·49	2·89	2·51	·60	1·51	1·16	1·85	4·30	1·48	3·53	5·24	28·80
		„ Holly Bank	1·21	2·47	2·84	2·55	·65	1·44	1·22	1·91	4·82	1·68	3·59	5·67	30·05
		„ Oaklands	1·24	2·54	2·42	2·40	·68	1·49	1·37	1·97	4·83	1·74	3·64	5·80	30·12
		„ Cassiobury	·88	2·15	3·09	2·39	·58	1·50	1·00	1·70	4·12	2·08	3·63	5·60	28·72
		„ Harwood's Farm	·58	2·65	3·03	2·42	·62	1·43	1·19	1·86	4·67	1·60	3·51	5·36	28·48
		Rickmansworth—Moor Park	1·45	2·75	3·63	2·32	·67	1·60	1·03	2·32	4·23	1·68	4·04	5·32	31·57
	Ver	St. Albans—Gorhambury	1·60	2·59	3·14	3·25	·67	1·26	1·27	2·34	5·29	1·41	3·67	5·83	32·32
		Harpenden—Rothamsted	1·59	2·79	2·42	3·24	·76	1·33	1·43	2·83	4·59	1·37	3·99	5·80	32·14
		„ „ (2nd gauge)	1·81	3·06	2·90	3·33	·78	1·35	1·46	2·98	5·02	1·52	4·20	6·00	34·41
	Bulborne	Dunstable—Kensworth	1·57	1·87	3·33	2·86	·88	1·23	1·50	2·75	5·68	1·40	4·20	5·85	33·12
		Hemel Hempsted—Nash Mills	1·57	2·81	3·39	3·10	·79	1·64	1·75	2·00	4·97	1·29	4·00	5·84	33·15
		Berkhampstead—High St.	1·79	3·06	3·04	3·10	·91	1·40	1·74	2·13	5·22	1·22	4·24	6·15	34·10
		„ Ashlyns	1·66	3·23	2·98	3·08	·84	1·03	1·69	1·61	6·17	1·25	5·17	6·66	35·44
LEA	Thame	Tring—Cowroast	1·75	3·02	3·02	2·85	·60	1·38	1·27	2·08	5·64	1·32	4·20	6·72	34·09
	Lower Lea	Holdesdon—Feildes Weir	·90	2·20	2·80	2·50	·79	1·30	1·05	2·20	3·30	1·25	3·00	5·50	26·60
	Upper Lea	Hertford—Bayfordbury	1·28	2·59	2·80	2·96	·77	1·20	1·07	2·38	4·34	1·42	3·60	6·07	30·50
	Minram	Welwyn	1·55	2·68	2·89	3·18	·92	1·15	·96	2·11	4·77	1·43	3·51	5·27	30·27
	Ash	Ware—Much Hadham	1·24	2·50	2·97	2·74	·71	1·08	·95	2·03	5·19	1·15	3·12	4·96	28·85
	Beane	Stevenage	1·62	2·33	2·78	3·00	·70	1·12	·99	1·90	4·35	1·17	3·63	5·33	28·93
	Rib	Buntingford—Aspenden	1·60	2·50	2·89	2·66	·71	1·61	1·21	2·55	4·16	1·11	3·35	5·02	29·36
OUSE	Ivel	Hitchin	1·86	2·38	2·97	2·81	·60	1·22	1·41	1·39	5·08	·97	3·89	5·57	30·26
	Cam	Royston	1·90	2·14	2·37	2·37	·60	1·64	·86	1·45	4·43	·85	2·86	5·31	26·78
		Mean	1·43	2·56	2·96	2·78	·73	1·37	1·23	2·12	4·79	1·39	3·73	5·68	30·77

on any one day in each month. To give this here would occupy too much space, but it may be interesting to know at what station there was the greatest fall in 24 hours in each month, with the day of the month on which it occurred and the amount of the fall.

	ins.		ins.
Jan. 21.—Berkhampstead (High Street)	1·10	July 31.—Berkhampstead (Ashlyns)	0·94
Feb. 14.—Rickmansworth	0·66	Aug. 15.—Harpenden	0·78
Mar. 12.—St. Albans	0·95	Sept. 5.—St. Albans	1·43
Apl. 13.—Stevenage	1·00	Oct. 10.—Rickmansworth	0·59
May 22.—Hemel Hempstead	0·39	Nov. 27.—Tring	0·90
June 15.—Buntingford	0·68	Dec. 23.—Hitchin	1·05

The wettest day in each month is in nearly every instance here shown—a fact which may be proved by taking all the dates given in the 18 returns as those on which the greatest depth of rain fell in each month, and giving under each date the number of times the date occurs—giving, that is to say, the number of stations at which, on any day, the greatest amount of rain is recorded to have fallen. The highest number given will therefore indicate the day on which a heavy fall of rain was most general over the county; and it will be seen that in only two months (August and November) was this not the day on which the greatest rainfall occurred at any one station. These days are indicated by italics.

January—21*st, the wettest day at* 17 *stations*; 22nd, at 1.
February—13th at 1; 14*th at* 12; 15th at 3; 22nd at 2.
March—12*th at* 10*; 27th at 7; 28th at 1.
April—10th at 4*; 11th at 1; 13*th at* 9*; 14th at 2; 18th at 1; 29th at 1.
May—22*nd at* 13; 23rd at 1; 24th at 2; 25th at 2.
June—15*th at* 15; 22nd at 2; 23rd at 1.
July—7th at 1; 11th at 1; 30th at 1; 31*st at* 15.
August—2nd at 1; 3rd at 1; 4th at 9; 15*th at* 5; 18th at 1; 19th at 1.
September—4th at 2; 5*th at* 15; 28th at 1.
October—5th at 2; 6th at 2; 10*th at* 10; 11th at 1; 12th at 3; 13th at 1.
November—11th at 8; 12th at 2; 26th at 1; 27*th at* 6; 28th at 1.
December—2nd at 2; 7th at 6; 8th at 1; 23*rd at* 8; 27th at 1.

We have seen that December was the wettest month in the year, and September the next. The 5th of September seems to have been the wettest day in the year, for the fall exceeded one inch at 10 stations, while on no other day did the fall reach an inch at more than one station. The amounts exceeding an inch on this day were:—at Holly Bank, Watford—1·13; Oaklands, Watford—1·08; St. Albans—1·43; Rothamsted—1·18; Hemel Hempstead—1·34; High Street, Berkhampstead—1·22; Ashlyns, Berkhampstead—1·33; Welwyn—1·27; Hitchin—1·12; and Royston—1·15.

I have endeavoured in this report to express, as briefly as possible, the main features brought out by the returns which have been communicated to me, and I have drawn no comparisons with previous years or with other districts. To compare our rainfall with that of other counties the record of a single year would not suffice, and to compare the rainfall of 1876 with that of previous years we have

* A snow storm.

not yet sufficient data. Moreover these and other questions of considerable interest are fully treated of in Mr. Symons' excellent annual publication 'British Rainfall.' As, however, a few observers have sent me the annual rainfall at their stations for some years past, and two have communicated the monthly fall for several years, I hope to embody these, and any other returns of past years that I may receive, in a future report.

APPENDIX.

As it is necessary for strict comparison that all observations be made upon one uniform plan, and as I have received returns which evidently were not carried out in accordance with Mr. Symons' rules, which all observers should comply with in order to secure uniformity, I here append, in a condensed form, those to which adherence is indispensable, referring observers, for full instructions, to Mr. Symons' 'British Rainfall.'

Gauges should be examined at 9 a.m. daily; or if read monthly at 9 a.m. on the 1st. [If weekly always also on the 1st of each month.]

The amount measured at 9 a.m. on any day is to be entered to *the previous day*. (This rule has been approved by the Meteorological Societies of England and Scotland and *cannot be altered*.)*

There must always be two figures to the right of the decimal point; thus seven-hundredths of an inch is to be entered as ·07, and ten-hundredths, or one-tenth, as ·10.

The amount should always be written down before the water is thrown away.

The unit of measurement being ·01, if the amount is under ·005, it should be thrown away; if it is ·005 to ·010 inclusive, it should be entered as ·01.

When snow falls, melt what is caught in the funnel and enter as rain; or, where the snow has not drifted, invert the funnel, and, turning it round, lift and melt what is enclosed; or, take one-twelfth of the average depth of snow as the equivalent of water (but this method is not to be adopted if it can be avoided).†

Small amounts of water deposited by fog or dew should be added to the amount of rainfall.

---

* It is to be regretted that all the observers in our county have not adhered to this rule. Where this has without doubt been the case the necessary correction has been made.

† " Snowdon pattern gauges are much the best."—Symons.

32.—Notes on a Remarkable Storm in Hertfordshire, April 4th, 1877.

By Lieut. R. B. Croft, R.N., F.L.S.

[Read 12th April, 1877.]

At about 4·30 p.m. on the 4th of April, 1877, during a very violent thunderstorm accompanied by heavy rain and a gale from the south-east, a remarkable and destructive whirlwind (?) passed over the town of Ware, and from descriptions given me by eye-witnesses, coupled with my own observation, I have collected the following information.

From the southern part of Amwell Bury grounds, about 100 yards to the westward of the main road, to and beyond Little Munden Church, a distance of about seven miles N.N.W., the storm may be traced by its effects. It is remarkable, however, that on the centre portion of this line—viz., from where it crosses the North road into Poles Park, to near Sacombe House, but little damage is done, while the two extremities of the line are marked by a great destruction of property, large trees being up-rooted, cottages unroofed, barns and sheds blown down, one man killed, and many slightly injured. I have seen and conversed with many people who watched this storm, and their accounts are most conflicting. Two men standing side by side describe it as "a white mass of steam rolling along like a wheel," and as "a jet black mass revolving like a teetotum." Others say they could distinguish no regular movement—"it was just like a mass of smoke;" "it was as big as a barn;" "I thought the other side of the street was on fire." All, however, agree that it lasted only a few seconds, and that it made a noise like an express train, only louder. I think there is no doubt that to persons at a certain distance the formation appeared like a waterspout, and from the twisted appearance of some of the boughs of the destroyed trees this appears likely. Whether at the base a white seething mass was visible is a matter for conjecture. On going over the ground next day, it appeared that the path of destruction did not exceed twenty yards (forty feet, according to some accounts); but, notwithstanding the course on the map being so direct, the storm appears to have deviated several degrees to either hand at different times. If these deviations could be accurately traced it would be very interesting. All trees, fences, etc., blown down, fell to the north-west, and railway tilts and other objects were carried a great distance. Slates blown off roofs were embedded in the ground like quoits. About the most remarkable things noticeable are the jumps made by the storm. Besides the long jump in the middle of its track before noticed, others equally remarkable are recorded.

33.—On Microscopic Fungi.

By E. M. Chater.

[Read 10th May, 1877.]

The subject of my paper, Microscopic Fungi, is one of such wide extent that it is only to a section of it that I propose to ask your attention this evening, viz. to those minute fungi which are found on living plants, and of these I shall select those that are most likely to be met with and are easily discovered. Should any of our members wish to make a study of these really interesting bodies, I would advise them (if they have not already done so) to procure Mr. Cooke's book on the subject, to which I am chiefly indebted for the information my sketch contains.

One of the earliest of our spring flowers, and one of the best known, is the lesser celandine or pilewort, *Ranunculus Ficaria*. If you examine a cluster of leaves of this plant, especially if it is growing in a low and damp locality, you are almost sure to find on the under surface of some of the leaves, as well as on the petioles, patches of a yellow colour, and at these spots the leaf or leaf-stalk is more or less thickened. On placing one of these yellow patches beneath a microscope, it is found to consist of a cluster of beautiful little cups having teeth at their margin, and containing a quantity of orange-coloured spores. This fungus is called *Æcidium ranunculacearum*. The genus *Æcidium* is included in the family of the *Coniomycetes* or dust fungi, so called because the spores are the principal feature. This fungus is also to be found in considerable abundance on the leaves of *Ranunculus repens*, the creeping crowfoot, and its presence is indicated by spaces of a paler green on the upper portion of the leaves. The stinging nettle, *Urtica dioica*, furnishes a home for another member of this genus, *Æcidium Urticæ*, and although it is scarcely to be found in such quantity as the preceding species, yet it is by no means uncommon. Its presence in the nettle gives rise to some very curious swellings and distortions of the leaves and petioles, so that it is often to be observed without difficulty on a cluster of these by no means favourite plants. The shape of the cups and the colour of the spores are very similar to those of the first-named fungus. The sweet and the dog violet have each of them their "cluster-cups." The latter are to be found in quantity in Oxhey Wood, and doubtless in many other places in the neighbourhood. The buckthorn, *Rhamnus catharticus*, furnishes us with a species in which the cups are longer than in those of which I have spoken. This is by no means uncommon, and almost every buckthorn bush will be found to have a few leaves bearing this fungus, which is called *Æcidium crassum*. Later in the year a cluster-cup is to be found on the under surface of the coltsfoot, its presence being indicated by a purple spot on the upper surface, and it is generally accompanied by groups of the orange-coloured spores of the coltsfoot rust, but

these however are not contained in cups as are those of the
Æcidium. The goatbeard, the wood sanicle, the spurge, and
several other plants have also their cluster-cups. A variety with
white spores is found on the leaves of the wood anemone. I have
not yet however been so fortunate as to find it in this neighbourhood.

The leaves of the hawthorn are visited with a fungus which
differs considerably in appearance from the *Æcidium*, and is referred to a distinct genus called *Rœstelia*. Instead of the margins
of the cups being divided into teeth, they are apparently torn into
shreds throughout their entire length, and the shreds themselves
are somewhat spirally twisted. This species is called the *Rœstelia
lacerata*, and one locality where it may be found in abundance is
near the railway crossing in Watford Fields. Two other members
of this genus are mentioned by Mr. Cooke; one in which the cups
are divided into shreds, the tips being united at the apex, which is
found on the leaves of the pear, and the other in which the cups
are long and cylindrical, but not split as in the former. This is
found on the mountain ash, and is called *Rœstelia cornuta*.

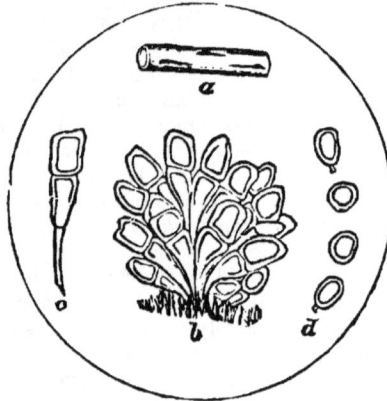

Fig. 1. Wheat Mildew—*Puccinia graminis*.
a. Straw with mature mildew.   *b*. A tuft of the mature mildew magnified.
c. A single spore.   *d*. Spores of the "rust" or early stage of the mildew.

When searching for specimens of the preceding we frequently
observe other appearances indicating the presence of fungi. For
instance, in looking over the leaves of the wood anemone for the
white-spored *Æcidium*, we often come across leaves which are
covered with little brown pustules, and on examining these we
find that the epidermis has been ruptured at these parts, and
clusters of spores have forced themselves through the opening;
these spores are found to be stalked and constricted in the middle
so as nearly to form two divisions, and they are covered with
spines. We have found the *Puccinia Anemones*, which we may take
to represent a large genus, in which the spores are divided into

two cells. The most important member of this group is the Puccinia graminis (Fig. 1), which attacks the wheat and other cereals, as well as various grasses. In its first stage it appears as a rusty powder on the leaves and stalks, and seems to consist of rounded yellow spores, but these are regarded now by many as a previous condition of the more fully developed two-celled spores of the Puccinia. In the same order we find some fungi with spores divided into more than two cells, and a very pretty one is to be met with on the leaves of the meadow sweet, Spiræa Ulmaria, in which the spores are divided into three cells. This fungus is called Triphragmium Ulmariæ. It is not very common, but I found some of it a few years ago near Bushey Mill.

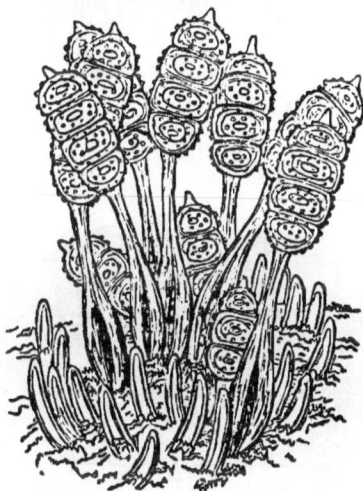

Fig. 2. Bramble Leaf Brand—*Aregma bulbosum.*

If in the autumn we examine a blackberry bush, we shall probably find some dark spots on the upper surface of some of the leaves, and on turning over the leaves so marked, we shall see on the under surface some little black specks looking very much like small spots of soot, which, when placed beneath an inch power of the microscope, are found to consist of tufts of little stalked bodies closely packed together. If we place some of them in a drop of spirit or water and view them as transparent objects, we find them to be spores which are divided transversely into three or four cells, and the stalks are found to be somewhat thickened below and to contain a granular core. A very similar variety containing rather a larger number of cells, and with a mucronate point, is found on the leaves of rose trees. These fungi are called *Aregma,* and the one on the bramble, *Aregma bulbosum* (Fig. 2). At the same time we shall find among the tufts some orange-coloured spores, which at one time were considered a distinct form and called *Lecythea,* but are now regarded by several writers on this subject as only a former stage of the same fungus.

The pilewort is attacked by another fungus besides the *Æcidium*, and as it is almost sure to attract the notice of those who may be looking for the cluster-cups, it should not be passed without remark. It is called the pilewort rust, *Uromyces Ficariæ*, and appears as a purplish brown powder bursting through the epidermis. The spores are small, one-celled, and stalked. Besides the brown rust there is also a white rust so common that it must have been noticed by most of us. It attacks cruciferous plants, and is seen very generally on the leaves and stalk of the shepherd's purse, *Capsella Bursa-pastoris*. It makes the plant look as if it had been splashed over with whitewash, and as the threads of the fungus gradually work their way among the tissues of the plant, they cause it to become swollen and distorted, so that plants attacked by this fungus present a very sickly and sorry appearance. It is called the *Cystopus candidus*. One of the most destructive of the fungi that attack living plants is the potato mould, which is the cause of the disease that does so much damage to this most important vegetable. The fungus is called *Peronospora infestans*.

Fig. 3. Maple Blight—*Uncinula bicornis*.
Lower figures—ends of appendages and spores.

The last group of fungi that I shall attempt to notice is that of the white mildews or blights. One of the most common is the maple blight, *Uncinula bicornis* (Fig. 3). As autumn approaches it is by no means uncommon to find the leaves of the maple looking as if they had been dusted over with some fine white powder. If we pluck a leaf and examine it carefully, we can make out, even with the naked eye, little black dots scattered over the white ground.

The white portion is the mycelium or vegetative part, while the little black dots are what are called conceptacles, that is to say, they are collections of sporangia or spore cases, each of which contains several spores. These conceptacles are furnished with certain appendages which differ in different species. The conceptacles of the maple blight are furnished with appendages the tops of which are bifid and hook-shaped. The appendages of the conceptacles of the gooseberry blight, and the hazel blight, and those of the berberry, form very beautiful objects for the microscope. The leaves of many other plants present similar appearances during the autumn, owing to the presence of white mildews; among the most common are the plantain and the knot grass, but the appendages in these cases are far less beautiful than in those previously mentioned.

The spores of several of the other parasitic fungi are sufficiently interesting to be worth preserving as permanent microscopic objects, and will keep for a long time if mounted in glycerine. The various species of cluster cups may be mounted as dry objects, but when so mounted do not keep well, and soon lose their bright colour.

In concluding this sketch I have to apologise for attempting to deal with a subject with which I have so very limited and insufficient acquaintance, but I hope I may have induced some members of our Society to give it more careful attention than I have done, feeling sure it is one that will afford much interest and pleasure.

34.—Notes on the Otter and Badger in Hertfordshire.

By Alfred T. Brett, M.D., President.

[Read 4th June, 1877.]

As the otter and the badger are becoming somewhat rare in this part of the country, I thought some notice of these animals might interest this Society.

The Otter.—I presume this animal was more common formerly than it is now, as we have two localities named after it—Otterspool and Little Otterspool. There is a curious pool at the former place, interesting to geologists, but I do not know of any pool at the latter.

The otter is not very frequent at Watford. Mr. J. King and other old inhabitants have never seen a wild otter. Mr. Alfred Dyson tells me that one was killed in the osier beds past Tolpits 20 years ago. In 1875 a young one was killed in the Colne above Watford. Mr. George Francis recollects his father shooting one which escaped at Piggott's End, in the Gade, 60 years since. Mr. Arthur H. Hibbert, of Munden Park, tells me that " a male otter was shot in February, 1875, at Munden; it weighed 32 lbs. and a few ounces, and it was 4 ft. 2½ ins. in length. It was shot after a heavy fall of snow had melted and the floods were out. The keeper had seen some strange tracks up and down the river Colne by Little Munden, and he had found the head and tail of a large jack. Mr. Haylock was going through the Grove, and the dog bringing the otter to bay, he shot it, about 100 yards from the water. The keeper looked out for the female, but could not find her, nor did he see any tracks of any more." Lately, a large fish—a carp—has been seen on the bank at Otterspool, partly consumed, as if it had been eaten by an otter. The same thing has been observed on a bank at Aldenham Abbey.

It is a question whether the otter does good or harm to a stream. By doing good or harm, does he, I mean, increase or decrease the absolute weight of fish in a stream? There can be no doubt but that the otter destroys a large quantity of fish; but the fecundity of fish is so enormous that almost any loss can be readily replaced, and by taking out the larger fish he may actually be doing good; for the large ones do not grow in proportion to the food they consume. Growth is more rapid in the young, and the food consumed would go to produce more weight. Besides, the otter would naturally catch those fish which were least active in avoiding his pursuit. The swifter and more healthy would get away, and in this manner the breed of fish would be improved, according to the law of the " survival of the fittest." I have no doubt the otter plays an important part in the plan of nature, and I hope he will not be exterminated from our county.

The Badger.—The badger appears to be more common in our county than the otter. Miss Hibbert informs me that she recollects two being killed at Munden at different times. A few years since one was caught in a trap at Langleybury. Mr. Loyd had it let loose, and it ran towards King's Langley. I am told they are common at that place, and at Ashridge, and also at Ashlyns. Mr. E. Ellis tells me that, in 1870, " a badger was caught in a trap in the grounds at Aldenham Abbey. The keeper found it an awkward creature to deal with. He could neither take it nor liberate it. He then provided himself with a sack or bag, which he threw over the animal, and removed it to the stable, where he tied it in a loose box, and it was kept four or five days. He failed to domesticate it in any degree; it refused food and pined away, and died. It was a full-grown badger, and had a formidable set of teeth." Some years ago an earth of theirs was dug out at Aldenham Lodge, and a litter of cubs found. An old man at Aldenham was a kind of purveyor of badgers for bating. I am not sure whence he drew his supplies for his patrons, but probably not far away. In 1875 a female badger and three young ones were caught at the "Temple of Pan," at The Grove, Lord Clarendon's. They were placed by the keeper in an out-house, and some one going there unexpectedly was so frightened as to run away, leaving the door open, and they all escaped but one. I am told that the best run they had in the Vale of Aylesbury last year with the foxhounds was after a badger. They did not discover it till after the run was over, and they killed. Mr. Samuel Betts, of Hadham Hall in this county, says: "Some years ago, two, with their young ones, were taken in one of the Hadham Hall woods, and I had them stuffed. Since then none have been seen or heard of, and I believe they are now extinct in this part of the county. Those referred to were taken out of a fox earth, and, being such rare animals, I have since felt very sorry that they were disturbed, but in those days everything had to give way to foxes, with which, however, I do not believe the badgers interfered at all." Mr. Forsdyke, senior, the keeper who has lived on the Cassiobury estate 60 years, says that 30 or 40 years ago there were badgers in the Badgers' Dell at Cassiobury, and they sold them to a man at Croxley Green, who kept a public-house, and who used to have one placed in a tub, and dogs set on it. At about this time, also, I am told one was baited annually at Sandridge Fair, near St. Albans. There have been several Acts of Parliament regarding cock fighting and badger baiting. The last was in 1849, and these sports are now illegal.

It is said that the "brock" or badger has legs on one side shorter than the other. I have brought a stuffed one for you to examine, and you can see if such is the case.

35.—MISCELLANEOUS NOTES AND OBSERVATIONS.

[Read 4th June, 1877.]

GEOLOGY.

The Coprolite Beds at Hinxworth.—My property in the parish of Hinxworth, the extreme northern boundary between Herts and Beds, is on the geological formation containing the now well-known Cambridgeshire coprolite bed, or, geologically speaking, the Cretaceous phosphatic nodules which are found in a thin seam of the Upper Greensand at the point of contact of the Chalk Marl with the Gault. In the years 1856–8 Mr. B. Denton carried out some drainage works for me in the parish of Hinxworth, over an area of 800 acres, the progress of which was fully reported by him in the 20th vol. of the 'Journal of the Royal Agricultural Society' (p. 273), where he thus described the geological character of the district:—"The estate lies at the bottom of the Chalk escarpment of the London Basin, and covers a portion of the lowest bed of the Chalk, the outcrop of the Greensand, and a portion of the Gault of the Greensand formation. In several parts a superficial deposit of drifted gravel and sand overlies the older beds. The Greensand separating the Chalk from the Gault is very thin, and, if collected in a distinct layer, would not exceed three inches in its thickest part." As I then myself occupied, and continued to occupy for some years later, 300 acres of the land lying upon the Gault and thoroughly drained, I necessarily became aware of the existence on my own property of the seam which contains the coprolite bed. The discovery by Liebig of dissolving bones in sulphuric acid for the purposes of manure had at that time given a commercial value to these phosphatic nodules, and they were eagerly sought for by the manufacturers of mineral phosphates for agricultural purposes.

The origin of these nodules appears still to be a *questio vexata.* An exhaustive paper "On the Relations of the Cambridge Gault and Greensand," by Mr. Jukes-Browne, was read in 1875 before the Geological Society, and appears in the 31st vol. of the Journal of the Society (p. 256), with a map which shows the course of the strata which contain the seam, between Tring and Cambridge, In this map the name of the parish of Hinxworth does not occur, but its position is on a projecting point of the Gault between Arlesey and Ashwell. This and other papers lately read before the Geological Society by Messrs. Jukes-Browne, Fisher, and Bonney, still leave open the question whether the phosphatic nodules "originated where they are now found, or have been derived from the underlying Gault." As regards the yield and money value of these nodules, some of these papers give the average yield as 140 tons per acre and 50s. per ton value—the land to be restored to its original level and condition by the contractor. The value of the seam, however, necessarily depends upon the depth below the surface, which at a certain depth, say 18 or 20 feet, fails to yield a profit to the digger. In Cambridgeshire, where the depth of the seam is inconsiderable, one hears of very large sums having been realised. In my own case the depth is so uncertain, and the nuisance of the coprolite diggers, an especially rough lot, so great, that I not long since declined an offer made for turning over some 10 acres during three years.

I am afraid that this hasty letter will not afford the Society either the amount or quality of information it deserves. At the time I occupied my farm at Hinxworth I felt probably more interest in carrying out the several agricultural operations, and, I trust, improvements, in which I was engaged, than in collecting materials which might assist the members of a Natural History Society in dealing with matters of a scientific nature.—*Robert Clutterbuck, London.*

BOTANY.

Fertilisation of Aucuba Japonica.—'The Times' of Feb. 22nd gave some extracts from an interesting lecture, delivered by Sir John Lubbock, M.P., at the Society of Arts, on "The Relations of Plants and Insects." Amongst other facts Sir John mentions the fertilisation of plants by insects, and produces several examples showing how plants are fertilised by winged insects. I have a remarkable instance of this in my garden at the present time. For many years I have had plants of the *Aucuba Japonica* in my garden, some of which are 8 feet high, but, not having a male plant among them, they never fruited. A friend gave me a male plant in the autumn of 1875, and last spring (1876) it flowered; the result being that all the fertile plants standing near are at the present time full of berries. This, however, would not surprise me so much as the fact that the plants in other parts of the garden, and separated by the house, are bearing a small quantity of fruit. This must have been occasioned by the agency of winged insects, the *Aucuba* being diœcious. I think it singular that the *Aucuba* should have been so long in the country (Loudon states since 1783) without the introduction of the male plant, which is not nearly so handsome, and wants the attractive blotch on the leaf—a sexual difference, I think, uncommon in vegetation. It is noticeable too, that the *Aucuba* requires 12 months to ripen its fruit, which I consider unusual in berry-fruiting plants.—*Rev. R. H. Webb, Essendon Rectory, Hatfield.*

ENTOMOLOGY.

Appearance of Colias Edusa. — The clouded yellow (*Colias Edusa*), a butterfly occasionally abundant both in the extreme south-east and extreme south-west of England, but never common in any other parts of the country, has been seen round this neighbourhood during the last few days in unusual numbers. It is occasionally taken both in Middlesex and Hertfordshire as a straggler, but only singly. Last Saturday my son saw one, a female, at Chalk Farm; on Sunday Mr. Fry saw one at Bushey, and I saw on the same day a male at Bushey also. On the same day my brother saw three together in a field at St. Albans, and on Monday I saw another on the railway bank at Bushey. The insect emerges from the chrysalis in August, and may be taken up to November if the weather keeps open; it then hybernates, and flies again in the summer. It is remarkable that it should appear now, and not have been noticed here last autumn. Its food-plant is clover, and it is usually to be found either in clover or lucerne fields.—*Arthur Cottam, Watford.*

ORNITHOLOGY.

Notes on the Owl.—We have at Watford the white owl and the brown or tawny owl. The white owl has built for more than 20 years in an old hollow elm tree at Mrs. Robins', The Elms, Watford. Last year most of the tree was blown down, and the gardener tells me he saw the owls come afterwards and look about, but not finding their old home, he thinks they have finally departed. They built in a barn at Wiggen Hall and also at Oxhey Lodge. The brown or tawny owl has built in a box placed in the fork of a tree on the lawn at Wiggen Hall. Four or five years ago Mr. King had one given to him, and it took up its abode in the box. A mate soon came, and they have bred there ever since. On the 25th of last May, he saw the old one and one young one in a larch tree on the lawn. Three young ones were hatched in the box, and they had been putting their heads out for some days. These brown owls ought to be prosecuted for breaking the Wild Birds Preservation Act, for they seem very destructive to birds. One, last week, tried to kill a skylark that was in a cage by the house. On hearing a great noise, the gardener's wife came out, and frightened the owl away. The same night he went to a blackbird's cage, tore out two strong wires and bent a third, and then took away the blackbird, which had been a favourite one for three years. The bird must have fought valiantly for his life, for the cage had a great many feathers in it. The nest of the long-tailed tit which I show you seems to have been injured by the owl, probably the hen was killed. Nine or ten other birds' nests have been found deserted, and Mr. King thinks it probable that the owl has destroyed the sitting bird. A young brown owl was caught in an apple tree last year in my garden. I kept it and another some months. I then gave them away because of the difficulty of getting food for them. A long-eared owl was shot in a turnip field near Royston, by Mr. Haylock, 40 years since, whilst he was partridge shooting.—*A. T. Brett, M.D., Watford House.*

INDEX.

Abbot's Langley, Tertiary outlier at, 127, 169.
Acherontia Atropos at Watford, 64.
Aldbury, visit to, xxi.
Aldenham, badger at, 237.
Alopecurus fulvus in Herts, 63.
Amwell Bury, height of, 146; storm at, 230.
Amwell End, height of, 147; well-section at, 170.
Anacharis Alsinastrum in the Colne, 173.
Anniversary Address, 1876, 113; 1877, 187.
Annual Meeting, 1876, report of, xxix; 1877, l.
Appearance of *Sphinx Convolvuli*, 108; of *Colias Edusa*, 239.
Archæo-geology, discoveries in, 190.
Aregma bulbosum figured, 233.
Ashbrook, height of, 149.
Ashley Green, source of Bourne near, in 1873, 137.
Ashlyns, Berkhampstead, rainfall at, in 1876, 227; badgers at, 237.
Ashridge Park, field meeting in, xxi; badgers in, 237.
Aspenden, rainfall at, in 1876, 227.
Aucuba Japonica, fertilisation of, 239.

Badger and otter in Herts, 236.
Bagshot beds, 103, 167.
Barkhausia taraxacifolia in Herts, 73.
Barnet, medicinal spring at, 109; height of, 144, 145; well-sections at, 170.
Barometer, instructions for reading, 211.
Barometric depression of 12th March, 1876, 220; of 4th December, 1876, 223.
Barrois, C., on the Chalk of England, 91.
Bayford, well-section at, 170.
Bayfordbury, rainfall at, in 1876, 227.
Beaufort's notation for weather observations, 216.
Bembridge series, 168.
Bedmont, Tertiary outlier at, 127, 169.

Bench Marks, Hertfordshire Ordnance, 141.
Bennet's End, London clay fossils found at, xlii; Tertiary outlier at, 169.
Berkhampstead, Chalk-rock at, 117; River Bourne near, 137; rainfall at, in 1876, 227.
Berkhampstead Common and Castle, visit to, xxii.
Bernard's Heath, brickfields at, xxxv.
Berry Wood, Aldenham, chalk pit in, xvi; conchology of, xvii.
Birds, list of, to be observed in connexion with phenological phenomena, 37; observation of, 52.
Birmingham to London, line of levelling, in Herts, 142.
Bishop's Stortford, Tertiary beds at, 101, 169; well-sections at, 171.
Boccius quoted, 185.
Botanical districts of Hertfordshire, 67.
Botanical work of the past season, 65.
Botany, notes on, 63, 108, 135, 173, 239.
Botany of Watford District, 21; of Hertfordshire, 63, 119; of West Suffolk, 108.
Botzen, earth pyramids near, xliii.
Boxmoor, field meeting at, xli; Chalk-rock at, 117.
Boulders near Buntingford, 172.
Bourne, the Hertfordshire, 137.
Bracklesham and Barton Beds, 167.
Bragbury End, height of, 148.
Bramble leaf brand, 233.
Brent botanical district, 67.
BRETT, Dr. A. T.: Mineral Spring at Watford, xx, 63; Notes on the Cuckoo, xl, 136; Is the *Anacharis Alsinastrum* dying out in the River Colne at Watford? xliv, 173; Notes and Queries on the River Colne, Watford, l, 175; Fish-hatching and Fish-culture in Hertfordshire, l, 179; On microscopic fungi, lvii; Notes on the Otter and Badger in Hertfordshire, lx, 236; Notes on the Owl, lx, 240; Notes on the Size and Growth of Trees at Watford, lx.

Brick earths, investigation of, 119.
Bricket Wood. field meetings in, xix, xxxviii; boulder clay of, 106.
British sedimentary rocks, relative thickness of, 3.
Broadfield, petrifying spring at, 111.
Broadwater, height of, 148.
Bromus arvensis in Herts, 73.
Broxbourne, height of, 146; well-section at, 171.
Broxbourne to Hoddesdon, line of levelling, 146.
Buckland, F., quoted, 179, 181.
Buntingford, boulders near, 172; rainfall at, in 1876, 227.
Bushey, Tertiary beds at, xviii, 12, 94, 97, 100, 105, 125, 169; London Clay fossils found at, 170; well-sections at, 171; *Colias Edusa* at, 239.
Bushey Grove, swallow-holes at, 128.
Bushey Station, rainfall at, in 1876, 227.

Cam botanical district, 67.
Cambridge, calendar of periodical natural phenomena at, 39.
Campanula latifolia, re-discovery of, in Herts, xliv, 187.
Calendar of periodical natural phenomena recommended for observation, 39.
Carduus tenuiflorus in Herts, 74.
Cassiobury House, visit to, lxiii; rainfall at, in 1875, 112; in 1876, 227; meteorological observations taken at, 132.
Cassiobury Park, field meeting in, lxiii; beeches of, 8; badgers in, 237.
Caterham valley, river Bourne in, 138, 140.
Chalk formation, 7; fossils of, 13.
Chalk marl near Hitchin, lxii.
Chalk, origin of, 8, 115.
Chalk-pit in Berry Wood, xvi; near Bushey Station, xviii; in Hatfield Park, xxxviii; on Rough Down, Boxmoor, xli; at Hitchin, lxi.
Chalk-rock, xli, 13; investigation of, 117.
Challenger Expedition, 9, 115.
Chalybeate spring, supposed, at Watford, 109.
CHATER, E. M.: On Microscopic Fungi, lvii, 231.
Chauncy quoted, 135, 175, 184.
Cheddington, coprolite pits near, lix.
Cheshunt, height of, 145, 146; well-sections at, 171.
Chipping Barnet, mineral spring at, 111; height of, 144, 145.
Chloritic marl near Hitchin, lxii.

Chœrocampa Nerii at Hemel Hempstead, 174.
Chorley Wood, Tertiary beds at, 97; well-section at, 171.
Clays, origin of, 10, 116.
Clouds, instructions for observing, 215.
CLUTTERBUCK, Rev. J. C.: The Geology and Water-supply of the Neighbourhood of Watford, xxxvi, 125.
CLUTTERBUCK, R.: The Coprolite Beds at Hinxworth, lix, 238.
Coffleys, medicinal spring at, 110.
Colias Edusa, appearance of, 239.
Colne, *Anacharis Alsinastrum* in, 173; notes and queries on, 175; origin of the word, l, 175.
Colne botanical district, 67.
Colne Valley Waterworks, visit to, xviii; effects of pumping at, 130; section at, 135.
Colney Butts gravel pits, xix.
Conchology of Berry Wood, xvii.
Conochilus volvox, lvii, lviii.
Coprolite beds, 7; at Hinxworth, 238.
Cossus ligniperda, destruction of oak tree by, 64, 135.
COTTAM, A.: Botanical Geography of Hertfordshire, xv; Notes on the Flora of the Watford District, xv, 14; Notes on the Observation of Insects in connexion with Investigations on Seasonal Phenomena, xvii, 50; Appearance of *Sphinx Convolvuli*, xxiii, 108; Microscopical Mounting, xxxiv; Appearance of *Colias Edusa*, lx, 239.
Council elected 11th February, 1875, xi; 10th February, 1876, xxx; 9th February, 1877, li.
Cowroast, Tring, rainfall at, in 1876, 227.
Cretaceous rocks of England, 1; extension of, in England, 5.
CROFT, Lieut. R. B.: Advantage of observing Phenological Phenomena, xxxix; The Ermine Street traced by its Vegetation, xl, 135; New Field-Naturalist's Microscope, xl; Notes on a Remarkable Storm in Herts, April 4th, 1877, lvi, 230.
Cuckoo, notes on, 136.
Cyclostoma elegans in North Herts, 172.

Darwin, C., on scarcity of holly-berries, 189; experiments on the fertilisation of plants, 201.
Death's head moth at Watford, 64.
Dentaria bulbifera at Red Heath, xviii.
De Ranee, C. E., quoted, 106.
Destruction of oak tree by larvæ of goat-moth, 64.

Development of fish, 181.
Dianthus armeria near Watford, xxiv.
Donations to the library in 1875, xxv; in 1876, xlv.
Drift, investigation of, 118.
Dunstable, height of, 142; rainfall at, in 1876, 227.
Dunstable to St. Albans, line of levelling, 142.

Earth pyramids near Botzen in the Tyrol, xliii.
Elstree, well-section at, 171.
Elstree reservoir, field meeting at, xlii; swallow-holes at, 127.
England, Cretaceous rocks of, 1; Eocenes of, 161.
Entomology, notes on, 64, 108, 135; 174, 239.
Eocenes of England, 90, 161; of Herts, 169.
Ermine Street traced by its vegetation, 135.
ESSEX, Earl of: Meteorological observations taken at Cassiobury House from May to December, 1875, xxix, 132; fish-hatching by, 182.
EVANS, Dr. J.: Inaugural Address delivered 11th February, 1875, xiii; Anniversary Address delivered 10th February, 1876, xxx, 113; On water supply, xxxvii; The Hertfordshire Bourne, xxxix, 137; On ascertaining flow of water in rivers, xl; On the Earth Pyramids near Botzen in the Tyrol, xliii; On the origin of the word Colne, 1; Anniversary Address delivered 9th February, 1877, li, 187.

Fairfield, Hitchin, visit to, lxi.
Ferns, our local, a few words about, 83.
Fertilisation of plants, 201; of *Aucuba Japonica*, 239.
Field Meetings, reports of, 1875, May 1, Berry Wood, xv; May 29, Bushey, xviii; June 9, Bricket Wood and Munden, xix; June 19, Aldbury, Ashridge, and Berkhampstead, xxi; 1876, April 29, St. Albans, xxxv; May 13, Hatfield, xxxvii; June 3, Bricket Wood, xxxviii; June 17, Boxmoor, xli; July 1, Elstree, xlii; 1877, May 5, Stanmore, lvii; May 26, Pinner, lviii; June 16, Hitchin, lxi; June 30, Cassiobury, lxiii.
Field-naturalist's microscope, description of a new, xl.
Fieldes Weir, Hoddesdon, rainfall at, in 1876, 227.

Fish-hatching and fish-culture in Herts, 179.
Flint, origin of, 116.
Flora of Watford district, 14; of Hertfordshire, 17.
Foraminifera of the Chalk, 9; of the Atlantic ooze, 9.
FORDHAM, H. G.: Supposed recent extinction of *Cyclostoma elegans* in North Herts, xliv, 172.
Friars Wash, height of, 142.
FRY, C. E.: Capture of *Chærocampa Nerii* at Hemel Hempstead, xliv, 174.
Fungi, microscopic, lvii, 231.

Galium erectum in Herts, 70.
Gault clay, 7; near Hitchin, lxii.
Geological Ordnance Survey Map of Hertfordshire purchased, xxv.
Geology, notes on, 63, 135, 172, 238.
Geology of Hertfordshire, 78; of the neighbourhood of Watford, 89.
Geology and water supply of Watford, 125.
Goodlake, Col., fish-hatching by, 182.
Goat moth, destruction of oak tree by larvæ of, 64, 135.
Gorhambury, St. Albans, rainfall at, in 1876, 227.
Grallatores, or wading birds, 57.
Great Offley, height of, 150, 151.
Greensand, Lower, 6; Upper, 7; origin of, 115; coprolite beds in, 238.
Greenwich, Meteorology of, 1876-77, compared with that of Watford, 219.
GREG, R. P.: Boulders in the Neighbourhood of Buntingford, xliii, 172.
Grindon, Leo, botanical discourses of, xlii.
Gryme's Dyke, Pinner, lviii.

Hadham, well-section at, 171.
Hadham Hall, badgers at, 237.
Harefield Park, well-section at, 171.
HARFORD, J. U.: The Polarisation of Light, xxxv, xliii, 152.
Harpenden, rainfall at, in 1876, 227.
Harratt's End, source of Bourne near, 137.
HARRISON, E.: Meteorological Observations taken at Oaklands, Watford, 1871-75, xxxix.
HARTING, J. E.: On the Pleasures and Advantages to be derived from a Study of Natural History, and more particularly from the Observation of Birds, xvii, 52.
Harwood's Farm, Watford, rainfall at, in 1875, 112; in 1876, 227.
Hatfield Park, field meeting in, xxxvii; Tertiary beds in, 97, 98, 169.

Headon series, 168.
Heat of 9th to 17th August, 1876, 222.
HEATHER, T.: On the Construction, Adjustment, and Use of Meteorological Instruments, xxix.
Hedges Farm, visit to, xxxvi.
Hemel Hempstead, rainfall at, in 1875, 63, 112; in 1876, 227; gravels of, 106; *Chœrocampa Nerii* at, 174.
HENSLOW, Rev. G.: The Fertilisation of Plants, lvi, 201.
Hertford, Tertiary beds near, 97, 99; height of, 148; well-section at, 171; rainfall at, in 1876, 227.
Hertford to Stevenage, line of levelling, 148.
Hertfordshire, flora of, 17; botany of, 63; botanical districts of, 67; plants new to, 76, 77; list of works on the geology of, 78; medicinal waters in, 109; Eocenes of, 169; well-sections in, 170; fish-hatching and fish-culture in, 179; pisciculture in, 185; rainfall in, in 1876, 225; remarkable storm in, 230; otter and badger in, 236.
Hertfordshire plum-pudding stone, 119; ordnance bench marks, 141.
Hibbert, Mrs., fish-hatching by, 182.
HIND, Rev. W. M.: Notes on the Plants on which the Meteorological Society invites observations as to their time of flowering, xvii, 43; Botany of West Suffolk, xxiv, 108.
High Down, Hitchin, visit to, lxii.
Highley Hill Tumulus, Ashwell, *Cyclostoma elegans* from, 173.
Hinxworth, coprolite beds at, 238.
Hitchin, field-meeting at, lxi; *Sphinx Convolvuli* at, 108; height of, 149, 150; well-section at, 171; snowstorm at, in April, 1876, 221; rainfall at, in 1876, 227.
Hitchin to Luton, line of levelling, 149.
Hoddesdon, height of, 146; well-section at, 171; rainfall at, in 1876, 227.
Hoddesdon to Ware, line of levelling, 146.
Holly Bank, Watford, visit to, xvii; meteorological observations taken at, 217; rainfall at, in 1876, 227.
Holly-berries, scarcity of, 189.
HOOD, Dr. P.: Notes on Pisciculture in Hertfordshire, l, 185.
HOPKINSON, J.: On the Observation of Periodical Natural Phenomena, xvii, 33; The Rainfall in 1875, xxiii, xxix, 63, 112; The Hertfordshire Ordnance Bench Marks, from the 'Abstracts of Levelling' of the

Ordnance Survey, xliii, 141; Meteorological Observations taken at Holly Bank, Watford, during the year ending 28th February, 1877, lvi, 217; Report on the Rainfall in Hertfordshire in 1876, lvi, 225.
Humbert, C. F., on scarcity of fish in the Colne, l.

Icknield Way, near Hitchin, lxii.
Impatiens fulva in Herts, xxiii, xxiv, 71.
Inaugural Meeting, 1875, report of, x.
Insects, list of, to be observed in connexion with phenological phenomena, 37; observation of, 50.
Insessores, or perching birds, 56.
Instructions for taking meteorological observations, 211.
Ivel botanical district, 67.

JAMES, J. H.: Destruction of an Oak Tree by the Larvæ of the Goat Moth, xxi, 64; The Death's Head Moth at Watford, xxi, 64; Note on the Larvæ of the Goat Moth, xl, 135.

Kensworth, Dunstable, rainfall at, in 1876, 227.
King, J., fish-hatching by, 180.

Langleybury, Watford, badgers at, 237.
Laws of the Society, xi, xxix.
Lea botanical district, 67.
Leighton sands, examination of, 115.
Le Notre, limes in Cassiobury Park planted by, lxiv.
Lepidium draba and *L. ruderale* in Herts, 73.
Letchmore Heath, swallow-hole at, 127.
Leverstock Green, Tertiary outlier at, 169.
Library, donations to, in 1875, xxv; in 1876, xlv.
Light, polarisation of, 152.
Lilley, height of, 151.
Lilley Hoo, Hitchin, geology of, lxii.
List of Works on Geology of Hertfordshire, 78.
LITTLEBOY, J. E.: A Few Words about our Local Ferns, xxiv, 83; Note on the Discovery of *Impatiens fulva* near Watford, xxiv; on coprolite beds, lix.
Little Munden, storm at, 230.
Little Wymondley, height of, 149.
LOBLEY, J. L.: The Cretaceous Rocks of England, xiii, 1; The Eocenes of England and their Extension in Hertfordshire, xlv, 161; on the geology of Pinner, lviii.

London Basin, section across, 11; physical structure of, 89.
London Clay, 100, 165.
London Colney, height of, 144, 145.
London to Dunstable, line of levelling in Herts, 145.
Longman, C., fish-hatching by, 182.
Lower Eocenes, 162.

Malacology, notes on, 172.
Maple blight, 234.
Marlborough, calendar of periodical natural phenomena at, 39.
Market Street, height of, 142.
MARRIOTT, W.: Instructions for taking Meteorological Observations, lvi, 211.
Medicinal waters in Herts, 109.
Meeting to found the Society, 1875, report of, ix.
Mentha citrata in Herts, 74.
Meteorological Observations, instructions for taking, 211.
Meteorological Observations taken at Cassiobury House, 132; at Holly Bank, Watford, 217.
Micklefield, Tertiary outlier at, 169.
Microscope, description of a new field-naturalist's, xl.
Microscopic fungi, 231.
Microscopic investigation, 122.
Middle Eocenes, 166.
Mimms, South, height of, 144.
Mineral spring at Watford, supposed, 63, 109.
Miscellaneous Notes and Observations, 63, 108, 135, 172, 238.
Molluscs, cultivation of, 183.
Moneybury Hill, Ashridge, barrow on, xxi.
Moor Park, Rickmansworth, rainfall at, in 1876, 227.
MORRIS, Prof. J.: The Physical Structure of the London Basin considered in its relation to the Geology of the Neighbourhood of Watford, xxiii, 89; remarks at field-meetings on the geology of Watford, xvi, xviii.
Much Hadham, rainfall at, in 1876, 227.
Munden Park, field meeting in, xix; badger and otter in, 236, 237.
Myosotis sylvatica in Herts, 63, 70.

Nash Mills, conversazione at, xxxii; visit to, xlii; rainfall at, in 1875, 63, 112; in 1876, 227.
Natatores, or swimming birds, 57.
Natural History, study of, 52.
Neocomian, or Lower Greensand, 6; near Hitchin, lxii.
Nether Wyld Farm, visit to, xxxix.

New England, height of, 150
Northaw, medicinal spring at, 110; Chalk inlier at, 169.
Notes and Observations, Miscellaneous, 63, 108, 135, 172, 238.

Oaklands, Watford, meteorological observations taken at, xxxix; rainfall at, in 1875, 112; in 1876, 227.
Observation of periodical natural phenomena, 33; of time of flowering of plants, 43.
Observation of insects, 50; of birds, 52.
Observations and Notes, Miscellaneous, 63, 108, 135, 172, 238.
Œnothera biennis near Watford, xxiv.
Oilley, Great, height of, 150, 151.
Oldhaven and Blackheath beds, 100, 164.
Orchids found near Hitchin, lxii.
Ordinary Meetings, 1875, reports of, xiii-xxv; 1876, xxix-xlv; 1877, l-lxi.
Ordnance Bench Marks, Hertfordshire, 141.
Ornithology, notes on, 136, 240.
Osborne or St. Helen's Series, 168.
Otter and badger in Herts, 236.
Otterspool, Aldenham, springs at, xvi, xix, 127; otter at, 236.
Our local ferns, a few words about, 83.
Owl, notes on, 240.
Oxhey Woods, visit to, lix.

Palæolithic age, 192.
Palæolithic implements found near Hitchin, lxi.
Papers read in 1875, list of, xxxi; in 1876, lii.
Pegsden Barns, Hitchin, combe at, lxii.
Pepper Hill, height of, 146.
Percolation of rain through the soil, investigation of, 122.
Periodical natural phenomena, observation of, 33.
Physical structure of the London Basin, 89.
Pinner, field-meeting at, lviii.
Pinner Hill, visit to, lviii.
Pisciculture in Herts, notes on, 185.
Plantago Timbali in Herts, 73.
Plants, list of, to be observed, 36; new to Watford, 173; fertilisation of, 201.
Plants of which the time of flowering should be observed, 43.
Plum-pudding stone, Hertfordshire, 119.
Polarisation of light, 152.
Poles Park, storm at, 230.
Potamogeton mucronatus in Herts, 71.
Potentilla argentea near Watford, xxiv.

Poterium muricatum in Herts, 63, 72.
Prestwich, Prof., quoted, 92, 93, 97, 100.
PRYOR, R. A.: Notes on a proposed re-issue of the Flora of Hertfordshire, with supplementary remarks on the Botany of the Watford District, xv, 17; Botany of Hertfordshire, xx, 63; On the Botanical Work of the Past Season, xxiv, 65; Note on the occurrence of *Impatiens fulva* in Herts, xxv; On the supposed Chalybeate Spring at Watford, and on other Medicinal Waters in Herts, xxix, 109; Plants new to the neighbourhood of Watford, xliv, 173; Recent blossoming of Spring Flowers, xliv, 174; Notes on some Hertfordshire Plants, lvii.
Puccinia graminis figured, 232.
Putteridge Bury, height of, 151.

Radlett, plum-pudding stone at, 103, 119.
Rainfall at Watford and Hemel Hempstead, 63; in Herts in 1875, 112; in 1876, 225; rules for observing, 229.
Rain-gauge, instructions for reading, 215.
Raptores, or birds of prey, 56.
Rasores, or scrapers, 56.
Redbourn, height of, 143.
Remarkable storm in Herts, 230.
Report of the Council for 1875, xxx; for 1876, li.
Rickmansworth, Tertiary beds at, 97, 169; rainfall at, in 1876, 227.
Roaring Meg, lxii.
Rothamsted, rainfall at, in 1876, 227.
Rough Down chalk-pit, xli.
Royston, rainfall at, in 1876, 227.
Rubi, fruticose, in Herts, 24.

St. Albans, field meeting at, xxxv; height of, 143; Tertiary outlier at, 169; rainfall at, in 1876, 227; botanical discoveries at, xliv, 187; *Colias Edusa* at, 240.
Salmon quoted, xxi, xxii.
Sarratt, Tertiary outlier at, 169.
Sedimentary rocks, British, relative thickness of, 3.
Shenley, Tertiary beds at, 169.
Six Hills, height of, 149.
Snowstorms of March and April, 1876, 220.
Societies, publications of, received in exchange, xlviii.
South Mimms, height of, 144.
Special Meeting, 1876, report of, xxix.
Sphinx Convolvuli, appearance of, 108.

Spring flowers, recent blossoming of, 174.
Standbridge, coprolite beds at, lix.
Standon, boulder at, 172.
Stanmore Common, field meetings on, xlii, lvii; gravels of, 104; Tertiary beds at, 125.
Stevenage, height of, 149; rainfall at, in 1876, 227.
Stevenage to Hitchin, line of levelling, 149.
Storm, remarkable, in Herts, 230.
Suffolk, West, botany of, 108.
Symons, J. G., on water supply, xxxvi.

Tertiary Basin, London, section across, 11.
Thame botanical district, 67.
Thanet sands, 92, 162.
Thermometers, instructions for reading, 213.
Tolpits, Watford, otter at, 236.
Tottenham, height of, 145.
Tottenham to Broxbourne, line of levelling, 145.
Totternhoe stone, xxii, 13.
Transactions, publication of, lii.
Trees near Watford, size and growth of, lx.
Tring, rainfall at, in 1876, 227.
Turner's Hill, height of, 145.
Turnford, height of, 146.

Uncinula bicornis figured, 234.
Upper Eocenes, 168.

VERINI, W.: Section of the strata passed through in boring at the Colne Valley Waterworks, xl, 135.
Volvox globator, xlii.

Waltham Cross, height of, 145; well-section at, 171.
Ware, height of, 147; rainfall at, in 1876, 227; storm at, 230.
Ware to Hertford, line of levelling, 147.
WARNE, H. A.: Exchange of North American for British Plants, xiv.
Water supply of Watford, 125.
Waterford, height of, 148.
Watford, chalk of, 7, 10, 12; mineral spring at, 63, 109; rainfall in, 1875, 63, 112; in 1876, 227; death's head moth at, 64; geology of the neighbourhood of, 89; *Sphinx Convolvuli* at, 108; supposed chalybeate spring at, 109; geology and water supply of, 125; meteorological observations taken at, xxxix, 132, 217;

well-section at, 171 ; plants new to, 173 ; otter at, 236 ; notes on the size and growth of trees at, lx.

Watford district, flora of, 14 ; botany of, 17 ; list of plants of, to be investigated, 22.

Watford Heath, Tertiary beds at, xviii, 95, 97, 169.

Watson, H. C., on distribution of *Impatiens fulva*, xxiv.

Watton, chalybeate spring at, 109 ; height of, 148.

Wealden formation, 4.

WEBB, Rev. R. H.: Fertilisation of *Aucuba Japonica*, lx, 239.

Wellhead, height of, 150.

Welwyn, chalybeate spring at, 110 ; rainfall at, in 1876, 227.

Westmill, boulders at, 172.

Wheat mildew, 232.

WHITAKER, W.: List of Works on the Geology of Hertfordshire, xxv, 78.

Whitaker, W., quoted, 93, 97-101, 103, 106.

White Hill, source of Bourne near, 137.

Wiggenhall, Watford, cuckoo in swallow's nest at, lx, 136 ; owls at, 240.

Wind, instructions for observing, and scale of velocity of, 215.

Woodcock Hill, Tertiary beds at, 97.

Woodhall, height of, 148.

Woolwich and Reading series, 96, 164.

Wormley, height of, 146 ; well-section at, 171.

Wormley End, well-section at, 171.

Works on Geology of Hertfordshire, list of, 78.

Wymondley, Little, height of, 149.

Zoology of Herts, investigation of, 120.

ERRATA.

Page lix, lines 5 and 10 from bottom, *for* " Chittenden " *read* " Cheddington."

„ 19, line 26, *for* "botryodes " *read* " botryoides."

„ 20, lines 3, 4, and 27, *for* " cœrulea " *read* " cœrulea."

„ 22, line 13 from bottom, for " *R. Homœophllyus*" read " *R. Homœophyllus*."

„ 63, in table, *for* " Cassiobury" *read* " Harwood's Farm, Cassiobury."

LIST OF SOCIETIES, &c., TO WHICH THE TRANSACTIONS ARE PRESENTED.

Bath Natural History and Antiquarian Field Club.
Bedfordshire Natural History Society and Field Club.
Belfast Natural History Society.
———— Naturalists' Field Club.
Birmingham Natural History and Microscopical Society.
————. Editors of the ' Midland Naturalist.'
Boston (U.S.A.) Society of Natural History.
Brighton and Sussex Natural History Society.
Bristol Naturalists' Society.
Cambridge Public Library.
Clifton College Scientific Society.
Croydon Microscopical Club.
Dublin. Library of Trinity College.
————. Royal Geological Society of Ireland.
Eastbourne Natural History Society.
Edinburgh Botanical Society.
———— Geological Society.
————. Library of the Faculty of Advocates.
————. Royal Physical Society.
Glasgow, Geological Society of.
———— Natural History Society.
———— Philosophical Society.
Hertford Public Library.
High Wycombe Natural History Society.
Huddersfield. Editors of the ' Naturalist.'
Liverpool Geological Society.
————, Literary and Philosophical Society of.
London. British Museum.
————. Entomological Society.
————. Geological Society.
————. Geologists' Association.
————. Linnean Society.
————. Meteorological Society.
————. Quekett Microscopical Club.
————. Royal Society.
————. Royal Microscopical Society.
————. Scientific Club.
————, West, Scientific Association and Field Club.
————. Editor of ' Nature.'
————. Editor of ' Science Gossip.'
Manchester Field-Naturalists' and Archæologists' Society.
———— Geological Society.
———— Literary and Philosophical Society.
Marlborough College Natural History Society.
New York (U.S.A.) State Library.
Norfolk and Norwich Naturalists' Society.
Oxford. Bodleian Library.
Rugby School Natural History Society.
Somersetshire Archæological and Natural History Society.
Washington (U.S.A.). Geological Survey of the Territories.
————. Smithsonian Institution.
Watford Public Library (2 copies).
Wiltshire Archæological and Natural History Society.
Winchester and Hampshire Scientific and Literary Society.

APPENDIX.

LIST OF MEMBERS

AND

CATALOGUE OF THE LIBRARY.

CORRECTED TO JULY, 1878.

HONORARY MEMBERS.

Year elected.

1875   Allman, George James, M.D., F.R.S., F.R.S.E., Pres.
       L.S., M.R.I.A., *Emeritus Professor of Natural History
       in the University of Edinburgh*, Sunny Hill, Park-
       stone, Dorset.

1877   Darwin, Charles, M.A., LL.D., F.R.S., F.R.S.E., F.L.S.,
       F.G.S., Hon. Memb. R.H.S., and R. Med. Chir. Soc.,
       etc., Down, Beckenham, Kent.

1875   Glaisher, James, F.R.S., F.R.A.S., F.M.S., *Superintendent
       of the Magnetic and Meteorological Department, Royal
       Observatory, Greenwich*, 1, Dartmouth Park, Black-
       heath.

1876   Hayden, Prof. Ferdinand Vandeveer, A.M., M.D., *United
       States Geologist in Charge*, Washington, U.S.A.

1877   Henslow, Rev. George, M.A., F.L.S., 6, Titchfield Terrace,
       Regent's Park, London, N.W.

1875   Hooker, Sir Joseph Dalton, C.B., K.C.S.I., M.D., D.C.L.,
       LL.D., Pres. R.S., F.L.S., F.G.S., *Director of the
       Royal Gardens*, Kew.

—   Lubbock, Sir John, Bart., M.P., D.C.L., LL.D., F.R.S.,
       F.L.S., F.G.S., High Elms, Farnborough, Kent;
       and 15, Lombard Street, London, E.C.

—   Morris, John, F.G.S., *Emeritus Professor of Geology and
       Mineralogy, University College, London*, 15, Upper
       Gloucester Place, Dorset Square, London, N.W.

1876   Symons, George James, F.R.S., Sec. M.S., 62, Camden
       Square, London, N.W.

—   Whitaker, William, B.A., F.G.S., *Geological Survey of
       England*, Museum, Jermyn Street, London, S.W.

ORDINARY MEMBERS.

An asterisk before a name indicates a Life Member.

Year elected.

1875 Ambler, Edward H., F.R.C.S., Hemel Hempstead.
1876 Arnold, Mrs., Redbourne Bury, St. Albans.
1877 *Attfield, John, Ph.D., F.C.S., *Professor of Practical Chemistry to the Pharmaceutical Society of Great Britain*, Ashlands, Watford; and 17, Bloomsbury Square, London, W.C.
1875 Austin, Stephen, Bayley Lodge, Hertford.

— Barber, William, M.A., Barrow Point, Pinner.
— Barber, Mrs., Barrow Point, Pinner.
1878 Barraud, Allan T., St. John's Villas, Watford.
1875 Benskin, John P., High Street, Watford.
1877 Bernard, G. P., Marlowes, Hemel Hempstead.
1875 Booth, Charles A., Westfield, Watford.
— *Brett, Alfred T., M.D., PRESIDENT, Watford House.
1877 Brightwen, Mrs. George, The Grove, Great Stanmore.

— Clarendon, Right Hon. the Earl of, The Grove, Watford.
1875 Capel, Hon. Arthur, Cassiobury Park, Watford.
— *Carew, R. Russell, F.C.S., F.R.G.S., M.R.I., Carpenders Hall, Watford.
— *Carew, Mrs., Carpenders Hall, Watford.
1876 *Carew, Robert Marcus, Carpenders Hall, Watford.
— *Carnegie, David, Eastbury, Watford; and 11, Hill Street, Berkeley Square, London, W.
1875 Cazalet, Miss Florence, St. Albans Road, Watford.
— Chater, E. M., High Street, Watford.
— Chater, Jonathan, High Street, Watford.
— Chippindale, George, 21, Upper Baker Street, London, W.
1877 Clayton, Oscar, Grove Cottage, Heathbourne, Bushey Heath.
1876 Clutterbuck, Robert, F.G.S., F.R.G.S., 8, Great Cumberland Place, Hyde Park, London, W.
1878 Clutterbuck, Thomas Meadows, Stanmore.
1875 Copeland, Alfred James, Dell Field, Watford.
— Copeland, Mrs. A. J., Dell Field, Watford.
— Cottam, Arthur, F.R.A.S., Eldercroft, Watford.

1876   *Croft, Lieut. Richard Benyon, R.N., F.L.S., F.R.M.S.,
        Fanhams Hall, Ware.
1878   *Croft, Mrs., Fanhams Hall, Ware.
1877   Cussans, John Edwin, 179, Junction Road, Upper Hollo-
        way, London, N.

1875   Dawson, John E., F.R.G.S., F.R.M.S., Oak Lodge,
        Watford.
—   Diggle, Miss, Napoleon Villa, Essex Road, Watford.
—   Dove, John R. B., M.B.(Lond.), Chesnut Cottage, Pinner.
—   Duncan, Major F., Royal Artillery, M.A., D.C.L., LL.D.,
        F.G.S., F.R.G.S., 29, The Common, Woolwich.
1876   Durham, Charles, Aldenham Abbey.

1875   Ebury, Right Hon. the Lord, F.R.G.S., F.M.S., Moor
        Park, Rickmansworth.
—   Essex, Right Hon. the Earl of, Cassiobury Park, Watford.
—   Eley, William Thomas, Oxhey Grange, Watford.
1878   Elsden, James Vincent, B.Sc., F.C.S., The North Crescent,
        Hertford.
1875   Etheridge, Robert, F.R.S., F.R.S.E., F.G.S., *Palæontolo-
        gist to H.M. Geological Survey*, Geological Museum,
        Jermyn Street, London, S.W.
1878   Ewing, Rev. John Aiken, M.A., Westmill, Buntingford.
1875   *Evans, John, D.C.L., LL.D., F.R.S., F.S.A., F.L.S.,
        F.G.S., F.M.S., etc., Nash Mills, Hemel Hempstead.
—   *Evans, Mrs. John, Nash Mills, Hemel Hempstead.
—   Evans, H. Sugden, F.R.M.S., F.C.S., Barham Lodge,
        Elstree.
—   Evans, Miss, Barham Lodge, Elstree.
—   Evans, Miss Beatrice, Barham Lodge, Elstree.

—   Fairman, John B., Station Road, Watford.
—   Falconer, Rev. W., M.A., F.R.A.S., The Rectory, Bushey.
—   Fawcett, W. M., Mardale House, Watford.
—   Fordham, H. George, F.G.S., Odsey Grange, Royston.
—   Fry, Clarence E., The Little Elms, Watford.

1877   Gaubert, Miss L. A., Chalk Hill, Bushey.
1875   Gee, Rev. Canon, D.D., The Vicarage, Windsor.
—   Gibbs, Surgeon-Major J. G., Braziers, Chipperfield, Rick-
        mansworth.
—   Gisby, George Henry, Widbury Hill, Ware.
1876   Goadby, Rev. F. W., M.A., St. Albans Road, Watford.
1875   Green, George, Field House, Watford.
—   Green, Walter J., High Street, Watford.
—   Green, Mrs. W. J., High Street, Watford.
—   Greg, Robert Philips, F.G.S., F.R.A.S., Coles Park,
        Buntingford.
—   Griffits, Mrs., Queen's Road, Watford.

1875 Groome, John Edward, King's Langley.
— Grosvenor, Hon. Norman, Moor Park, Rickmansworth.

— *Halsey, Thomas F., M.P., Gaddesden Place, Hemel Hempstead.
— Harford, James U., Upper Nascot, Watford.
— Harrison, Edward, Upper Nascot, Watford.
— Harting, James Edmund, F.L.S., F.Z.S., Ladymead, Harting, Petersfield.
— Healey, Miss Laura, Lady's Close, Watford.
— Heather, Thomas, Queen's Road, Watford.
— Heaton, Mrs., Verulam House, Watford.
— Heaton, Clement, Verulam House, Watford.
— Henson, Charles, Rutland Lodge, Watford.
— Hibbert, A. H. Holland, Munden House, Aldenham.
1878 Hill, Mrs. Joseph, Frogmore House, Watford.
1876 Hobson, William Henry, M.D., Berkhampstead.
1875 Holland, Stephen Taprell, Otterspool, Aldenham.
— Hollingsworth, C. F., Hyde Lodge, Watford.
— Hood, Peter, M.D., Upton House, Watford.
— Hopkinson, James, Holly Bank, Watford.
— Hopkinson, Mrs. James, Holly Bank, Watford.
— *Hopkinson, John, F.L.S., F.G.S., F.R.M.S., F.M.S., Hon. Sec., Wansford House, Watford.
— *Hopkinson, Mrs. John, Wansford House, Watford.
— Humbert, Charles F., F.G.S., Treasurer, Little Nascot, Watford.
— Humbert, Mrs., Little Nascot, Watford.
1877 Humbert, Sydney, Little Nascot, Watford.

1875 Iles, F. H. Wilson, M.D., High Street, Watford.

— James, J. Henry, Kingswood, Watford.
— James, Rev. R. Lee, LL.B., The Vicarage, Watford.
— Jeffreys, J. Gwyn, LL.D., F.R.S., F.L.S., F.G.S., F.Z.S., F.R.G.S., Ware Priory; and 33, Grosvenor Street, London, W.
1878 Johnson, Miss, Langley Hill, King's Langley.

1876 King, Jonathan, Wiggenhall, Watford.

— *Lambert, George, F.S.A., Coventry Street, Haymarket, London, W.
— Laurie, Milton, 145, Gloucester Road, Regent's Park, London, N.W.
1875 Lavin, M. Drury, M.D., Bushey.
— Littleboy, John E., Hunton Bridge, Watford.
1876 Lemon, Oliver, Langley Hill House, East Langley.
1875 Lobley, J. Logan, F.G.S., F.R.G.S., 59, Clarendon Road, London, W.

1875   Loyd, William Jones, Langleybury, Watford.
—   Loyd, Mrs., Langleybury, Watford.
1876   *Lucas, Francis, Hitchin.
—   *Lucas, William, The Firs, Hitchin.

—   Marfitt, Miss, Aldenham Abbey.
1877   Marnham, Henry, Beech Lodge, Watford.
1876   Marnham, John, The Hollies, Boxmoor.
1877   Marnham, Francis John, The Hollies, Boxmoor.
1875   *Marshall, Frank E., M.A., Harrow.
1876   McFarlane, Robert, Kildare, Rickmansworth.
—   McFarlane, W. McMurray, Loudwater, Rickmansworth.
1875   McGill, H. J., Aldenham.
—   Moggridge, Matthew, F.G.S., 8, Bina Gardens, South
         Kensington, London, S.W.

—   Noakes, Simpson, Bushey Heath.
1876   Nunn, Charles W., Hertford.

1875   Perkins, Rev. C. M., M.A., Abbey Gateway, St. Albans.
—   Piffard, Bernard. Hill House, Hemel Hempstead.
—   Piffard, Mrs., Hill House, Hemel Hempstead.
1876   *Pollard, Joseph, High Down, Hitchin.
1875   Pryor, Reginald A., B.A., F.L.S., Baldock.
—   Pryor, Robert, High Elms, Watford.
1877   Pugh, Miss S., High Street, Watford.

—   *Ransom, William, Fairfield, Hitchin.
1875   Ransom, Mrs., Essex Road, Watford.
—   Richards, W. F., Commercial Travellers' Schools, Pinner.
—   Rooper, George, F.Z.S., Nascot House, Watford; and
         20, Hyde Park Square, London, W.
—   Roper, Freeman C. S., F.L.S., F.G.S., F.R.M.S.,
         Palgrave House, Eastbourne.
—   Rudyard, Alfred T., M.D., St. Albans Road, Watford.

1876   Saunders, Charles Edward, M.D., 21, Lower Seymour
         Street, London, W.
1877   Saunders, H. Demain, Brickendon Grange, Hertford.
1875   Scholz, Miss, Chalk Hill, Bushey.
—   Sedgwick, Alfred O., North End House, Watford.
—   Sedgwick, Mrs. A. O., North End House, Watford.
—   Sedgwick, Frederick J., High Street, Watford.
—   Sedgwick, John, Elmcote, Watford.
1878   Selby, Miss, Batler's Green, Aldenham.
—   Selby, Miss Nellie, Batler's Green, Aldenham.
1875   Silvester, Frank W., Hedges, St. Albans.
—   Smith, C. King, The Hawthorns, Watford.
1876   Smith, Miss H. M. K., The Hawthorns, Watford.
1875   Smith, John James, Southfield House, Watford.

1875   *Smith, W. Lepard, Southfield House, Watford.
—   Smith, Joseph G., Hamper Mills, Watford.
—   Snowing, Charles, Holywell Farm, Watford.
1878   Spedding, Mrs., St. Peter's, St. Albans.
—   Stevenson, Miss, Chalk Hill, Bushey.
1877   Stone, George, Cassio Bridge, Watford.
1875   Stone, W. T., Watford Heath.

—   Thairlwall, F. J., 169, Gloucester Road, Regent's Park, London, N.W.
—   Tidcombe, George, jun., Chalk Hill, Bushey.
1876   Tidcombe, Mrs. G., Chalk Hill, Bushey.
1875   *Tooke, William A., Pinner Hill.
1878   *Tuke, James Hack, Hitchin.
1877   Turnbull, George, M.I.C.E., Rose Hill, Abbot's Langley.

1875   Verini, William, The Ferns, Bushey Heath.

—   Wailes, George, Park Road, Watford.
—   Walker, J. Watson, jun., Fairfield House, Watford.
—   Ward, Miss, Chalk Hill, Bushey.
—   Waterman, George, Queen's Road, Watford.
1876   Webb, Rev. R. H., M.A., Essendon Rectory, Hatfield.
1875   Wilkie, Miss, Bushey Grange.
—   Wilson, John, 159, New Bond Street, London, W.
1877   Wilson, Miss, Nutfield, Watford.
1875   Wilson, Miss Mary, Nutfield, Watford.
—   Wilson, Miss Rose, Nutfield, Watford.
—   Wiltshire, Rev. Thomas, M.A., F.L.S., F.G.S., F.R.A.S., 25, Granville Park, Lewisham, London, S.E.
1877   Woolrych, W. R., Croxley Green, Rickmansworth.
1875   Wotton, Charles, M.D., King's Langley.
1878   Wyman, Henry, Hemel Hempstead.

CATALOGUE OF THE LIBRARY.

Allen, J. A. North American Rodentia. See Coues, E.

Anon. Minstrelsy of the Woods. 8vo. London, 1832.

—— Physiognomy. 2 vols. 8vo.

Arago, François. Meteorological Essays. 8vo. London, 1855.

Attfield, Prof. John. Chemistry: General, Medical, and Pharmaceutical. 6th Edition. 8vo. London, 1875.

Bath Natural History and Antiquarian Field Club. Proceedings. Vol. iii. 8vo. Bath, 1877.

Bentham, George. Handbook of the British Flora. (Illustrated Edition.) 2 vols. 8vo. London, 1865.

Boston (U.S.) Society of Natural History. Proceedings. Vols. xvii-xviii. 8vo. Boston, 1875-77.

Botany, Journal of. New Series. Vol. vi. 8vo. London, 1877.

Brande, Prof. W. T. Manual of Chemistry. 2nd Edition. 3 vols. 8vo. London, 1821.

Bristol Naturalists' Society. Proceedings. New Series. Vol. i. 8vo. London and Bristol, 1876.

Buckton, G. B. Monograph of the British Aphides. Vol. i. (*Ray Society.*) 8vo. London, 1876.

Capel, C. C. Trout Culture. 8vo. London, 1877.

Carpenter, Dr. W. B. Valorous Expedition. See Jeffreys, Dr. J. Gwyn.

Coleman, Rev. W. H. Flora Hertfordiensis. See Webb, Rev. R. H.

Coleman, W. S. British Butterflies. 8vo. London, 1860.

——. Our Woodlands, Heaths, and Hedges. 8vo. London, 1869.

Conybeare, Rev. W. D., and William Phillips. Outlines of the Geology of England and Wales. 8vo. London, 1822.

Cooke, M. C. Our Reptiles. 8vo. London, 1865.

——. A Plain and Easy Account of the British Fungi. 8vo. London, 1866.

——. Handbook of British Fungi. 2 vols. 8vo. London, 1871.

COPE, E. D. The Vertebrata of the Cretaceous Formations of the West. (*U.S. Geol. Surv.*) 4to. Washington, 1875.

COUES, ELLIOTT. Birds of the Northwest. (*U.S. Geol. Surv.*) 8vo. Washington, 1874.

——— . Fur-bearing Animals : a Monograph of North American Mustelidæ. (*U.S. Geol. Surv.*) 8vo. Washington, 1877.

———, and J. A. ALLEN. Monographs of North American Rodentia. (*U.S. Geol. Surv.*) 4to. Washington, 1877.

CURTIS, JOHN. Farm Insects. 4to. London, 1867.

CUVIER, BARON. Discours sur les Révolutions de la Surface du Globe. 8vo.

DAVIES, THOMAS. The Preparation and Mounting of Microscopic Objects. 2nd Edition. Edited by John Matthews. 8vo. London, 1873.

DRUMMOND, DR. JAMES L. First Steps to Botany. 3rd Edition. 12mo. London, 1831.

EDINBURGH BOTANICAL SOCIETY. Transactions and Proceedings. Vol. xii. 8vo. Edinburgh, 1876.

ENTOMOLOGICAL SOCIETY. Proceedings. 1871-75. 8vo. London, 1872-76.

ENTOMOLOGIST. Vol. x. 8vo. London, 1877.

EVANS, JOHN. The Ancient Stone Implements, Weapons, and Ornaments of Great Britain. 8vo. London, 1872.

FERGUSON, DR. ROBERT M. Electricity. 8vo. London and Edinburgh, 1868.

GANNETT, HENRY. List of Elevations West of the Mississippi River. (*U.S. Geol. Surv.*) 8vo. Washington, 1877.

GEOGRAPHICAL MAGAZINE. Vols. ii-iv. 4to. London, 1875-77.

GEOLOGISTS' ASSOCIATION. Proceedings. Vol. iv. 8vo. London, 1876.

GLASGOW NATURAL HISTORY SOCIETY. Proceedings. Vols. i-ii. 8vo. Glasgow, 1869-76.

———, PHILOSOPHICAL SOCIETY OF. Proceedings. Vols. ix-x. 8vo. Glasgow, 1875-77.

GOSSE, P. H. Fishes. 8vo. London, 1851.

GREG, R. P., and W. G. LETTSOM. Manual of the Mineralogy of Great Britain and Ireland. 8vo. London, 1858.

HARRISON, W. J. A Sketch of the Geology of Hampshire. 8vo. Sheffield, 1877.

——— . A Sketch of the Geology of Leicestershire and Rutland. 8vo. Leicester, 1877.

HARTING, J. E. The Ornithology of Shakespeare. 8vo. London, 1871.

HARTING, J. E. A Handbook of British Birds. 8vo. London, 1872.

———. Our Summer Migrants. 8vo. London, 1875.

———. Rambles in Search of Shells, Land and Freshwater. 8vo. London, 1875.

HAYDEN, DR. F. V. Final Report of the United States Geological Survey of Nebraska. 8vo. Washington, 1872.

———. First, Second, and Third Annual Reports of the United States Geological Survey of the Territories, for the years 1867, 1868, and 1869 (*Reprint*). 8vo. Washington, 1873.

———. Fourth Report, for 1870. (Wyoming.) *ib.* 1872.

———. Fifth Report, for 1871. (Montana.) *ib.* 1872.

———. Sixth Report for 1872. (Montana, &c.) *ib.* 1873.

———. Seventh Report, for 1873. (Colorado.) *ib.* 1874.

———. Eighth Report, for 1874. (Colorado.) *ib.* 1876.

———. Ninth Report, for 1875. (Colorado.) *ib.* 1877.

HEATHER, J. F. Mathematical Instruments. 12mo. London, 1872.

HENSLOW, REV. J. S. Descriptive and Physiological Botany. 8vo. London, 1839.

HERSCHEL, SIR JOHN F. W. Discourse on the Study of Natural Philosophy. 8vo. London, 1830.

———. Manual of Scientific Enquiry. 2nd Edition. 8vo. London, 1851.

———. Meteorology. 8vo. Edinburgh, 1861.

———. Familiar Letters on Scientific Subjects. 8vo. London, 1866.

HITCHCOCK, PROF. E. The Religion of Geology and its connected Sciences. 8vo. London, 1851.

INTELLECTUAL OBSERVER. Vols. i-iv. 8vo. London, 1868-69.

IRELAND, ROYAL GEOLOGICAL SOCIETY OF. Journal. Vols. i-iii. 8vo. Dublin, 1867-73.

JEFFREYS, DR. J. GWYN, and DR. W. B. CARPENTER. The Valorous Expedition. 8vo. London, 1876.

JOHNS, REV. C. A. The Forest Trees of Britain. Vol. ii. 8vo. London, 1849.

JOHNS, DR. WILLIAM. Practical Botany. 8vo. London, 1840.

JUKES, J. BEETE. The Student's Manual of Geology. 2nd Edition. 8vo. Edinburgh, 1862.

KIRBY, REV. W., and W. SPENCE. An Introduction to Entomology. 8vo. London, 1870.

LANDSBOROUGH, REV. D. A Popular History of British Zoophytes. 8vo. London, 1852.

LARDNER, DR. The Microscope Explained. 12mo.

LEIDY, JOSEPH. Contributions to the Extinct Vertebrate Fauna of the Western Territories. (*U.S. Geol. Surv.*) 4to. Washington, 1873.

LESQUEREUX, LEO. Contributions to the Fossil Flora of the Western Territories. Part 1. The Cretaceous Flora. (*U.S. Geol. Surv.*) 4to. Washington, 1874.

———. Part 2. The Tertiary Flora. *ib.* 1878.

LETTSOM, W. G. Mineralogy of Great Britain. See Greg, R. P.

LIEBIG, JUSTUS VON. Familiar Letters on Chemistry. 3rd Edition. 8vo. London, 1851.

———. Letters on Modern Agriculture. 8vo. London, 1859.

———. Natural Laws of Husbandry. 8vo. London, 1863.

LINDLEY, PROF. JOHN. School Botany. 8vo. London, 1847.

LINDSAY, W. LAUDER. A Popular History of British Lichens. 8vo. London, 1855.

LINNEAN SOCIETY. Journal. Zoology, Vols. xii-xiii. Botany, Vols. xv-xvi. 8vo. London, 1876-78.

LIVERPOOL, LITERARY AND PHILOSOPHICAL SOCIETY OF. Proceedings. Vols. xxx-xxxi. 8vo. London and Liverpool, 1876-77.

LOBLEY, J. LOGAN. Mount Vesuvius. 8vo. London, 1868.

LUBBOCK, SIR JOHN. On British Wild Flowers considered in Relation to Insects. 8vo. London, 1875.

LYELL, SIR CHARLES. The Principles of Geology. 9th Edition. 8vo. London, 1853.

———. The Student's Elements of Geology. 12mo. London, 1871.

MANCHESTER, LITERARY AND PHILOSOPHICAL SOCIETY OF. Memoirs. Third Series. Vols. i-v. 8vo. Manchester, 1862-76.

———. Proceedings. Vols. iv-xv. 4 vols. 8vo. *ib.* 1865-76.

MARLBOROUGH COLLEGE NATURAL HISTORY SOCIETY. Reports for 1867 to 1876. 5 vols. 8vo. Marlborough, 1867-1877.

MAWE, J. Woodarch's Introduction to the Study of Conchology. 3rd Edition. 8vo. London, 1825.

McINTOSH, DR. W. C. Monograph of the British Annelids. Part I. The Nemerteans. (*Ray Society.*) 4to. London, 1873-74.

MEEK, F. B. Report on the Invertebrate Cretaceous and Tertiary Fossils of the Upper Missouri Country. (*U.S. Geol. Surv.*) 4to. Washington, 1876.

MELVILLE, J. C. The Flora of Harrow. 12mo. London, 1874.

METEOROLOGICAL SOCIETY. Quarterly Journal. New Series. Vol. iii. 8vo. London, 1877.

MICROSCOPICAL, MONTHLY, JOURNAL. Vols. xv-xviii. 8vo. London, 1876-77.

MILLER, HUGH. My Schools and Schoolmasters, or the Story of my Education. 4th Edition. 8vo. Edinburgh, 1855.

MUDIE, ROBERT. The Feathered Tribes of the British Islands. 2 vols. 8vo. London, 1834.

NATURALIST. Vols. i-iii. 8vo. London and Huddersfield, 1865-67.

NEWMAN, E. A History of British Ferns. 8vo. London, 1840.

NICHOLSON, PROF. A. H. Introductory Text Book of Zoology. 2nd Edition. 8vo. Edinburgh and London, 1875.

PACKARD, DR. A. S. A Monograph of the Geometrid Moths or Phalœnidæ of the United States. (*U.S. Geol. Surv.*) 4to. Washington, 1876.

PAGE, DAVID. The Earth's Crust. 4th Edition. 8vo. Edinburgh, 1868.

PATTERSON, ROBERT. Introduction to Zoology. Part 1. Invertebrate Animals. 12mo. London, 1846.

PHILLIPS, PROF. JOHN. Treatise on Geology. 2 vols. 12mo. London, 1837-39.

———. Notices of Rocks and Fossils in the University Museum, Oxford. 8vo. Oxford, 1863.

PHILLIPS, WILLIAM. Elementary Introduction to the Knowledge of Mineralogy. 12mo. London, 1816.

———. Geology of England and Wales. See Conybeare, Rev. W. D.

POPULAR SCIENCE REVIEW. Vols. i-ii. 8vo. London, 1862-63.

PORTLOCK, MAJOR-GENERAL. Rudimentary Treatise on Geology. 4th Edition. 12mo. London, 1859.

POWELL, REV. PROF. BADEN. History of Natural Philosophy. 8vo. London, 1834.

PRESTON, REV. T. A. Flora of Marlborough. 8vo. Marlborough, 1870-76.

QUEKETT MICROSCOPICAL CLUB. Journal. Vol. iv. 8vo. London, 1877.

RAMSAY, PROF. A. C. The Old Glaciers of Switzerland and North Wales. 8vo. London, 1860.

———. The Physical Geology and Geography of Great Britain. 8vo. London, 1863.

RAY SOCIETY. See G. B. Buckton, and Dr. W. C. McIntosh.

SCHLEIDEN, DR. J. M. Principles of Scientific Botany. 8vo. London, 1849.

SCIENCE GOSSIP, 1877. 8vo. London, 1877.

SCOTT, R. H. Instructions in the use of Meteorological Instruments. 8vo. London, 1875.

SMITH, SIR J. E. An Introduction to Physiological and Systematic Botany. 6th Edition. 8vo. London, 1827.

SMITHSONIAN INSTITUTION. Annual Reports or the Board of Regents for 1874-76. 3 vols. 8vo. Washington, 1875-77.

SOMERSETSHIRE NATURAL HISTORY AND ARCHÆOLOGICAL SOCIETY. Proceedings. New Series. Vols. i-ii. 8vo. Taunton, 1876-77.

SOMERVILLE, MARY. The Connexion of the Physical Sciences. 5th Edition. 8vo. London, 1840.

SPENCE, W. Introduction to Entomology. See Kirby, Rev. W.

SWAINSON, WILLIAM. A Preliminary Discourse on the Study of Natural History. 8vo. London, 1834.

———. A Treatise on the Geography and Classification of Animals. 8vo. London, 1835.

———. On the Natural History and Classification of Quadrupeds. 8vo. London, 1835.

———. On the Natural History and Classification of Birds. 2 vols. 8vo. London, 1836.

———. On the Habits and Instincts of Animals. 8vo. London, 1840.

SYMONS, G. J. British Rainfall (Extracts from) 1860-70. 8vo. London, 1862-71.

———. British Rainfall, 1875-77. 3 vols. 8vo. London, 1876-78.

———— Reports of the Rainfall Committee of the British Association, for 1860-65, and 1870-75. 8vo. London, 1863-76.

———. Monthly Meteorological Magazine. Vols. xi-xii. 8vo. London, 1876-77.

TATE, RALPH. The Land and Fresh-water Mollusks of Great Britain. 8vo. London, 1866.

TAYLOR, J. E. Geological Stories. 8vo. London, 1873.

THOMAS, Dr. CYRUS. Synopsis of the Acrididæ of North America. (U.S. Geol. Surv.) 4to. Washington, 1873.

UNITED STATES GEOLOGICAL AND GEOGRAPHICAL SURVEY OF THE TERRITORIES. Bulletin. Vol. iii. 8vo. Washington, 1877.

———. The Grotto Geyser of the Yellowstone National Park. Folio. Washington, 1877.

———. Illustrations of Cretaceous and Tertiary Fossils of the Western Territories. 4to. Washington, 1878.

———. See also E. D. Cope, E. Coues, H. Gannett, F. V. Hayden, J. Leidy, L. Lesquereux, F. B. Meek, A. S. Packard, and C. Thomas.

URE, DR. ANDREW. Dictionary of Chemistry. 8vo. London, 1821.

VARLEY, D.   Rudimentary Treatise on Mineralogy.   4th Edition. 12mo.   London, 1859.

WALKER, HENRY.   The Glacial Drifts of Muswell Hill and Finchley. 12mo.   London, 1874.

WARINGTON, GEORGE.   The Phenomena of Radiation.   8vo.   London, 1865.

WATFORD NATURAL HISTORY SOCIETY.   Transactions.   Vol. i.   8vo. Watford and London, 1878.

WATTS, DR. J.   The Knowledge of the Heavens and the Earth made easy.   5th Edition.   8vo.   London, 1752.

WEBB, REV. R. H., and REV. W. H. COLEMAN.   Flora Hertfordiensis. 12mo.   London and Hertford, 1849-59.

WHITAKER, WILLIAM.   The Geology of Parts of Middlesex, Hertfordshire, Buckinghamshire, Berkshire, and Surrey (sheet 7 of the Map of the Geological Survey).   8vo.   London, 1864.

————.   Guide to the Geology of London and the Neighbourhood. 8vo.   London, 1874.

————.   Geological Record for 1874-76.   8vo.   London, 1875-78.

WHITE, REV. GILBERT.   The Natural History of Selborne.   Edited by the Rev. J. G. Wood.   8vo.   London, 1853.

WILTSHIRE ARCHÆOLOGICAL AND NATURAL HISTORY SOCIETY.   Magazine.   Vols. xvi-xvii.   8vo.   Devizes, 1876-78.

WINCHESTER AND HAMPSHIRE SCIENTIFIC AND LITERARY SOCIETY. Journal of Proceedings.   Vol. i.   8vo.   Winchester, 1875.

WITHERING, DR. W.   A Systematic Arrangement of British Plants. Edited by W. Macgillivray.   4th Edition.   12mo.   London, 1837.

WOODWARD, DR. JOHN.   An Essay towards a Natural History of the Earth, especially Minerals: as also of the Sea, Rivers, and Springs.   With an Account of the Universal Deluge: and of the Effects that it had upon the Earth.   3rd Edition. 8vo.   London, 1723.

ZOOLOGIST.   3rd Series.   Vol. i.   8vo.   London, 1877.

PAMPHLETS.   Vol. I.   Geology.   8vo.
Contents:

EVANS, JOHN.   Address delivered at the Anniversary Meeting of the Geological Society of London, on the 19th of February, 1875.   (*Quart. Journ. Geol. Soc.* 1875.)

HOPKINSON, JOHN.   On British Graptolites.   (*Journ. Quek. Micr. Club*, 1869.)
————.   On Dexolites gracilis, a new Silurian Annelide.   (*Geol. Mag.* 1870.)
————.   On the Structure and Affinities of the Genus Dicranograptus.   (*ib.* 1870.)
————.   On Dicellograpsus, a new Genus of Graptolites.   (*ib.* 1871.)
————.   On a Specimen of Diplograpsus pristis with Reproductive Capsules. (*Ann. Nat. Hist.* 1871.)
————.   On Callograptus radicans, a new Dendroid Graptolite.   (*ib.* 1872.)
————.   On some New Species of Graptolites from the South of Scotland. (*Geol. Mag.* 1872.)

HOPKINSON, JOHN. The Graptolites of the Arenig Rocks of St. David's, South Wales. (*Proc. Liverpool Geol. Soc.* 1873.)
———. On some Graptolites from the Upper Arenig Rocks of Ramsey Island, St. David's. (*ib.* 1874.)
———. Report of the Proceedings of the Geological Section of the British Association at Edinburgh, 1871. (*Proc. Geol. Assoc.* 1872.)
———. Excursion of the Geologists' Association to Watford, April 13th, 1872. (*ib.* 1873.)
———. Excursion of the Geologists' Association to Eastbourne and St. Leonards, May 23rd and 24th, 1873. (*ib.* 1874.)
JOHNSON, M. H. Flint. London, 1871.
———. The Nature and Formation of Flint and Allied Bodies. *ib.* 1874.
———. On the Microscopic Structure of Flint and Allied Bodies. (*Journ. Quek. Micr. Club*, 1874.)
LOBLEY, J. L. The Cretaceous Rocks of England. (*Trans. Watford Nat. Hist. Soc.* 1875.)
PHILLIPS, PROF. J. Address to the Geological Section of the British Association, Bradford, Sept. 18th, 1873.
TYLOR, ALFRED. On Quaternary Gravels. (*Quart. Journ. Geol. Soc.* 1869.)
WHITAKER, W. On Subaërial Denudation, and on Cliffs and Escarpments of the Chalk and the Lower Tertiary Beds. (*Geol. Mag.* 1867.)
———. On the Connection of the Geological Structure and the Physical Features of the South-East of England with the Consumption Death-rate. (*ib.* 1869.)
———. On the Chalk of the Cliffs from Seaford to Eastbourne, Sussex. (*ib.* 1871.)
———. On the Chalk of the Southern Part of Dorset and Devon. (*Quart. Journ. Geol. Soc.* 1871.)
———. On the Cliff-sections of the Tertiary Beds west of Dieppe in Normandy, and at Newhaven in Sussex. (*ib.* 1871.)
———. On the Occurrence of the "Chalk Rock" near Salisbury. (*Mag. Wiltshire Nat. Hist. Soc.* 1871.)
———. On the Occurrence of Thanet Beds and of Crag at Sudbury, Suffolk. (*Quart. Journ. Geol. Soc.* 1874.)
WOODWARD, HENRY. Man and the Mammoth. (*Proc. Geol. Assoc.* 1869.)

PAMPHLETS. Vol. II. Geology. 8vo.

Contents:

EVANS, JOHN. Address delivered at the Anniversary Meeting of the Geological Society of London, on the 18th of February, 1876. (*Quart. Journ. Geol. Soc.* 1876.)
HICKS, HENRY. On the Succession of the Ancient Rocks in the Vicinity of St. David's, Pembrokeshire. (*Quart. Journ. Geol. Soc.* 1875.)
HOPKINSON, JOHN, and C. LAPWORTH. Descriptions of the Graptolites of the Arenig and Llandeilo Rocks of St. David's. (*Quart. Journ. Geol. Soc.* 1875.)
LOBLEY, J. L. Two Days in a Mining District. (*Proc. Geol. Assoc.* 1871.)
———. On the Stratigraphical Distribution of the British Fossil Brachiopoda. (*ib.* 1871.)
———. On the Stratigraphical Distribution of the British Fossil Lamellibranchiata. (*Quart. Journ. Geol. Soc.* 1871.)
———. Excursion of the Geologists' Association to Malvern, July 21st, 1873, and five following days. (*Proc. Geol. Assoc.* 1874.)
MORRIS, PROF. JOHN. The Physical Structure of the London Basin, considered in its Relation to the Geology of the Neighbourhood of Watford. (*Trans. Watford Nat. Hist. Soc.* 1876.)
REDGRAVE, GILBERT R. A Short Account of Mountsorrel, and the Working of its Granite Quarries. Leicester, 1870.
RICHARDSON, RALPH. The Ice Age in Britain. Edinburgh, 1876.
RICKETTS, CHARLES. The Cause of the Glacial Period, with reference to the British Isles. (*Geol. Mag.* 1875.)

WHITAKER, W.   List of Works on the Geology of Hertfordshire.   (*Trans. Watford Nat. Hist. Soc.* 1876).

WOODWARD, HENRY.   On a new Species of Rostellaria from the Gray Chalk, Folkestone.   (*Geol. Mag.* 1872.)

————.   Further Remarks on Xiphosura.   (*Quart. Journ. Geol. Soc.* 1872.)

PAMPHLETS.   Vol. III.   Botany.   4to.

Contents :

CURREY, F.   Notes on British Fungi.   (*Trans. Linn. Soc.* 1864.)

HANBURY, DANIEL.   On the Species of Garcinia which affords Gamboge in Siam.   (*ib.*)

KIRK, DR. JOHN.   On a new Genus of Liliaceæ from East Tropical Africa.   (*ib.*)

MANN, GUSTAV, and HERMANN WENDLAND.   On the Palms of Western Tropical Africa.   (*ib.*)

MIERS, JOHN.   On the Conantherœ.   (*ib.*)

OLIVER, DANIEL.   Note on the Structure and Mode of Dehiscence of the Legumes of Pentaclethra macrophylla, Benth.   (*ib.*)

TRIANA, DN. J.   Les Mélastomacées.   (*ib.* 1871.)

PAMPHLETS.   Vol. IV.   Zoology.   4to.

Contents :

BAIRD, DR. W.   Description of a new Species of Annelide belonging to the Family Amphinomidæ.   (*Trans. Linn. Soc.* 1864.)

————.   On a new Species of British Annelides belonging to the Family Chætopteridæ.   (*ib.*)

BRADY, HENRY B.   Contributions to the Knowledge of the Foraminifera.— On the Rhizopodal Fauna of the Shetlands.   (*ib.*)

HALIDAY, A. H.   Iapyx, a new Genus of Insects belonging to the Stirps Thysanura, in the Order Neuroptera.   (*ib.*)

HANCOCK, ALBANY.   On the Structure and Homologies of the Renal Organ in the Nudibranchiate Mollusca.   (*ib.*)

MOXON, WALTER.   Notes on some Points in the Anatomy of Rotatoria.   (*ib.*)

MURRAY, ANDREW.   Monograph of the Family of Nitidulariæ.   (*ib.*)

WILLIAMS, JOHN.   On a Species of Chætopteris (C. insignis, Baird) from North Wales.   (*ib.*)

WRIGHT, DR. PERCIVAL.   On a new Genus of Teredininæ.   (*ib.*)

₊ Unbound pamphlets, serial publications, etc., which are not available for circulation, are not included in this Catalogue.

www.ingramcontent.com/pod-product-compliance
Lightning Source LLC
Chambersburg PA
CBHW021123270326
41929CB00009B/1023